Frommer's®

Alaska Cruises & Ports of Call

2011

by Fran Wenograd Golden & Gene Sloan

Wiley Publishing, Inc.

Published by:

Wiley Publishing, Inc.

111 River St.
Hoboken, NJ 07030-5774

ISBN 978-0-470-87612-1 (paper); ISBN 978-1-118-00559-0 (ebk);
ISBN 978-1-118-00560-6 (ebk); ISBN 978-1-118-00561-3 (ebk)

Editor: Ian Skinnari
Production Editor: Lindsay Conner
Cartographer: Anton Crane
Photo Editor: Richard Fox
Production by Wiley Indianapolis Composition Services

Front cover photo: Coral Princess cruising the Inside Passage © Danny Lehman / Courtesy Princess Cruises
Back cover photo (inset): Bald Eagle © Wolfgang Kaehler / Alamy Images

For information on our other products and services or to obtain technical support, please contact our Customer Care Department within the U.S. at 877/762-2974, outside the U.S. at 317/572-3993 or fax 317/572-4002.

Wiley also publishes its books in a variety of electronic formats. Some content that appears in print may not be available in electronic formats.

Manufactured in the United States of America

5 4 3 2 1

Contents

5 The Cruise Lines, Part 1: The Big Ships 64

6 The Cruise Lines, Part 2: The Small Ships 138

7 The Ports of Embarkation 157

Ports & Wilderness Areas Along the Inside Passage 196

9 Ports & Wilderness Areas Along the Gulf Route 241

10 Cruisetour Destinations 247

Appendix A: Alaska in Depth 256

Appendix B: Alaska on the Wild Side 261

Index 269

List of Maps

Acknowledgments

The authors wish to thank contributing writers Art Sbarsky and Nicola Hassapis.

About the Authors

Fran Wenograd Golden is a well-known cruise and travel writer, and Travel News Columnist for AOL Travel. Former travel editor of the *Boston Herald,* she also writes for numerous newspapers, magazines and websites, including the *Miami Herald, TravelandLeisure.com,* and *Porthole,* and has her own popular blog, www.getawaywithfran.com. She lives in Boston and is the proud parent of Erin and Eli.

Gene Sloan writes about cruising for *USA TODAY* and oversees *USA TODAY's* online cruise site, The Cruise Log (cruises.usatoday.com). Sloan's stories also are distributed by the Gannett News Service to more than 80 other U.S. newspapers. He has written about travel for more than 15 years and has spent more than 1,000 days on the road. Prior to writing about travel, Sloan covered the television industry for *USA TODAY,* and he also has served as an editor in the paper's Life section.

How to Contact Us

In researching this book, we discovered many wonderful places—hotels, restaurants, shops, and more. We're sure you'll find others. Please tell us about them, so we can share the information with your fellow travelers in upcoming editions. If you were disappointed with a recommendation, we'd love to know that, too. Please write to:

Frommer's Alaska Cruises & Ports of Call 2011
Wiley Publishing, Inc. • 111 River St. • Hoboken, NJ 07030-5774

An Additional Note

Please be advised that travel information is subject to change at any time—and this is especially true of prices. We therefore suggest that you write or call ahead for confirmation when making your travel plans. The authors, editors, and publisher cannot be held responsible for the experiences of readers while traveling. Your safety is important to us, however, so we encourage you to stay alert and be aware of your surroundings. Keep a close eye on cameras, purses, and wallets, all favorite targets of thieves and pickpockets.

Travel Resources at Frommers.com

Frommer's travel resources don't end with this guide. **Frommers.com** has travel information on more than 4,000 destinations. We update features regularly, giving you access to the most current trip-planning information and the best airfare, lodging, and car-rental bargains. You can also listen to podcasts, connect with other Frommers.com members through our active-reader forums, share your travel photos, read blogs from guidebook editors and fellow travelers, and much more.

What's New in Alaska Cruising in 2011

In 2011, the big news for vacationers looking for an Alaska cruise is the presence of four new lines. Arriving in the state for the first time in the line's 13-year history is the family-focused Disney Cruise Line, and 9-year-old Oceania Cruises also is making its first appearance here. On the luxury end, returning after many years away is Crystal Cruises, and Alaska also will be home in 2011 to a new start-up small-ship adventure cruise line called InnerSea Discoveries. The arrival of all these brands is good news for the state's tourism sector, which has suffered a blow the past couple years. In 2009 and 2010, Alaska cruising took a big hit in a depressed U.S. economy. Low demand, combined with a particularly contentious controversy over a $50 per passenger head tax approved by Alaska voters in 2006, caused several lines to decide that enough is enough. Cruise lines decided to cut ships, and the number of cruise passengers decreased from 1 million in 2008 to an estimated 860,000 in 2010.

Cruise lines filed suit against the state over the head tax, and the governor and legislature listened. A reduction to $34.50 was approved and signed, and the cruise lines dropped their suit.

There was even word that lines like Holland America, which cut a ship for 2011, would look kindly on Alaska in terms of their 2012 itinerary planning—the line's President and CEO Stein Kruse told reporters he was "more positively inclined to bring back capacity" with the tax reduced.

Meanwhile, the cuts had a pretty drastic impact on hotels and tour operations—fewer cruisers meant less revenue, period.

Alaska remains one of the world's premier destinations. But just like the glaciers, the world of Alaska travel is always changing. In addition to the new lines cruising here this year, cruise lines have added new shore excursions and land packages, and enhanced their onboard offerings. During our travels, we're constantly finding interesting new changes in the tourism industry of the 49th state. In writing this book, we've tried to keep track of the latest and greatest developments.

THE CRUISE INDUSTRY IN GENERAL While cruise lines are notoriously reluctant to publicize their passenger loads, it's safe to say 2010 was not the best year for cruising in Alaska, as the lines cumulatively had reduced capacity for 2010. But the capacity is increasing this year over last. The goal of the lines, of course, is to increase both demand and fares. With the added capacity we expect there will be some deals in 2011 (of a last-minute variety). Meanwhile, though, the cruise lines' brochures reflect an early booking discount, which they now consider to be the de facto brochure price. We still believe your best bet for getting a good deal on a cruise in 2011, as always, is to book early, by mid-February—or earlier, if possible. Early booking discounts can be very attractive, especially if you're flexible and prepared to sail in the shoulder season (May or Sept). Chances are that you'll still be able to get a deal even after that date, though (especially if you're a past passenger of one of the lines; cruise lines offer all sorts of deals for repeat passengers).

You can take your chances and wait for special offers to come later in 2011, but if you do, be prepared to miss out, because those offers are likely to be limited as the lines try to make up for a difficult 2010.

CRUISE LINES & THEIR SHIPS As we noted, the cruise industry cut back on capacity in the region for 2010, and in 2011 the two biggest operators in Alaska will have even less capacity in the state than they did in 2010. Holland America is sending seven ships to Alaska in 2011 (one fewer than in 2010) and Princess is sending just six ships this year (down from seven in 2010 and eight in 2009). Decisions on 2011 itineraries, we should note, were made before the state reduced the head tax.

Still, both Holland America and Princess—the two 800-pound gorillas of Alaska cruising—will continue to have a hefty presence in the region and offer nearly all of the itineraries they have in the past. Two of Princess' biggest ships, the ***Golden Princess*** and ***Sapphire Princess,*** once again are sailing round-trip voyages out of Seattle, while three more large Princess ships—***Diamond, Island,*** and ***Coral***—once again will be in the Gulf. The ***Sea Princess,*** meanwhile, is back for another season of 10-day Inside Passage cruises out of San Francisco.

The big change for Princess in 2011 is the removal of the intimate, 680-passenger ***Royal Princess*** from the market, bringing an end to the line's unusual "Connoisseur Cruise" schedule of 14-day sailings that include the Gulf ports plus the seldom-visited Kodiak, southwest of Anchorage (the *Royal Princess* has been transferred to one of Princess' sister lines in Europe).

Like Princess, Holland America has trimmed its presence in the state for 2011 by one vessel, but with seven ships in Alaska it's still the king of the hill. Despite the disappearance of the *Ryndam* from the market (repositioned to Europe), the line is for the most part offering the same line-up of itineraries in 2011 as it did in 2010 (including, for a second year, an unusually long, 14-night Inside Passage itinerary out of Seattle operated by the *Amsterdam* that includes a stop in Anchorage).

Making up for the departures of the Holland America and Princess ships is the arrival of several new vessels in the state, including the family-friendly Disney Cruise Line's ***Disney Wonder.*** The 83,000-ton, 2,400-passenger vessel—the first Disney ship to visit Alaska—will sail 7-night voyages to the state out of Vancouver, B.C. Also debuting in the region for the first time in 2011 is upscale Oceania Cruises, which is sending the 684-passenger ***Regatta.*** And another line that hasn't sailed in the region for many years, luxury operator Crystal Cruises, is revisiting the state with the deployment of the 960-passenger ***Crystal Symphony.***

Still, perhaps the most talked-about new entrant into the Alaska market for 2011 is small-ship adventure line **InnerSea Discoveries.** As this book went to press, the two-ship operator had yet to sail its first cruise (scheduled for May 2011). But the line comes with a strong pedigree (it's an off-shoot of small-ship Alaska luxury operator American Safari Cruises, which has three vessels in the state, none with capacity for more than 36 passengers), and its focus—getting adventure-minded vacationers into the most beautiful and wildlife-filled corners of Southeast Alaska's Inside Passage—has many Alaska tourism-watchers excited.

One of several lines that aren't changing a thing for 2011 is Carnival, which returns with a single ship, the ***Carnival Spirit,*** sailing out of Seattle to the Inside Passage.

Also sticking with the status quo for 2011 are Norwegian Cruise Line and Royal Caribbean, which both are sending the same two ships to Alaska that they did in 2010 (Norwegian is back with the ***Norwegian Pearl*** and ***Norwegian Star;*** Royal Caribbean once again is deploying the ***Rhapsody of the Seas*** and ***Radiance of the Seas***). Both lines had cut back their Alaska operations sharply in 2010 by removing one ship each. On the high end, Regent Seven Seas Cruises is back with the 490-passenger ***Navigator*** for a second year, and Silversea is sending its ***Silver Shadow*** to Alaska for a fourth year in a row.

On the small-ship side, one of the most storied names in Alaska cruising, Cruise West, shut down in September 2010—a victim of the economic downturn of recent years. The small-ship line founded by the late Chuck West—a pioneer of tourism in the state and known as "Mr. Alaska"—had operated as many as eight ships in the state as recently as 2008 (though by last year it was down to just four Alaska-based vessels). Known for visiting smaller Alaska ports such as Petersburg that bigger cruise ships couldn't reach, Cruise West operated a fleet of 78- to 138-passenger vessels that offered an unusual option for adventuresome (and wealthier) travelers, and its disappearance is no doubt a blow for Alaska tourism. But all is not lost for small-ship lovers: Perhaps not coincidentally, Cruise West collapsed just as another small-ship operator with a Cruise West connection—InnerSea Discoveries—geared up to begin its first sailings. Several of the top executives at InnerSea Discoveries are Cruise West alumni, and the two-ship line offers some similarities in format.

PORTS OF EMBARKATION Vancouver had boasting rights as host of the 2010 Winter Olympics, but as it no longer has them, Seattle now boasts top dog title as it continues to grow as a jumping-off point for voyages to Alaska. Carnival's one Alaska ship, the ***Carnival Spirit,*** cruises from Seattle instead of Vancouver. Norwegian Cruise Line is also an all-Seattle-based line. In 2011, 10 big ships will be at home port in Seattle, representing the above fleets as well as Princess Cruises, Royal Caribbean, Celebrity Cruises, and Holland America. All this is amazing when you consider Seattle didn't even host one Alaska-bound cruise ship a decade ago.

Conveniently located Seward and tiny Whittier continue to operate as the turnaround ports for Gulf of Alaska cruises; and in both, rail tracks extend right up to the piers, enabling passengers to board their transportation to Anchorage (of course, it is also possible to get there by motorcoach, still the most common transfer medium). Holland America broke new ground in 2010 by offering cruises on the ***Amsterdam*** that called in Anchorage proper (the ship docked about 2 miles from downtown)—because the cruises are for 14 days, they can afford the extra time it takes to get around the Kenai Peninsula to Anchorage. The itinerary will be repeated in 2011.

ONBOARD CHANGES In 2010, Holland America significantly revamped one of its old standbys in Alaska, 1,258-passenger ***Statendam.*** The 18-year-old vessel—the second oldest in the Holland America fleet—underwent a massive dry dock that saw the addition of a more contemporary lounge area called Mix, an Italian eatery called Canaletto, and a new showroom. The line also revamped every cabin on the ship with new fixtures, fabrics, and bedding, and completely overhauled cabin bathrooms with new vanities and cabinetry. A number of cabins near the spa were converted into "spa staterooms" with special amenities.

CRUISETOURS Celebrity Cruises is upping the ante this year when it comes to add-on cruisetours by offering what it is calling "The Ultimate Cruisetour—Canadian Rockies and Alaska." The 18-night package is being offered to passengers on the ***Millennium*** and features a 6-night Canadian Rockies tour, a 7-night northbound Alaska cruise, and a 5-night post-cruise Alaska land tour.

Also making changes for 2011 is Princess Cruises, which is adding new "On Your Own" cruisetour options designed for independent-minded travelers that do not include any pre-planned excursions, giving travelers time to create their own experience. Princess is also expanding its Connoisseur line of cruisetours, which include the services of a professional tour director and allow additional time for passengers to explore. At press time, Princess was making a big push to promote affordability with its cruisetours, noting that it is offering add-on land tours for 2011 for as little as $299 per person for three days in the Denali area.

SHORE EXCURSIONS One thing we've noticed when it comes to shore excursions is that prices last year appeared to stabilize and in some cases even went down. We expect the same trend in 2011.

Cruise lines are increasingly regarding Alaskan ports as just the starting points for land exploration. They have to—how else to disperse crowds of thousands? Toward that end, the lines have beefed up their offerings. **Carnival,** for instance, has a brochure that lists over 120 shore excursions; and **Princess** has so many that it now presents them in Special Interest categories on its website—such as Foodie, Fitness-focused, and Water Activities. This year, we've added to our suggested tours more ways to learn about Mother Nature on small group tours. Examples include a cool new Bear & Wildlife Expedition in Ketchikan, where 12 passengers head off with a naturalist to a recently opened rainforest trail to safely view bears doing their thing: picking salmon out of a creek. In Juneau, 16 passengers can head out on a Whales & Glaciers Citizen Science Adventure to experience what it's like to be a research scientist in Alaska.

Continuing to prove popular is one of the most intriguing excursions, inspired by the Discovery Channel's documentary series *Deadliest Catch,* a 3½-hour tour in a Bering Sea crab boat—in the considerably calm waters off Ketchikan. During the cruise, crew members go through exactly the same procedures as they would in the Bering Sea, dropping pots, hauling them in, sizing and counting the catch—and releasing the marine creatures back to the deep. As with other popular tours, if you want to book this trip, book it early.

Increasingly creative excursions in the traditional ports (Ketchikan, Skagway, Juneau, and Sitka) are on the rosters as well. In Ketchikan, several lines offer a Harley-Davidson Motorcycle Tour, even though there are not a lot of roads in Ketchikan. There are 4 x 4 tours and other ways to 'vroom around the 49th state, too. For those who like quieter pursuits, try exploring on a horseback excursion in Seward, to see bald eagles nesting. For those with big bucks and traveling as a group, some lines, including **Holland America** and **Norwegian Cruise Line,** offer private tours of the pricey, luxury variety, including booking a private boat tour.

EXPLORING The biggest upgrade in tourist attractions can be found at the Anchorage Museum.

Just in time for last season, the museum opened its $106-million expansion, which includes the new Smithsonian Arctic Studies Center—with 600 Native Alaska artifacts imported from the Smithsonian museums in Washington and most never before displayed. Also newly moved to the enhanced museum space are the Thomas Planetarium and Imaginarium Discovery Center.

In tiny Haines, the American Bald Eagle Foundation Natural History Museum also got an upgrade in the form of a new building for rehabilitated bald eagles, which allows visitors to view them in their enclosed aviary.

CRUISE ITINERARIES The most notable itinerary news for 2011 is the new roundtrip offerings from upscale line Oceania Cruises and luxury line Crystal Cruises out of San Francisco—an enticing option for West Coasters who want to visit Alaska without getting on an airplane. Oceania's *Regatta* will sail a series of 14-night roundtrip voyages from the California city to Alaska in May and August that include stops in Victoria and Vancouver, B.C.; Astoria, Ore.; and Sitka, Skagway, Hoonah, and Juneau in Alaska. The voyages also include a visit to Hubbard Glacier and Tracy Arm. Crystal's new cruises to Alaska are 12-nighters out of San Francisco, roundtrip, that visit Victoria, Vancouver, Sitka, Skagway, Juneau, Ketchikan, and either Glacier Bay or Hubbard Glacier

Oceania also is offering 12-night, one-way voyages between San Francisco and Vancouver that include stops in Victoria, Astoria, Wrangell, Juneau, Hoonah, Sitka, and Ketchikan.

Other than that, itineraries for 2011 are much as they were in 2010. As we mentioned earlier, Holland America made waves in 2010 with a new, 14-night Inside Passage itinerary out of Seattle that includes a stop in Anchorage—the first call in the city by a major line in 25 years—and the line will repeat that itinerary in 2011. The unusually long round-trip voyages on the ***Amsterdam*** also include port calls in rarely visited Homer and Kodiak, as well as Sitka, Ketchikan, Juneau, Skagway, and Victoria, B.C. The hit-it-all-in-one-trip itinerary also includes scenic cruising in Tracy Arm and a visit to the Hubbard Glacier, though famed Glacier Bay National Park is not included.

Also newly appearing on cruise itineraries is Nanaimo, a historic port town on Vancouver Island, 38 nautical miles west of Vancouver. Norwegian, Royal Caribbean, and Celebrity are all visiting in 2011—diving, arts and crafts, and small-town charm are the attractions.

THE GLACIER BAY ACCESS DEBATE The ecological issues involving passenger ship entry into Glacier Bay continue to pit environmentalists (who want to limit the number of cruise ships allowed into the bay) against the cruise lines. But the subject of how many ships can safely enter the vast wilderness area without upsetting the whales and other forms of aquatic life inhabiting it during summer is hotly debated. The environmentalists would like to prohibit *all* big cruise ships from visiting Glacier Bay in June, July, and August; the cruise lines, naturally, feel that more ships should be granted access during those peak travel months.

Again in 2011, **Holland America** will have more ships with access to the park than any other line in the market, and **Princess Cruises** will have the biggest ships there. Other cruise lines awarded concession agreements through 2019 are Norwegian Cruise Line and Crystal Cruises.

Don't worry if your cruise doesn't include a visit to Glacier Bay; there are plenty of other equally delightful—and in our opinion, sometimes even more attractive—glacier areas to visit. The cruise lines have found ways to live with the Glacier Bay–entry restrictions by substituting visits to Hubbard Glacier, Icy Bay, Misty Fjords, or Tracy Arm. We would rather visit active Hubbard Glacier any day of the week!

ENVIRONMENTAL CONCERNS In response to popular demand, the Alaska State Legislature has enacted a series of pollution-mitigating restrictions on cruise ships, including increased environmental reporting requirements and stricter rules about where cruise ships may legally discard treated wastewater.

It is that last item—dumping wastewater at sea—that has gotten the cruise lines riled up. They argue, among other things, that with current technology half the ships cannot meet limits on the pollutant ammonia, which was to go in effect last year. They got a delay. In April, the *Juneau Empire* reported the state Department of Environmental Conservation had created new limits for five types of treatment systems currently on ships, and would not require the cruise lines to add newer systems. The industry said it was pleased with the change, but this news came much to the chagrin of environmentalists, some of whom were threatening a suit at press time.

1

The Best of Alaska Cruising

Alaska is one of the top cruise destinations in the world, and when you're sailing through the calm waters of the Inside Passage or across the Gulf of Alaska, it's easy to see why: The scenery is simply breathtaking.

Much of the coastline is wilderness, with snowcapped mountain peaks, immense glaciers that create a thunderous noise as chunks break off into the sea (a process known as calving), emerald rainforests, fjords, icebergs, soaring eagles, lumbering bears, and majestic whales—all easily visible from the comfort of your ship.

Visit the towns and you'll find people who retain the spirit of frontier independence that brought them here in the first place. Add Alaska's colorful history and heritage, with its European influences, its spirit of discovery, and its rich Native cultures, and you have a destination that is utterly, endlessly fascinating. Even thinking about it, we get chills of the good kind.

Two years ago, the state celebrated its 50th anniversary of statehood. It was in January 1959 that the Union accepted what had once been a territory as a fully fledged state—the 49th. Every city, town, and hamlet seemed to hold celebrations in honor of the event, showing their Alaska spirit.

The number of cruise passengers visiting the state topped the one million mark in 2008, and even though the numbers dipped to about 860,000 last year, in summer some towns still turn into tourist malls. We're talking seasonal vendors, including jewelry stores geared towards the cruise crowd and shelves filled with imported souvenirs. However, the port towns you'll visit—from Juneau, the most remote state capital in the country, to Sitka, with its proud reminders of Native and Russian cultures—also manage to retain much of their rustic charm and historical allure. Sure, you may have to jostle for a seat in Juneau's popular Red Dog Saloon (a must-do beer stop, and the oldest tourist attraction in the state) or ask other visitors to step out of the way as you try to snap a picture of Skagway's historic gold-rush buildings or Ketchikan's picturesque Creek Street, but these are minor hassles for cruise-ship passengers. If you want to get away from the crowds by taking an organized shore excursion, touring on your own, or booking a small-ship cruise that goes to more remote parts, there's opportunity for that, too. In addition, by signing up for the cruise lines' pre- or post-cruise land-tour packages (known as "cruisetours"), you can also visit less populated inland destinations such as Denali National Park, Fairbanks, the Kenai Peninsula, the Yukon Territory, or the Canadian Rockies.

Even before you cruise, we can predict you'll want to visit again. This is a place that puts a spell on you. Our writer Fran Golden first visited a dozen years ago and found her view of the world was forever changed. She quickly put the state at the top of her list of cruise destinations; numerous visits since have just confirmed her initial impression. In 2010, she even visited in winter for the first time, attending the Fur Rendezvous

(Fur Rondy) in Anchorage, and discovered a whole new side to Alaska (where they know how to have fun even in the cold). Our coauthor Gene Sloan is more of a newbie to Alaska, but has become a big fan of the cruising scene—he found himself doing three cruises in 3 months at one point. Alaska is like that. It grabs you by the scruff of the neck and won't let you go.

Whether you're looking for pampering and resort amenities or a "you and the sea" adventure experience, you'll find it all on cruise ships in Alaska. Here are some of our favorites, along with our picks of the best ports, shore excursions, and sights.

1 The Best of Alaska's Ships

- **The Best Ships for Luxury:** Luxury in Alaska is defined in 2011 by **Regent Seven Seas, Silversea,** and **Crystal.** If you want a more casual kind of luxury (a really nice ship with a no-tie-required policy), Regent's *Seven Seas Navigator* offers just that on an all-suite vessel (most cabins have private balconies) with excellent cuisine. **Silversea,** on the other hand, with its *Silver Shadow,* represents a slick, Italian-influenced, slightly more formal luxury experience with all the perks—big suite cabins and excellent food, linens, service, and companions. Both Regent and Silversea include fine wine and booze in their cruise fares. **Crystal,** on the *Crystal Symphony,* offers the glitz and glamour of a luxury experience on a bigger ship—complete with show productions and a lively casino. For the ultimate Alaska experience in a small-ship setting, check out the yachts of **American Safari Cruises,** where soft adventure comes with luxury accoutrements.
- **The Best of the Mainstream Ships:** The newest ships of every cruise line are beautiful, but Celebrity's *Infinity* is a stunner, as is its sister ship, *Millennium.* These modern vessels, with their extensive art collections, cushy public rooms, and expanded spa areas, give Celebrity a formidable presence in Alaska. And Princess' late-model *Sapphire Princess* and *Diamond Princess* have raised the art of building big ships to new heights. The *Sapphire* sails out of Seattle for a second year, while the *Diamond* will again sail the Inside Passage between Vancouver, B.C., and Whittier.
- **The Best of the Small Ships: American Safari Cruises** is the most intimate and luxurious of a dwindling number of small-ship players, now that Cruise West, Clipper, Glacier Bay Cruiseline, and Majestic America Line have all vanished from the scene. You can't get much more personal or pampering than the line's 12-person *Safari Spirit,* a favorite of such stars as Kate Winslet, Emma Thompson, and their families. The only hiccup for would-be Alaska adventurers: the price, which can run well in excess of $500 per person, per day.
- **The Best Ships for Families:** All the major lines have well-established kids' programs, with Carnival, Royal Caribbean, and Norwegian Cruise Line leading the pack in terms of facilities and activities. Princess gets a nod for its National Park Service Junior Ranger program designed to teach kids about glaciers and Alaska wildlife—the kids can even earn a Junior Ranger badge—and last year increased its shore excursions geared for families. Holland America's Culinary Arts program includes cooking classes that are a favorite of teens. But no one can beat Disney in 2011, with

the *Disney Wonder* making its debut in the Alaska market this year.

- **The Best Ships for Pampering:** It's a toss-up—Celebrity's *Infinity* and *Millennium* have wonderful AquaSpas, complete with thalassotherapy pools and a wealth of soothing and beautifying treatments; and the solariums on Royal Caribbean's *Rhapsody of the Seas* and *Radiance of the Seas* have relaxing indoor pool retreats. We are also big fans of the thermal suite (complete with hydrotherapy pool) in the Greenhouse Spas on Holland America's *Zuiderdam* and *Westerdam.* Luxury line Regent Seven Seas, of course, pampers all around. Ditto for the very posh Silversea Cruises.
- **The Best Shipboard Cuisine:** Regent Seven Seas and Oceania's *Regatta,* new in the Alaska market and with culinary inspiration from celebrity chef Jacques Pepin, will appeal to foodies, especially in the creative department. They share the top-tier with Silversea, with its emphasis on preparation—if you want your filet rare, you'll get it rare. And while this may surprise some people, of the mainstream lines, we are most impressed by the buffet and flavorful dining room cuisine on Carnival. The *Carnival Spirit* in Alaska also boasts the Nouveau Supper Club ($30 service charge per person), where you can enjoy as fine a meal as you'll likely find anywhere. The *Crystal Symphony* has a restaurant operated by top sushi chef Nobu (at no extra charge). Norwegian Cruise Line's Teppanyaki restaurant ($25 per person charge) is also an experience not to be missed—yummy food and a show by knife-wielding chefs.
- **The Best Ships for Onboard Activities:** The ships operated by Carnival and Royal Caribbean have rosters teeming with onboard activities that range from the sublime (such as lectures) to the ridiculous (such as contests designed to get passengers to do or say outrageous things). Princess' ScholarShip@Sea program is a real winner, with exciting packaged classes in such diverse subjects as photography, computers, cooking, and even ceramics, so you can make your own take-home souvenirs. Holland America Line has particularly impressive culinary classes.
- **The Best Ships for Entertainment:** Look to the big ships here. Carnival and Royal Caribbean are tops when it comes to an overall package of shows, nightclub acts, lounge performances, and audience-participation entertainment. Princess also presents particularly well-done—if somewhat less lavishly staged—shows. Holland America has made recent improvements in this area, including adding comedians and magicians to its roster. Of course newcomer to Alaska, Disney, is also tops in this area with its family-oriented fare.
- **The Best Ships for Whale-Watching:** If the whales come close enough, you can see them from any ship in Alaska—Fran spotted a couple of orcas from her balcony cabin on a Holland America ship. But smaller ships—such as those operated by Lindblad, American Safari, and the new InnerSea Discoveries—might actually change course to follow a whale. Get your cameras and binoculars ready!
- **The Best Ships for Cruisetours:** With their own fleets of deluxe motorcoaches and railcars, Princess, Holland America, and more recently Royal Caribbean Cruises (which owns Royal Caribbean and Celebrity) are the market leaders in getting you

Alaska

0
200 mi
0
200 km
N
RUSSIA
CHUKCHI SEA
Chukchi Peninsula
Diomede Is.
Bering Strait
International Date Line
Arctic Circle
65° N
60° N
55° N
Savoonga
St. Lawrence
St. Matthew
Nunivak
BERING SEA
St. Paul
Pribilof Islands
St. George
Barrow
Pt. Barrow
C. Halkett
Teskekpuk L.
Icy Cape
C. Lisburne
Pt. Hope
Colville R.
BROOKS
Noatak R.
Noatak N.Pres.
Gates of the Arctic N.P. & Pres.
Cape Krusenstern N.M.
Kobuk Valley N.P.
Kotzebue
Ambler
Noorvik
Selawik
Coldfoot
Bering Land Bridge N.Pres.
Kotzebue Sound
Kobuk R.
Bettles
Koyukuk R.
Wales
Teller
Seward Peninsula
Nome
Norton Sound
Galena
Manley Hot Springs
Yukon R.
Unalakleet
Stebbins
Emmonak
Kotlik
Alakanuk
Kuskokwim Mts.
Denali N.P. & Pres.
Mt. McKinley
McGrath
Innoko R.
Mountain Village
St. Marys
Hooper Bay
Chevak
Talkeetna
Kuskokwim R.
ALASKA
Baird Inlet
Houston
Bethel
Lake Clark N.P. & Pres.
Nushagak R.
Hope
Kenai
Soldotna
Kenai Pen.
Kipnuk
Quinhagak
Iliamna L.
Range
Homer
Cook Inlet
Seldovia
Togiak
Dillingham
C. Newenham
C. Constantine
King Salmon
BRISTOL BAY
Naknek L.
Aleutian
Katmai N.P. & Pres.
Shelikof Strait
Afognak
Becharof L.
Kodiak
Aniakchak N.M. & Pres.
Alaska Peninsula
Trinity Is.
Chirikof
Unimak
King Cove
Sand Point
Shumagin Islands
Akutan
Sanak
Umnak
Unalaska
Unalaska

ARCTIC OCEAN
BEAUFORT SEA
C. Bathurst
C. Dalhousie
NUNAVUT
Bluenose L.
Prudhoe Bay
Deadhorse
DALTON HWY.
Inuvik
Great Bear Lake
RANGE
Porcupine R.
Mackenzie R.
DEMPSTER HWY.
NORTHWEST TERRITORIES
Ft. Yukon
Circle
STEESE HWY.
Yukon R.
CANADA
MACKENZIE
Yukon-Charley Rivers N.Pres.
FAIRBANKS
Eagle
College
North Pole
Nenana
Delta Jct.
Mertie Mts.
Ogilvie Mountains
Dawson
YUKON TERRITORY
GEORGE PARKS HWY.
RANGE
Tok
Tanana R.
Pelly Mountains
Susitna R.
RICHARDSON HWY.
TOK CUT-OFF
ALASKA HWY.
KLONDIKE HWY.
Talkeetna Mts.
Glennallen
GLENN HWY.
Wrangell Mts.
Teslin R.
Palmer
Wasilla
ANCHORAGE
Chugach Mountains
Wrangell-St. Elias N.P. & Pres.
Kluane L.
Whitehorse
Watson Lake
Whittier
Valdez
St. Elias Mountains
Carcross
COAST MOUNTAINS
BRITISH COLUMBIA
Kenai Mts.
Cordova
Seward
Prince William Sd.
Kayak
Montague
Skagway
Haines
Atlin L.
Yakutat
Kenai Fjords N.P.
Glacier Bay N.P. & Pres.
Gustavus
JUNEAU
Stikine R.
Hoonah
Admiralty I. N.M.
GULF OF ALASKA
Chicagof
Kupreanof
Sitka
Kake
Petersburg
Wrangell
Misty Fjords N.M.
Baranof
Revillagigedo
C. Ommaney
Kuiu
Klawock
Craig
Pr. of Wales
Ketchikan
Metlakatla
Hydaburg
PACIFIC OCEAN
Dall
Prince Rupert
Dixon Entrance
Masset
Hecate Strait
Graham
Queen Charlotte

into the Interior of Alaska, either before or after your cruise. Princess and Holland America also own lodges and hotels, and some of the other lines actually buy their land-product components from these lines. One of Holland America's strengths is its shortened 3- and 4-night cruises combined with an Alaska/Yukon land package. (You get on a regular 7-night cruise, but disembark early to continue on your land tour.) The company offers exclusive entry into the Yukon's Kluane National Park, and another Yukon gem has been added—Tombstone Territorial Park, near Dawson City, a region of staggering wilderness beauty, Native architecture, stunning vistas, and wildlife. Princess is arguably stronger in 7-night Gulf of Alaska cruises in conjunction with Denali/Fairbanks or Kenai Peninsula cruisetour arrangements, and has been emphasizing its availability of 3-night land options combined with weeklong cruises in addition to longer options.

2 The Best Ports

Juneau and Sitka are our favorite ports this year. Juneau is one of the most visually pleasing small cities anywhere and certainly the prettiest capital city in America (once you get beyond all the tourist shops near the pier). It's fronted by the Gastineau Channel and backed by Mount Juneau and Mount Roberts, has the very accessible Mendenhall Glacier, and is otherwise surrounded by wilderness—and it's a really fun city to visit, too. Recently, an addition to the tourist attraction roster is a drive past the governor's mansion, residence of the current governor Sean Parnell.

Sitka's Russian architecture, totem pole park, and Raptor Rehabilitation Center are all top-flight attractions. And what we like most about Sitka is that it hasn't been overrun with stuff for tourists—it still feels like a small-town place. (In fact, on a visit a few years ago, Fran heard plenty of complaints from locals about a chain tourist store that somehow snuck into the town—the locals vowing not to allow such shops anymore). Sitka is the kind of place real travelers (as opposed to tourists) will adore.

No town in Alaska is more historically significant than Skagway (which used to be one of our favorites), and the old buildings are so perfect you might think you stepped into a Disney version of what a gold-rush town should look like. However, you must first get over the presence of a Starbucks at the Mercantile Center, 15 or so upscale jewelry shops that have followed cruise passengers from the Caribbean (like some locals, we were thrilled to discover that one such shop, Little Switzerland, had actually pulled up stakes and moved on after an unsuccessful run in Skagway), and all the other tourist shops and attractions. Skagway has become hokey and touristy. But if you can get yourself into the right frame of mind, if you can recall the history of the place, the gold-rush frenzy that literally put the town on the map, it's easier to capture its true spirit.

For a more low-key Alaska experience, take the ferry from Skagway to Haines, which reminds us of the folksy, frontier Alaska depicted on the TV show *Northern Exposure,* and is a great place to spot eagles and other wildlife. Some ships also stop at Haines as a port of call, usually for a few hours after Skagway, and we're pleased to report this is one town that has not been changed by the advent of cruise-ship visitors.

3 The Best Shore Excursions

Flightseeing by floatplane or helicopter in Alaska is an unforgettable way to check out the scenery, if you can afford it: Airborne tours tend to be pretty pricey, from $215 to about $600 per head. A helicopter trip to a dog-sled camp at the top of a glacier (usually among the priciest of the offerings) affords both incredibly pretty views and a chance to try your hand at the truly Alaskan sport of dog sledding, and it's a great way to earn bragging rights with the folks back home.

For a less extravagant excursion, nothing beats a ride on a clear day on the White Pass & Yukon Route Railway out of Skagway to the Canadian border—the route was recently expanded so that some of the trains go not just to Fraser, at the border, but on to Carcross (formerly known as Caribou Cross) in the Yukon Territory, some 30 more miles into Canada. The steep train route is the same one followed by the gold stampeders of 1898. While you're riding the rails, try to imagine what it was like for those gold seekers crossing the same path on foot!

We also like to get active with kayak and mountain-biking excursions offered by most cruise lines at most ports. In addition to affording a chance to work off those shipboard calories, these excursions typically provide optimum opportunities for spotting eagles, bears, seals, and other wildlife. Ziplining is just plain fun for those who want to try soaring on a wire above the treetops—the adrenaline rush can be addictive.

Another, less hectic shore excursion that's become increasingly popular is whale-watching. On one evening excursion from Juneau in May, passengers on one of the small whale-watching boats got the thrill of seeing an entire pod of orcas, more than a dozen of the giant creatures, frolicking before their eyes. For those with big bucks or big groups, some lines are offering private tours. For example, Holland America passengers can spend $2,099 for a private luxury boat with captain that can take up to 18 people exploring from Juneau, or $1,765 for private Alaska touring in a DeHavilland Beaver floatplane in Ketchikan (for up to 6 people).

2

Choosing Your Ideal Cruise

Just like clothes, cars, and gourmet coffee, Alaska cruises come in all different styles to suit all different tastes; so the first step in ensuring that you have the best possible vacation is to match your expectations to the appropriate itinerary and ship.

In this chapter, we explore the advantages of the two main Alaska itineraries, examine the differences between big-ship cruising and small-ship cruising, pose some questions you should ask yourself to determine which cruise is right for you, and give you the skinny on cruisetours, which combine a cruise with a land tour that gets you into the Alaska Interior.

1 The Alaska Cruise Season

Alaska is very much a seasonal, as opposed to year-round, cruise destination; the season generally runs from May through September, although some smaller ships start up in late April. May and September are considered the shoulder seasons, and lower brochure rates and more aggressive discounts are offered during these months. We particularly like cruising in May, before the crowds arrive, when we've generally found locals to be friendlier than they are later in the season, at which point they're pretty much ready to see the tourists go home for the winter.

Also, at the Inside Passage ports, May is one of the driest months in the season. On a recent late-May cruise, temperatures were in the 70s (low to mid-20s Celsius), perfect for hiking and biking. Late September, though, also offers the advantage of fewer fellow cruise passengers clogging the ports. The warmest months are June, July, and August, with temperatures generally around 50°F to 80°F (10°C–27°C) during the day and cooler at night. Some years the temperature has soared higher—Juneau has been known to hit the 90s. When this happens, there is much local speculation about global warming. You may not need a parka, but you will need to bring along some outerwear and rain gear. Pack some T-shirts, too. The trick in coping with Alaska weather is to dress in layers, with a lightweight waterproof jacket on top and a sweater and T-shirt underneath. June tends to be drier than July and August. (We have experienced trips in July when it rained nearly every day.) April and May are drier than September, although in early April you may encounter freezing rain and other vestiges of winter. If you are considering traveling in a shoulder month, keep in mind that some shops and a few visitor attractions don't open until Memorial Day, and the visitor season is generally considered over on Labor Day (although cruise lines operate well into September).

2 The Inside Passage or the Gulf of Alaska?

For the purposes of cruising, Alaska can be divided into two separate and distinct areas, known generically as "the Inside Passage" and "the Gulf."

Shore Excursions: The What, When & Why

Shore excursions offered by the cruise lines provide a chance for you to get off the ship and explore the sights up close. You'll take in the history, nature, and culture of the region, from exploring gold-rush-era streets to experiencing Native Alaskan traditions such as totem carving.

Some excursions are of the walking-tour or bus-tour variety, but many others are activity-oriented: Cruise passengers have the opportunity to go sea kayaking, mountain-biking, horseback riding, salmon fishing, ziplining, and even rock climbing. There are tours by motorcycle and ATV. You can see the sights by seaplane or helicopter—and maybe even land on a glacier and go for a walk or dog-sled ride. Occasionally, with some of the smaller cruise lines, you'll find quirky excursions, such as visits with local artists in their studios. Some lines even offer scuba diving and snorkeling.

With some lines, shore excursions are included in your cruise fare, but with most lines they are an added (though very worthwhile) expense. See chapters 8 and 9 for details on the excursions available at the various ports. For more information, see section 4, "Cruisetours: The Best of Land & Sea," later in this chapter, and chapter 10, "Cruisetour Destinations."

THE INSIDE PASSAGE

The Inside Passage runs through the area of Alaska known as Southeast (which the locals also call "the Panhandle"). It's the narrow strip of the state—islands, mainland coastal communities, and mountains—that runs from the Canadian border in the south to the start of the Gulf in the north, just above the Juneau/Haines/Skagway area. The islands on the western side of the area afford cruise ships a welcome degree of protection from the sea and its attendant rough waters (hence the name "Inside Passage"). Because of that shelter, such ports as Ketchikan, Wrangell, Petersburg, and others are reached with less rocking and rolling, and thus less risk of seasickness. Sitka is not on the Inside Passage (it's on the Pacific Ocean side of Baranof Island) but is included in a fair number of Inside Passage cruise itineraries because it is a beautiful little port, with architecture and historical sites strongly reflective of Alaska's Russian past.

Southeast encompasses the capital city, **Juneau,** and townships influenced by the former Russian presence in the state (**Sitka,** for instance), the Tlingit and Haida Native cultures (**Ketchikan**), and the great gold rush of 1898 (**Skagway**). It is a land of rainforests, mountains, inlets, and glaciers (including Margerie, Johns Hopkins, Muir, and the others contained within the boundaries of **Glacier Bay National Park**). The region is rich in wildlife, especially of the marine variety. It is a scenic delight. But then, what part of Alaska isn't?

THE GULF OF ALASKA

The other major cruising area is the **Southcentral** region's Gulf of Alaska, usually referred to by the cruise lines as the "Glacier Discovery Route" or the "Voyage of the Glaciers," or some such catchy title. "Gulf of Alaska," after all, sounds pretty bland.

The coastline of the Gulf is that arc of land from just north of Glacier Bay to the Kenai Peninsula. Southcentral also takes in **Prince William Sound;** the **Cook Inlet,** on the northern side of the peninsula; **Anchorage,** Alaska's biggest city; the year-round **Alyeska Resort** at Girdwood, 40 miles from Anchorage; the **Matanuska** and **Susitna** valleys (the "Mat-Su"), a fertile agricultural region renowned for the record size of some of its garden produce; and part of the Alaska Mountain Range.

The principal Southcentral terminus ports are **Seward** or **Whittier** for Anchorage. Rarely do ships actually head for Anchorage proper because that adds another full day to the route (but in 2011, Holland America for a second year will visit the city regularly on its new 14-night itinerary on the *Amsterdam* from Seattle—last year it became the first big ship to visit in 25 years); instead, they carry passengers from Seward or Whittier to Anchorage by bus or train.

Let us stress that going on a Gulf cruise does not mean that you don't visit any of the Inside Passage. The big difference is that, whereas the more popular Inside Passage cruise itineraries run 7 nights round-trip to and from Seattle or Vancouver, B.C., the Gulf routing is one-way—either northbound or southbound—between Vancouver and Seward or Vancouver and Whittier. A typical Gulf itinerary still visits such Inside Passage ports as **Ketchikan, Juneau,** and **Skagway.**

The Gulf's glaciers are quite dazzling and every bit as spectacular as their counterparts to the south. **College Fjord,** for instance, is lined with glaciers—16 of them, each one grander than the last. On one cruise, Fran saw incredible calving at **Harvard Glacier,** with chunks of 400- and 500-year-old ice falling off and crashing into the water to thunderous sounds every few minutes. (Worries about the display being caused by global warming aside, it was spectacular.) Another favorite part of a Gulf cruise is the visit to the gigantic **Hubbard Glacier**—at 6 miles, Alaska's longest—at the head of Yakutat Bay, where the chunks in the water may remind you of ice in a giant punch bowl. Nothing beats a sunny day watching the glacier—hyperactive, popping and cracking, and shedding tons of ice into the bay. We should mention that on a recent visit to Hubbard Glacier, we couldn't even get into the bay because another ship was blocking our path (and hogging the optimum views). Our fear is that, with so many new ships in Alaska, glacier viewing could become a blood sport.

And then there's the fact that, sadly, what you're really seeing is Alaska's glaciers in retreat, some receding quite rapidly.

WHICH ITINERARY IS BETTER?

It's a matter of personal taste. Some people don't like open-jaw flights (flying into one city and out of another)—which can add to the ticket price—and prefer the round-trip Inside Passage route. Others don't mind splitting up the air travel because they want to enjoy the additional glacier visits on the Gulf cruise itineraries. It's entirely up to you. Cruise enthusiasts should not limit themselves to one itinerary; they should try both.

It wasn't so long ago that you wouldn't have had a choice. A few years back, there were practically no Gulf crossings. Then Princess and its tour-operating affiliate decided to accelerate the development of its land components (lodges, railcars, motorcoaches, and so on), particularly in the Kenai Peninsula and Denali National Park areas, for which Anchorage is a logical springboard. To feed these land services with cruisetour passengers, Princess beefed up its number of Gulf sailings and the line will still have three ships in the Gulf this year—as well as having a formidable Inside Passage capacity. One of the line's newest ships, and one with the most amenities, the

2,670-passenger *Diamond Princess* is doing the Gulf in 2011, while sister ship *Sapphire Princess* is doing a second year of Inside Passage rotation out of Seattle. The other Alaska cruise giant Holland America Line (HAL), will have five of its seven vessels in the Inside Passage (two out of Vancouver, three out of Seattle), and two vessels cruising across the Gulf (out of Vancouver). HAL tends to go more heavily into the Inside Passage than Princess because it is arguably stronger in Yukon Territory land services, which are more accessible from Juneau or Skagway.

3 Big Ship or Small Ship?

Picking the right ship is the most important factor in ensuring that you get the vacation you're looking for. Cruise ships in Alaska range from **small, adventure-type vessels** to **really big, resortlike megaships,** with the cruise experience varying widely depending on the type of ship you select. There are casual cruises and luxury cruises; there are educational cruises, where you attend lectures; and entertainment-focused cruises, where you attend musical revues; there are adventure-oriented cruises, where hiking, kayaking, and exploring remote areas are the main activities; and resortlike cruises, where aquatherapy and mud baths are the order of the day.

Besides the availability (or nonavailability) of the programs, the spas, the activities, and the like, there is another question you have to answer before deciding on a ship. Do you want, or do you need, to be with people and, if so, in an intimate daily setting or only on an occasional basis? On a small ship, there's no escape. The people you meet on a 12-passenger or even a 138-passenger vessel are the ones you're going to be seeing every day of the cruise. And woe betide you if they turn out to be boring, or bombastic, or slow-witted, or in some other way not to your taste. Some people may think that the megaships are too big, but they do have at least one saving grace. On a 2,670-passenger ship, there's plenty of room to steer clear of people who turn you off. And because all of these big, newer ships have lots of alternative restaurants, it's even easier to avoid those types at mealtimes, something that's not so easy on a smaller ship. Personal chemistry plays a big part in the success or failure of any cruise experience—especially a small-ship cruise experience.

You'll need to decide what overall cruise experience you want. Itinerary and type of cruise are even more important than price. After all, what kind of bargain is a party cruise if you're looking for a quiet time? Or an adventure-oriented cruise if you're not physically in the best of shape? Your fantasy vacation may be someone else's nightmare, and vice versa.

Unlike the Caribbean, which generally attracts people looking to relax in the sun or possibly to party 'til the cows come home, Alaska attracts visitors with a different goal: They want to experience Alaska's glaciers, forests, wildlife, and other natural wonders. All the cruise lines recognize this, so almost any cruise you choose will give you opportunities to see what you've come for. The main question, then, is how you want to see those sights. Do you want to be down at the waterline, viewing them from the deck of an adventure vessel, or do you want to spot them from a warm lounge or your own private veranda?

The hotel director on a Holland America ship once noted, "If you want to stay out until 4am, gamble wildly, and pass out in a lounge, you don't come on Holland America." And he's right. Picking the ship that's right for you is the key to a successful Alaska cruise experience.

In this section, we'll run through the pros and cons of the big ships and the small and alternative ships. (See chapters 5 and 6 for detailed descriptions of the ships cruising in Alaska.)

THE BIG SHIPS

Big ships operating in Alaska vary in size, amenities, and activities, and include really big and really new megaships (the *Diamond Princess* and the *Sapphire Princess* are the biggest; the *Norwegian Pearl* the newest). All the big ships provide a comfortable experience, with virtual armies of service employees overseeing your well-being, and ship stabilizers ensuring smooth sailing.

The size of the current crop of ships may keep Alaska's wildlife at a distance (you may need binoculars to see the whales), but they have plenty of deck space and comfy lounge chairs for relaxing as you take in the gorgeous mountain and glacier views, and sip a cup of coffee or cocoa (and on Holland America the famous Dutch pea soup). Due to their deeper drafts (the amount of ship below the waterline), the big ships can't get as close to the sights as the smaller ships, and they can't visit the more pristine fjords, inlets, and narrows. However, the more powerful engines on these ships do allow them to visit more ports during each trip—generally popular ports where your ship may be one of several, and where shopping for souvenirs is a main attraction. Some of the less massive ships in this category may also visit alternative ports, away from the cruise crowds.

It should be noted that the bigger ships being built nowadays are equipped with some pretty powerful stabilizers—something to think about if you have the occasional bout with seasickness.

The big-ship cruise lines put a lot of emphasis on **shore excursions,** which often take you beyond the port city to explore different aspects of Alaska—nature, Native culture, and so on. (See the shore excursion listings in chapters 8 and 9 for more information.) Dispersing passengers to different locales on these shore trips is a must. When 8,000 passengers from several visiting ships disembark on a small Alaska town, much of the ambience goes out the window. On particularly busy days, there are more cruise passengers in some ports than locals. Take Skagway, for instance: In midsummer, even counting the influx of seasonal tourist services–related employees, its population is far short of 1,000. One large cruise ship will deposit at least twice that many people onto the streets—and on busy days there may be as many as *four* ships in port! The larger ships in the Alaska market fall into two categories: midsize and megaships.

Carrying as many as 2,670 passengers, the **megaships** look and feel like floating resorts. Big on glitz, they have loads of activities, attract many families and seniors, have many public rooms (including fancy casinos and fully equipped gyms and spas), and provide a wide variety of meal and entertainment options. And though they may feature one or two formal nights per trip, the ambience is generally casual. The Alaska vessels of the Carnival, Celebrity, Princess, and Royal Caribbean fleets all fit in this category, as do Norwegian Cruise Line's *Star* and newer *Pearl,* Holland America's *Oosterdam, Zuiderdam,* and *Westerdam,* and Disney's *Wonder.* But a word of caution: Due to the number of people involved, debarkation from the biggest ships can be a lengthy process.

Midsize ships in Alaska for 2011 fall into two segments: the luxurious Silversea's *Silver Shadow,* Crystal's *Symphony,* and Regent Seven Seas' *Navigator;* and the modern midsize *Volendam, Amsterdam, Zaandam,* and *Statendam,* of the Holland America

Ship Size Comparisons

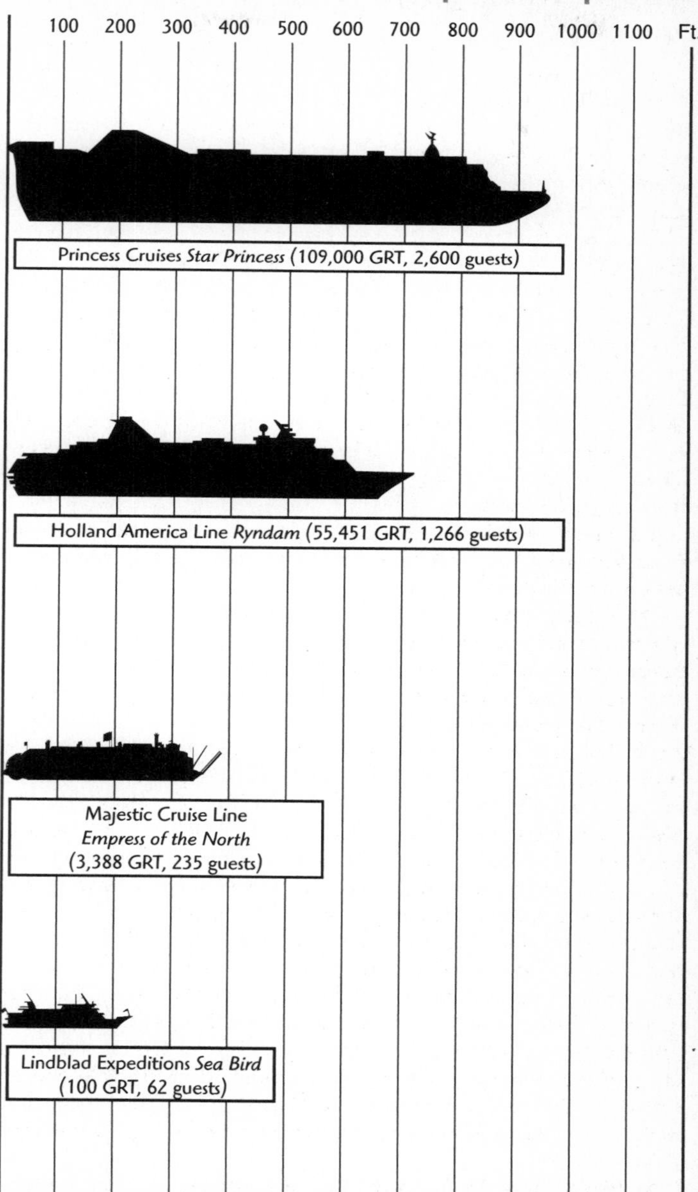

Ships in this chart represent the various size vessels sailing in Alaska. See ship reviews in chapters 5 and 6 for comparative sizes of ships not shown here. (GRT means gross register tons, which is not a literal measure of weight, but rather a measure of interior space on ships.)

Weighing the Dining Options on Various Cruises

Smaller ships usually serve dinner at a certain time, with open seating, allowing you to sit at any table you want but at a set time. Large ships may offer only two fairly rigid, set seating times, especially for dinner. This means that your table will be preassigned and remain the same for the duration of the cruise. However, increasingly, there are exceptions to the rule in the large-ship category. The ships of Norwegian Cruise Line, Oceania, Regent Seven Seas, and Silversea serve all meals with open seating—dine when you want and sit with whom you want (within the restaurants' open hours and sometimes requiring reservations to be made in the morning for dinner). Princess, Holland America, Carnival, Royal Caribbean, and Celebrity have their own systems, allowing guests to choose before the cruise between traditional early or late seating, or open restaurant-style seating. Most large ships today also offer multiple alternative-dining options, featuring casual buffets and specialty restaurants, some with an additional charge (as a gratuity) of up to $35. See "Choosing Your Dining Options," in chapter 3, for more information on dining choices, and see the individual ship reviews in chapters 5 and 6 for ship-specific dining information.

Line, and *Regatta* of Oceania. In general, the size of these ships is less significant than the general onboard atmosphere. Holland America's midsize ships all have a similar calm, adult-oriented feel: the *Navigator* offers a casual form of luxury (think country-club set) and the *Silver Shadow* affords ultraluxury with a sleek, Italian flair, for instance. Both the midsize ships and the megaships have a great range of **facilities** for passengers. There are swimming pools, health clubs, spas (of various sizes), nightclubs, movie theaters, shops, casinos, bars, and special kids' playrooms. In some cases, especially on the megaships, you'll also find sports decks, virtual golf, computer rooms, and cigar clubs, as well as quiet spaces where you can get away from it all. There are so many public rooms that you more than likely won't feel claustrophobic. **Cabins** range from cubbyholes to large suites, depending on the ship and the type of accommodations you book. They provide TVs and telephones, and some have minibars, picture windows, and private verandas.

These ships have big dining rooms and buffet areas and serve a tremendous variety of **cuisine** throughout the day, often with 24-hour-a-day food service. There may also be additional dining venues, such as pizzerias, hamburger grills, ice cream parlors, alternative restaurants (typically for an extra service charge), wine bars, cigar bars, champagne bars, caviar bars, and patisseries.

In most cases, there are lots of **onboard activities** to keep you occupied when you're not whale- or glacier-watching, including games, contests, and classes and lectures (sometimes by naturalists, park rangers, or wildlife experts; sometimes on topics such as line dancing and napkin folding). These ships also have a variety of entertainment options that may even include celebrity headline acts and usually include stage-show productions, some pretty extravagant (those of Carnival come to mind). These ships carry a lot of people and, as such, can at times feel crowded—there may be lines at the buffets and in other public areas, and it may take a while to disembark in port.

THE SMALL & ALTERNATIVE SHIPS

While big cruise ships are mostly for people who want every resort amenity, small or alternative ships are best suited for people who prefer a casual, crowd-free cruise experience that gives passengers a chance to get up close and personal with Alaska's **natural surroundings** and **wildlife.**

Thanks to their smaller size, these ships, carrying fewer than 138 passengers (American Safari Cruises' *Safari Spirit* carries only 12), can go places where larger ships can't, such as narrow fjords, uninhabited islands, and smaller ports that cater mostly to small fishing vessels. Due to their shallow draft, they can nose right up to sheer cliff faces, bird rookeries, bobbing icebergs, and cascading waterfalls that you can literally reach out and touch. Also, sea animals are not as intimidated by these ships, so you might find yourself having a rather close encounter with a humpback whale, or watching other sea mammals bobbing in the ship's wake. You may catch excellent glimpses of land animals, too—while on a small ship in the Misty Fjords (a place big ships can't even go), Fran and her fellow passengers watched through binoculars as a brown bear shoreside stood to its full height, the captain positioning the ship a safe distance from the creature for a good half-hour so everyone could take in the sight. The decks on these ships are closer to the waterline, too, giving passengers a more intimate view than they would get from the high decks of the large cruise ships. Some of these ships stop at ports on a daily basis, like the larger ships, while some avoid ports almost entirely, exploring natural areas instead. Small ships also have the flexibility to change direction as opportunities arise—say, to go where whales have been sighted and to linger awhile once a sighting has been made.

The alternative-ship experience is all about a sense of **adventure** (usually of a soft rather than rugged sort) and it's a generally casual cruise experience: There are no dress-up nights and food may be rather simply prepared. (Although there are notable exceptions: American Safari's fare is excellent.) Because there are so few public areas to choose from—usually only one or two small lounges—camaraderie tends to develop more quickly between passengers on these ships than aboard larger vessels, which can be as anonymous as a big city. **Cabins** on these ships don't usually offer TVs or telephones and tend to be very small and, in some cases (not in the case of American Safari), downright spartan. Meals are generally served in a single open seating (seats are not assigned, but there is a set dinner time), and dress codes are usually nonexistent.

None of these ships has the kind of significant exercise or spa facilities that you'll find on the big ships—your best exercise bet is usually a brisk walk around the deck after dinner—but many compensate by providing more **active off-ship opportunities,** such as hiking or kayaking. The alternative ships are also more likely to feature in-depth **lectures** on Alaska-specific topics, such as marine biology, history, and Native culture.

There are little or no stabilizers on most of these smaller ships, and the ride can be bumpy in open water—which isn't much of a problem on Inside Passage itineraries, since most of the cruising area is protected from sea waves. These ships are also difficult for travelers with disabilities as there are no elevators. And the alternative-ship lines do not offer specific activities or facilities for children, although you will find a few families on some of these vessels.

4 Cruisetours: The Best of Land & Sea

Most folks who go to the trouble of getting to a place as far off the beaten path as Alaska try to stick around for awhile once they're there, rather than jetting home as soon as they hop off the boat. Knowing this, the cruise lines have set themselves up in the land-tour business as well, offering a number of great land-based excursions that can be tacked onto your cruise experience.

We're not just talking about an overnight stay in Anchorage or Juneau before or after your cruise. Almost any cruise line will arrange an extra night of hotel accommodations for you; but enjoyable as that may be, it doesn't begin to hint at the real opportunities available in Alaska. No, the subject here is **cruisetours,** a total package with a cruise and a structured, prearranged, multi-day land itinerary already programmed in—for instance, a 7-day cruise with a 5-day land package. There are any number of combinations between 9 and 21 days in length.

In this section, we'll discuss the various cruisetour itineraries that are available through the lines. See chapter 10 for details on the various cruisetour destinations.

CRUISETOUR ITINERARIES

Many parts of inland Alaska can be visited on cruisetour programs, including Denali National Park, Fairbanks, Wrangell–St. Elias, Nome, and Kotzebue. If you're so inclined, you can even go all the way to the oil fields of the North Slope of Prudhoe Bay, hundreds of miles north of the Arctic Circle.

Three principal tour destination areas can be combined with your Inside Passage or Gulf of Alaska cruise—two major ones, which we'll call the **Anchorage/Denali/Fairbanks** corridor and the **Yukon Territory,** and one less-traveled route that we'll call the **Canadian Rockies Route,** which is an option due to Vancouver's position as an Alaska cruise hub.

ANCHORAGE/DENALI/FAIRBANKS CRUISETOUR

A typical Anchorage/Denali/Fairbanks cruisetour package (we'll use Princess as an example, since it is heavily involved in the Denali sector) might include a 7-day Vancouver-Anchorage cruise, followed by 2 nights in Anchorage, and a scenic ride in a private railcar to **Denali National Park** for 2 more nights at Princess' Denali Lodge or Mount McKinley Lodge (or 1 night at each), before heading on to Fairbanks. On a clear day, the McKinley property affords a panoramic view of the Alaska Mountain Range and its centerpiece, **Mount McKinley,** which, at 20,320 feet, is North America's highest peak. A full day in the park allows guests to explore the staggeringly beautiful wilderness expanse and its wildlife before reboarding the train and heading into the Interior of Alaska, to **Fairbanks,** for 2 more nights. Fairbanks itself isn't much to look at, but the activities available in outlying areas are fantastic—the *Riverboat Discovery* paddle-wheel day cruises on the Chena and Tanana rivers and an excursion to a gold mine are two excellent activity options in the area. Passengers on that particular cruisetour fly home from Fairbanks.

A shorter variation of that itinerary might be a cruise combined with an overnight (or 2-night) stay in Anchorage along with the Denali portion, perhaps with rail transportation into the park and a motorcoach back to Anchorage, skipping Fairbanks. Princess also recently introduced cruisetours that include visits to a hitherto largely inaccessible area, **Wrangell–St. Elias National Park,** where they have built the Copper River Princess Wilderness Lodge, the fifth hotel in the company's lodging network.

Should You Take Your Cruisetour Before or After Your Cruise?

Though the land portion of both the Denali and the Yukon itineraries can be taken either before or after the cruise, we feel that it's better to take the land portion pre-cruise rather than post-cruise. Why? After several days of traveling around in the wilderness, it's nice to be able to get aboard a ship to relax and be pampered for awhile.

Because of the distances that must be covered on some wilderness cruisetour itineraries, passengers often have to be roused out of bed and ready to board the motorcoach by, say, 7:30am. And the day may seem to go on forever, with a stop to view this waterfall, or that river, or mountain. Then, upon arrival at the next stop—in the early evening usually—the request is, "Hurry and get cleaned up for dinner." By the time you've crawled into your new bed often quite late at night, you're beat. It's a nice kind of tired, as the saying goes, but it's tired nevertheless. After a few days of that, it's great to get on a luxurious cruise ship, unpack just once, and rise when you feel like it, comfortable in the knowledge that you haven't missed your transportation and that you'll still make it in time to have a leisurely breakfast.

That, at any rate, is the conventional wisdom, and there's more of a demand for pre-cruise land packages than for post-cruise. As the lines obviously can't always accommodate everybody on a land itinerary before the cruise (they're hoping to even out the traffic flow by having a like number of requests to go touring after the voyage), it's smart to get your bid in early.

YUKON TERRITORY CRUISETOUR

Another popular land itinerary offered along with Alaska cruises typically involves a 3- or 4-day cruise between Vancouver and Juneau/Skagway (you either join a 7-day sailing late or get off early), combined with a land program into the **Klondike,** in Canada's Yukon Territory, then through the Interior of Alaska to Anchorage. En route, passengers experience a variety of transportation modes, which may include rail, riverboat, motorcoach, and possibly air. There are multiple variations.

The Yukon, although located in Canada, is nevertheless an integral part of the overall Alaska cruisetour picture, due to its intimate ties to Alaska's gold-rush history. The overnight stops are **Whitehorse,** the territorial capital, and **Dawson City,** a remote, picture-perfect gold-rush town near the site where gold was found in 1896. Holland America offers a drive through Canada's **Kluane National Park,** a Yukon Territory wilderness area designated a UNESCO World Heritage Site, and also through Tombstone Territorial Park, about 90 minutes' drive from Dawson City, an area of stunning scenery, Native architecture, and abundant wildlife. Kluane Park contains 5 of North America's 10 tallest peaks. If it's wilderness scenery you want, you'll be hard-pressed to find anything more awesome than that seen on these two exclusive tours from Holland America.

After heading north through the Yukon, cruisetour passengers cross the Alaska border near Beaver Creek, travel to Fairbanks, and from there go through Denali to Anchorage. Again, the tour can be taken in either direction and on a pre- or post-cruise basis.

CANADIAN ROCKIES CRUISETOUR

A Canadian Rockies tour is easily combined with a Vancouver-originating (or terminating) Inside Passage or Gulf cruise. In 5-, 6-, or 7-day chunks, you can visit such scenic wonders as **Banff, Lake Louise,** and **Jasper National Park** in conjunction with an Alaska sailing.

The Canadian Rockies have some of the finest **mountain scenery** on earth. It's not just that the glacier-carved mountains are astonishingly dramatic and beautiful; it's also that there are hundreds and hundreds of miles of this wonderful wilderness high country. Between them, Banff National Park and Jasper National Park preserve much of this mountain beauty. Other national and provincial parks make accessible more vast and equally spectacular regions of the Rockies, as well as portions of the nearby Columbia and Selkirk mountain ranges. The beautiful Lake Louise, colored deep green from its mineral content, is located 35 miles north of Banff.

BATTLE OF THE TOP PLAYERS

If we talk in this section more about **Princess** and **Holland America (HAL)** than we do about other lines, it's because their investments of tens of millions of dollars in land components of Alaskan tourism have allowed them to become the 800-pound gorillas duking it out for dominance in Alaska. Other lines offer some of the same cruisetours as these two, but many of them buy at least some of their cruisetour components from Princess and/or Holland America's land operations. It may seem odd to have companies buying from (or selling to) competitors, but with tourism in Alaska, there's practically no other way. As recently as the early 1980s, when Holland America–Westours owned the bulk of the land-tour components, Princess, its number-one rival, was also its number-one customer! Hey, a 4-month season makes for strange bedfellows.

It was partly to carve out a niche for itself and at the same time to lessen its reliance on the services of a competitor that Princess plunged heavily into the lodging and transportation sectors. Princess is arguably stronger in the Denali corridor than any other line, while Holland America could be said to have the upper hand in the Yukon/Klondike market. But each line offers tours to both of these areas, among other options.

Princess owns railcars (the *Midnight Sun Express*) in the Denali corridor. Holland America also owns railcars there (the *McKinley Explorer*). Both, incidentally, rely on the Alaska Railroad to pull them. Princess owns wilderness lodges; Holland America owns primarily city hotels. Both Princess and Holland America have a fleet of motorcoaches. HAL's fleet was enhanced 2 years ago with 39 luxurious 45-seat beauties. For the technically minded, they are MCI LX models, the very latest, with as much legroom as in most first-class airplane cabins and, according to the operator, 50% more legroom than on its coaches previously. Other coaches in the fleet are being retired or retrofitted to provide the same level of comfort as the newcomers.

But HAL and Princess have not gone unchallenged. With its Royal Caribbean International and Celebrity Cruises brands, Royal Caribbean has become the third well-established player in the game, though it did cut a ship for 2011. The company will have two Royal Caribbean ships and three Celebrity ships in the 49th state this summer. A few years ago, it formed Royal Celebrity Tours to operate its own land packages; in 2011, the land affiliate will provide several dozen cruisetour options. Its motorcoaches are luxurious and its railcars are truly state-of-the-art, featuring glass-domed tops so you don't miss any views on the Denali Park run. The railcars have comfortable, airline-style leather seats at least on par with the business-class seating of most major airlines, a fine kitchen on the lower level (meals are extra, with a variety of menus), and a friendly, knowledgeable staff. Plus, the railcars are more accessible for travelers with disabilities than those run by Princess or HAL (each of Royal Caribbean's is equipped with a mechanical lift that can carry two wheelchairs at a time to the second level from the station platform).

5 Quiz Time: Questions to Ask When Choosing Your Cruise

After you've decided which itinerary and what kind of ship appeal to you, we suggest you ask yourself some questions about the kind of experience you want, and then read through the cruise line and ship reviews in chapters 5 and 6 to see which ones match your vision of the perfect Alaska cruise vessel.

When looking at the attributes of the various ships to make your choice, some determining factors will be no-brainers. For instance, if you're traveling with kids, you'll want a ship with a good kids' program. If you're a foodie, you'll want a ship with gourmet cuisine. If you're used to staying at a Ritz-Carlton hotel when you travel, you'll probably want to cruise on a luxury ship. If you usually stay at B&Bs, you'll probably prefer one of the small ships.

Also ask yourself whether you require resortlike amenities, such as a heated swimming pool, spa, casino, aerobics classes, and state-of-the-art gym. Or do you care more about having an adventure or an educational experience? If you want the former, choose a large cruise ship; if you prefer the latter, a small ship may be more your speed.

Here are some more pertinent questions to help you narrow the field:

How do you get a deal and what's not included? The best way to get a deal on a cruise in Alaska is to book early. Virtually all the lines (with the exception of some of the small-ship lines) offer early booking discounts. The numbers and dates may vary a bit, but the formula has been fairly standard: When you **book in advance,** in a typical year, you can expect to save 25% to 50% off the brochure rate if you book your Alaska cruise by mid- to late February of the year of the cruise. If the cabins do not fill up by the cutoff date, the early-bird rate may be extended. We were seeing starting early-bird brochure prices for 2011 as low as $529 for an inside cabin on an early-season weeklong cruise.

If the cabins are still not full as the cruise season begins, cruise lines typically start marketing special deals, usually through their top-producing travel agents. In 2010, there were some last-minute offers below $399 for a weeklong cruise, but far fewer than in 2009—such bargain basement fares generally are for the lowest category of inside cabins, and very limited in terms of how many cabins are offered at that price. With additional lines in the market in 2011, it's our feeling that such last-minute discounts, which can run as high as 50% to 75%, will be less common than in some previous years. We suggest you book your Alaska cruise, and particularly your Alaska cruisetour (because these are increasingly popular), as early as possible.

Cruise fares cover accommodations, meals, shipboard entertainment, and most shipboard activities. There are, however, a number of expenses not covered in the typical cruise package, and you should factor these in when planning your vacation budget. Airfare to and from your port of embarkation and debarkation is usually extra (though cruise lines sometimes offer reduced rates). Necessary hotel stays before or after the cruise are also usually not included. Gratuities, taxes, and trip insurance are typically extra as well. Shore excursions are rarely included in the cruise fare (Regent Seven Seas is the only big ship line that includes them); and if you opt for pricey ones, such as flightseeing, you can easily add $600 to $1,000 per person to your total. Alcohol is typically extra (though Regent and Silversea include all drinks in the cruise fare), as is soda and such incidentals as laundry, Internet access (which can run as much as 75¢ per minute!), telephone calls from the ship, and babysitting. And then there are such optional splurges as beauty and spa services, wine tastings, dining in alternative restaurants, select fitness classes, fancy ice cream sundaes, and photos taken by ship photographers.

Because travel agents constantly keep abreast of the latest bargains, we believe they are best equipped to advise you on the best Alaska cruise deals.

See chapter 3 for more information on when to book for the best prices.

How much time is spent in port and how much at sea? Generally, ships on 7-night itineraries spend 3 days in port, and cruise in natural areas such as Glacier Bay, College Fjord, or Tracy Arm during the other 4 days.

Coming into port, ships generally dock right after breakfast, allowing you the morning and afternoon to take a shore excursion or explore on your own. They usually depart in the early evening, giving you an hour or two to rest up before dinner (although some ships do stay in Juneau as late as 10pm, allowing you a chance to sample a halibut burger, salmon steak, or similar local fare off the ship for dinner, if you so choose). On rare occasions, a ship might cruise through a glacier area in the morning and dock at the next port in the early afternoon, not leaving until 10 or 11pm.

On days at sea, the emphasis will be on exploring natural areas, viewing glaciers, and scanning for wildlife. Big ships stick to prearranged schedules on these days, but on small-ship, soft adventure–type cruises, days at sea can be unstructured, with the captain choosing a destination based on reports of whale sightings, for example. Some small-ship itineraries include almost no ports, sticking instead to isolated natural areas that passengers explore by kayak, by Zodiac boat, or on foot.

Is the cruise formal or casual? If you don't care to get dressed up, select a less formal cruise, such as those offered by many of the small ships, by Regent's luxurious but casual *Seven Seas Navigator,* and by the Norwegian Cruise Line ships, which do not have official formal nights (though there's a night when you can dress up if you like). If, on the other hand, having the chance to put on your finery appeals to you, select one of the more formal premium lines such as Princess, Celebrity, or Holland America (and, to a lesser extent, mass-market lines such as Royal Caribbean and Carnival), or the posh *Silversea* and *Crystal.* These ships will have casual and formal nights, meaning women can show off everything from a sundress to an evening gown (though on formal nights, most show up in cocktail dresses) over the course of a week, and men will go from shirtsleeves one night, to jacket and tie the next (you can wear a tuxedo if you like, but many men are now opting for dark suits). All the lines also now have an option for those who do not want to dress up on formal nights—you can skip the dining room and eat casually at the buffet.

What are the other passengers usually like? Each ship attracts a fairly predictable type of passenger. On small ships, you'll find a more physically active bunch that's highly interested in nature, but you'll find fewer families and single travelers. Larger ships cater to a more diverse group—singles, newlyweds, families, and couples over 55. Alaska sailings from Seattle attract a younger, more family-oriented crowd. If you're looking for nightlife, you may want to look at Carnival, Norwegian Cruise Line, and Royal Caribbean cruises from this port. We've included information on typical passengers in all the cruise-line reviews in chapters 5 and 6.

I'll be traveling alone. Will I have fun? And does it cost more? A nice thing about cruises is that you needn't worry about dining alone because you'll be seated with other guests. (If you don't want to be, seek a ship with alternative-dining options, although a steady diet of "Table for one, please" is likely to raise a few eyebrows among your shipmates.) You also needn't worry much about finding people to talk to because the general atmosphere on nearly all ships is very congenial and allows you to find conversation easily, especially during group activities. Some ships host a party to give singles a chance to get to know one another, and some ships provide social hosts as dance partners.

The downside is that you may have to pay for the privilege of traveling solo. Because their rates are based on two people per cabin, some lines charge a "single supplement" rate (aka an extra charge) that ranges from 110% to an outrageous 200% of the per-person, double-occupancy fare. As a single person, you have two choices: Find a line with a reasonable single supplement rate or ask if the line has a cabin-share program, under which the line will pair you with another single so you can get a lower fare. Some lines also have a single-guarantee program, which means if they can't find you a roommate, they'll book you in a cabin alone, but still honor the shared rate. Singles seeking real savings have the option on some ships of cramming into a shared quad (a room for four). Single cabins would be for one person and available on some ships; however, they tend to be small and to sell out fast.

Is shipboard life heavily scheduled? That depends to a certain extent on you and the ship you choose. Meals are generally served during set hours; though on larger ships, you'll have plenty of alternative options if those hours don't suit you. On smaller ships, you may be out of luck if you miss a meal, unless you can charm the cook. On both large and small ships, times for disembarking and reboarding at the ports are strict: If you miss the boat, you miss the boat. (See chapter 4 for tips on what to do in this situation.) Other than these two considerations, the only schedule you'll have to follow on board is your own. It all depends on how busy you want to be.

What are the cabins like? Cabins come in all sizes and configurations. See "Choosing Your Cabin" in chapter 3 for a detailed discussion.

What are meals like? Meals are a big part of the cruise experience. The larger the ship, the more dining options you'll find. When booking on large ships that feature two dining-room seatings each evening, you'll be asked ahead of time to decide on your preferred dinner hour, with tables assigned. On Princess, Royal Caribbean, Carnival, Holland America, and Celebrity ships, you choose in advance whether to dine traditional- or restaurant-style. Norwegian, Silversea, and Regent ships have open, restaurant-style seating, meaning that you can dine when you want, with whomever you choose; but you are encouraged to make reservations each morning for tables at dinner. On smaller ships, you can sit where you want, but dinner will be called for a set time. In the reviews in chapters 5 and 6, we discuss dining options for each line.

If you have any special dietary requirements (vegetarian, kosher, low salt), be sure the line is informed well in advance, preferably at the time you book your cruise. Almost all ships have vegetarian, vegan, and low-fat options available at every meal, and those that don't can usually meet your needs with some advance warning. With low-carb diets so popular, the lines are getting into these options as well. Carnival, for instance, has a nightly low-carb menu.

What activities and entertainment does the ship offer? On small ships, activities are limited by the available public space and are usually up to the passengers to organize—maybe a game of Scrabble or Trivial Pursuit. There may be a showing of a video or two and there will typically also be a lecture series dealing with the flora, fauna, and geography of Alaska, usually conducted by a naturalist. These lectures are also becoming more popular on the larger ships.

The big ships have activities such as fitness, personal finance, photography, and art classes; Ping-Pong and bingo tournaments; audience-participation games; art auctions; and parties. Glitzy floor shows at night are almost *de rigueur.* Cooking classes and demonstrations are the *in* thing. (See the general big-ship and small-ship descriptions earlier in this chapter for more information on activities and entertainment.)

Does the ship have a children's program? Many parents are taking their kids with them on vacation. The lines are responding by adding youth counselors and supervised programs, fancy playrooms, teen centers, and even video-game rooms to keep kids entertained while their parents relax. Some lines offer special shore excursions for children and teens, and most ships provide babysitting (for an extra charge). Some lines have reduced rates for kids, though most discourage parents from bringing infants.

It's important to ask whether a supervised program will be available on your specific cruise, as sometimes the programs operate only if a certain number of children are onboard. If your kids are TV addicts, you may want to make sure that your cabin will have a TV and VCR. Even if it does, though, channel selection will be very limited (consider bringing along a portable DVD player and your own selection of movies).

I have a disability; will I have any trouble taking a cruise? It's important to let the cruise line know about any special needs when you make your booking. If you use a wheelchair, you'll need to know if wheelchair-accessible cabins are available (and how they're equipped), as well as whether public rooms are accessible and can be reached by elevator, and whether the cruise line has any special policy regarding travelers with disabilities. For instance, some lines require that you be accompanied by a fully mobile companion. We've noted all this information in the cabin sections of the ship reviews in chapters 5 and 6. Note that newer ships tend to have the largest number of wheelchair-accessible cabins.

Travelers with disabilities should inquire when booking whether the ship docks at ports or uses "tenders" (small boats) to go ashore. Tenders cannot always accommodate passengers with wheelchairs; in most cases, you can't wheel yourself, but instead will need crew assistance. One exception is Holland America, which uses a special lift system to get passengers into the tenders without requiring them to leave their wheelchairs.

Once aboard the ship, travelers with disabilities will want to seek the advice of the tour staff before choosing shore excursions, as not all will be wheelchair-friendly.

If you have a chronic health problem, we advise you to check with your doctor before booking the cruise and, if you have any specific needs, to notify the cruise line in advance. This will ensure that the medical team on the ship is properly prepared to offer assistance. There is another, somewhat sensitive, consideration for some would-be small-ship passengers: obesity. We mention this only because we once met, on a small ship, a charming young lady who stood a little over 5 feet tall and weighed about 250 pounds. She told us that she had been advised by the cruise line not to book passage on the ship she first chose because she wouldn't fit in the shower. The company put her instead on one for which her girth would not be such a problem. Understand, please, that the cruise operator is not being judgmental. But if you don't mention such things and end up on an inappropriate ship, you're in for a miserable time. So assess the situation realistically.

What if I want to take a cruise for my honeymoon? One-week Alaska cruises start not only on Saturdays and Sundays, but also on Mondays, Wednesdays, Thursdays, and Fridays, which should help you find an appropriate departure date so that you won't have to run out of your wedding reception to catch a plane. You will want to make sure that the ship you choose has double, queen-, or king-size beds; and you may want to also request a cabin with a Jacuzzi. Rooms with private verandas are particularly romantic. You can take in the sights in privacy and even enjoy a quiet meal, assuming the veranda is big enough for a table and chairs (some are not) and the weather doesn't turn chilly. If you want to dine alone, make sure the dining room has tables for two or the ship provides room service. Your travel agent can fill you in on these matters. You may also want to inquire as to the likelihood that there will be other honeymooners your age on the ship. Some ships—among them those of Princess, Royal Caribbean, Carnival, Celebrity, and Holland America—offer special honeymoon packages and sometimes honeymoon suites. Most lines provide special perks such as champagne and chocolates if you let them know in advance that you'll be celebrating your honeymoon on the ship.

Can I get married onboard? Yes. You can get married at sea in the chapel on any of the Princess ships, with the nuptials conducted by the ship's captain. You can also get married at sea on the *Carnival Spirit,* which has a nice wedding chapel. Other big ships permit you to get married onboard, but only if you're willing to bring your own clergyman along with you at full price. Of course, you can also get married while the ship is in port, but you will have to provide your own officiate (since sea captains are only able to legally marry couples in international waters). Ships without wedding chapels will usually agree to clear a public room for your nuptials and may provide flowers and light refreshments.

Will I get seasick? On Inside Passage itineraries, most of your time will be spent in protected waters, where there are islands between you and the open sea, making for generally smooth sailing. However, there are certain points, such as around Sitka and at the entrance to Queen Charlotte Strait, where there's nothing between you and Japan but a lot of wind, water, and choppy seas. Ships with sailing itineraries on the Gulf of Alaska and those sailing from San Francisco, out of necessity, will spend more time in rough, open waters. Although ships that ply these routes tend to be very stable, you'll probably notice some rocking and rolling. Keep in mind that big ships tend to be more stable than smaller ships.

Unless you're particularly prone to seasickness, you probably don't need to worry much. But if you are, there are medications that can help, including Dramamine, Bonine, and Marezine, which are available over the counter and also stocked by most ships—the purser's office may even give them out free. Another option is the Transderm patch, available by prescription only, which is applied behind your ear and has time-released medication. The patch can be worn for up to 3 days, but you should be aware that it comes with a slew of warnings about side effects. Some people have also had success in curbing seasickness by using ginger capsules, which are available at health food stores, or acupressure wristbands, which are available at most pharmacies. Our best advice is to ask your doctor before your cruise what he or she recommends. If you do get sick onboard, the ship's doctor may have additional recommendations.

Is there smoking on ships? The short answer is yes. But cruise lines have recently been reevaluating their smoking policies and some, including Celebrity Cruises, Oceania, and Regent Seven Seas, now ban smoking in cabins and on cabin balconies. Royal Caribbean and Disney Cruise Line do not allow smoking in cabins, but do allow it on cabin balconies. Smoking is generally not allowed in shipboard theaters, show lounges, or dining rooms, and may be restricted to certain bars (many ships now have cigar lounges) or even certain sides of the ship (open decks on starboard side only on Royal Caribbean vessels, for instance). Smoking is generally allowed in ship casinos. Small ships typically allow smoking only in certain outdoor areas. If you are a smoker, check with your line in advance, as several lines were considering stricter policies at press time. If you are not a smoker, you will no doubt be relieved by the new policies being adopted.

3

Booking Your Cruise & Getting the Best Price

Okay, you've thought about what type of cruise vacation experience you have in mind. You've decided when and for how long you'd like to travel. You know what sort of itinerary interests you. And after reading through our ship reviews in chapters 5 and 6, and narrowing your focus down to a couple of cruise lines that appeal to you, you'll be ready to get down to brass tacks and make your booking.

1 Booking a Cruise: The Short Explanation

Every cruise line has a brochure, or sometimes many different brochures, full of beautiful glossy photos of beautiful glossy people enjoying fabulous vacations. They're colorful! They're gorgeous! They're enticing! They're confusing!

You'll see low starting rates on the charts, but look further and you'll realize those are for tiny inside cubicles; most of the cabins sell for much more. Sometimes the brochures have published rates that are nothing more than the pie-in-the-sky wish of cruise lines for the rate at which they'd like to sell the cruise (most customers will pay less). We strongly suggest you look at the early-bird savings column and book your cruise early (by mid-Feb for an average savings of 25%–30%, and sometimes as much as 50%). In reality, you may be able to get the cruise for a lot less at the last minute. In 2010, though, we did not see the widespread discount pricing we saw in 2009, when the analysts were calling Alaska "bargain basement" (at the time, of course, the country was in the midst of an economic turndown and the cruise lines were fighting with Alaska over the passenger head tax). So what does this mean for 2011? Keep in mind the cruise lines will like Alaska a lot more this year, now that the passenger tax has been reduced. But how this will reflect in prices is anyone's guess. You may be able to save by taking your chances, but if you don't reserve space early, you may also be left out in the cold (cold in Alaska, get it?). Keep in mind that the most expensive and cheapest cabins tend to sell out first. As they say in the cruise business, ships sell out from the top and bottom first. Aggressive marketing by the cruise lines may add to an increase in early booking—for instance, Princess' offer of a weeklong cruise plus 3 nights in Denali from $899. Many of the most intense deals are geared towards past passengers. Speaking of which, if you've cruised at all before—Caribbean, Europe, Bermuda—check with the cruise line to see if you qualify for a past-passenger deal.

So how do you book your cruise? Traditionally (meaning over the past 30 years or so), people have booked their cruises through **travel agents.** But you may be wondering: Hasn't the traditional travel agent gone the way of typewriters and eight-track tapes and been replaced by the **Internet?** Not exactly. Travel agents are alive and kicking, though the Internet has indeed staked its claim alongside them and knocked some of them out of business. In an effort to keep pace, most traditional travel agencies now have their own websites.

So which is the better way to book a cruise these days? Good question. The answer can be both. If you're computer savvy, have a good handle on all the elements that go into a cruise, and have narrowed down the choices to a few cruise lines that appeal to you, websites are a great way to trawl the seas at your own pace and check out deals, which can be dramatic. On the other hand, you'll barely get a stitch of personalized service searching for and booking a cruise online. If you need help getting a refund or arranging special meals or other matters, or deciding which cabin to choose, you're on your own. In addition, agents usually know about cruise and airfare discounts that the lines won't necessarily publicize on their websites.

However you arrange to buy your cruise, what you basically have in hand at the end is a contract for transportation, lodging, dining, entertainment, housekeeping, and assorted other miscellaneous services that will be provided to you over the course of your vacation. That's a lot of services, involving a lot of people. It's complex, and like any complex thing, it pays (and saves) to study up. That's why it's important that you read the rest of this chapter.

2 Booking Through a Travel Agent

The majority of cruise passengers still book through agents. The cruise lines are happy with this system and have only small reservations staffs themselves (unlike airlines). In some cases, if you try to call a cruise line to book your own passage, you may be advised by the line to contact an agent in your area. The cruise line may even offer you a choice of names from its list of preferred agencies, and there are often links to preferred agencies on some of the lines' websites.

A good travel agent can save you both time and money. If you're reluctant to use an agent, consider this: Would you represent yourself in court? Perform surgery on your own abdomen? Tackle complicated IRS forms without seeking help? You may be the rare type that doesn't need a travel agent, but most of us are better off working with one.

Good agents can give you expert advice, save you time, and (best of all) will usually work for you for free or a nominal fee—the bulk of their fees are paid by the cruise lines. (Many agents charge a consultation fee—say, $25—which is refunded if you eventually give them the booking.) In addition to advising you about the different ships, an agent can help you make decisions about the type of cabin you will need, your dining room seating choices, any special airfare offerings from the cruise lines, pre- and post-cruise land offerings, and travel insurance. All of these can have a big impact on your cruise experience. We recently saw a complaint by someone who booked a really cheap inside cabin and was very angry that it was "a noisy cabin." Had they asked an experienced agent, they might have been advised that the cabin was cheap because it was practically in the engine room—and that if they had paid only a few bucks more, they would have had a nice, quiet cabin.

It's important to realize that not all agents represent all cruise lines. In order to be experts on what they sell, and to maximize the commissions the lines pay them (they're often paid more based on volume of sales), some agents may limit their offerings to, say, one luxury line, one midprice line, one mass-market line, and so on. If you have your sights set on a particular line or have narrowed down your preferences

Watch Out for Scams

It can be difficult to know whether the travel agency you're dealing with to make your Alaska cruise booking is or isn't reliable, legitimate, or, for that matter, stable. The travel business tends to attract more than its share of scam operators trying to lure consumers with incredible come-ons. If you get a solicitation by phone, fax, mail, or e-mail that just doesn't sound right, or if you are uneasy about an agent you are dealing with, call your state consumer-protection agency or the local office of the Better Business Bureau. Or you can check with the cruise line to see whether they have heard of the agency in question. Be wary of working with any company, be it on the phone or Internet, that won't give you its street address.

- **Get a referral.** A recommendation from a trusted friend or colleague is one of the best ways to hook up with a reputable agent.
- **Use the cruise lines' agent lists.** Many cruise-line websites include agency locator lists, naming agencies around the country with which they do business. These are by no means comprehensive lists of all good or bad agencies, but an agent's presence on these lists is usually another good sign of experience.
- **Beware of snap recommendations.** If an agent suggests a cruise line without first asking you a single question about your tastes, beware. Because agents work on commissions from the lines, some may try to shanghai you into cruising with a company that pays them the highest rates, even though that line may not be right for you.
- **Always use a credit card to pay for your cruise.** A credit card gives you more protection in the event the agency or cruise line fails. (Trust us! It happens occasionally.) When your credit card statement arrives, make sure the payment was made to the cruise line, not the travel agency. If you find that payment was actually made to the agency, it's a big red flag that something's wrong. If you insist on paying by check, you'll be making it out to the agency, so it may be wise to ask if the agency has default protection. Many do.
- **Always follow the cruise line's payment schedule.** Never agree to a different schedule the travel agency comes up with. The lines' terms are always clearly printed in their brochures and usually require an initial deposit, with the balance due no later than 45 to 75 days before departure, depending on the cruise line. If you're booking 2 months or less before departure, the full payment is often required at the time of booking (but cruise lines have been making changes in this regard, so read the fine print carefully).
- **Keep on top of your booking.** If you ever fail to receive a document or ticket on the date it's been promised, inquire about it immediately. If you're told that your cruise reservation was canceled because of overbooking and that you must pay extra for a confirmed and rescheduled sailing, demand a full refund and/or contact your credit card company to stop payment.

to a couple of lines, you'll have to find an agent who handles your choices. As we mentioned above, you can call the lines themselves to get the name of an agent near you. It's also a good idea to ask the agent you are working with if he has actually been to Alaska. The cruise lines have been clamping down on agents who give rebates, and there are fewer of these deals out there than there were a few years ago. The cruise lines themselves post Internet specials on their websites, and the same deals are usually also available through travel agents. The lines don't want to upset their travel-agent partners and generally try not to compete against them.

Travel agents are frequently in contact with the cruise lines and are continually alerted by the lines about the latest and best deals and special offers. The cruise lines tend to communicate such deals and offers to their top agents first, before they offer them to the general public, and some of these deals will never appear in your local newspaper, on bargain travel websites, or even on the websites of the cruise lines themselves.

Experienced agents know how to play the cruise lines' game and get you the best deals. As an example, the lines run promotions that allow you to book a category of cabin rather than a specific cabin, and guarantees that you'll be placed in that category or better. An informed agent will not only know about these offers, but may be able to direct you to a category on a specific ship in which your chances of an upgrade are better. The cruise lines will also sometimes upgrade passengers as a favor to their top-producing agents or agencies.

To keep their clients alert to specials, agencies may offer newsletters or communicate through other means, such as postcards or e-mail, or post specials on their websites. Depending on the agency you choose, you may run across other incentives for booking through an agent. Some agencies buy big blocks of space on a ship in advance and offer it to their clients at a group price available only through that agency. These are called group rates, although "group" in this case means savings, not that you have to hang out with the other people booking through the agency. In addition, some agencies are willing to negotiate, especially if you've found a better deal somewhere else. It never hurts to ask. Finally, some agencies are willing to give back to the client a portion of their commissions from the cruise line in order to close a sale. This percent may be monetary, or it might take the form of a perk such as a free bottle of champagne or a limo ride to the ship (hardly reasons to book in and of themselves, but nice perks nevertheless).

FINDING A GREAT AGENT

If you don't know a good travel agent already, try to find one through your friends, preferably those who have cruised before. For the most personal service, look for an agent in your area, and for the most knowledgeable service, look for an agent who has cruising experience. It's perfectly okay to ask an agent questions about his or her personal knowledge of the product, such as whether he or she has ever cruised in Alaska or with one of the lines you're considering. The easiest way to be sure that the agent is experienced in booking cruises is to work with an agent at a **cruise-only agency** (that's all they book) or to find an agent who is a cruise specialist within a full-service agency. If you are calling a full-service travel agency, ask for the **cruise desk.** A good and easy rule of thumb to maximize your chances of finding an agent who has cruise experience and who won't rip you off is to book with an agency that's a member of the **Cruise Lines International Association** (**CLIA;** ✆ **754/224-2200;** www.cruising.org), the main industry association. Members are cruise specialists. Membership in the

American Society of Travel Agents (ASTA; ✆ 800/275-2782; www.astanet.com) ensures that the agency is monitored for ethical practices, although it does not designate cruise experience. You can tap into the websites of these organizations to find reliable agents in your area.

BOOKING WITH DISCOUNTERS

Keep in mind that discounters, who specialize in great-sounding, last-minute offers (usually without airfare) and whose ads you can find in Sunday papers and all over the Internet, don't necessarily offer service that matches their prices. Their staffs are more likely to be order takers than advice givers. Go to these companies to compare prices only when you are certain about what you want.

BOOKING A SMALL-SHIP CRUISE

The small-ship companies in Alaska—American Safari Cruises, InnerSea Discoveries, and Lindblad Expeditions—all provide real niche-oriented cruise experiences, attracting passengers who have a very good idea of the kind of experience they want (usually educational or adventurous, and always casual and small scale). In many cases, a large percentage of passengers on any given cruise will have sailed with the line before. Because of all this, and because the passenger capacity of these ships is so low (12–138 passengers), in general you don't find the kind of deep discounts that you do with the large ships. For the most part, these lines rely on agents to handle their bookings, taking very few reservations directly. All of the lines have a list of agents with whom they do considerable business, and they can hook you up with one of them if you call or e-mail the cruise line and ask for an agent near you.

3 Cruising on the Internet

For those who know exactly what they want (we don't recommend online shopping for first-time cruisers), there are deals to be had on the Internet. Those sites that sell cruises include top online travel agencies (Travelocity.com, Expedia.com, Orbitz.com), agencies that specialize in cruises (icruise.com, Cruise.com, Cruise411.com, 7blueseas.com), travel discounters (Bestfares.com, Onetravel.com, Lowestfare.com), search engines (www.kayak.com), and auction sites (Allcruiseauction.com, Priceline.com). For more Internet options, check out the cruise listings at Johnnyjet.com.

There are also some good sites on the Internet that specialize in providing cruise information rather than selling cruises. The best site dedicated to cruising in general (rather than linked with one line) is **Cruisecritic.com** (now owned by Expedia). On this website, there are reviews by professional writers, ratings and reviews by cruise passengers, plus useful tips, frequent chat opportunities, and message boards. For updated cruise news, no one does it better than Gene, at his USA Today Cruise Log Blog (www.cruises.usatoday.com), where you'll also find a very active discussion forum. **Alaskacruisingreport.com** tracks what's happening specifically in Alaska. In addition, nearly all the cruise lines have their own sites, which are chock-full of information—some even give virtual tours of specific ships. You'll find the website addresses for the various cruise companies in our cruise line reviews in chapters 5 and 6.

4 Cruise Costs

In chapters 5 and 6, we've included the brochure rates for every ship reviewed, but as noted above, these prices may actually be higher than any passenger will pay. Prices constantly fluctuate based on any special deals the cruise lines are running. The volume of travelers interested in cruising Alaska heavily influences rates. If the sales season (Sept–Jan are the key months) fails to achieve certain predetermined passenger volume goals, the lines are very quick to start slashing rates to goose the market. The prices we've noted are for the following three basic types of accommodations: inside cabins (without windows), outside cabins (with windows), and suites. Remember that cruise ships generally have several different categories of cabins within each of these three basic divisions, all priced differently. That's why we give a range. See "Choosing Your Cabin," later in this chapter, for more information on cabin types.

The price you pay for your cabin represents the bulk of your cruise vacation cost, but there are other costs to consider. Whether you're working with an agent or booking online, be sure that you really understand what's included in the fare you're being quoted. Are you getting a price that includes the cruise fare, port charges, taxes, fees, and insurance, or are you getting a cruise-only fare? Are airfare and airport transfers included, or do you have to book them separately (either as an add-on to the cruise fare or on your own)? One agent might break down the charges in a price quote, while another might bundle them all together. Make sure you're comparing apples with apples when making price comparisons. Read the fine print!

It's important when figuring out what your cruise will cost to remember what extras are not included in your cruise fare. The items discussed in the section below are not included in most cruise prices and will add to the cost of your trip.

SHORE EXCURSIONS

The priciest additions to your cruise fare, particularly in Alaska, will likely be shore excursions. Rates range from about $35 to $99 for a sightseeing tour by bus (the higher priced tours usually include visits to museums or other local attractions), to $500 and up (sometimes as high as $600) for a lengthy helicopter or seaplane flightseeing excursion. Although these sightseeing tours are designed to help cruise passengers make the most of their time at the ports the ship visits, they can add a hefty sum to your vacation costs, so be sure to factor these expenses into your budget. Of course, whether you take the excursions is a personal choice, but we suggest you set aside at least $600 per person for trips in port, which might just about cover a short flightseeing trip, a kayak or jeep safari, and a bus tour.

TIPS

You'll want to add tips for the ship's crew to your budget calculations. Crewmembers are usually paid low base wages with the expectation that they'll make up the difference in gratuities. Exceptions in Alaska this year, as far as the big ships are concerned, are Regent Seven Seas and Silversea Cruises, which include tips in the cruise fare (but you can still leave a few bucks for your favorite crew members if you want to).

Because some people find the whole tipping process confusing, a couple of years ago, some lines began automatically adding tips to guests' shipboard accounts. Carnival, Holland America, Norwegian Cruise Line, and Princess, for instance, all add a standard tip of $10 to $12 per passenger, per day. In all these cases, you are free to adjust the amount up or down as you see fit, based on the service you received.

Tips are given at the end of the cruise, and passengers should set aside at least $10 per passenger per day for tips for the room steward, waiter, and busperson. In practice, we find that most people tend to give a little more. Additional tips to other personnel, such as the headwaiter or maitre d', are at your discretion. If you have a room with a butler, slip him or her $5 a day. Most lines automatically add 15% to bar bills, so you don't have to tip your bartender. There may be an automatic tip of 15% for spa services. If not, you can add a tip to the bill.

You can tip in cash or, on most lines, add gratuities to your shipboard account. On small ships, tips are typically pooled among the crew: You hand over a lump sum in cash, and they divvy it up. Because tipping etiquette on small ships varies, we include information on tipping specifics for small-ship lines on p. 140 in chapter 6, and general guidelines in "Tips on Tipping," on p. 61 in chapter 4.

BOOZE & SODA

Most ships charge extra for alcoholic beverages (including wine at dinner) and soda. Nonbubbly soft drinks, such as lemonade and iced tea, and hot drinks such as coffee and tea are included in your cruise fare. Soda will cost about $2.50, beer $3.50 and up, and mixed drinks $5.95 and up. A bottle of wine with dinner will run anywhere from $15 to upward of $300.

PORT CHARGES, LOCAL TAXES & FEES

Every ship has to pay docking fees at each port. It also has to pay some local taxes per passenger in some places. Port charges, taxes, and other fees are sometimes included in your cruise fare, but not always, and these charges can add on average between $200 and $250 to the price of a 7-day Alaska cruise. The recently reduced $34.50 per passenger head and berth tax imposed by the State of Alaska, and $7 and $8 taxes in Juneau and Ketchikan, respectively, are usually melded into this figure and not paid by passengers separately. Make sure you know whether these fees are included in the cruise fare when comparing rates.

FUEL SURCHARGES

With the high cost of fuel in 2008, most lines instituted fuel surcharges. These added significantly to the cost of the cruise. The charges went away for the first 6 months of 2009, with fuel costs lower. But the cruise lines reserved the right to institute them again whenever oil prices exceed $70 per barrel. Sample surcharges were $11 per person, per day on Norwegian Cruise Line, $9 on Holland America and Princess, and $8 on Royal Caribbean and Celebrity. The fees are less for a third or fourth person in the cabin.

5 Money-Saving Strategies

EARLY-BIRD & LAST-MINUTE DISCOUNTS

As we said earlier, the best way to save on an Alaska cruise is to **book in advance.** In a typical year, lines offer early-bird rates, usually 25% to 30% off the brochure rate, to those who book their Alaska cruise by mid-February of the year of the cruise. If the cabins do not fill up by the cutoff date, the early-bird rate may be extended, but it may be lowered slightly—say, a 15% or 20% savings. Offers made to past cruisers may present even bigger discounts. In preparation for 2011, Holland America Line and Princess seemed more determined than ever to get people booking early, reducing their starting fares. For the 2011 season, early-bird fares started at $699 on Holland America ($50 less than the 2010 starting fare) and $649 on Princess ($100 less than the year before). Just when we thought we were seeing a trend, though, other lines raised their early-bird fares, which for 2011 were $569 on Norwegian Cruise Line, $599 on Royal Caribbean, and $529 on Carnival. Keep in mind that all of these fares are designed to fill up the ships as quickly as possible, and offered on a limited basis.

If the cabins are still not full as the cruise season begins, cruise lines typically start marketing special deals, usually through their top-producing travel agents, and sometimes, but rarely, with crazy savings of up to 75%. Still, there was less craziness last year, with cruise lines offering only sporadic last-minute sales of under $399 for weeklong cruises (after touting many more of the deals in 2009). Planning your Alaska cruise vacation in advance and taking advantage of early booking discounts is still the best way to go, in our opinion.

SHOULDER-SEASON DISCOUNTS

You can also save by booking a cruise in the shoulder months of **May** or **September,** when cruise pricing is usually lower than during the high-season summer months (though in 2010 there were deals even in July and August). Typically, Alaska cruises are divided into budget, low, economy, value, standard, and peak seasons, but since these overlap quite a bit from cruise line to cruise line, we can lump them into three basic periods:

1. **Budget/Low/Economy Season:** May and September
2. **Value/Standard Season:** Early June and late August
3. **Peak Season:** Late June, July, and early to mid-August

THIRD- & FOURTH-PASSENGER DISCOUNTS

Most ships offer highly discounted rates for third and fourth passengers sharing a cabin with two full-fare passengers, even if those two have booked at a discounted rate. You can add the four rates together and then divide by four to get your per-person rate. This is a good option for families (or very good friends) on a budget; but remember that it'll be a tight fit, as most cabins aren't all that big. Some lines, including Norwegian Cruise Line, also have **special rates for kids,** usually on a seasonal or select-sailing basis. In 2010, Norwegian was offering kids' fares from $199.

GROUP DISCOUNTS

One of the best ways to get a cruise deal is to book as a group, so you may want to gather family together for a reunion or convince your friends or colleagues they need a vacation, too. A "group," as defined by the cruise lines, is generally **at least 16 people** in at least eight cabins. Not only do the savings include a discounted rate, but at least the cruise portion of the 16th ticket will be free. On some upscale ships, you can negotiate a free ticket for groups of 10 or more. Crystal Cruises for one has a group special, Crystal Family Memories, geared towards families of 10 or more in five cabins. The gang can split the proceeds from the free berth or hold a drawing for the ticket, maybe at a cocktail party on the first night. If your group is large enough, you may even be able to get that cocktail party for free, and perhaps some other onboard perks as well.

Some travel agencies buy big blocks of space on a ship in advance and offer it to their clients at a group price available only through that agency. These are called group rates, although, as we mention earlier in the chapter, "group" in this case means savings, not that you have to hang out with (or even know) the other people booking through the agency.

SENIOR CITIZEN & MILITARY DISCOUNTS

Senior citizens might be able to get extra savings on their cruise. Some lines will take 5% off the top for those 55 and older on select sailings, and the senior rate applies even if the second person in the cabin is younger. Membership in groups such as AARP is not required, but such membership may bring additional savings. Discounts may also be available for active or retired military personnel, so tell your travel agent if you fit into this category.

OTHER DEALS

Check each line's website for the latest savings plans.

If you like your Alaska cruise so much that you decide to take a vacation there again, consider booking your next cruise on the spot. Cruise lines have become smart about the fact that when you're on a ship, you're a captive audience, so they may propose that you make future vacation plans onboard. Before you sign on the dotted line, though, make sure the on-the-spot discount can be combined with other offers you might find later. Keep in mind that if you do choose to book onboard, you can still do the reconfirmation and ticketing through your travel agent by giving the cruise line his or her name.

Lines tend to offer cut rates when they are introducing a new ship or moving into a new market. So it pays to keep track of what's happening in the cruise industry—or have your agent do so—when looking for a deal.

6 Airfares & Pre-/Post-Cruise Hotel Deals

Also see the information on cruisetours in chapter 10.

AIR ADD-ONS

Unless you live within driving distance of your port of embarkation, you'll probably be flying to Vancouver, Anchorage, Seattle, or one of the other ports to join your ship. Your cruise package may include airfare, but if not, you'll have to make other arrangements. You can book air travel separately, but remember that those attractive starting discount fares you see in the newspapers and on the Web may not apply, especially if your cruise departs on the peak travel days of Friday or Saturday. A better option is usually to take advantage of the cruise lines' air add-ons. Why? First of all, as frequent customers of the airlines, cruise lines tend to get decent (if not the best) discounts on airfare, which they pass on to their customers. Second, booking air flight with the cruise line also allows the line to keep track of you. If your plane is late, for instance, they may hold the boat, though not always. When you book air travel with your cruise line, most lines will include **transfers** from the airport to the ship, saving you the hassle of getting a cab. (If you do book the air travel on your own, you may still be able to get the transfers separately—ask your agent about this.) Be aware that once the air ticket is issued by the cruise line, you usually aren't allowed to make changes.

The only times it may pay to book your own air transportation is if you are using frequent-flier miles and can get your air travel for free, or if you are particular about which carrier you fly or which route you take. You are more or less at the mercy of the cruise line in terms of carrier and route if you take their air deals. Princess, for one, last year launched a program that does let you choose on what airline you want to fly, but other lines may charge a "deviation" fee if you want to fly a specific airline or route. The deadline for these requests is usually 60 days before the sailing date or, if you book later, on the day your cruise reservations are made. ***Tip:*** If you're determined to book your own plane ticket and your travel schedule is flexible, it's often easier to get the carrier and the flight time you prefer if you choose a cruise that leaves on a Wednesday or Thursday—or other times considered nonpeak by the airlines.

If airfare is part of the cruise package, but you choose not to book your air transportation with the cruise line, you will be refunded the air portion of the fare.

PRE- & POST-CRUISE HOTEL DEALS

Even if you don't take a cruisetour, you may want to consider spending a day or two in your port of embarkation or debarkation either before or after your cruise. (See details on exploring the port cities in chapters 8 and 9.) An advantage to coming in a day or two early is that you don't have to worry if your flight is running late. (Our coauthor Gene has a personal policy of always flying into his embarkation port at least a day early, just to be safe; he's never missed a ship!) Plus, Vancouver, Anchorage, and Seattle, the cities into which most passengers fly, happen to be great cities to explore.

Just as with airfare, you need to decide whether you want to buy your hotel stay from the cruise line or make arrangements on your own. The cruise lines negotiate **special deals with hotels** at port cities, so you will often get a bargain by booking through the cruise line.

When evaluating a cruise line's hotel package, make sure you review it carefully to see what's included. See whether the line provides a transfer from the airport to the hotel and from the hotel to the cruise ship (or vice versa); make sure that the line offers a hotel that you will be happy with in terms of type of property and location; and inquire if any escorted tours, car rental deals, or meals are included. You'll also want to compare the price of booking on your own. (See chapter 7 for information on hotels in the various ports.) Keep in mind that cruise lines usually list rates for hotels on a per-person basis, whereas hotels post their rates on a per-room basis.

7 Choosing Your Cabin

Once you've looked at the ship descriptions in chapters 5 and 6, talked over the options with your travel agent, and selected an itinerary and ship, you'll have to choose a cabin. The cruise lines have improved things a bit since Charles Dickens declared that his stateroom reminded him of a coffin, but cramped, windowless spaces can still be found. On the other hand, so can penthouse-size suites with expansive verandas, Jacuzzis, and butler service. Most cabins on cruise ships today have twin beds that are convertible to queen-size (you can request which configuration you want), plus a private bathroom with a shower. Some cabins have bunk beds, which are obviously not convertible. Most ships also have cabins designed for three or four people, which will include two twin beds plus one or two bunks that fold down from the wall in some way. In some cases, it is possible to add a fifth bed to the room. Some lines have special cabins designed for families, with "regular" twin beds that can be pushed together to create a double bed, plus fold-down bunks. Families may also be able to book connecting cabins (although they'll have to pay for two cabins to do so).

Most cabins, but not all, have televisions. Some also have extra amenities, such as safes, minifridges, VCRs or DVD players, bathrobes, and hair dryers. A bathtub is considered a luxury on ships and will usually be found only in more expensive cabins. Some cabin choice considerations:

1. Note the location of the ship's disco and other loud public areas, and try not to book a cabin that's too close or underneath.
2. Cabins on upper decks can be affected by the motion of the sea. If you're abnormally susceptible to seasickness, keep this in mind.
3. Ditto for cabins in the bow.

MODEL CABIN LAYOUTS

Typical Outside Cabins

- Twin beds (can usually be pushed together)
- Some have sofa bed or bunk for third passenger
- Shower (tubs are rare)
- TV and music
- Window or porthole, or veranda

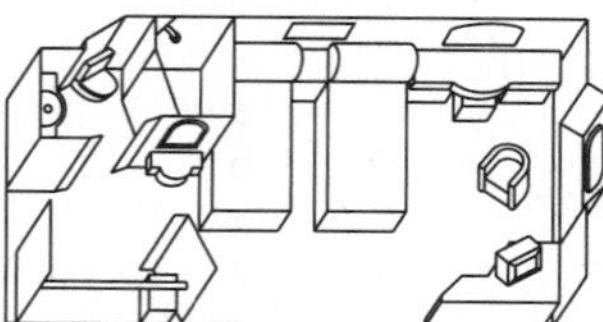

Outside Cabin

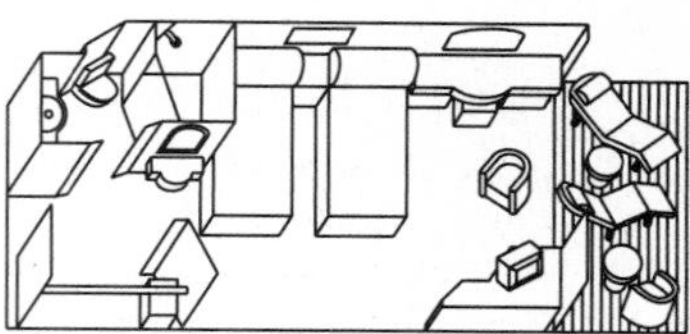

Outside Cabin with Veranda

Typical Suites

- King, queen, or double beds
- Sitting areas (often with sofa beds)
- Large bathrooms, usually with tub, sometimes with Jacuzzi
- Refrigerators, sometimes stocked
- TVs w/VCR and stereo
- Large closets
- Large veranda

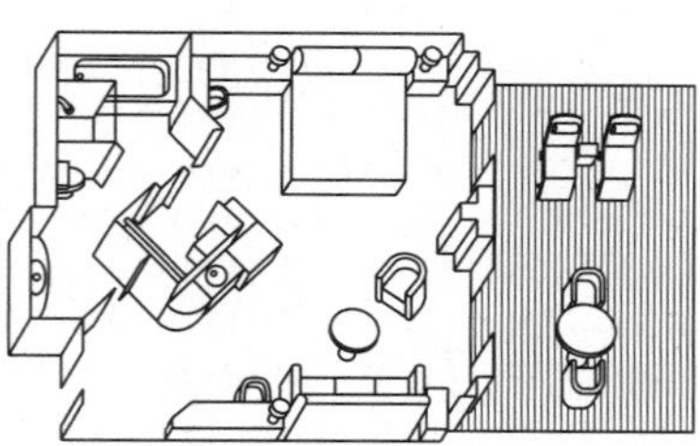

Suite with Veranda

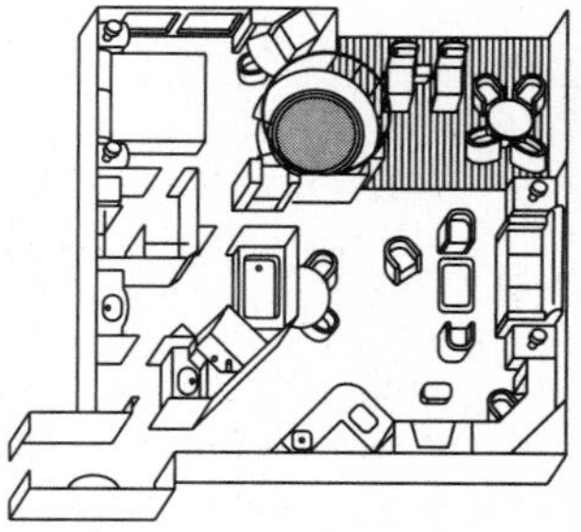

Grand Suite with Veranda

Thanks to Princess Cruises for all photos and diagrams.

4. Outside cabins without verandas appear as solid blocks of space.
5. Outside cabins with verandas are shown with a line dividing the two spaces.
6. Inside cabins (without windows) can be real money-savers.
7. Cabins midship are the least affected by the motion of the sea, especially if they're on a lower deck.
8. Cabins that adjoin elevator shaftways might be noisy (though proximity makes it easier to get around the ship).
9. Cabins in the stern can be affected by the motion of the sea and tend to be subject to engine vibration.
10. Cabins near children's facilities may not be the quietest places, at least during the day.
11. Check that lifeboats don't block the view from your cabin.
12. Cabins for travelers with disabilities are ideally located near elevators and close to the ship's entrances.

CABIN TYPES

What kind of cabin is right for you? Price will likely be a big factor here, but so should the vacation style you prefer. The typical ship has several types of cabins, which are illustrated by floor plans in the cruise line's brochure. The cabins are usually described by **price** (highest to lowest), **category** (suite, deluxe, superior, standard, economy, and other types), and **furniture configuration** ("sitting area with two lower beds.") The cabins will also be described as being **inside** or **outside.** Simply put, inside cabins do not have windows (or even portholes) and outside cabins do. However, views from some outside cabins may be obstructed—usually by a lifeboat—or look out onto a public area; an experienced travel agent should be able to advise you on which cabin to choose if full views and privacy are important. On the big ships, deluxe outside cabins may also come with **verandas** (also referred to as **balconies**) that give you a private outdoor space to enjoy the sea breezes. This is a great thing to have in Alaska. You can throw on your bathrobe and view the glaciers and wildlife. But remember that the verandas vary in size, so if you're looking to do more than stand on your balcony, make sure the space is big enough to accommodate deck chairs, a table, or whatever else you require. Also keep in mind that these verandas are not completely isolated—your neighbors may be able to see you and vice versa. With few exceptions, veranda cabins will not have obstructed views.

Noise can be a factor that may influence your cabin choice. If you take a cabin on a lower deck, you may hear engine noises; in the front of the ship, anchor noises; and in the back of the ship, thruster noises. A cabin near an elevator may bring door opening and closing sounds; and a cabin above or below the disco may pulse until all hours of the night. The loudest areas of a ship vary depending on how well insulated the different areas are, so if noise will be a problem for you, ask what the quietest part of the ship is when you are booking your cabin. We would say that, generally, midship on a higher deck will be the quietest part of the ship (unless, of course, you're near a disco).

If you plan to spend a lot of quiet time in your cabin, you should probably consider booking the biggest room you can afford, and you should also consider taking a cabin with a picture window or, better still, a private veranda. If, conversely, you plan to be off on shore excursions or on deck checking out the glaciers and wildlife, and using your cabin only to change clothes and collapse in at the end of the day, you might be happy with a smaller (and cheaper) cabin. Usually, cabins on the higher decks are more expensive and much nicer, with plusher amenities and superior decor, even if

Bed Lingo

On cruise ships, "lower beds" refer to standard twin beds, while "bunks" (or, less commonly, "upper beds") refer to beds that passengers pull out from the wall to sleep in.

they are the same size as cabins on lower decks. **Luxury suites** are usually on upper decks. The top suites on some ships are actually apartment size, and you'll get lots of space to stretch out. A quirky thing about cabin pricing is that the most stable cabins during rough seas are those in the middle and lower parts of the ship.

On the small ships, cabins can be truly tiny and spartan, though some give the big-ship cabins a run for their money. Generally, the difference lies in the orientation of the cruise line: Those promising a real adventure experience tend to feature somewhat utilitarian cabins.

Aboard both large and small ships, keep in mind that the most expensive and least expensive cabins tend to sell out fast. Also keep in mind that, just as with real estate, it's sometimes better to take a smaller cabin in a nicer ship than a bigger cabin in a less pleasant ship.

CABIN SIZES

The size of a cabin is described in terms of square feet. This number may not mean a lot unless you want to mark it out on your floor at home. But to give you an idea: 120 square feet and under is low end and cramped, 180 square feet is midrange (and the minimum for people with claustrophobia), and 250 square feet and up is suite size.

8 Choosing Your Dining Options

Smaller ships usually serve dinner at a certain time, with unassigned seating, allowing you to sit at any table you want. So if you plan to sail on one of the smaller lines, you don't have to read this section at all. Because most dining rooms on **larger ships** are not large enough to accommodate all passengers at once, large ships typically offer the option of traditional seating, which means two different seating times, especially for dinner. In this case, your table will be preassigned and remain the same for the duration of the cruise. You will generally make your choice of seating time and table size when you book your cruise. You will also have the option of open seating, as noted in the "Open Seating" portion of this section.

MEALTIMES

If you choose traditional seating, there are set dinner times, with early or main seating typically at 6pm and late seating at 8:30pm. There are advantages and disadvantages to both times, and it basically comes down to personal choice. **Early seating** is usually less crowded and the preferred time for families and seniors. The dining experience can be a bit more rushed (the staff needs to make way for the next wave of guests), but food items may be fresher. You can see a show right after dinner and have first dibs on other nighttime venues as well. And you just may be hungry again in time for the midnight buffet.

Late seating, on the other hand, allows you time for a good long nap or late spa appointment before dining. Dinner is not rushed at all. You can sit as long as you want, enjoying after-dinner drinks—unless, that is, you choose to go catch a show, which will usually start at 10:15 or 10:30pm.

If you also choose to eat **breakfast** and **lunch** in the dining room as opposed to more casual venues on the ship, you are theoretically supposed to eat at assigned times as well—typical mealtimes for breakfast are 7 or 8am for the early seating and 8:30 or 9am for the late; for lunch, it's usually noon for the early seating and 1:30pm or so for the late. We've found, though, that most ships aren't hard and fast on this. Crowds in the dining room are typically an issue only at dinner. If you show up outside of your assigned time for breakfast or lunch and your assigned table is full, the staff will probably just seat you elsewhere. Most cruise lines, in fact, operate their dining rooms on a de facto "open seating" basis for both of these meals.

Most large ships today also have **alternative dining options.** Most have a casual, buffet-style cafe restaurant, usually located on the Lido Deck, with indoor and outdoor poolside seating and an extensive spread of both hot and cold food items at breakfast, lunch, and dinner (as a casual alternative to the dining room). Some ships also have **reservations-only restaurants,** seating fewer than 100, where—except on some luxury ships—a small fee is charged, mainly to cover gratuities.

TABLE SIZE

Do you mind sitting with strangers? Are you looking to make new friends? Your dinner companions can make or break your cruise experience. Most ships have tables configured for two to eight people. For singles or couples who want to socialize, a table of eight seats generally provides enough variety so that you don't get bored and also allows you to steer clear of any individual you don't particularly care for (tables are assigned, not seats). Couples may choose to sit on their own, but singles may find it hard to secure a table for one. A family of four may want a table for four, or request to sit with another family at a table for eight.

You need to state your table size preference in advance, unless you are on a ship with an open-seating policy, but don't worry if you change your mind once you're onboard. You'll probably be able to move around. Just tell the dining-room maitre d' and he or she will review the seating charts for an opening.

OPEN SEATING

Put off by all this formality? Want guaranteed casual all the way? Norwegian Cruise Line's ships, Regent's *Seven Seas Mariner,* and Silversea's *Silver Shadow* serve all meals with open seating—dine when you want (within the restaurants' open hours, of course) and sit with whom you want. The catch is, particularly with Norwegian, you are best off deciding in the morning where you want to have dinner and making a reservation or you may find the restaurant of your choice is full when you decide to eat. Princess, Carnival, Royal Caribbean, Holland America, and Celebrity all have their own version of this system, allowing guests to choose traditional early or late seating, or open restaurant-style seating (you make your choice before the cruise, but may be able to change your mind once you're onboard).

SPECIAL MENU REQUESTS

The cruise line should be informed at the time you make reservations about any special dietary requirements you have. Some lines provide kosher menus, and all have vegetarian, vegan, low-fat, low-salt, and sugar-free options.

SMOKE-FREE DINING

Most ships now have smoke-free dining rooms, but if smoking is a particular concern to you, check this out with your travel agent. If the dining room isn't nonsmoking, you can request a nonsmoking table. On the other hand, smokers can request a smoking table.

9 Deposits & Cancellation Policies

You'll be asked by your travel agent to make a **deposit,** either a fixed amount or some percentage of your total cruise cost. You'll then receive a receipt in the mail from the cruise line. You'll typically be asked to pay the remaining fare usually no later than 2 months before your departure date.

Cruise lines have varying policies regarding **cancellations,** and it's important to look at the fine print in the line's brochure to make sure you understand the policy. Most lines allow you to cancel for a full refund on your deposit and payment anytime up to 75 days before the sailing, after which you have to pay a penalty. Norwegian Cruise Line, for one, instituted a new policy in 2009 based on the difficult economic climate—if you book a cruise and then get laid off from your job, you qualify for a full refund.

10 Travel Insurance

There are three kinds of travel insurance: trip-cancellation, medical, and lost-luggage coverage. Rule number one: Check your existing policies before you buy any additional coverage. **Trip-cancellation insurance** is a good idea if you have paid a large portion of your vacation expenses up front—as is the case with cruises. It gives protection if, for some reason, you're not able to take your cruise or your trip is interrupted. For trip-cancellation insurance information, contact one of the following insurers: **Access America** (✆ **800/729-6021;** www.accessamerica.com), **Travel Guard** (✆ **800/826-4919;** www.travelguard.com), **Travel Insured International** (✆ **800/243-3174;** www.travelinsured.com), or **Travelex Insurance Services** (✆ **888/457-4602;** www.travelex-insurance.com).

Health insurance doesn't make sense for most travelers. Your existing health insurance should cover you if you get sick while on vacation (though if you belong to an HMO, you should check to see whether you are fully covered when away from home). If you require additional medical insurance, try **MEDEX International** (✆ **800/527-0218** or 410/453-6300; www.medexassist.com) or **Travel Assistance International** (✆ **800/821-2828;** www.travelassistance.com; for general information on services, call the company's Worldwide Assistance Services, Inc., at ✆ **800/777-8710**).

Onboard Medical Care

Large ships usually have a fully equipped medical facility and staff (a doctor and a nurse or two) on board to handle any emergency. They work from a medical center that typically offers set office hours but is also open on an emergency basis 24 hours a day. A fee (sometimes a steep one) is charged. They're equipped to do some surgery, but in cases of major medical emergencies, passengers may be airlifted off the ship by helicopter to the nearest hospital.

MedJetAssist (✆ **800/527-7478;** www.medjetassist.com) is a leader in medical evacuation insurance, which you may want to consider if you are traveling to particularly remote destinations.

Small ships may have someone on staff with nursing skills, though they rarely have a doctor, but such ships in Alaska never get so far from civilization that a plane can't be summoned by radio to airlift a sick passenger to a hospital.

Lost-luggage insurance doesn't make much sense for most travelers, either. On domestic flights, checked baggage is covered up to $2,800 per ticketed passenger. On international flights (including U.S. portions of international trips), baggage is limited to about $1,500 per checked bag. If you plan to check items more valuable than the standard liability, see if your valuables are covered by your homeowner's policy, get baggage insurance as part of your comprehensive travel-insurance package (contact one of the travel insurance providers listed above), or buy Travel Guard's BagTrak product. Don't buy insurance at the airport, as it's usually overpriced. Be sure to take any valuables or irreplaceable items with you in your carry-on luggage, as many valuables (including books, money, and electronics) aren't covered by airline policies.

If your luggage is lost, immediately file a lost-luggage claim at the airport, detailing the luggage contents. For most airlines, you must report delayed, damaged, or lost baggage within 4 hours of arrival. The airlines are required to deliver luggage, once found, directly to your house or destination free of charge.

The cruise line may also offer its own insurance policies, including trip-cancellation insurance, lost-baggage insurance, and death and dismemberment insurance. It may pay to compare these policies with the plans offered by insurance companies (this is another area where your travel agent can be of assistance).

FAST FACTS: Alaska

Area Code Almost all of Alaska is in area code **907.** The tiny community of Hyder, about 90 miles northeast of Ketchikan, lies on the Alaska/British Columbia border. For practical and technical reasons, Hyder uses the same area code as nearby Stewart, B.C.: **250.** In the Yukon Territory, the area code is **867.** When placing a toll call within the state, you must dial 1, the area code, and the number. See "Telephone," below, for an important tip on phone cards.

Banks & ATMs There are banks and automated teller machines (ATMs) in all but the tiniest towns. They may charge a nominal fee.

Business Hours In the larger cities, major **grocery stores** are open 24 hours a day and carry a wide range of products (even fishing gear) in addition to food. At a minimum, stores are open Monday through Friday from 10am to 6pm and Saturday afternoons, but closed on Sunday. However, many are open for longer hours, especially in summer. **Banks** may close an hour earlier and, if open on Saturday, it's only in the morning. Under state law, **bars** don't have to close until 5am, but many communities have earlier closing times (around 2am).

Cellphone Coverage Most of the populated portion of the state has cellular coverage. The largest provider is an Alaska company called ACS, which posts maps of its coverage area at **www.acsalaska.com**. AT&T has the second-best network. We've found that usable coverage is often less than what the companies claim.

Emergencies Generally, you can call ✆ **911** for medical, police, or fire emergencies. On remote highways, there sometimes are 911 coverage gaps, but dialing 0 will generally get an operator, who can connect you to emergency services. Citizens-band channels 9 and 11 are monitored for emergencies on most highways, as are channels 14 and 19 in some areas.

Holidays Besides the normal national holidays, banks and state and local government offices close on two state holidays: Seward's Day (the last Mon in Mar) and Alaska Day (Oct 18, or the nearest Fri or Mon if it falls on a weekend).

Liquor Laws The minimum drinking age in Alaska is 21. Most restaurants sell beer and wine, and a minority have full bars that serve hard liquor as well. Packaged alcohol, beer, and wine are sold only in licensed stores, but these are common and are open long hours every day. More than 100 rural communities have laws prohibiting the importation and possession of alcohol (this is known as being "dry") or only the sale but not possession of alcohol (known as being "damp"). With a few exceptions, these are tiny bush communities off the road network; urban areas are all "wet." Of the communities featured in this book, Kotzebue and Barrow are damp, and the rest are wet. Before flying into a Native village with alcohol, ask about the law—bootlegging is a serious crime (and serious bad manners), or check a list online at **www.dps.state.ak.us/abc**.

Lost or Stolen Credit Cards Be sure to tell all of your credit card companies the minute you discover your wallet has been lost or stolen, and file a report at the nearest police precinct. Your credit card company or insurer may require a police report number or record of the loss. Most credit card companies have an emergency toll-free number to call if your card is lost or stolen; they may be able to wire you a cash advance immediately or deliver an emergency credit card in a day or two. **Visa**'s U.S. emergency number is ✆ **800/847-2911** or 410/581-9994. **American Express** cardholders and traveler's check holders should call ✆ **800/221-7282. MasterCard** holders should call ✆ **800/307-7309** or 636/722-7111. For other credit cards, call the toll-free number directory at ✆ **800/555-1212.**

If you need emergency cash over the weekend when all banks and American Express offices are closed, you can have money wired to you via **Western Union** (✆ **800/325-6000;** www.westernunion.com).

Identity theft or fraud are potential complications of losing your wallet, especially if you've lost your driver's license along with your cash and credit cards. Notify the major credit-reporting bureaus immediately; placing a fraud alert on your records may protect you against liability for criminal activity. The three major U.S. credit-reporting agencies are **Equifax** (✆ **800/766-0008;** www.equifax.com), **Experian** (✆ **888/397-3742;** www.experian.com), and **TransUnion** (✆ **800/680-7289;** www.transunion.com). Finally, if you've lost all forms of photo ID, call your airline and explain the situation; they might allow you to board the plane if you have a copy of your passport or birth certificate and a copy of the police report you've filed.

Newspapers The state's dominant newspaper is the ***Anchorage Daily News*** (www.adn.com); it's available everywhere, but is harder to find in Southeast Alaska. Seattle newspapers and ***USA Today*** are often available, and in Anchorage you can get virtually any newspaper.

Taxes There is no state sales tax, but most local governments have a sales tax and a bed tax on accommodations.

Telephone We have been assured that all major calling cards will work in Alaska, but this hasn't been the case in the past. To make sure, contact your long-distance company, or buy a by-the-minute card.

Time Zone Although the state naturally spans five time zones, in the 1980s, Alaska's middle time zone was stretched so almost the entire state would lie all in one zone, known as Alaska Time. It's 1 hour earlier than the U.S. West Coast's Pacific Standard Time and 4 hours earlier than Eastern Standard Time. Crossing over the border from Alaska to Canada adds an hour and puts you at the same time as the West Coast. As with almost everywhere else in the United States, daylight saving time is in effect from 2am on the second Sunday in March (turn your clocks ahead 1 hour) until 2am on the first Sunday in November (turn clocks back again).

Water Unpurified river or lake water may not be safe to drink. Hand-held filters available from sporting-goods stores for around $75 are the most practical way of dealing with the problem. Iodine kits and boiling also work.

4

The Cruise Experience

Now that you've made most of the hard decisions—choosing and booking your cruise—the rest of your vacation planning should be relatively easy. From this point on, the cruise lines take over much of the work, particularly if you've booked a package that includes air travel.

You should carefully read the pretrip information sent to you by your chosen cruise line, because most lines' pretrip packets include sections that address commonly asked questions. Most of this information can also be found on each line's website. In this chapter, we'll add our own two cents' worth on these matters and provide some practical hints that'll help you be prepared for all you'll find in the 49th state, both aboard ship and in the ports of call.

1 Packing for Your Cruise

PREPARING FOR THE WEATHER

The sometimes extreme and always unpredictable Alaska weather will be a big factor in the success of your vacation. During your summertime cruise, you may experience temperature variations from the 40s to the 80s or even low 90s (single digits to low 30s Celsius). The days will be long, with the sun all but refusing to set, especially in the more northern ports, and people will be energized by the extra daylight hours. You'll likely encounter some rain, but there could also be weeks of sunny skies with no rain at all. You're less likely to encounter snow, but it is a remote possibility, especially in the spring.

Weather plays a factor in what you need to pack, with the must-haves on an Alaska cruise including a raincoat, an umbrella, and comfortable walking shoes that you don't mind getting wet or muddy. A swimsuit is also a must if your ship has a pool (sometimes covered, sometimes heated) or hot tubs.

Even in the summer, temperatures in Alaska may not go much higher than the 50s or 60s (low or high teens Celsius), although they also may go into the 70s or 80s (low to high 20s Celsius). Having **layers of clothing** that you can peel off if the weather is hot and add if the weather is cold is the most convenient approach.

ESSENTIALS

What you choose to pack obviously involves a lot of personal choice, but here's a checklist of some items that everyone should bring along:

- A waterproof parka or jacket or lightweight raincoat (big enough to fit a sweater underneath)
- Two sweaters or fleece pullovers, or substitute a warm vest for one
- A warm hat and gloves

- Two to four pairs of pants or jeans
- Two pairs of walking shoes (preferably waterproof)
- Sunscreen (SPF 15 or higher)
- Bug spray (Alaska has 55 different kinds of mosquitoes, although the Inside Passage ports in the south are not as affected as the areas farther north.)
- Sunglasses
- Binoculars (Some small ships stock them for free guest use, but on the bigger ships, it will cost you—if they even have pairs for rent.)
- A camera, preferably with a telephoto or zoom lens
- Film (bring more than you think you'll need), or extra flash cards and batteries if you use digital
- Formal wear (with accessories) if your ship has formal nights (not all do)
- Semiformal wear if your ship has informal nights (not all do)
- Long underwear if you're on a shoulder-season cruise

ALASKA'S CLIMATE, BY MONTHS & REGIONS

Anchorage: Southcentral Alaska

	May	June	July	Aug	Sept
Average high/low (°F)	54/39	62/47	65/52	63/50	55/42
Average high/low (°C)	12/4	17/8	18/11	17/10	13/6
Avg. hours of light	17:45	19:30	18:15	15:30	12
Avg. sunny days	11	10	9	9	9
Avg. rainy days	7	8	11	13	14
Avg. precipitation (in.)	.7	1.1	1.7	2.4	2.7

Juneau: Southeast Alaska

	May	June	July	Aug	Sept
Average high/low (°F)	55/39	61/45	64/48	63/47	56/43
Average high/low (°C)	13/4	16/7	18/9	17/8	13/6
Avg. hours of light	17	18:15	17:30	15:30	12:30
Avg. sunny days	8	8	8	9	6
Avg. rainy days	17	15	17	17	20
Avg. precipitation (in.)	3.4	3.1	4.2	5.3	6.7

PACKING FOR FORMAL, INFORMAL & CASUAL EVENTS

Some people agonize over what to pack for a cruise, but there's no reason to fret. Except for the addition of a formal night or two, a cruise vacation is really no different from any resort vacation. And in some cases, it's much more casual.

Don't feel you have to go out and buy "cruise wear." Sweatshirts, jeans, and jogging outfits are the norm during the day. Dinner is dress-up time on most ships, although several have begun to offer more casual alternatives. And the small adventure-type ships are all casual, all the time.

Generally, ships describe proper dinner attire as formal; informal or semiformal (the two terms mean the same thing in this case); or casual. There are usually 2 formal nights and 2 informal (or semiformal) nights during a weeklong cruise, with the rest casual; check with your line for specifics. **Formal,** although the term has gotten somewhat more relaxed in recent years, generally means a tuxedo or dark suit with tie for

Cleaned & Pressed

Many ships offer dry-cleaning and laundry services (for a fee, of course; look for deals where they will wash whatever you can squeeze into a laundry bag for a set price, usually around $25), and some offer coin-operated laundry facilities (usually requiring quarters so having some handy is helpful). Check your line's brochures for details. Using these services can save you a lot of packing.

men, and a nice cocktail dress, long dress, gown, or dressy pantsuit for women. **Informal** (or semiformal) is a jacket, tie, and dress slacks, or a light suit, for men (jeans are frowned upon), and a dress, skirt and blouse, or pants outfit for women (the ubiquitous little black dress is appropriate here). **Casual** at dinner means a sports shirt or open-collar dress shirt with slacks for men (some will also wear a jacket), and a casual dress, pants outfit, or skirt and blouse for women. You may also come across country-club casual; in our experience, this is pretty much the same as informal without the tie. For casual nights, dress as you would to go out to dinner at a midrange restaurant.

Men who don't own a **tuxedo** may be able to rent one in advance through the cruise line's preferred supplier, who will deliver the tux right to the ship. In some cases, the ship will keep a limited supply of tuxes onboard. But if you attend a formal evening wearing a dark business suit instead of a tux, you won't be alone (you'll find some people don't even bother with a suit these days).

2 Money Matters

There are few forms of travel that are as easy as a cruise, at least as far as money is concerned. That's because you've already paid the lion's share of your all-inclusive vacation by the time you board the ship.

When you check in for a large-ship cruise, either at the terminal or online, the cruise line will ask for a major credit card to charge your onboard expenses (although most lines now allow you to also process this information in advance online). They will typically preauthorize your account (with your credit card company) for $50 to $60 per person, per day, an amount refunded if you don't spend it. On some ships, you must report to the purser's office once onboard to establish your onboard credit account. On all cruises, you also have the option of paying your account with cash, traveler's checks, or, in some cases, a personal check. Check the cruise line's brochure for specific rules on this. You may be asked to leave a deposit if you are paying with cash, usually $250 for a 1-week sailing. You should let the cruise line know as early as possible if you wish to pay with cash or checks (some lines like to know at the time you make your cruise reservations). One thing to keep in mind if you plan to put down a deposit in cash and you're departing out of Vancouver in Canada, is that you need to have enough U.S. dollars—the accepted currency of the ships in Alaska—with you before leaving home. The ATMs in Vancouver, as you might expect, dispense Canadian dollars, not U.S. dollars. As obvious as that would seemingly be, our coauthor, Gene Sloan, ran into one woman last year on a cruise who admitted to arriving in Vancouver without her cash deposit in hand, assuming she could withdraw it from her bank at the last minute. (Luckily, she was able to borrow the necessary U.S. dollars from a traveling companion and hit an ATM once the ship arrived in Alaska.)

The Cost of Common Cruise Incidentals	US$
Alternative dining (service charge)	10.00–30.00
Babysitting (per hr.)	
Group	6.00–8.00
Private	10.00
Beverages	
Beer (domestic/imported)	3.50–6.00
Latte	3.75–4.25
Mineral water	2.00–3.95
Mixed drink	5.95–7.75 (more for fine liquors)
Soft drink	2.50–2.75
Wine with dinner	15.00–300.00 per bottle
Cruise-line logo souvenirs	3.00–50.00
E-mail (per min.)	0.40–0.75
Haircuts	
Men's	29.00–35.00
Women's	52.00–77.00
Laundry	1.25–7.00 per item
Massage (50 min.)	129.00–169.00
Phone calls (per min.)	4.95–12.00
Photos	9.95–17.95

Whether you check in online (which the lines are encouraging to speed up the process) or at the terminal, the staff at the check-in counter will give you a special **ship charge card** (sometimes called a "signature card") that you will use for the length of your cruise. From this point on, on most ships, your time aboard is virtually cashless, except for any gambling you do in the casino. On many ships, you can even put your crew tips on your credit card, though on some you're expected to use cash (more on tipping later in this chapter). The same electronic card, by the way, also will likely serve as your cabin key.

On most small ships, things aren't so formal. Because there are so few passengers, and because the only places to spend money aboard are at the bar and the small gift counters, the staff will just mark down your purchases and you'll settle your account at the end of the week.

In all cases, you will need some cash on hand for when you stop at a port, in order to pay for cabs, make small purchases, buy sodas and snacks, tip your tour guides, and so on. Having bills smaller than $20 is useful for these purposes (especially some $1 bills). At all the ports described in this book (even the Canadian ones), U.S. dollars are accepted, as are major credit cards. If you prefer to deal in Canadian currency in Canada, there are exchange counters, banks, and ATMs at most ports you will visit. Ships in Alaska do not usually offer currency-conversion services.

Some ships have their own ATMs aboard, most often located, not surprisingly, in the casino. These give out U.S. dollars. A fee may be involved.

It's recommended that you not leave large amounts of cash in your room. All ships have some sort of safes available, either in-room or at the purser's desk, and passengers are wise to use them. You should also store your plane ticket and passport or ID papers there.

BUDGETING

Before your trip, you may want to make a tentative budget. You should set aside money for shore excursions ($600 per person or more if you plan to do several) and tips (about $10 per passenger per day).

Extras that should also be included in your planning are bar drinks, dry cleaning, phone calls, massage and other spa services, salon services, babysitting, photos taken by the ship's photographer, wine at dinner, souvenirs, and costs for any other special splurges your particular ship might offer (items at the caviar bars or cigar bars, time on the golf simulator, and so on). Above are some rough prices for the more common incidentals.

We suggest that you keep careful track of your onboard expenses to avoid an unpleasant surprise at the end of your cruise.

On big ships, a final bill will be slipped under your door on the last night of your cruise. If everything is okay and you're paying by credit card, you don't have to do anything but keep the copy. If there's a problem on the bill, or if you are paying by cash, traveler's check, or personal check, you will have to go down to the purser's or guest relations desk and wait in what will likely be a very long line. On small ships, you usually have to settle up directly with the purser on the last full day of the cruise.

3 Your Very Important Papers

About 1 month (and no later than 1 week) before your cruise, you should receive in the mail your **cruise documents,** including airline tickets (if you purchased them from the cruise line), a boarding document with your cabin and dining choices on it, boarding forms to fill out, luggage tags, and your prearranged bus-transfer vouchers from the airport to the port (if applicable). Also included will likely be a description of shore excursions available for purchase either onboard or, in some cases, in advance, as well as additional material detailing things you need to know before you sail. Most lines also now allow you to download this information online.

All this information is important. Read it carefully. Make sure that your cabin category and dining preference are as you requested and also check your airline tickets to make sure everything is okay in terms of flights and arrival times. Make sure that there is enough time to arrive at the port no later than a half-hour before departure time, and preferably a lot earlier. Be sure to carry these documents in your carry-on rather than in your luggage, since you can't board without them.

IMPORTANT RULE CHANGE

A Department of Homeland Security regulation requires cruise ships to deliver a final passenger manifest at least an hour before sailing, and most lines are now requiring passengers to check in at least 1½ hours before sailing and to complete a check-in form online (with your name, address, and passport information) at least 3 days prior to sailing. If you do not complete the form, you may be required to show up at least 3 hours before your sailing so that the cruise line has time to prepare and transmit your information. If you don't comply, you may be denied boarding (with no refund).

PASSPORTS & NECESSARY IDENTIFICATION

With the Western Hemisphere Travel Initiative (WHTI), travel ID requirements were recently changed, though some of those changes were subject to debate. As of June 1, 2009, you are to have a valid passport (whereas a photo ID and birth certificate used to suffice) for all Alaska cruises that visit Canada. If you are not a U.S. citizen, but live in the United States, you will have to carry your alien registration card and passport. Foreign-born travelers who do not reside in the U.S. will be required to show a valid visa to enter the U.S. through Canada. For more information about passports and to find your regional passport office, consult the Department of State website (http://travel.state.gov) or call the **National Passport Information Center**'s automated service at ✆ **877/487-2778.**

Even if your cruise doesn't visit Canada, you'll still be required to show photo ID when boarding the ship; in this case, however, a driver's license is sufficient.

4 Getting to the Ship & Checking In

Before you leave for the airport, attach to each of your bags one of the luggage tags sent by the cruise line. Make sure that you correctly fill in the tags with your departure date, port, cabin number, and so forth. You can find all this information in your cruise documents. Put a luggage tag on your carry-on as well.

AIRPORT ARRIVAL

If you booked your air travel and/or transfers with the cruise line, you should see a **cruise-line representative** holding a card with the name of the line, either when you get off the plane or at the baggage area. (If you're arriving on a flight from the United States to Vancouver, you will need to clear Customs and Immigration. Follow the appropriate signs. The cruise-line rep will be waiting to greet you after you've cleared.) Check in with this person. If you are on a precruise package, the details of what to do at the airport will be described in the cruise line's brochure.

When you arrive at your gateway airport, you will be asked by a cruise-line representative to identify your luggage, which will then go straight to the ship for delivery to your cabin. It won't necessarily go in the same bus as you, and it may not (almost certainly will not) be waiting for you when you board, but it'll arrive eventually, have no fear. Make certain that your bags have the cruise line's tags on them, properly filled out, before you leave the airport for the ship.

You'll have to turn over to the bus driver the **transportation voucher** received with your cruise documents, so do have it handy.

If you're flying independent of the cruise line, claim your luggage at the baggage area and proceed to the pier by cab, rental car, or whatever other transportation you

Where's My Luggage?!

Don't panic if your bags aren't in your cabin when you arrive: Getting all the bags on board is a rather slow process—on big ships, as many as 6,000 bags need to be loaded and distributed. If it gets close to sailing time and you're concerned, call guest relations or the purser's office. If your luggage really is lost rather than just late, the cruise line's customer-relations folks will track it down and arrange for it to be delivered to the ship's first port of call.

Safety at Sea in the New World (Dis)Order

Traditionally, safety-at-sea issues have included the occasional hurricane, fire, gastrointestinal bug, petty theft, and rogue iceberg. But in the wake of the September 11, 2001, terrorist attacks, the threat of terrorism immediately assumed a high place on that list, prompting cruise lines, port authorities, and the U.S. Coast Guard to implement a number of new security measures throughout their destination areas—including Alaska.

Logistically, ships are more difficult to protect than planes because of their larger passenger loads; their numerous labyrinthine public and "crew only" areas; their regular presence at public port facilities; the access they offer to the numerous contractors who come aboard on turnaround days to refresh flowers, service machinery, and perform other needed functions; and their multi-country itineraries—Alaska cruises usually include Canadian ports as well. For these reasons, all the major cruise lines have their own dedicated onboard security forces, and events over the years have periodically forced enhancements to security procedures. These have included the hiring of ex–Navy SEALs as top-level security consultants, the drilling of deck officers in how to react to takeover attempts, and a mandate that ships have alternative onboard command sites, making it difficult for a small number of terrorists to take and maintain control of a ship. Following 9/11, all cruise ships adopted heightened security measures required by the Coast Guard, but because stringent security measures were already in place, onboard changes were relatively few. The cruise lines already were using metal detectors at the gangways, requiring that anyone boarding be on a preapproved list, and employing computerized systems that could tell instantly who was aboard at any given time. Recent additions to these regulations dictate a no-visitors policy; a 300-foot (or more) security zone around all cruise ships; the use of sniffer dogs, concrete barriers, Coast Guard patrol boats, and other security measures at some ports; and the screening of all luggage, ship's stores, mail, and cargo. Many cruise lines have begun photographing passengers digitally at embarkation and matching faces to pictures every time travelers get back aboard in port.

Because Coast Guard guidelines apply only to U.S. ports, the cruise lines have been working diligently with foreign port officials to beef up security around the ships and protect passengers on shore excursions. Measures include tightening access to ports and increasing local law enforcement patrols in the water around the vessels.

have arranged. And again, remember to put the luggage tags provided by the cruise line on your bags at this point if you haven't already, because when you get to the pier, your bags will be taken from you by a porter for loading onto the ship. The porter who takes your bags may expect a tip of $1 per bag (some will be more aggressive than others in asking for it).

On the question of identifying your luggage, don't rely simply on appearances; one Samsonite looks just like another, even though yours may have a distinctive yellow ribbon on its handle. Check the ID tags as well! There's nothing worse than getting on a cruise that starts with 2 days at sea and you have somebody else's luggage and only the clothes on your back.

WHAT TO DO IF YOUR FLIGHT IS DELAYED

First of all, tell the airline personnel at the airport that you are a cruise passenger and that you're sailing that day. They may be able to put you on a different flight. Second, have the airline folks call the cruise line to advise them of your delay. There should be an emergency number included in your cruise documents. Keep in mind that you may not be the only person delayed, and the line just may hold the ship until your arrival.

WHAT TO DO IF YOU MISS THE BOAT

Don't panic. Go directly to the cruise line's port agent at the pier (the name, phone number, and address of the port agent should be listed in your cruise documents). You may be able to get to your ship via a chartered boat or tug, assuming that the vessel isn't too far out at sea by that time. (Be aware that if you do follow in a small boat, you'll have to transfer from it to a moving ship at sea—not an exercise to be taken lightly!) Or you may be put up in a hotel for the night and flown or provided with other transportation to the next port the next day. If you booked your flight on your own, you will likely be charged for this service.

AT THE PIER

Most ships start embarkation in the early afternoon, and depart between 4 and 6pm. You will not be able to board the ship before the scheduled embarkation time, usually about 3 or 4 hours before sailing, and even then it's likely that you'll have to wait in line unless you're sailing on a small ship carrying very few passengers. If you've booked a suite, you may get priority boarding at a special desk. Special-needs passengers may also be processed separately. Ship personnel will check your boarding tickets and ID and collect any documents you've been sent to fill out in advance. You will then be given a boarding card and your cabin key. (On some lines, your key may be waiting in your cabin.)

You have up to 90 minutes before departure to board (see "Important Rule Change," above), but there are some advantages to boarding earlier, like getting first dibs on spa-treatment times. Plus, if you're early enough, you can eat lunch on the ship.

Protocol for establishing your **dining-room table assignment,** if one is required (you may instead have open seating), varies by ship. You may be given your assignment in advance of your sailing (shown on your tickets), you may be advised of your table number as you check in, or a card with your table number may be waiting for you in your cabin. If you do not receive an assignment by the time you get to your cabin, you will be directed to a maitre d's desk, set up in a convenient spot onboard. This is also the place to make any changes if your assignment does not meet with your approval.

5 Keeping in Touch with the Outside World

GETTING THE NEWS & KEEPING IN TOUCH

Newshounds don't have to feel out of touch on a cruise ship. Most big ships offer CNN on in-room TVs, and nearly every ship—even small ships without TVs—will post the latest news from the wire services outside the purser's office. Some lines excerpt information from leading newspapers each day and deliver the news to your room (if you are British, you may even be able to get British news).

Most ships will provide the opportunity to make satellite phone calls, but these can be exorbitantly expensive—usually anywhere from $6.95 to $12 per minute. You should be able to use your cellular phone in some of the more populated areas of Alaska (see "Fast Facts: Alaska," in chapter 3). Check with your cellular provider for details. Many ships have added service that allows you to use your cellphone at sea, although you do have to pay what can be expensive roaming rates—again, check with your provider for details (and smartphone users should be aware that even if you have calling capability, your e-mail service and Internet access may not work).

Another alternative is shipboard e-mail, which all the big ships now have. Rates range from 40¢ to 75¢ per minute. It is generally cheaper if you buy a set plan; for instance, paying in advance for 4 hours of usage throughout your cruise (plans vary by line, so check with your ship's Internet cafe to see what plans are available; special discounts may be offered if you sign up the first day of your cruise). In recent years, some lines, including Holland America, have been offering discount packages toward the end of the cruise as well (on a recent Norwegian Cruise Line cruise, there was an offer of free bingo cards if you booked certain Internet packages). Some of the small ships also provide e-mail access. The port cities you'll be visiting are also likely to have Internet cafes—usually charging cheaper rates than ships.

SENDING MAIL

If you want to send mail from the ship, you should be able to find postage stamps and a mailbox at the purser's office.

6 Visiting the Ports of Call

Here's where the kind of ship you chose for your cruise, and the itinerary, comes into play. On a big ship, you will likely visit the popular ports of Skagway, Juneau, and Ketchikan (and possibly Sitka or Victoria, depending on your itinerary) and will have several days at sea to enjoy the glorious glaciers, fjords, and wildlife, as well as participate in shipboard activities and relax. On a smaller ship, you may also visit several smaller ports of call and head into wilderness areas that cannot accommodate larger vessels.

On **days in port,** you need a plan for what you want to see on land (more on that in this section). On **days at sea,** you will probably want to be out on deck much of the time looking for whales and listening to the commentary of glacier and wildlife experts. There will be plenty of activities offered, but these may be reduced at certain times—for instance, when the ship is scheduled to pass one of the famous glaciers.

Nearly every ship in Alaska has naturalists and other Alaska experts onboard to share their expertise on glaciers, geography, plant life, and wildlife. Sometimes these experts are on for the entire cruise and give lectures complete with slides or films. Other times they are National Park Service rangers who come onboard at glacier sites (particularly in Glacier Bay) to provide commentary, usually over the ship's PA system. Depending on the ship, local fishermen, Native Alaskans, teachers, photographers, librarians, historians, and anthropologists may come onboard to teach about local history and culture.

Religion on the High Seas

Religious services depend, of course, on the ship and the clergy onboard. Most ships have a nondenominational service on Sunday and a Friday-night Jewish Sabbath service, usually run by a passenger. On Jewish and Christian holidays, clergy are typically onboard large ships to lead services, which are usually held in the library or conference room. If you are looking for a daily Catholic Mass, you may have to visit churches at the ports.

Cruise lines carefully arrange their itineraries to visit places that have a little something for everyone, whether your interest is nature, museum hopping, barhopping, or no hopping at all. You can take in the location's ambience and natural beauty, learn about the local culture and history, eat local foods, and enjoy sports activities. And you'll have the opportunity to shop to your heart's content.

SHORE EXCURSIONS

When the ship gets into port, you'll have the choice of going on a shore excursion organized by the cruise line or going off on your own. The shore excursions are designed to help you make the most of your limited time at each port of call, to get you to the top natural or historical attractions, and to make sure you get back to the ship on time. But shore excursions are also a moneymaking area for the cruise line, and they can add a hefty sum to your vacation costs. Whether you choose to take one of these prearranged sightseeing trips is a matter of both personal preference and budgetary concerns; you should in no way feel that you must do an excursion in every port. Our picks of some of the best shore excursions in Southeast and Southcentral Alaska, as well as in Vancouver and Victoria, are included with all the port listings in chapters 8 and 9, along with advice on exploring on your own.

At most ports, the cruise lines have **guided tours** to the top sights, usually by bus. The most worthwhile tours take you outside the downtown area or include a meal, a dance or music performance, or a crafts demonstration (or sometimes all of the above). There's a guide on each bus, and the excursion price includes all incidental admission costs. The commentary is sometimes hokey, other times educational.

In most Alaska ports, it's easy to explore the downtown area on your own. There are advantages to independent exploration: Walking around is often the best way to see the sights, and you can plan your itinerary to steer clear of the crowds. In some ports, however, there's not much within walking distance of the docks, and it's difficult to find a cab or other transportation. In these cases, the cruise line's excursion program may be your best and most cost-effective option. For instance, a typical **historical tour** in Sitka will take in the Russian St. Michael's Cathedral in the downtown area plus two great sights a little way out of downtown: Sitka National Historic Park, with its totem poles and forest trails; and the Alaska Raptor Rehabilitation Center, where injured bald eagles and other birds of prey are nursed back to health. The tour may also include a Russian dance performance by the all-female New Archangel Dancers. Although you could visit the church on your own, it's a long walk to the park, and the bus is the best way to get to see the eagles (otherwise you're talking a $22 cab fare each way).

There are plenty of shore excursions in Alaska for those who want to get active, such as **mountain-bike trips, fishing, snorkeling,** and **kayak voyages,** all of which get you close to nature and afford stunning views. These trips are generally worth taking. They usually involve small groups of passengers, and by booking your activity through the cruise line, you have the advantage of knowing that the vendors have been prescreened: Their prices may be slightly higher than those offered by the outfitters that you'll find once you disembark at the port, but you can be assured that the outfitters the cruise lines work with are reputable.

For those who enjoy trips in small planes or helicopters and are willing to pay for the experience (they are on the pricey side), **flightseeing trips,** offered as shore excursions at many of the ports of call, are a fascinating way to see the Alaska landscape. Again, the ship's tours may be priced slightly higher than those offered at the port, but by booking the ship's package, you should be able to avoid touring with Reckless Mike and His Barely Flying Machine. The extra few bucks you pay will be worth it.

That said, in some cases you can lock in the exact same tour your cruise line is selling you (with the exact same outfitter) at a lower price by cutting out the middle man (the line) and going straight to the source (the outfitter). The trick is finding the same operator, which takes a fair amount of legwork. But it's doable, and it can result in significant savings. One summer, for instance, during an Alaskan cruise with his family, our coauthor Gene decided to splurge on one of the flightseeing trips offered on Alaska cruises (something he feels every Alaska visitor should do at least once). But the particular outing he was eyeing cost nearly $400 a person through the cruise line! By tracking down the outfitter that arranges the tour for the line, and talking with them directly, he was able to get the price knocked down about 20%, or $80 per person—a significant savings (and note, he never mentioned his affiliation with Frommer's or *USA Today;* as far as they were concerned, he was just another cruiser looking for a deal).

If you try the direct route, keep in mind that a fair number of the outfitters in Alaskan towns won't budge from quoting you the same price whether you book on the ship or off it. It's no secret that the cruise lines discourage their preferred outfitters from undercutting them by taking bookings directly from cruisers at lower prices, and the last thing an outfitter in Alaska wants is to be put on the naughty list of a cruise line that's one of its biggest customers. The outfitters that do offer you a discount often will ask you not to mention it to anyone back at the cruise line—lest they find themselves in the hot seat.

As for tracking down the operators that cruise lines use, the secret is to examine in great detail the tour you're interested in on your cruise line's website, noting the wording of the description and even the photos you find there, and then comparing that to the descriptions and photos of tour options you'll find on the websites of Alaska's main port towns such as Juneau and Skagway (in many cases, you'll find an exact match). In some of the towns that are small, such as Skagway, it's fairly obvious once you do a little digging which particular outfitter does what for the cruise lines. Keep in mind that some of the port towns, such as Skagway, are so small that they might only have one operator offering such activities as hiking, biking, and climbing tours and the like, so no matter where you book, you're probably going to end up with the same folks.

A new trend is private shore excursions—the cruise line arranges a guide just for you and anyone else you want to invite along. Norwegian Cruise Line, for instance, provides this option in Juneau and Ketchikan; and Holland America in Juneau, Sitka, and Ketchikan. It's the best of both worlds—you get to see what you want to see with an experienced guide—but naturally these tours are pricey.

Regular shore excursions usually range in price from about $35 to $99 for a bus tour, to $215 and up for elaborate trips such as flightseeing by floatplane or helicopter (sometimes $600 and up if you add in thrills such as dog sledding on a glacier). You may be in port long enough to book more than one option or to take an excursion and still have several hours to explore the port on your own. You may very well find that you want to do a prearranged shore excursion at one port and go it on your own at the next.

The best way to decide which shore excursions you want to take is to do some research in advance of your trip. In addition to our descriptions in chapters 8 and 9, which detail the most common and popular excursions offered in the various ports, your cruise line will probably send you a booklet listing its shore excursions with your cruise tickets. You can compare and contrast. You are best off booking shore excursions online before your trip as the most popular ones tend to sell out fast. But if you wait until you are onboard, you'll find a shore-excursion order form in your cabin, available at the purser's desk or shore-excursion desk, or at the shore-excursion lecture that will be offered the first day of your cruise. To make your reservations, check off the appropriate places on the shore-excursion order form, sign the form (make sure to include your cabin number), and drop it off as directed, probably at the ship's shore-excursion desk or at the purser's office. Your account will be automatically charged, and tickets will be sent to your cabin before your first scheduled tour. The tickets will include such information as where and when to meet for the tour. Carefully note the time: If you are not at the right place at the right time, the tour will probably leave without you.

Remember: The most popular excursions (such as flightseeing trips) sell out fast. For that reason, you're best off booking your shore excursions online before your cruise or at least by the first or second day of your cruise.

ARRIVING IN PORT

When the ship arrives in port, it will either dock at the pier or anchor slightly offshore. You may think that when the ship docks right at the pier, you can walk right off, but you can't. Before the gangway is open to disembarking passengers, lots of papers must be signed, and local authorities must give their clearance, a process that can take as long as 2 hours. Don't bother going down to the gangplank until you hear an announcement saying the ship has been cleared.

If your ship anchors rather than docks (as in Sitka, for instance), you will go ashore in a small boat called a launch or tender, which ties up next to your ship and shuttles passengers back and forth all day. Getting on the tender may require a helping hand from crew members, and the waves may keep the tender swaying, sometimes requiring passengers to literally jump to get aboard. (The tenders, by the way, are part of the ship's ample complement of lifeboats, lowered into the water, usually four at a time, for the day in port.)

Whether the ship is docked or anchored, you are in no way required to get off at every port of call. The ship's restaurants will remain open, and there will still be activities, though usually on a limited basis.

If you do disembark, before you reboard, you may want to use the pay phones at the docks to call home. This is much cheaper than making calls from the ship. But be prepared to wait for a phone. No matter how many telephones there are on the pier, you will invariably find that off-duty members of the crew, who generally get off the ship earlier than passengers, have beaten you to them. It's an interesting exercise to stand near a dozen public telephones and listen to the Filipino, cockney, French, Norwegian, and other languages and dialects being spoken by the users. The same goes for Internet cafes near the pier—crew members may flock there—though without the audio aspect.

TIPS FOR YOUR PORT VISITS

THE ESSENTIALS: DON'T LEAVE THE SHIP WITHOUT 'EM

You must bring your **ship boarding pass** (or shipboard ID) with you when you disembark or you will have trouble getting back onboard. (You probably have to show it as you leave the ship anyway, so forgetting it will be hard.) You may also be required to show a photo ID (such as your passport or driver's license). The ship will let you know if you have to carry this as well. And don't forget to bring a little cash—although your ship operates on a cashless system, the ports do not. Many passengers get so used to carrying no cash or credit cards while aboard the ship that they forget them when going ashore. (Coauthor Gene admits to doing just this last summer when popping off a ship in Ketchikan; luckily, all he had planned was a long hike, so there was little need for paper money, though he says it was a bit disconcerting when he realized halfway out of town that he was wandering off sans wallet.)

WATCH THE CLOCK

If you're going off on your own, whether on foot or on one of the alternate tours or transportation options that we've listed, remember to be very careful about timing. You're generally required to be back at the dock at least a half-hour before the ship's scheduled departure. Passengers running late on one of the line's shore excursions needn't worry: If an excursion runs late, the ship accepts responsibility and won't leave without the late passengers.

If you're on your own and do miss the boat, immediately contact the cruise-line representative at the port. (Most lines list phone numbers and addresses for their port agent at each stop in the newsletter they put in your cabin each day; be sure to take it ashore if you are going any distance from the ship!) You'll probably be able to catch your ship at the next port of call, but you'll have to pay your own way to get there.

7 Tipping, Packing & Other End-of-Cruise Concerns

A few hints that should save you time and aggravation at the end of your cruise:

TIPS ON TIPPING

Tipping is a subject that some people find confusing. First, let's establish that you are expected on most ships to tip the crew at the end of the cruise—in particular, your cabin steward, server, and busperson—and not to tip is bad form. Recently, lines including Carnival, Holland America, Princess, and Norwegian Cruise Line have made the process easier, adopting a system whereby they automatically add tips of $10 to $12 per passenger, per day, to your shipboard account. You can visit the purser's office and ask to increase or decrease the amount, depending on your opinion of the service you received. Other lines may suggest that you tip in cash, but some also allow you to tip via your shipboard account. Bar bills usually automatically include the tip (usually 15%), but if the dining-room wine steward, for instance, has served you exceptionally well, you can slip him or her a few bucks, too.

If there is no automatic tip, the cruise line will give suggested tip amounts in the daily bulletin and in the cruise director's debarkation briefing, but these are just suggestions—you can tip more or less, at your own discretion. Keep in mind, though, that stewards, servers, and buspersons are often extremely underpaid (some lines pay their waiters $1 a day base pay) and that their salaries are largely dependent on tips. Many of these crew members support families back home on their earnings.

We think the **minimum tip** you should consider is $4 per passenger per day for your room steward and your waiter, and $2 per passenger per day for your busperson. That's a total of up to $70 per passenger for a 7-night cruise (you don't have to include debarkation day). We also recommend leaving about half of these amounts on behalf of child passengers 12 and under. Some lines recommend more, some a little less. Of course, you can always tip more for good service or simply to round out the number. You'll also be encouraged to tip the dining room maitre d', the headwaiter, and other better salaried employees. Whether to tip these folks is your decision. If you have a cabin with butler service, tip the butler about $5 per person, per day, provided he has been visible throughout your cruise (if he hasn't, reduce that amount). The captain and his officers should not be tipped—it'd be like tipping your doctor.

Regent Seven Seas Cruises and Silversea Cruises include tips in the cruise fare, although some people choose to tip key personnel anyway—it's really up to you. The small-ship lines do recommend tips. (See details in chapter 6.)

If you have spa or beauty treatments, you can tip at the time of service (just add it to your ship account; be aware some ships add 15% automatically) and you can hand a bartender a buck if you like, but otherwise tips are usually given on the last night of your cruise. On some ships (especially small ships), you may be asked to submit your tips in a single sum that the crew will divide among itself after the cruise, but generally you reward people individually, usually in little preprinted envelopes that the ship distributes.

If a staff member is particularly great, a written letter to a superior is always good form and may earn that person an employee-of-the-month honor, and maybe even a bonus.

SETTLING YOUR SHIPBOARD ACCOUNT

On big ships, your shipboard account will close just before the end of your cruise, but before that time you will receive a preliminary bill in your cabin. If you are using a credit card, just make sure the charges are correct. If there is a problem, you will have to go to the purser's office, where you will likely encounter long lines. If you're paying by cash or traveler's check, you'll be asked to settle your account during the day or night before you leave the ship. This will also require you to go to the purser's office. A final invoice will be delivered to your room before departure.

On small ships, the procedure will be simpler. Often you can just mosey over to the purser's desk on the last evening, check to see that the bill they give you looks right, and sign your name.

LUGGAGE PROCEDURES

With thousands of suitcases to deal with, big ships have established the routine of requiring guests to pack the night before they disembark, if they don't want to carry their bags off the ship themselves. You will be asked to leave your bags (except for your carry-ons) in the hallway before you retire for the night—usually, you will be required to leave them in the hallway by midnight. The bags will be picked up overnight and placed in the cruise terminal before passengers are allowed to disembark. It's important to make sure that your bags are tagged with the luggage tags given to you by the cruise line toward the end of your cruise. These are not the same tags you arrived with; rather, they're color-coded to indicate deck number and debarkation order—the order in which they'll likely be arranged on the dock. If you need more tags, alert your cabin steward or the purser's staff. You may also have the option of carrying your own bags off if they are not too heavy for you to do so.

If you booked your air travel through the cruise line, you may be able to check your luggage for your flight at the cruise terminal (or even onboard the ship for a small fee). Make sure you receive your luggage claim checks. You may even be able to get your flight boarding passes at the cruise terminal, saving you a wait in line at the airport. A bus will then take you to the airport.

If you're signed up for a post-cruise tour, special instructions will be given by the cruise line.

DEBARKATION

You won't be able to get off the ship until it is cleared by Customs and other authorities, a process that usually takes 90 minutes or more. In most cases, you'll be asked to vacate your cabin by 8am and wait in one of the ship's lounges. If you have a flight home on the same day, you will disembark based on your flight departure time. Passengers with mobility problems, those who booked suites, and travelers who will be staying on in the port will often disembark early. If you have booked a land package through the cruise line, there will be transportation waiting to take you from the ship to your hotel.

CUSTOMS & IMMIGRATION

If your cruise begins or ends in Canada, you'll have to clear Canadian Customs and Immigration, which usually means that your name goes on a list that is reviewed by authorities. You must fill out a Customs declaration form, and you may be required to show your passport.

When disembarking in U.S. ports after starting out from Vancouver, non-U.S. citizens (including green-card holders) will be required to meet with U.S. Immigration authorities, usually in a lounge or theater, when the ship arrives at the port. Bring your passport receipt, and all family members must attend.

The U.S. Customs & Border Protection Service has a preclearance program in Vancouver that allows cruise passengers to go through Customs before boarding their flights home. The procedure in Vancouver—purely because of the lower number of travelers to be processed—is generally a lot faster than at LAX, JFK, or other U.S. airport facilities, where a half-dozen flights arrive close together.

5

The Cruise Lines, Part 1: The Big Ships

Here's where the rudder hits the road: It's time to choose the ship that will be your home away from home for the duration of your Alaska cruise.

As we said earlier, your biggest decision is whether you want to sail on a big ship or a small ship. So that you can more easily compare like with like, in this chapter we'll deal with the big and midsize ships; in chapter 6, we'll discuss the small ships.

For some years, the ships in Alaska have been getting bigger and bigger, and in terms of total tonnage, Princess ships still lead. Indeed, three of the six vessels the company is sending to Alaska in 2011 are over 100,000 tons, putting them among the biggest cruise ships in the world. The largest two, the 116,000-ton *Diamond Princess* and *Sapphire Princess,* both in their seventh Alaska season, are capable of carrying 2,670 passengers, and at 109,000 tons, the *Golden Princess* is not far behind. Princess' three other ships in the region also are relatively large at 77,000 to 92,000 tons. (Starting in 2011, Princess no longer will be sending one of its smaller, 30,000-ton ships to Alaska.)

There are other megaships that don't sport the Princess colors. Celebrity Cruises' returning *Millennium* and *Infinity* each measure 91,000 tons and carry 1,950 passengers. Royal Caribbean's 90,000-ton, 2,112-berth *Radiance of the Seas* will be spending its eighth summer in Alaska, joined by the slightly smaller *Rhapsody of the Seas.* Norwegian Cruise Line is sending two large ships to Alaska in 2011, the 93,000-ton *Norwegian Pearl* and 91,700-ton *Norwegian Star.* And as in past years, even Caribbean-focused Carnival Cruise Lines is positioning one ship in Alaska, the 88,500-ton, 2,124-passenger *Carnival Spirit.*

For those looking for a slightly more intimate experience, midsize ship–focused Holland America Line has seven vessels in Alaska this year. The largest of the lot—the *Zuiderdam* and *Westerdam*—are "only" a little in excess of 80,000 tons and carry fewer than 2,000 passengers apiece, while several other Holland America ships, such as the *Statendam,* are under 60,000 tons. (By today's standards, such ships are definitely midsize!)

Perhaps the biggest news in Alaska cruising for 2011 is the arrival of the Disney Cruise Line, which is sending a ship to the region for the first time in its 12-year history. The family-friendly operator's 83,000-ton, 2,400-passenger *Disney Wonder* will sail 7-night voyages to the state out of Vancouver, B.C.

Also debuting in the region for the first time in 2011 is upscale Oceania Cruises, which is sending the 684-passenger *Regatta.* And another line that hasn't sailed in the region for many years, luxury operator Crystal Cruises, is revisiting the state with the deployment of the 960-passenger *Crystal Symphony.*

The *Crystal Symphony* is joining two other luxury ships that are returning to Alaska, Regent Seven Seas' *Seven Seas Navigator* and Silversea's *Silver Shadow.* Both of the latter are tiny compared to most of the vessels we mention here. However, they're a good bit bigger than the ships in the next chapter, and they have a full range of big-ship amenities, so we've kept them in with the big guys.

The beauty of some of the latter-day megaships is that they're designed so that you won't feel as if you're sharing your vacation with thousands of others. There are lots of nooks and crannies in which to relax and hide far from the maddening crowd, so to speak.

The evolution of cruise ships is almost worth a chapter all by itself, but we'll address it here in shorter order. Two decades ago, major cruise lines operated ships that ranged from about 20,000 to 40,000 gross registered tons (GRT). These were considered "big" ships. Their cabins had portholes or, at best, picture windows that didn't open. The ships had one dining room, with two seatings for lunch and dinner, and a snack bar/buffet as pretty much the only alternative. Many of them had large numbers of inside cabins, and all of their cabins, inside and outside, tended to be rather basic (in some cases, downright spartan). Only the very best half-dozen or so suites on some of them had private balconies.

Things began changing in the 1980s, when ships began getting bigger—and debuting with not just a few but rows of balcony cabins. As the demand for cruises grew—stoked by the popular TV show *The Love Boat*—the lines also began looking for ways to make life at sea more enjoyable for their passengers, adding everything from larger showrooms with more sophisticated acts to more deck-top amenities. Advances in shipbuilding technology allowed them to move up from 45,000 tons to 70,000 tons and, by the middle of the 1990s, more than 100,000 tons, and they were adding ever more onboard attractions (from miniature golf courses to climbing walls) along the way. But the growth of cruise ships wasn't over. Early last decade, lines such as Cunard and Royal Caribbean rolled out ships as big as 160,000 tons, and in 2009 Royal Caribbean upped the ante again with the unveiling of the 225,282-ton *Oasis of the Seas*—by far the biggest ship ever built. (***Note:*** None of these biggest-of-the-big vessels—aimed primarily at the Caribbean market—sail in Alaska.)

All the new ships, but especially those built this century, have more technologically advanced showrooms, million-dollar collections of original art, better trained and higher paid entertainment directors, flashy and extensive children's and teens' centers—and alternative dining facilities. Lots and lots of alternative dining facilities! Nowadays, the roster of available food choices on cruise ships would do credit to the Manhattan telephone directory. Depending on your ship, you can have Italian, Tex-Mex, Cajun, Asian fusion, top-flight steakhouse, French, even good old British fish and chips. More and more cruise ships are also going to an open seating policy (come when you like, eat with whom you like). On some ships, it is possible nowadays to eat dinner in a different restaurant every night of your cruise.

The ships featured in this chapter vary in size, age, and amenities, but share the common thread of having scads of activities and entertainment. You will not be roughing it. On these ships, you'll find swimming pools, health clubs, spas, nightclubs, movie theaters, shops, casinos, multiple restaurants and bars, special kids' playrooms (in most cases, special club spaces for teens as well), sports decks, virtual golf, computer rooms, martini and cigar bars, as well as the aforementioned quiet spaces where you can get away from it all. Onboard activities generally include games, contests, classes, and lectures, plus a variety of entertainment options and show productions, some very sophisticated. There's usually a vast array of shore excursions for which you will have to pay extra. Cabins vary in size and amenities, but are usually roomy enough for the time you'll be spending aboard. And with all the public rooms, you won't be spending much time in your cabin anyway.

1 Some Components of Our Cruise-Line Reviews

Each cruise line's review begins with a quick word about the line in general and a short summation of the kind of cruise experience you can expect to have aboard that line. The text that follows fleshes out the review, providing all the details you need to get a feel for what kind of vacation the cruise line will provide.

The individual ship reviews following the general cruise-line description then get into the nitty-gritty, giving you all the details on the ships' accommodations, facilities, amenities, comfort levels, and upkeep.

People feel very strongly about ships. For centuries, mariners have imbued their vessels with human personalities, usually referring to an individual ship as "her." In fact, an old (really old) seafaring superstition holds that women should never be allowed aboard a ship because the ship, being a woman herself, will get jealous. It's a fact that people bond with the ships aboard which they sail. They find themselves in the gift shop loading up on T-shirts with the ship's name emblazoned on the front. They get to port and the first question they ask other cruisers they meet is "Which ship are you sailing on?" They engage in a (usually) friendly comparison, and both parties walk away knowing in their hearts that their ship is the best. We know people who have sailed the same ship a dozen times or more and feel as warmly about it as their

New Cruisers

There is a saying in the industry that nobody should cruise just once. On any voyage, a ship could encounter bad weather. On any given day at sea, the only seat left in the show lounge might be behind an unforgiving pillar. Or a technical problem might affect the enjoyment of the onboard experience. Our coauthor Gene Sloan remembers vividly one occasion when the air-conditioning on a ship on which he was traveling—which shall remain nameless—went out for a half-day. It was an uncomfortable time and could have turned a neophyte off cruising forever. That would have been a mistake. In travel, there is liable to be an occasional snafu. Your hotel room may not be available, even though you have a valid confirmation number. Your flight might be canceled. The luxury car you thought you rented might not be on the lot, and all that's available is a miniature subcompact. But you don't stop flying, you don't refuse to stay in a hotel ever again, and you don't stop renting cars. Nor should one unforeseen problem on a cruise ship cause you to swear off the product forever. Give it another go, on a different cruise line, if you prefer. If you still haven't had the enjoyable experience that millions of others have discovered, then, and only then, is it perhaps time to abandon hope of becoming a cruise aficionado.

summer cottage. That's why, when looking at the reviews, you want to look for a ship that says "you."

We've listed some of the ships' vital statistics—ship size, years built and most recently refurbished, number of cabins, number of crew—to help you compare. Size is listed in tons. Note that these are not actual measures of weight, but gross register tons (GRTs), a measure of the interior space used to produce revenue on a ship. One GRT equals 100 cubic feet of enclosed, revenue-generating space. Among the crew/officers statistics, an important one is the **passenger/crew ratio,** which tells you, in theory, how many passengers each crew member is expected to serve and, thus, how much personal service you can expect.

Note: When several vessels are members of a class—built on the same design, with usually only minor variations in decor and attractions—we've grouped the ships together into one class review.

STARS

THE RATINGS

To make things easier on everyone, we've developed a simple ratings system that covers those things that vary from vessel to vessel—quality and size of the cabins and public spaces, comfort, cleanliness and maintenance, decor, number and quality of dining options, gyms/spas (and for the small-adventure lines that don't have gyms and spas, a slightly different system, see p. 139), and children's facilities—plus a rating for the overall enjoyment of the onboard experience. We've given each ship an overall **star rating** (for example, ★★★) based on the combined total of our poor-to-outstanding ratings, translated into a 1-to-5 scale:

1	=	**Poor**	**4**	=	**Excellent**
2	=	**Fair**	**5**	=	**Outstanding**
3	=	**Good**			

In instances when the category doesn't apply to a particular ship (for example, none of the adventure ships have children's facilities), we've simply noted "not applicable" (N/A) and absented the category from the total combined score, as these unavailable amenities will be considered a deficiency only in certain circumstances (for instance, if you plan to travel with kids).

Now for a bit of philosophy: The cruise biz today offers a profusion of experiences so different that comparing all ships by the same set of criteria would be like comparing a Park Avenue apartment to an A-frame in Aspen. That's why, to rate the ships, we've used a sliding scale, rating ships on a curve that compares them only with others in their category—big vs. small (more mainstream vs. adventure). Once you've determined what kind of experience is right for you, you can look for the best ships in that category based on your particular needs.

ITINERARIES

Each cruise-line review includes a chart showing itineraries for each ship the line has assigned to Alaska for 2011. Often a ship sails on alternating itineraries—for instance, sailing southbound from Seward or Whittier to Vancouver, B.C. one week and doing the same route in reverse the next. When this is the case, we've listed both and noted that they alternate. These one-way cruises are known as Gulf of Alaska cruises, as opposed to Inside Passage cruises, which generally are round-trip out of either Seattle or Vancouver, B.C. (Some longer round-trip cruises depart from San Francisco.) All

Weddings at Sea

Lovers long have known that there is nothing as romantic as cruising. Luxury cruise ships have been vastly popular honeymoon vehicles for decades. And recently, with the growing popularity of cruises, they have assumed new significance in the marriage business. Ship operators now make it easier to tie the knot either in a port of call during the voyage or onboard the vessel. Most lines will help you set it all up—for a fee, of course (and assuming you give them enough advance notice). They will provide the music, photographer, bouquets, champagne, hors d'oeuvres, cake, and other frills and fripperies. All you have to do is bring somebody to share your "I do" moment. The wedding package might cost you $1,000 or so over the price of your cabin.

In Alaska this year, Carnival, Celebrity, Norwegian Cruise Line, Royal Caribbean, and Holland America Line allow you to hold your marriage ceremony in a specially decorated lounge onboard while in port, officiated by a local clergyman or justice of the peace. Princess goes one better: Whereas before you could be married only on the *Diamond, Sapphire, Island,* and *Coral Princess,* all of them equipped with wedding chapels in which the captain himself can conduct the ceremony, now you can be wed on any ship in the Princess fleet, including those in Alaska in 2011. It's all perfectly legal. The ships now sail under a Bermuda registry, the authority under which your nuptials will be certified.

If you want guests to attend your special onboard moment while in port, the ship line must be notified well in advance, and your guests will be required to produce valid ID and to go through the same kind of screening process that passengers go through. Princess makes it easy for friends and family on shore to share the event by filming the entire process and then posting it on a special webcam found on its website (www.princess.com). Click on "Ships" and then "Bridge Cams." And, no, it's not really live. The images are there for all to see long after the rites are concluded.

No matter where you wed, you have to have a valid U.S. marriage license (or a Canadian license, if you want to bid farewell to the single life in one of the British Columbia ports). The cruise line's wedding planner will help you set that up. Just remember to plan in advance—these things take time.

itineraries are subject to change. Consult the cruise line websites or your travel agent for exact sailing dates.

The variety of cruise itineraries and of ports of embarkation (and debarkation, for that matter) also demonstrates the maturing of the cruise industry and growth in demand for the product. Not so long ago, just about the only thing you could do in Alaska cruising was a Vancouver to Vancouver Inside Passage loop. Very few lines had one-way Gulf itineraries. It was simply easier for the ship operators to stick with the tried and true. People wanted it. Ships' crews got into a rhythm—arrive in Vancouver,

B.C. at 8am, discharge passengers, take on new ones, and start all over again. But demand began to outstrip the available berths. San Francisco became an attractive alternative, then Seattle. People who had done the Inside Passage round-trip began to demand a new experience—a cruise across the Gulf. Princess and Holland America, sister companies in the Carnival Corp. family who had invested heavily on a physical presence in Alaska (hotels/lodges, motorcoaches, railcars for land tour add-ons in the Denali Park corridor btw. Anchorage and Fairbanks), began to see that route as the way to go. Princess tweaked the itinerary further using Whittier rather than Seward as the northern terminal of its Gulf cruises because it's closer to Anchorage. (Not much, but when you're on vacation, every minute counts!) Royal Caribbean Cruises also has invested heavily in Denali railcars and motorcoaches for its Royal Caribbean International and Celebrity brands. Those lines that do not have a strong investment in Alaska land components still tend to stick with the Vancouver, B.C. (or Seattle) originating round-trip.

For your convenience, we've listed the **cruisetours and add-ons** you can book with your cruise, and we've provided brochure prices for these as well where possible—though some lines make their plans (and set their prices) early, others do not. Therefore, at press time, some of the numbers were not available.

PRICES: DON'T GET STICKER SHOCK

We've listed the prices for cabins and suites. We stress that all of the prices listed reflect the line's **brochure rates,** so depending on how early you book and on any special deals the lines are offering, you may get a rate substantially below what we've listed. (Discounts can run as high as 60% or thereabouts.) Rates are per night for a 7-night cruise, per person, and are based on double occupancy. If the ship does not sail 7-night itineraries, we've noted that and given per diem rates for whatever itineraries it does sail. (The *Sea Princess,* for instance, operates a 10-night round-trip Inside Passage pattern out of San Francisco.)

Our rates are based on the basic types of accommodations:

- Inside cabin (without windows)
- Outside cabin (with windows)
- Suite

Remember that cruise ships generally have several different categories of cabins within each of these three basic divisions, all priced differently, which is why, on some ships, you'll see a rather broad range in each category.

Please keep something else in mind. As they say in the business, "Buy as much cruise as you can afford." If you go in with the attitude that you refuse to buy anything but the least expensive inside cabin, you may be doing yourself a disservice. The idea that "Oh, I'm not going to spend any time in my cabin anyway, so what does it matter if it's inside or outside, big or small?" isn't really valid. You *will* spend time in your cabin, and sometimes having no exposure to the outside world can be awfully claustrophobic. You may find that for a few hundred dollars more, you can upgrade to an outside room. Or, if you're planning to pay for an outside cabin, you may find that you could reserve a room with a balcony if you dug just a little deeper into the purse. This is not to say you have to go deeply into debt to buy the best—just that you should investigate the possibility of buying something a little better.

2 Carnival Cruise Lines

Carnival Place, 3655 NW 87th Ave., Miami, FL 33178-2428. ✆ **800/CARNIVAL** [227-6482]. Fax 305/471-4740. www.carnival.com.

THE LINE IN A NUTSHELL Almost the definition of mass market, Carnival is the Big Kahuna of the industry, boasting a modern fleet of flashy megaships that cater to a fun-loving crowd. Nonstop entertainment (if you have the energy after a busy day of Alaska cruising) is the name of the game onboard.

THE EXPERIENCE Carnival ships are known for spectacularly glitzy, over-the-top decor that some people love and others find overwhelming (and that's putting it nicely). Translating the line's warm weather, fun-in-the-sun experience to Alaska has meant combining the "24-hours of good times" philosophy with opportunities to experience the natural wonders of the state, so you may find yourself bellying up to the rail with a multicolored umbrella drink to gawk at a glacier. The casino is nearly always hopping, although the party scene is not as hearty in Alaska as on the line's Caribbean sailings. This, of course, is either a plus or a minus, depending on your taste. Carnival does not pretend to be a luxury experience. It doesn't claim to have gourmet food (although it's routinely praised for serving some of the best meals of any mass-market ship) and it doesn't promise 'round-the-clock pampering. The motto is "fun," and with a big focus on entertainment, friendly service, and creative cruise directors (they can be corny sometimes, but at least they're lively), that's what Carnival delivers.

Pros

- **Entertainment.** Carnival's entertainment is among the industry's best, with each ship boasting a large cast of dancers and singers who perform lively production numbers in a big theater, along with comedians, jugglers, and numerous live bands, including a resident jazz trio, as well as a big casino.
- **Children's program.** Carnival long has had one of the best children's programs in the industry, and it keeps getting better. The line now has separate facilities, counselors, and nearly around-the-clock activities for each of three different age groups. Carnival's Alaska cruises, moreover, include Alaska-specific activities thrown into the mix, including a special series of shore excursions designed for teens.

Cons

- **Service.** The international crew doesn't provide the type of service typically found on higher-end brands, but that's not the point here, is it?
- **Crowds.** This is a big ship with lots of people onboard, and you are occasionally aware of that fact, like when you want to get off at a port and have to wait in line.

THE FLEET The 2,124-passenger megaship *Carnival Spirit* returns to Alaska in 2011. It has plenty of activities, great pool and hot tub spaces (some covered for use in chillier weather), a big oceanview gym and spa, and more dining options than your doctor would say are advisable.

PASSENGER PROFILE Overall, Carnival has some of the youngest demographics in the industry. But it's far more than age that defines the line's customers. Carnival executives are fond of using the word spirited to describe the typical Carnival passenger, and indeed it's right on target. The line's many fans increasingly come from a wide range of ages as well as occupations, backgrounds, and income levels, but what they

Carnival Fleet Itineraries

Ship	Itineraries
Carnival Spirit	**7-night Inside Passage:** Round-trip from Seattle, visiting Skagway, Juneau, Ketchikan, and Victoria, and cruising Tracy Arm Fjord (May–Aug).

share is an unpretentious, fun-loving, and outgoing demeanor. This is a line for people who don't mind at all that their dinner will be interrupted by the loud music and flashing lights of a dance show starring their waiters. If anything, the typical Carnival passenger will want to jump right into the fray. On Carnival, you'll find couples, a few singles, and a good share of families (in fact, the line carries more than 650,000 kids a year—the most in the cruise industry). But the bottom line is this is not your average sedentary, bird-watching crowd. Passengers want to see whales, but they will also dance the Macarena.

DINING Food is bountiful, and the cuisine is traditional American: Red meat is popular on these ships. In addition, there are delicious preparations of more "nouvelle" dishes such as broiled Chilean sea bass with truffle butter, and smoked turkey tenderloin with asparagus tips. The line features fresh salmon on Alaska sailings. Gourmet Spa Carnival Fare is on menus, for those seeking healthier options. Pasta and vegetarian choices are also served nightly. Until recently, meals always were served at assigned tables, with two seatings per meal. But over the past year, the line has been rolling out an alternative, eat-when-you-want dining option for passengers called Your Time dining. Passengers must sign up for Your Time dining in advance, in lieu of fixed seatings. The casual lunch buffets include international (Japanese, Indian, and so on, with a different cuisine featured daily), deli, rotisserie, and pizza stations; and the breakfast buffet, in the same location—La Playa Grill, on Lido Deck—has everything from made-to-order egg dishes to cold cereals and pastries. Many passengers prefer to eat their meals in La Playa rather than in the main dining room. The *Carnival Spirit* also adds the special treat of a truly superb reservations-only steakhouse, where for a fee of $30 per person, you can dine on a great steak and other upscale culinary choices.

ACTIVITIES If Atlantic City and Las Vegas appeal to you, Carnival will, too. What you'll get is fun—lots of it, professionally and consistently delivered and spangled with glitter. Cocktails inevitably begin to flow before lunch. You can learn to country line dance, take cooking lessons, learn to play bridge, watch first-run movies, and practice your golf swing by smashing balls into a net. Among the newer offerings is a photo safari in Juneau led by a professional photographer. Plus, there are always the onboard staple activities of eating, drinking, and shopping, and the Alaska-specific naturalist lectures that are delivered daily. Once in port, Carnival lives up to its "more is more" ethos by providing more than 120 shore excursions in Alaska. These are divided into categories of easy, moderate, and adventure. Internet cafes allow Internet access for 75¢ a minute, with a 10-minute minimum (discounted bulk-use packages also are available). The ships in the fleet also have been outfitted with Wi-Fi for those who bring their own laptops (for the same fee as above).

The ships also now have technology that allows you to use your own cellphone at sea, rather than having to pay steep shipboard phone rates.

CHILDREN'S PROGRAM Camp Carnival is an expertly run program for children ages 2 to 11, and it's loaded with kid-pleasing activities, allowing Mom and Dad some downtime. In Alaska, these activities include everything from Native American arts-and-crafts sessions to lectures conducted by wildlife experts. On the *Carnival Spirit,* parents of little kids even can request beepers so that they can keep in touch. In recent years, Carnival also has added separate programs called Circle "C" for 12- to 14-year-olds and Club O2 for children ages 15 to 17, each with dedicated facilities and separate staffs.

ENTERTAINMENT Carnival consistently has the most lavish entertainment extravaganzas afloat, spending millions on stage sets, choreography, and acoustical equipment that leave many other floating theaters in their wake. Each Carnival megaship carries flamboyantly costumed dancers and singers (on the *Carnival Spirit,* there's a cast of about 20) and a 10-piece orchestra, plus comedians, jugglers, acrobats, rock-'n'-roll bands, country western bands, classical string trios, jazz trios, pianists, and big bands.

SERVICE As we said before, Carnival service isn't exactly "refined" in the way you'd find on a luxury line, but it is certainly friendly and professional. A Carnival ship is a well-oiled machine, and you'll certainly get what you need—but not much more. When you board the ship, for instance, you're welcomed by polite staff at the gangway, given a diagram of the ship's layout, and then pointed in the right direction to find your cabin on your own, carry-on luggage in tow. On Carnival, gratuities of $10 per passenger per day are automatically charged to your shipboard account, but you can increase or decrease the amount by visiting the guest services desk onboard.

There is a laundry service onboard (for washing and pressing only) that charges by the piece, as well as a handful of self-service laundry rooms with irons and coin-operated washing machines and dryers. Dry cleaning is not available.

CRUISETOURS & ADD-ON PROGRAMS None.

Carnival Spirit

The Verdict

The *Carnival Spirit* is glitzy Vegas, with more bars and lounges than you'll be able to visit. The dining room is multistory, and there are such cool extras as a reservations-only steakhouse and a wedding chapel.

Carnival Spirit *(photo: Gero Mylius, Indav Ltd.)*

Specifications

Size (in Tons)	88,500	Crew	930
Passengers (Double Occ.)	2,124	Passenger/Crew Ratio	2.3 to 1
Space/Passenger Ratio	41.7 ft. to 1	Year Launched	2001
Total Cabins/Veranda Cabins	1,062/682	Last Major Refurbishment	N/A

Frommer's Ratings (Scale of 1–5) ★★★★½

Cabin Comfort & Amenities	5	Dining Options	4
Ship Cleanliness & Maintenance	4	Gym, Spa & Sports Facilities	5
Public Comfort/Space	4	Children's Facilities	5
Decor	4	Enjoyment Factor	4

THE SHIP IN GENERAL The *Carnival Spirit* is big and impressive, even if some may find the interior a bit over the top (but after a few days onboard, it may grow on you). Rooms reflect a purposeful mismatch of styles, including Art Nouveau, Art Deco, Empire, Gothic, and Egyptian, with the decor featuring expensive materials, such as burled wood, marble, leather, copper, and even gold gilt. In other words, legendary Carnival designer Joe Farcus has shown little restraint. Love it or not, you'll certainly be wowed.

CABINS Some 80% of the cabins on this ship boast ocean views, and of those, 80% have private balconies, a big plus in a market like Alaska where views are the main draw. Cabins are larger than those you'll find on other lines in the same price category, and they are mostly furnished with twin beds that can be converted to king size. (A few have upper and lower berths that cannot be converted.) All cabins come with a TV, wall safe, and telephone; oceanview cabins also come with bathrobes and coral-colored leather couches with nifty storage drawers underneath. There are connecting cabins available for families or groups traveling together. Suites are offered at several different levels, each with separate sleeping, sitting, and dressing areas, plus double sinks, a bathtub, and a large balcony. Sixteen cabins are wheelchair-accessible. Carnival features the Carnival Comfort Bed sleep system with plush mattresses and fluffy duvets (no more scratchy wool blankets for this line). And not to miss a marketing opportunity, if you fall in love with the new linens and more, you can buy them online at www.carnivalcomfortcollection.com.

Cabins & Rates

Cabins	Per Diem Rates	Sq. Ft.	Fridge	Hair Dryer	Sitting Area	TV
Inside Passage						
Inside	$125	185	yes	yes	no	yes
Outside	$161	220–260*	yes	yes	yes	yes
Suites	$261	340–430*	yes	yes	yes	yes
Gulf of Alaska						
Inside	$128	185	yes	yes	no	yes
Outside	$164	220–260*	yes	yes	yes	yes
Suites	$264	340–430*	yes	yes	yes	yes

**Includes veranda*

PUBLIC AREAS The ship's soaring atrium spans 11 decks. There are dozens of bars and lounges, including a piano bar, a sports bar, and a jazz club. A lobby bar provides live music and a chance to take in the vast dimensions of the ship. A particularly fun room is the two-level Jackson Pollock–inspired disco, with paint-splattered walls; depending on your particular Alaska sailing, it may be hopping until dawn or may just host a few stragglers late at night. A better hangout spot, we think, is the nearby Deco bar, where a combo plays nightly and cigar smoking is allowed (we've even seen the captain hanging out here).

The ship, which debuted as a new class for Carnival, consciously offers the best features of the line's earlier ships, including an expansive outdoor area with four swimming pools (there is a retractable dome over the main pool so that you can take a dip no matter what the weather), four whirlpools, and a water slide; a high-tech children's play center with computers and wall of video monitors; a multilevel oceanview fitness facility; numerous clubs and lounges; and a variety of eating and entertainment options. Among the interesting features is the line's original wedding chapel (you can get married at sea on this ship when it sails in Canadian waters, same-sex marriages included), as well as a mostly outdoor promenade (if you are doing a full tour around the ship, you have to take a few steps inside). The ship also has ultramodern engines and waste treatment and disposal systems to make it more environmentally friendly. And the *Carnival Spirit* offers more space per passenger than most ships in the Alaska market.

The hundreds of onboard activities for which Carnival is famous, including Vegas-style shows and casino action (the ship's Louis XIV casino is one of the largest at sea), keep passengers on the *Carnival Spirit* on the fast track to that famous and oft-mentioned fun. It's up to you to find time to stop and catch the scenery, which you can do both from the generous open-deck spaces and from some (but not many) indoor spaces. For kids, there's a children's playroom, children's pool, and video arcade. The *Carnival Spirit*'s library doubles as an Internet cafe and the clicking of computers may be annoying to those who want to read a book. Shoppers will find plenty of enticements at the ship's shopping arcade, including Fendi and Tommy Hilfiger products.

Carnival passengers also have the capability of using their personal cellphones anywhere at sea.

DINING OPTIONS The ship's handsome atrium is topped with a red stained-glass dome that is part of the Nouveau steakhouse, a reservations-only ($30 per person supplement) restaurant. Some people might consider the nightspot a little pricey, but this is not your run-of-the mill restaurant operating by filling tables with two or three changes of customers in the evening. Rather, it's an intimate room in which passengers are encouraged to linger and savor a truly elegant and enjoyable experience. The two-level main dining room is done up in Napoleonic splendor, and a 24-hour poolside pizzeria and 24-hour room service will keep you from getting hungry.

POOL, FITNESS, SPA & SPORTS FACILITIES The ship has three pools, including one with a retractable dome, as well as a children's splash pool. There is a freestanding water slide on the top deck. The gym has an interesting tiered design and more than 50 exercise machines, as well as a spacious aerobics studio. There are windows, so you won't miss the scenery. The spa has a dozen treatment rooms and an indoor sunning area with a whirlpool. The ship also has three additional whirlpools and a jogging/walking track (10 laps = 1 mile).

3 Celebrity Cruises

1050 Caribbean Way, Miami, FL 33132. ✆ **800/437-3111** or 305/262-8322. Fax 800/437-5111. www.celebritycruises.com.

THE LINE IN A NUTSHELL With a premium fleet that's among the best designed in the cruise industry, Celebrity Cruises offers a great experience: classy, tasteful, and luxurious. You'll be pampered at a relatively reasonable price.

THE EXPERIENCE Each of the Celebrity ships is spacious and comfortable, mixing modern and Art Deco styles, and with an astoundingly cutting-edge art collection. The line's genteel service is exceptional: Staff members in our experience are polite and professional, and contribute greatly to the cruise experience. Dining-wise, Celebrity shines, offering innovative cuisine that's a cut above the fare served by some of the other mainstream lines.

Celebrity gets the "best of" nod in a lot of categories: The AquaSpas on the line's megaships are tops for mainstream lines, the art collections fleetwide are the most compelling, and the onboard activities are among the most varied. Like all the big-ship lines, Celebrity has lots for its guests to do, but it focuses on mellower pursuits and innovative programming.

It's interesting to note that Celebrity (and its sister company, Royal Caribbean International) has created the new port of Icy Strait Point. The port is growing—it was created from a cannery dock—and lies between Juneau and Glacier Bay, with a prime vantage point for whale- and wildlife-watching and easier access to the Alaskan wilderness.

Pros

- **Spectacular spas and gyms.** Beautiful to look at and well stocked, the spas and gyms on *Celebrity Infinity, Celebrity Century,* and *Celebrity Millennium* (and Celebrity's other non-Alaska megaships) are among the best at sea today, and set the standard followed by other lines.
- **Fabulous food.** Celebrity cuisine is rated highly among mainstream cruise lines.
- **Innovative everything.** Celebrity's entertainment, art, service, spas, and cuisine are some of the most groundbreaking in the industry. Its ships were among the first in the industry to display major art collections onboard, and its menus have long recognized the need for vegetarian, low-sodium, heart-conscious, and other dishes.

Cons

- **Occasional crowding.** Pack a couple thousand people onto a ship (pretty much any ship), and you'll get crowds at times, such as during buffets and when disembarking.

THE FLEET Celebrity's current Alaska fleet comprises *Celebrity Infinity* and *Celebrity Millennium* (both 91,000 tons, 1,950 passengers), and the slightly older *Celebrity Century* (71,545 tons, 1,814 passengers). All three ships have a high degree of decorative panache and just the right combination of elegance, artfulness, excitement, and fun.

PASSENGER PROFILE The typical Celebrity guest is one who prefers to pursue his or her R&R at a relatively relaxed pace, with a minimum of aggressively promoted group activities. The overall atmosphere leans more toward sophistication and less to the kind of orgiastic Technicolor whoopee that you'll find aboard, say, a Carnival ship. Celebrity passengers are the type who prefer wine with dinner and maybe a tad more decorum than on some other ships, but they can kick up their heels with the beer-and-pretzels crowd just fine if the occasion warrants. Most give the impression of being prosperous but not obscenely rich, congenial but not obsessively proper, animated and fun but not the type to wear a lampshade for a hat. You'll find everyone from kids to retirees, with a good number of couples in their 40s.

Celebrity Fleet Itineraries

Ship	Itineraries
Celebrity Infinity	**7-night Tracy Arm Fjord:** Round-trip cruises from Seattle visiting Ketchikan, Juneau, Victoria, B.C., and Skagway, in addition to cruising the Inside Passage and beside Sawyer Glacier (May–Sept).
Celebrity Century	**7-night Hubbard Glacier:** Round-trip cruises from Vancouver, B.C. visiting Ketchikan, Hubbard Glacier, Icy Strait Point, Juneau, and Inside Passage (May–Sept).
Celebrity Millennium	**7-night North- and Southbound Gulf of Alaska:** Sails from Vancouver, B.C. to Seward and reverse, visiting Juneau, Skagway, Icy Strait Point, Ketchikan, and Hubbard Glacier (May–Sept).

DINING Celebrity's cuisine, plentiful and served with style, is extra special, and leans toward American/European. This means that dishes are generally not low-fat, although the line has eliminated trans-fats, and more healthy alternatives are always available. The company's dining program is under the leadership of Jacques Van Staden, a highly talented and experienced head chef and restaurateur who was once nominated as a "rising star" by the prestigious James Beard Foundation.

Alaska cruises serve an array of Pacific Northwest regional specialties, and vegetarian dishes are featured at both lunch and dinner. If three meals a day in both informal and formal settings are not enough for you, Celebrity has one of the most extensive 24-hour room-service menus in the industry, plus themed lunch buffets and one to two (depending on the itinerary length) special brunches. Meals in the alternative dining rooms on *Century, Millennium,* and *Infinity,* served on a reservations-only basis, are worth the $30 charge of admission (primarily for gratuities, given the service-intensive nature of the venues); they may be the best romantic restaurants at sea.

You can dine formally in the dining room or informally at buffets for breakfast and lunch, with a sushi bar and made-to-order pastas and pizzas served nightly in the Casual Dining Boulevard. Dinner is served at two seatings in the main dining room. Last year, the line also introduced the option of open seating in the dining room (you choose either traditional or open seating Celebrity Select Dining before your cruise). The Spa Café in a corner of the thalassotherapy pool area serves low-cal treats, including raw veggie platters, poached salmon with asparagus tips, vegetarian sushi, and pretty salads with tuna or chicken (this is a hidden secret worth finding).

ACTIVITIES The line offers a laundry list of activities through "Celebrity Life," its relatively new, all-encompassing enrichment program. A typical day might involve a Rosetta Stone language course, bridge, a culinary demonstration, a chef's cook-off, distinct wine tastings in partnership with the renowned Riedel Crystal, an art auction, and a volleyball tournament. Lectures on the various ports of call, some by Smithsonian speakers, the Alaska environment, glaciers, and Alaska culture are given by resident naturalists, who also provide commentary from the bridge as the ships arrive in port and, at other times, are available for one-on-one discussions with passengers. Cybercafes allow e-mail access for 65¢ a minute, with discount packages also available. The line was among the first to offer an Acupuncture at Sea program.

CHILDREN'S PROGRAM For children, Celebrity ships employ a group of counselors who direct and supervise a camp-style children's program with activities geared toward different age groups. There's an impressive kids' play area and a separate lounge area for teens. Private and group babysitting are both available.

ENTERTAINMENT Although entertainment is not generally cited as a reason to sail with Celebrity, the line's stage shows are none too shabby. You won't find any big-name entertainers, but you also won't find any obvious has-beens either—there's just a whole lot of singin' and dancin'. If you tire of the glitter, you can always find a cozy lounge or piano bar to curl up in, and if you tire of that, the disco and casino stay open late.

SERVICE In the cabins, service is efficient and so unobtrusive that you might never see your steward except at the beginning and end of your cruise. In the dining rooms, service is polite, professional, and cheerful. Five-star service can be had at the onboard beauty salon or barbershop, and massages can be scheduled at any hour of the day in the AquaSpa. Laundry, dry cleaning, and valet services are also available. If you stay in a suite, you really will be treated like royalty with a tuxedo-clad butler at your beck and call. The butler will serve you afternoon tea (or free cappuccino or espresso) and bring predinner hors d'oeuvres. And yes, the butler will gladly shine your shoes too, at your request. Also available for those who can't quite afford a suite are Concierge Class rooms that come with such perks as fresh flowers and fruit, a choice of pillow types, and oversize towels.

CRUISETOURS & ADD-ON PROGRAMS Celebrity offers 21 cruisetours in conjunction with its sailings on *Celebrity Millennium* in 2011, ranging in length from 9 to 18 nights and priced from $1,349 per person double to $4,649 per person double, depending on the season and the staterooms chosen. Sixteen of the tours include a ride in Royal Celebrity Tours' luxurious domed railcars on the Denali Corridor and 2- or 3-night stays in the park area. Other packages feature the Kenai Peninsula and the 650,000-acre Kenai Fjords National Park. New in 2011 is a vacation-of-a-lifetime experience, "The Ultimate Cruisetour—Canadian Rockies and Alaska," an 18-night package being offered to passengers on *Celebrity Millennium.* The experience features a 6-night Canadian Rockies tour, a 7-night northbound Alaska cruise, and a 5-night post-cruise Alaska land tour. Celebrity also offers pre- and post-cruise hotel packages from $249 per person per night, double occupancy, in Anchorage; from $149 per person per night, double occupancy, in Vancouver, B.C.

Celebrity Infinity • Celebrity Millennium

The Verdict

These ships are true winners, combining the kind of luxury you'd expect at a great contemporary hotel with all the leisure, sports, and entertainment options of megaships. If these ships were high school seniors, they'd be heading to Harvard. They are the best in their class.

Infinity *(photo: Celebrity Cruises)*

Specifications

Size (in Tons)	91,000	Crew	999
Passengers (Double Occ.)	1,950	Passenger/Crew Ratio	2 to 1
Space/Passenger Ratio	46 ft. to 1	Year Launched	2001
Total Cabins/Veranda Cabins	975/590	Last Major Refurbishment	N/A

Frommer's Rating (Scale 1–5) ★★★★★

Cabin Comfort & Amenities	5	Dining Options	5
Ship Cleanliness & Maintenance	5	Gym, Spa & Sports Facilities	5
Public Comfort/Space	5	Children's Facilities	4
Decor	5	Enjoyment Factor	5

THE SHIPS IN GENERAL When *Celebrity Millennium* debuted in 2000, it was hailed as one of the most spectacular ships afloat; guests were equally struck by the debut of its sister ship *Celebrity Infinity* in 2001. Their designs include lots of glass through which to view the spectacular Alaska vistas.

CABINS The smallest inside cabins are 170 square feet and boast minibars, sitting areas with sofas, and entertainment units with TVs. Premium oceanview cabins measure 191 square feet, and large oceanview cabins with verandas are indeed large—271 square feet, with floor-to-ceiling sliding-glass doors leading outside. Suites come in several sizes and offer such accoutrements as whirlpool tubs, DVD players, and walk-in closets. The fanciest suites also have whirlpools on the veranda. The two apartment-size Penthouse Suites (1,432 sq. ft. each), designed to evoke Park Avenue apartments, have all of the above plus separate living and dining rooms, a foyer, a grand piano, a butler's pantry, a bedroom, exercise equipment, outbound fax, and—sure to be a favorite accessory—motorized drapes. Twenty-six cabins are wheelchair-accessible.

Cabins & Rates

Cabins	Per Diem Rates	Sq. Ft.	Fridge	Hair Dryer	Sitting Area	TV
Celebrity Infinity						
Inside	$150–$320	170	yes	yes	no	yes
Outside	$178–$414	170–191	yes	yes	yes	yes
Suites	$800–$1,257	251–1,432	yes	yes	yes	yes
Celebrity Millennium						
Inside	$150–$291	170	yes	yes	yes	yes
Outside	$178–$414	170–191	yes	yes	yes	yes
Suites	$1,028–$1,456	251–1,432	yes	yes	yes	yes

PUBLIC AREAS Highlights on *Celebrity Infinity* and *Celebrity Millennium* include the flower-filled botanical conservatories located on top of each ship. Pull up a rattan chair, sit under a ceiling fan, and enjoy a drink. You won't miss the Alaska views from this oasis, thanks to two-story-high windows. The conservatories have classes in flower arranging. Want more? How about Acupuncture at Sea, a shopping center, pizzeria, casino, champagne bar, martini bar, cinema, theater, beauty salon, medical center, library, cybercafe, children's center, teen room, and arcade?

DINING OPTIONS Both ships have two-tier dining rooms that feature live music by a pianist or a quartet. And they also provide gourmet dining experiences in wonderfully intimate and romantic alternative restaurants: the SS United States on *Infinity* and the Olympic Restaurant on *Millennium.* (A fee of $30 is charged to dine in these, primarily for gratuities, and reservations are required.) Breakfast, lunch, and dinner also are served in both formal and informal venues. Dinner is served in the main dining room in two seatings, as well as in the Casual Dining Boulevard and the Spa Café. After dinner, Michael's Club (on both ships), decorated like the parlor of a London men's club and devoted to the pleasures of live jazz and piano entertainment and fine cognac, comes into its own. Each ship also has a coffee bar, Cova Café, which becomes a wine bar with light, live music by night; and if you're looking to spend the evening socializing with friends, there are various other bars tucked into nooks and crannies throughout the ship.

POOL, FITNESS, SPA & SPORTS FACILITIES Spa aficionados, listen up: The *Infinity* and *Millennium* will not disappoint. The 25,000-square-foot AquaSpa complexes on both ships provide a range of esoteric hydrotherapy treatments; site-specific attractions, such as the Persian Garden; a suite of beautiful New Age steam rooms and saunas; and a huge free-of-charge thalassotherapy whirlpool. In addition, there is the usual array of massage and beauty procedures, plus some unusual ones, such as an Egyptian ginger-and-milk treatment. Next door to the spa, there's a very large, well-equipped cardio room and a large aerobics floor. On the top decks are facilities for basketball, volleyball, quoits (a game akin to horseshoes), and paddle tennis; a jogging track; a golf simulator; two pools; four whirlpools; and a multi-tiered sunning area. The swimming pool features a waterfall.

Celebrity Century

The Verdict

One of the most all-around attractive ships out there; a real winner.

Century *(photo: Celebrity Cruises)*

Specifications

Size (in Tons)	71,545	Crew	860
Passengers (Double Occ.)	1,814	Passenger/Crew Ratio	2 to 1
Space/Passenger Ratio	41 ft. to 1	Year Launched	1995
Total Cabins/Veranda Cabins	639/220	Last Major Refurbishment	2006

Frommer's Rating (Scale 1-5) ★★★★½

Cabin Comfort & Amenities	5	Dining Options	4
Ship Cleanliness & Maintenance	4	Gym, Spa & Sports Facilities	5
Public Comfort/Space	5	Children's Facilities	4
Decor	5	Enjoyment Factor	5

THE SHIP IN GENERAL It's hard to say what's most striking about *Celebrity Century.* The elegant spa and its 15,000-gallon thalassotherapy pool? The twin three- and four-story atria with serpentine staircases that seem to float without supports and domed ceilings of painted glass? The two-story, classically designed dining room set back in the stern, with grand floor-to-ceiling windows, allowing diners to spot the glow of the wake under moonlight? The industry's first "ice" martini bar? The Murano specialty restaurant? An intriguing modern-art collection? Take your pick: Any one points to a winner. We really like this ship!

CABINS Inside cabins are about par for the industry standard, but outside cabins are larger than usual, and suites, which come in five different categories, are particularly spacious. Some, such as the Penthouse Suites, have more living space than you find in many private homes, and the Sky Suites have verandas that, at 179 square feet, are among the biggest aboard any ship. During the ship's 2006 dry-dock, 314 new verandas were added.

All cabins are accented with wood trim and outfitted with built-in vanities. Closets and drawer space are roomy, and all standard cabins have twin beds that, when pushed together, convert into one full-size bed. Bathrooms are sizable and stylish. Celebrity is fond of high-tech gizmos, and you can actually order food, gamble, or check your bill from the comfort of your cabin via your interactive TV.

Butler service is provided to suite guests. Ten cabins are wheelchair-accessible.

Cabins & Rates

Cabins	Per Diem Rates	Sq. Ft.	Fridge	Hair Dryer	Sitting Area	TV
Inside	$128–$277	175	yes	yes	no	yes
Outside	$150–$343	210	yes	yes	yes	yes
Suites	$757–$1,757	1,433	yes	yes	yes	yes

PUBLIC AREAS The interior of this ship is the product of a collaboration between a dozen design firms that have created a diverse yet harmonious whole providing just the right atmosphere without resorting to glitz. Our favorite is the champagne bar with champagne bubbles etched into the wall.

Throughout the ship, artwork from a multimillion-dollar art collection sometimes greets you at unexpected moments. Read the tags and you'll be impressed to find names such as Sol LeWitt, who designed a mural specifically for the vessel. There is a coffee bar for those craving caffeine, and various other bars pepper the ship and are great venues for spending time with friends.

There's a two-deck theater with an unobstructed view from every seat if you want to take in a stage show, and there's a cinema if you're in the mood for film. If you're looking for more active pleasures, there's always the disco and casino. For kids, there's a children's playroom, a children's pool, a teen center, and a video arcade. When the ship was refurbished in 2006, in addition to adding 314 new verandas, Celebrity added a specialty restaurant called Murano, a new Spa Café and new Martini "ice" bar, as well as a new reception area in the AquaSpa and 10 new sea-view treatment rooms.

DINING OPTIONS In addition to a main dining room for breakfast, lunch, and dinner, the ship has a Lido Buffet that serves up breakfast, lunch, and a more casual dinner (the latter with menu as well as buffet service). The Lido Buffet also is home to a made-to-order pasta and pizza bar. But the most unusual venue on the ship is Murano, a specialty restaurant. There's also a 54-seat Spa Café.

POOL, FITNESS, SPA & SPORTS FACILITIES *Century*'s AquaSpa features a Moorish theme, with ornate tile work and latticed wood. There is a large hydrotherapy pool, plus steam rooms and saunas. The spa also features sometimes-pricey Elemis of London health and beauty services, including hairdressing, pedicures, manicures, massages, and various herbal treatments. We highly recommend the Rasul mud treatment for two. It's both relaxing and giggle-inducing—in the right company! The attached fitness area has exceptionally large cardiovascular floors and a full complement of exercise machines. An 18-member fitness staff is on hand in the spa and gym area to assist you. Prearranged spa packages that you book before your cruise are available and are a wise idea, as some services (including Rasul) sell out fast.

The Resort Deck features a pair of good-size swimming areas rimmed with teak benches for sunning and relaxation. Even when the ship is full, these areas don't seem particularly crowded. A basketball court, jogging/walking track, fitness center, golf simulator, and volleyball court also are available.

4 Crystal Cruises

2049 Century Park E., Ste. 1400, Los Angeles, CA 90067. ✆ **800/446-6620** or 310/785-9300. Fax 310/785-3891. www.crystalcruises.com.

THE LINE IN A NUTSHELL Crystal's brand of luxury cruising appeals to a discerning clientele. Everything is first class, with fine attention paid to detail and to making guests feel comfortable. The line has been sailing for just over 2 decades and has received widespread recognition for providing a truly luxurious experience with the largest ships in the category. Their ships, which debuted in 1995 and 2003, have been beautifully refurbished and the line is always looking for ways to update and embellish the onboard experience. Crystal has revamped its pricing policy, offering many 2-for-1 fares, onboard spending credits, and a Price Guarantee program.

THE EXPERIENCE The luxurious *Crystal Symphony* (the line's ship in Alaska in 2011) and its sister ship, *Crystal Serenity,* operate on a formula of offering all the amenities of much bigger ships but in a more luxurious and intimate atmosphere, with only 960 and 1,100 passengers respectively. At the same time, they strive to provide the intimate luxurious experience of the smaller ships in the category.

Japanese-owned and Los Angeles-based Crystal works extremely hard with its training program to make everyone on board feel like they are VIPs. Crystal is happy to offer you the chance to dress up and act like a millionaire (even if you're not one really).

Pros

- **The best of everything.** Superb cuisine, elegant service, handsome public areas, sparkling entertainment, excellent guest quarters—this ship has it all.
- **Great itinerary.** Another of *Crystal Symphony*'s selling points is its itinerary: It is the only luxury ship offering a series of 12-night Alaska sailings round-trip from San Francisco.

Cons

- **Rigid dining schedule.** For many upscale travelers, *Crystal Symphony*'s biggest failing used to be that, like all biggish ships, it has two seatings at dinner, locking passengers into 6:30 or 8:30pm appointments in the main dining room. But their Perfect Choice Dining and Open Dining by Reservation programs, put into effect for 2011, should solve this.

- **Stateroom size.** The non-suites are considered small by comparison to the rooms on certain luxury competitors such as *Seven Seas Navigator*.

THE FLEET Plush, streamlined, extravagantly comfortable, and not as overwhelmingly large as the megaships being launched by less glamorous lines, the 960-passenger *Crystal Symphony* (1995) offers a broad choice of onboard diversions and distractions, more than you'd expect on a luxury vessel. The ship underwent a major $25-million refurbishment to both public spaces and staterooms/suites in late 2009, making the ship sparkle all over again with beautiful new features and fittings.

PASSENGER PROFILE Generally, the passengers aboard Crystal are people of some discernment—say, successful businesspeople who can afford to pay for the best. Whereas, at one time, that couple might have been closer to the average age on an Alaska cruise (meaning fairly old), they no longer are. Probably thanks to Crystal's innovative shore-excursion program and its entertainment package, *Crystal Symphony* will attract a younger breed of cruiser, many under 50. The average age has, in fact, dropped considerably since the line's early days, making for a very sociable mix of age groups on board. And, while the entire cruise industry, including the luxury segment, is more casual than it used to be, a "colder" weather destination such as Alaska does seem to attract those that, whatever their age, tend to be people who like to dress up rather than down. Casual nights don't mean the same to Crystal guests as they do to some others.

DINING Cuisine aboard *Crystal Symphony* is widely considered to be as good as it gets anywhere on the high seas. Every meal is superbly prepared and professionally served, with dinner in the main dining room offering a choice of at least four entrees, health-conscious vegetarian dishes, and a pasta offering nightly. The Lido Café, an indoor/outdoor area that was gorgeously redone in late 2009, puts on a lavish breakfast and lunch buffet daily, and the poolside Trident Grill serves up hot dogs, hamburgers, pizza, and sandwiches from lunchtime throughout the afternoon. Those that want to be casual in the evening and enjoy the stay-light-late Alaska evening can, on select nights, enjoy dining at an open-air grill. The two alternative restaurants, Prego for Italian and Silk Road for Japanese cuisine, may just be the best pair of alternative restaurants at sea. Both are open on a reservations-only basis and only a modest service charge ($7 per person) is suggested. It's amazing to consider going to the Silk Road sushi bar and having a complete meal of specialties under the auspices of famed chef, Nobu Matsuhisa. On the other hand, at Prego, the menus are under the supervision of Piero Selvaggio known for his celebrated restaurant, Valentino's in Los Angeles.

There's also an ice-cream and frozen yogurt bar and 24-hour room service. The wine cellar features some 25,000 bottles of some 171 varieties.

ACTIVITIES *Crystal Symphony* will carry a battery of **Alaska naturalists,** environmentalists, and National Park Service rangers to educate and entertain passengers in the wilderness areas of the 49th state. For 2011, *Crystal Symphony* Alaska cruises will feature the line's Emerging Artists program.

Crystal Cruises has a superb activities program under the banner of Computer University@Sea for computer skills, photography, and so on. Their Creative Learning Institute has Berlitz language classes and Yamaha piano lessons, offered complimentarily.

Crystal Fleet Itineraries

Ship	Itinerary
Crystal Symphony	12-night Inside Passage: Round-trip from San Francisco, visiting Victoria, Vancouver, B.C., Sitka, Skagway, Juneau, Ketchikan, and either Glacier Bay or Hubbard Glacier.

A PGA-approved golf pro accompanies practically every *Crystal Symphony* cruise, conducting clinics along the way; there's also tai chi and yoga for those interested. As well, there's a flourishing **computer room** onboard, with training for the uninitiated, and Internet access for a fee ($50 for two hr., or $200 for 10 hr.).

CHILDREN'S PROGRAM Summer cruises see the most children on board, and *Crystal Symphony*'s purpose-built Fantasia and Waves kids' and teens' facilities—unique in luxury cruising—are equipped with arts and crafts, games, the latest video games, movies, and more. Junior Activities Directors are also on hand for organized activities for kids ages 3 to 17, with destination-related enrichment and other fun behind-the-scenes events. Babysitting services also are available for a fee.

ENTERTAINMENT Although it's certainly not the high point for everyone on a cruise, Crystal's onboard entertainment is excellent and plentiful, largely considered to be the best in the luxury category. Shows in the Galaxy Lounge encompass everything from classical concertos by accomplished pianists to comedy to a troupe of dancers and a pair of lead singers doing Vegas-style performances. After dinner each night, a second large, attractive lounge is the venue for ballroom-style dancing to a live band; gentlemen hosts are available to dance with single ladies. There's also a small, separate (and usually empty) disco featuring karaoke a couple of nights per cruise and a pianist plays popular show tunes and pop hits before and after dinner in the dark, paneled, and romantic Avenue Saloon. A movie theater shows first-run movies several times a day, and cabin TVs feature a wonderfully varied and full movie menu as well.

Gamblers will have no problem feeling at home in the roomy Crystal Casino with Las Vegas-odds (extremely nice for dice players) offering the bonus—unusual on ships—of free drinks for players.

SERVICE Service on the ship is nothing short of superb. Crystal has a corporate philosophy since it first sailed in 1990 called "The Crystal Attitude." It's a service philosophy that actually works. You can usually tell when service people are faking it: the plastic smiles, the looks meant to say "I care" while the actions clearly demonstrate "I don't give a hoot." That doesn't happen on Crystal. From the officers to the dining room staff, through the cabin stewards and the reception-desk employees to the guys who swab the deck and paint the rails, these people are genuinely glad to welcome passengers and to accommodate them in every way possible. It's not obsequiousness. It's not overpowering. It's just the right attitude.

In addition to laundry and dry-cleaning services, self-service laundry rooms are available.

CRUISETOURS & ADD-ON PROGRAMS Pre- and post-cruise and/or land packages were not available at press time. Check the Crystal Cruises' website at www.crystalcruises.com.

Crystal Symphony

The Verdict

An oustanding way to luxuriously enjoy the 49th state for those looking for superb service, dining, and entertainment. Having undergone a major $25-million refurbishment in late 2009, *Crystal Symphony* is the largest luxury ship in the market, sailing a series of nine 12-night round-trip cruises to and from San Francisco.

Crystal Symphony *(photo: Crystal Cruises)*

Specifications

Size (in Tons)	51,044	Crew	545
Passengers (Double Occ.)	960	Passenger/Crew Ratio	1.7 to 1
Space/Passenger Ratio	53.2 ft. to 1	Year Launched	1995
Total Cabins/Veranda Cabins	480/260	Last Major Refurbishment	2009

Frommer's Ratings (Scale 1–5)

★★★★½

Cabin Comfort & Amenities	4.5	Dining Options	5
Ship Cleanliness & Maintenance	5	Gym, Spa & Sports Facilities	4.5
Public Comfort/Space	5	Children's Facilities	4.5
Decor	4.5	Enjoyment Factor	4.5

THE SHIP IN GENERAL A handsome ship by any standard, *Crystal Symphony* was designed by an international team. Even though the ship debuted way back in 1995, its beauty is timeless in quality and elegance. A $25-million refurbishment in late 2009 made an excellent ship even better. On the pool deck alone, the main pool area was redone and the new seating areas are beautiful. Lido Café was redone to have serving stations rather than buffet lines, the smaller pool was removed, and more sitting area allowed for. The outstanding Italian restaurant was redesigned—gone are the Venetian gondola poles in favor of an elegant color palette of burgundy and chocolate. All staterooms and penthouses also have been redone.

The ship has one of the highest passenger-space ratios (an esoteric measurement of the amount of cubic space throughout the ship, public and private rooms, divided by the number of passengers) of any cruise ship. In industry parlance, that ratio is 55, a fact that may not mean much to the layperson, at least until he or she cruises on the ship. Then, the spaciousness becomes obvious. Combined with an excellent guest-to-crew ratio of 1.7, it makes for a special voyage.

CABINS The cabins are nice but not overly large. But, they are very well appointed (Frette bathrobes and Egyptian-cotton linens are just a couple of examples) and tastefully decorated with quality fittings and in agreeable color tones. Slightly more than half of them have private verandas (Crystal was the first line to break the 50% barrier in terms of verandas with their first ship, *Crystal Harmony,* in 1990). One small criticism is that the space to hang clothes is a little tight in some of the lower cabin categories.

The very smallest of the *Crystal Symphony's* cabins is just over 200 square feet, while the upper-end guest quarters are quite large, the biggest measuring 982 square feet. And these figures do not include the verandas! There are two Crystal penthouses on *Crystal Symphony*, each with a large sitting room, a wet bar, a big Jacuzzi with a view of the ocean (ah, bliss!), a dining area, a massive bedroom, two bathrooms, and walk-in closets.

Crystal Symphony's 19 penthouse suites are a little less than 500 square feet each and the 44 staterooms designated as penthouses are 367 square feet each. All of these, like the Crystal Penthouses, come with butler service and verandas. Be careful with the terminology when buying a cruise on *Crystal Symphony:* Crystal Penthouse, Penthouse Suite, and Penthouse sound awfully similar, but they're all different categories.

Four cabins are handicapped-accessible, two on the Penthouse Deck and two on the Promenade Deck.

Cabins & Rates

Cabins	Per Diem Rates	Sq. Ft.	Fridge	Hair Dryer	Sitting Area	TV
Deluxe Stateroom	$388 to $476	202	yes	yes	yes	yes
Deluxe Stateroom w/veranda	$528 to $554	246	yes	yes	yes	yes
Penthouses	$923 to $2,230	367 to 982	yes	yes	yes	yes

PUBLIC AREAS Let's hear it for *Crystal Symphony's* public areas. Like the rest of the ship, they're pure class. It's our opinion that Palm Court is the prettiest public space afloat. Bright, airy, with enticing and comfortable wicker furniture and natural greenery all around, it's the kind of room that reeks of that good old-fashioned "understated elegance." There's also the large, well-designed casino; the intimate midship bistro and piano bar; and the two-story lobby, the Crystal Atrium, that's such a refreshing change from the garishness of some of the lobbies on the new ships entering service. The elegance carries over to the rest of the ship: Sip a glass of wine in the Crystal Cove, in the lobby alongside the atrium, or in the snug Avenue Saloon, one deck up, and you'll see what we mean.

Crystal Symphony's two **alternative restaurants,** Prego (Italian, mostly northern) and Silk Road (Japanese, including sushi), introduce a variety to the dining experience not found on all ships. The meals there are included in the fare (except for the tip of $7 a head), and dining is by reservation only.

The dramatic wall-to-ceiling windows around the ship are perfect for wildlife and glacier viewing. And to occupy the kids while you're doing that, there's a playroom.

DINING OPTIONS Dining on board *Crystal Symphony* is simply outstanding. The main dining room for breakfast, lunch, and dinner serves delicious menu options. Dinner is set up as either traditional two sittings (which used to be considered a bit of a negative for Crystal) or, new for 2011, a combination of Perfect Choice Dining or Open Dining by Reservation (this should alleviate any negatives). The ship has two alternative restaurants for which reservations are needed. There's no charge other than a miniscule $7-per-person suggested service charge. Imagine going to Silk Road for a Japanese dinner or to the sushi bar, both run by famed chef Nobu Matsuhisa, for one of his special meals and only paying $7. Wow! The same applies at Prego, the Italian restaurant, where the menus were designed by famed L.A. restaurant expert, Piero Selvaggio of Valentino's fame. And the room, refurbished in late 2009, is as yummy as the food.

On Lido Deck, the Lido casual restaurant has been redesigned to eliminate the traditional buffet lines in favor of a series of serving stations. Outside is the Trident Bar & Grill, serving perhaps the best range of deck menu options in Alaska. On some nights, the area is set up for a casual dinner, perfect for those Alaska evenings when it stays light so late.

And more, there's the ice-cream and yogurt bar and of course, 24-hour room service at no charge.

POOL, FITNESS, SPA & SPORTS FACILITIES *Crystal Symphony* offers a lot of outdoor activities and spacious areas in which to do them. The redone outdoor pool deck has tons of really comfy seating. The main pool is now accompanied by a massive whirlpool. The area where the smaller pool used to be is now a great seating area covered by a retractable roof, ideal for the weather changes for which Alaska is known. The gym and separate aerobics area are positioned for a view over the sea, and the adjacent feng shui-inspired spa and beauty salon are sizable. There's also a pair of golf-driving nets, a putting green, a large paddle-tennis court, and Ping-Pong tables. For runners and walkers, just under four laps equals 1 mile on the broad teak Promenade Deck that completely encircles the ship.

5 Disney Cruise Line

P.O. Box 10210, Lake Buena Vista, FL 32820. ✆ **800/951-3532** or 888/325-2500. Fax 407/566-3541. www.disneycruise.com.

THE LINE IN A NUTSHELL Disney's cruising arm isn't large (with just two ships as of late 2010), but the company is the Big Kahuna when it comes to family-geared cruising. Though a number of big lines including Royal Caribbean, Carnival, and Norwegian Cruise Line have long offered wonderful programs for children, it was Disney that first set out to create a family-vacation that would be as relaxing for parents as their offspring. If you love Disney's resorts on land, you'll love the company's ships.

THE EXPERIENCE Both classic and ultra-modern, the line's two ships (only one of which will be in Alaska in 2011) are like no others in the industry, designed to evoke the grand trans-Atlantic liners of old but also boasting some truly innovative features such as extra-large cabins for families and a trio of restaurants through which passengers rotate on every cruise. Disney is known for entertainment, of course, and its ships don't disappoint, with Disney-inspired shows. The vessels also boast separate adult pools and lounges, and the biggest kids' facilities at sea. In many ways, the experience is more Disney than it is cruise (for instance, there's no casino); but, on the other hand, the ships are surprisingly elegant and well laid out, with little Disney touches sprinkled all around.

Pros

- **Great children's program.** Would you expect anything less from Disney? In both the size of facilities and range of activities, this is a line that's hard to beat.
- **Disney-quality entertainment.** The line shows family-oriented musicals that are some of the best onboard entertainment today.

- **Family-style cabins.** It's rare in the cruise business to find so many large, family-friendly cabins that can sleep three, four, or even five people.

Cons

- **Limited adult entertainment.** Forget about a night out gambling, as this is one of just a few ships at sea without a casino. There's an adult-only night entertainment area on board, but it's often quiet.
- **Crowded pools.** Disney's ships are kid magnets, and that has a downside on sunny days when children come out of the woodwork to hit the pools.
- **The cost.** Compared to other big-ship lines such as Carnival and Norwegian, Disney is pricey, running at least a few hundred dollars more per person for a week. In short, you pay a premium for The Mouse.

THE FLEET The 1,754-passenger *Disney Wonder* will be the line's first and only ship in Alaska in 2011. The streamlined vessel is chock full of activities for kids, with great pools (including one shaped like Mickey's head) and adult-only areas, too.

PASSENGER PROFILE Disney's ships attract a wide mix of passengers, from honeymooners to seniors, but as one might expect a big percentage is made up of young American families with children. (This isn't a big line for foreign passengers, though you'll see a few.) Because of the allure to families with younger children, the average age of passengers tends to be lower than aboard most other cruise ships. Many adult passengers are in their 30s and early to mid-40s. The bulk of the line's passengers are first-time cruisers, and because the line attracts so many families (sometimes large ones), more than half of its bookings are for multiple cabins.

DINING Disney offers a traditional fixed-seating type plan for dinners, but with a twist. There are three main restaurants—each with a different theme—among which passengers (and their servers) rotate over the course of a cruise. On one night, passengers dine on dishes such as roasted duck or garlic-roasted beef tenderloin in a green peppercorn sauce in the nautical-themed Triton's restaurant. On another night, they enjoy the likes of potato-crusted grouper, baby back pork ribs, or mixed grill in the tropical Parrot Cay restaurant. And then it's on to Animator's Palate, a bustling eatery with a gimmick: It's a sort of living animation cell with walls decorated with black-and-white sketches of Disney characters that over the course of the meal gradually become filled in with color. Video screens add to the illusion, and even the waiter's outfits change as the evening wears on. Disney also offers a romantic, adults-only Italian specialty restaurant on board its ships called Palo that comes with an extra charge ($10 per person). Breakfast and lunch are served in several restaurants, both sit-down and buffet. Pluto's Dog House, on the main pool deck, serves up kid-friendly basics such as chicken fingers, fries, burgers, and nachos. Nearby Goofy's Galley offers wraps, fresh fruit, and other more healthful fare.

ACTIVITIES Disney offers a similar array of activities to other big ship lines, with one big exception: There's no casino. (Disney executives apparently decided a casino just didn't fit with the line's family-friendly image.) Besides lounging at the pool or (for kids) heading to the kids' program, the array of options on board include basketball, Ping-Pong, and shuffleboard tournaments; sports trivia contests; weight-loss, health, and beauty seminars; bingo, Pictionary, and other games; wine tastings; and singles mixers (though these family-focused cruises aren't the best choice for singles).

Disney Fleet Itineraries

Ship	Itineraries
Disney Wonder	**7-night Inside Passage:** Round-trip from Vancouver, B.C., visiting Skagway, Juneau, and Ketchikan, and cruising Tracy Arm Fjord (May–Aug).

Each ship also has a spa and gym, and there are enrichment activities including galley tours, backstage theater tours, informal lectures on nautical themes and Disney history as well as current Disney productions, animation and drawing classes, and home entertainment and cooking demonstrations. All these activities come with no extra charge except for wine tastings, which cost a hefty $12 per person. There also are dance classes and movies, and all voyages include a captain's cocktail party with complimentary drinks once per cruise, where the master of the ship and (this being Disney) a gaggle of characters make an appearance.

CHILDREN'S PROGRAM Disney's kids' facilities are, famously, the most extensive at sea, spreading across a good part of an entire deck (what the ship lacks in casino space it makes up for with extra kids' space). The ships carry dozens of children's counselors who look after groups split into five age groups. Split into several areas, the children's zone generally is open between 9am and midnight. The **Oceaneer Club,** for ages 3 to 7, is a kiddie-size playroom themed around Captain Hook. Kids can climb and crawl on the bridge, ropes, and rails of a giant pirate ship, as well as on jumbo-size animals, barrels, and a sliding board; get dressed up from trunks full of costumes; dance with Snow White and listen to stories by other Disney characters; or play in the kiddie computer room on PlayStations. The interactive **Oceaneer Lab** offers kids ages 8 to 12 a chance to work on computers, learn fun science with microscopes, do arts and crafts, hear how animation works, and direct their own TV commercial.

For teens, there's a teen hangout called Aloft on the Wonder that has two separate rooms, one with video screens for movies and the other a teen disco with a teens-only Internet center. Dance parties, karaoke, trivia games, improv comedy lessons, and workshops on photography are offered for teens on every voyage.

One thing Disney doesn't do is private babysitting. Instead, Flounder's Reef Nursery for kids ages 3 months to 3 years operates from 6pm to midnight daily, and also for a few hours during the morning and afternoon ($6 per hour for the first child, $5 per each additional child; hours vary depending on the day's port schedule, and space is limited, so book well in advance). No other line offers such extensive care for babies.

ENTERTAINMENT Family-friendly entertainment is one of the highlights of being on a Disney ship, and as one might expect Disney characters and movies often are front and center in the line's onboard productions. Performances by Broadway-caliber entertainers in the nostalgic Walt Disney Theatre include *Disney Dreams,* a musical medley of Disney classics from *Peter Pan* to *The Lion King,* and *Golden Mickeys,* a tribute to Disney films through the years that combines song and dance, animated films, and special effects. Family game shows (including a trivia contest called "Mickey Mania") and karaoke take place in the **Studio Sea family nightclub.** Adults 18 years and older, meanwhile, have their own play zone, an **adults-only entertainment area** in the forward part of Deck 3 with three themed nightclubs. Another nightspot is the **Promenade Lounge,** where live music is featured daily. The **Buena Vista Theater** shows movies day and evening.

SERVICE Just as at its parks, Disney's cruise ships feature staff that come from around the globe. Service in the dining rooms is efficient and precise, but leans toward friendly rather than formal. The crew keeps the ship exceptionally clean and well maintained. Overall, things run very smoothly.

Services include laundry and dry cleaning. (The ship also has self-service laundry rooms and 1-hr. photo processing.) Tips can be charged to your onboard account, for which most passengers opt, or you can give them out in the traditional method: cash.

CRUISETOURS & ADD-ON PROGRAMS None.

Disney Wonder

The Verdict

Whether you're a Disney fanatic or just someone looking for a heavily family-focused experience while sailing in Alaska, this is your ship. Just keep in mind you'll be paying a bit of a "Disney premium" for the privilege.

Disney Wonder *(photo: © Disney Cruise Line)*

Specifications

Size (in Tons)	83,000	Crew	950
Passengers (Double Occ.)	1,754	Passenger/Crew Ratio	1.8 to 1
Space/Passenger Ratio	47.3 ft. to 1	Year Launched	1999
Total Cabins/Veranda Cabins	877/378	Last Major Refurbishment	2006

Frommer's Ratings (Scale of 1–5) ★★★★½

Cabin Comfort & Amenities	5	Dining Options	4.5
Ship Cleanliness & Maintenance	5	Gym, Spa & Sports Facilities	3
Public Comfort/Space	4	Children's Facilities	5
Decor	5	Enjoyment Factor	5

THE SHIP IN GENERAL This sleek homage to ocean liners of old carries 1,754 passengers at "double occupancy"—the standard industry measuring stick for passenger capacity that assumes two people per cabin. But with all the kids packing into rooms with their parents, the double occupancy rating for this particular vessel is less indicative of the crowds that will be on many sailings. Built to be family-friendly, many cabins can hold four or even five people (some two-bedroom family cabins can hold up to seven!), and theoretically the *Wonder* could carry 3,325 people if every possible berth was filled. Though service is a high point of a Disney cruise and the ships are well laid-out, the large numbers of passengers mean some areas of the ship can feel crowded at times, most notably the kids' pool area and the buffet eatery.

CABINS As noted above, the *Disney Wonder* is all about family-friendly cabins, and the rooms on the ship have a number of features that make them unusually appealing to parents with kids. In addition to being able to hold up to five people in some cases (a rarity in the cruise world), cabins are about 25% larger on average than the industry standard. All of the 877 cabins have at least a sitting area with a sofa bed to sleep families of three. Some cabins also have one or two pull-down bunks to sleep families of four or five. Nearly half have private balconies. One-bedroom suites have balconies and sleep four or five comfortably; two-bedroom suites sleep up to seven. Outside cabins that don't have balconies have large-size porthole windows.

One big twist aimed at families: The majority of cabins have two bathrooms—a sink and toilet in one and a shower/tub combo and sink in the other.

As for decor, it's virtually identical from cabin to cabin, combining modern design with nostalgic ocean-liner elements such as a steamer-trunk armoire for kids, globe- and telescope-shaped lamps, map designs on the bedspreads, and a framed black-and-white shot of Mr. and Mrs. Walt Disney aboard the fabled ocean liner *Rex.* Warm wood tones predominate, with Art Deco touches in the metal and glass fittings and light fixtures.

Cabins & Rates

Cabins	Per Diem Rates	Sq. Ft.	Fridge	Hair Dryer	Sitting Area	TV
Inside	$117	184-214	yes	yes	yes	yes
Outside	$193	226–268	yes	yes	yes	yes
Suites	$407	259–1,029	yes	yes	yes	yes

PUBLIC AREAS The *Wonder* has several theaters and lounges, including an adults-only area with three venues: a piano/jazz lounge, disco, and sports-pub-cum-karaoke bar. There's also a family-oriented entertainment lounge called Studio Sea for game shows, karaoke, and dancing; the Promenade Lounge for classic pop music in the evenings; and a 24-hour Internet cafe with eight flatscreen stations. The Cove Café is a comfy place for gourmet coffees (for a price) or cocktails in a relaxed setting with books, magazines, Internet stations, Wi-Fi access, and TVs. A 270-seat cinema shows mostly recent-release Disney movies. The ship also has a jumbo 336-square-foot screen attached to the forward funnel outside on Deck 9 that shows classic Disney animated films. The children's facilities, as you'd expect, are the largest of any ship at sea. In preparation for its Alaska sailings, the *Wonder* received a new venue in dry dock called Outlook Café. Located high atop Deck 10, the 2,500-square-foot observation lounge is designed as a place passengers in Alaska can relax with a drink as they peer out through floor-to-ceiling, curved glass windows at the region's vistas. A spiral staircase connects Outlook Café with the existing Cove Café one deck below.

DINING OPTIONS Disney's unique rotation dining system has passengers tasting three different eateries at dinner over the course of their cruise, with an adults-only specialty restaurant also available, by reservation. At breakfast and lunch, the buffet-style spread in *Wonder*'s Beach Blanket restaurant offers deli meats, cheeses, and rice and vegetable dishes, as well as a carving station, a salad bar, and a dessert table with yummy chocolate-chip cookies. Though the culinary offerings are par for the course in the cruise business, an oft-heard critique of the buffet area is that it's too small for the number of people who are on board and poorly designed for passenger flow, resulting in bottlenecks—particularly during the morning rush.

Options for grabbing a bite next to the pool include Pinocchio's Pizzeria, Pluto's Dog House (for hot dogs, hamburgers, chicken tenders, fries, and more), and an ice-cream bar (which also includes a generous selection of toppings). There's 24-hour room service from a limited menu, but no midnight buffet.

POOL, FITNESS, SPA & SPORTS FACILITIES The pool deck has three pools: Mickey's Kids' Pool, shaped like the mouse's big-eared head, with a great big white-gloved Mickey hand holding up a snaking yellow slide (expect a crowd at this pool!); Goofy's Family Pool, where adults and children can mingle; and the Quiet Cove Adult Pool, with whirlpools, gurgling waterfalls, teak deck and lounge chairs with plush cushions, a poolside bar, and a coffee spot called Cove Café. For families with young children, adjacent is a splash pool with circulating water for diaper-wearing babies and toddlers. It's the only one at sea, as the lines' official party line is no diaper-wearing children are allowed in any pool (and that includes Pull-Ups and swim diapers).

Just behind the pool at the stern is a spa and gym, which was refurbished a few years ago and expanded to twice its original size. The Steiner-managed Vista Spa & Salon is impressive, with attractive tile treatment rooms and a thermal suite with a sauna, steam room, misting shower, and heated contoured tile chaise lounges. Among the many treatments is a selection geared to teens.

The *Wonder* also has an outdoor Sports Deck with basketball and paddle tennis. There are also shuffleboard and Ping-Pong, and joggers and walkers can circuit the Promenade Deck.

6 Holland America Line

300 Elliott Ave. W, Seattle, WA 98119. ✆ **800/426-0327** or 206/281-3535. Fax 206/286-7110. www.hollandamerica.com.

THE LINE IN A NUTSHELL More than any other cruise company in Alaska, Holland America Line (HAL) has managed to hang onto some of its seafaring history and tradition, with its moderately priced, classic, casual yet refined, ocean-liner-like cruise experience. The line also has somewhat smaller, more intimate vessels than its main competitors, Princess and Celebrity.

THE EXPERIENCE In Alaska terms, everybody else is an upstart when it comes to the cruise and cruisetour business. The line calls itself Alaska's most experienced travel operator, and the key to that claim is HAL's 1971 acquisition of the tour company Westours, founded in 1947 by the late Charles B. "Chuck" West, often called "Mr. Alaska" and widely recognized as the absolute pioneer of tourism to and within the state.

Cruising with HAL is less hectic than cruising on most other ships. The line strives for a quieter, sometimes almost sedate, presentation, although it has brightened up its entertainment package and its menus in recent years. Overall, the ships tend to be more evocative of the days of grand liners, with lots of dark wood and displays of nautical artifacts.

A few years ago, the company embarked on a Signature of Excellence product- and service-enhancements program aimed at elevating the quality of the dining experience, service, and enrichment programs on older ships. One problem that always faces cruise lines is ensuring that their newly built vessels—which are invariably fitted with all of the latest bells and whistles—don't overshadow their existing, older fleetmates. HAL's now completed $525-million investment was one way to minimize the disparity between the old and the new.

Under the Signature of Excellence program, HAL has spent much of the upgrade dollars on such items as new amenities in all staterooms—massage showerheads, lighted magnifying makeup mirrors, hair dryers, extra-fluffy towels, terry-cloth robes, upgraded mattresses, and Egyptian-cotton bed linens. Guests in all rooms are welcomed with a complimentary fruit basket. Suites have plush duvets on every bed, VCR/DVD player, access to a well-stocked library of tapes and discs, and a fully stocked minibar.

A recent focus also has been culinary arts, with free cooking demonstrations several times during each cruise in a Culinary Arts Center, where video cameras allow you to watch every move the chefs make. For those who prefer a more hands-on experience, cooking classes cost $29 per person. (The classes are limited to about 12 people and highly popular, so sign up early on your cruise.)

Pros

- **Expertise that comes with experience.** The company's ships are young, but Holland America's experience is apparent. The company was formed in 1873 as the Netherlands-America Steamship Company. In 135-plus years, it figures that you'd get to know a little about operating oceangoing vessels.
- **Warm interiors.** Holland America ships, especially the more recent ones, tend to be understated, inviting, and easy on the eye; nothing garish here.
- **Signature of Excellence.** That mega-upgrade has really made HAL's accommodations much more attractive.

Cons

- **Sleepy nightlife.** If you're big on late-night dancing and barhopping, you may find yourself partying mostly with the entertainment staff, although the company is making an effort to offer more for night owls on its newer ships. You'll find more piano lounges, a bigger casino, and the like on the line's new ships.
- **Homogenous passenger profile.** To a certain degree, passengers tend to be a pretty homogenous group of low-key, 55-plus North American couples who aren't overly adventurous. However, this profile is changing as younger passengers and families come aboard.

THE FLEET Over the years, Holland America Line has picked up a lot of "stuff"—Holland America Tours (formed by the merger of Westours and Gray Line of Alaska); Westmark Hotels; the *Yukon Queen II* river/day boat that operates between Eagle, on the Alaska/Canada border, and Dawson City on the Yukon River; the *MV Ptarmigan* day boat that visits Portage Glacier outside Anchorage; a fleet of railcars (some built in the Old West style but with better viewing opportunities, and some built in more contemporary style); an almost completely new fleet of motorcoaches; and a lot more.

HAL's control of so many of the components of tour packages once gave the cruise company a position of preeminence in the Alaska market, though that's been well and truly challenged in the past decade by Princess, which now has a heavy presence in the accommodations and ground-transportation business as well. (Actually, the similarities don't end there: Both lines have large fleets of primarily late-model ships, both strive for and achieve consistency in the cruise product, and both are pursuing and acquiring younger passengers and families. And both are owned by Carnival Corp.) HAL's philosophy is to stick with ships of fewer than 2,000 passengers—many of them significantly smaller—eschewing the 2,500- to 5,000-passenger megaships being built by some other lines, including Princess.

The company's 1,260-passenger Statendam-class ships—the *Statendam* (1993), *Maasdam* (1993), *Ryndam* (1994), and *Veendam* (1996)—are virtual carbon copies of the same attractive, well-crafted design, with a dash of glitz here and there. The 1,432-passenger *Volendam* officially debuted in 1999, and the 1,432-passenger *Zaandam* debuted in 2000. Brighter and bolder than the earlier ships, the *Volendam* and *Zaandam* share many features of the Statendam-class ships, though they are slightly larger in size (63,000 tons, as opposed to 59,652) and carry more passengers (1,432, against the Statendam class's 1,260). The 1,380-passenger *Amsterdam* is 61,000 tons and is one of two flagships in the fleet. (The other is the *Amsterdam*'s sister ship, the *Rotterdam*.) The *Westerdam* (2004), *Oosterdam* (2003), and *Zuiderdam* (2000) are representing the newer Vista class in Alaska this summer, each at 85,000 tons and carrying 1,916 passengers—sister ship *Noordam* (2006) is cruising elsewhere. The company's smallest ship is the luxurious *Prinsendam,* just 38,000 tons and with a passenger capacity of under 800. The Signature-class ships include the 2,104-passenger *Eurodam* (2008) and the 2,106-passenger *Nieuw Amsterdam.*

Holland America has never shown any inclination to plunge into the 100,000-plus-ton megaship market. Keeping the size down allows HAL to maintain its high service standards and a degree of intimacy while enabling the line's ships to offer all of the amenities of its larger brethren.

In 2011, the line will have 125 cruises on eight vessels on either Inside Passage or Gulf of Alaska patterns. The line continues its unusually long Gulf of Alaska itinerary that lasts 14 days (twice as long as the line's typical 7-night offering in the region) and it includes a regular stop in Anchorage—a first for a major line in Alaska. Offered on just one of Holland America's eight ships in Alaska, the *Amsterdam,* the round-trip voyages out of Seattle also include two other relatively rare ports of call in Alaska—Homer and Kodiak—as well as Sitka.

PASSENGER PROFILE Holland America's passenger profile used to reflect a somewhat older crowd than on other ships. Now the average age is dropping, thanks to both an increased emphasis on the line's Club HAL program for children and some updating of the onboard entertainment offerings. HAL's passenger records in Alaska show a high volume of middle-age and older vacationers (the same demographic as aboard many of its competitors' ships), but on any given cruise, records are also likely to list a hundred or more passengers between the ages of, say, 5 and 16. This trend gathered its initial momentum a few years ago in Europe, a destination that, parents seem to think, has more kid appeal. It's spilled over into Alaska more recently, mainly thanks to the cruise line's added emphasis on generational travel with programs such as Club HAL, the Culinary Arts Center, and family reunion travel, a growing segment of the market.

The more mature among Holland America's passengers are likely to be repeat HAL passengers, often retirees. They are usually not Fortune 500 rich—they are looking for solid value for their money, and they get it from this line.

DINING Years ago, HAL's meals were as traditional as its architecture and its itineraries—almost stodgy. In the last few years, though, it's become a lot more adventurous in all three areas. The variety of dishes on the menu is as good as on any other premium line, and the quality of the food is generally high throughout the fleet. Don't look for lots of pastas; do look for excellent soups. Vegetarian options are available at every meal, and the line has excellent veggie burgers at the on-deck grill.

Holland America Fleet Itineraries

Ship	Itineraries
Amsterdam	**14-night Alaskan Adventurer:** Round-trip from Seattle, visiting Ketchikan, Juneau, Icy Strait Point, Anchorage, Homer, Kodiak, Sitka, and Victoria, B.C., and scenic cruising in Tracy Arm and at Hubbard Glacier (May–Sept).
Westerdam/Oosterdam	**7-night Alaskan Explorer:** Round-trip from Seattle, visiting Victoria, B.C., Ketchikan, Juneau, and Sitka, and either Glacier Bay or Hubbard Glacier (May–Sept).
Volendam/Zuiderdam	**7-night Inside Passage:** Round-trip from Vancouver, B.C., visiting Juneau, Skagway, Ketchikan, Glacier Bay, and Tracy Arm (May–Sept).
Volendam/Zuiderdam	**7-night Glacier Bay Inside Passage:** North- and southbound between Vancouver, B.C. and Skagway, visiting Ketchikan and Glacier Bay (May–Aug.).
Amsterdam	**7-night Alaskan Explorer:** Round-trip from Seattle, visiting Juneau, Sitka, Ketchikan, Glacier Bay, and Victoria, B.C. (Sept. 16, 2011).
Zaandam	**7-night Alaskan Explorer:** Round-trip from Vancouver, B.C., visiting Juneau, Skagway, Ketchikan, and Glacier Bay, and scenic cruising in Tracy Arm (Sept. 18, 2011).
Statendam	**11-night Alaska Collector:** Between Vancouver, B.C. and San Diego, visiting Juneau, Skagway, Ketchikan, Glacier Bay, and Victoria, B.C. (Sept. 19, 2011).
Statendam/Zaandam	**7-night Glacier Discovery:** North- and southbound between Vancouver, B.C. and Seward/Anchorage, visiting Juneau, Ketchikan, Skagway or Haines, College Fjord, and Glacier Bay (May–Sept).

The kids' menu usually includes spaghetti, pizza, hamburgers, fries, and hot dogs. In addition, a few variations on what's being offered to the adults at the table are often served.

Buffets are offered at the Lido Restaurant as an alternative to breakfast and lunch in the main dining room. HAL also has expanded its dinner options to include a casual table-service dinner on the Lido Deck (served on all but the final night of the cruise), in addition to its formal dining-room dinner service. The Pinnacle Grill, an excellent steak and seafood venue on all the ships, is priced at $20 for dinner and $10 for lunch; reservations required. It's money well spent. Canaletto is an Italian restaurant open for dinner on the Lido Deck for which there is no extra charge (though reservations are recommended).

ACTIVITIES Young swingers need not apply. Holland America's ships are heavy on more mature, less frenetic activities and light on boogie-till-the-cows-come-home, party-hearty pursuits. You'll find good bridge programs and music to dance to or listen to in the bars and lounges, plus health spas and all of the other standard activities found on most large ships—bingo, golf-putting contests (on the carpet in the lobby), dance lessons, art auctions, and the like. All ships provide Internet access for 75¢ a minute.

Local travel guides sail on all Alaska-bound ships. The guides bring their knowledge of local culture, history, art, and flora and fauna, giving lectures and interacting one-on-one with guests. They also sell artwork by Alaska Natives who engage in ivory and soapstone carving, basket weaving, and mask making. In addition, a Tlingit cultural interpreter from Hoonah boards ships at Glacier Bay and Hubbard Glacier to give talks explaining the origins of the Huna people—a tribe that has called Glacier Bay home for centuries. At the glaciers, there is also commentary by National Park Service employees.

CHILDREN'S PROGRAM Club HAL is more than just one of those half-hearted give-'em-a-video-arcade-and-hot-dogs-at-dinner efforts. This children's program has expert supervisors, a fitness center, and dedicated kids' rooms and teen club rooms (adults, keep out!).

Kids' activities are arranged in three divisions, by age—3 to 7, 8 to 12, and teens. The youngest group might have, say, storytelling and fabric painting, golf putting and disco parties for 'tweens, and, for the older kids, a chance to try their hand at karaoke and teen sports tournaments. When there are more than 100 kids onboard, a Talent Show is presented. On the *Statendam, Volendam,* and *Zaandam* in Alaska, teens also get their own outdoor sunning area called The Oasis.

ENTERTAINMENT The line has improved its nightly show lounge entertainment, which was once, frankly, not so hot. The change, to a large extent, reflects the tastes of the younger passengers who are starting to book in greater numbers with HAL. The quality of the professional entertainers on HAL ships has perceptibly improved over the last 5 or 6 years. And then there are the amateurs! Each week includes a crew talent show in which the international staff members perform their countries' songs and dances. Even if that sounds a bit corny, try it—many of the staff members are fabulous!

SERVICE The line employs primarily Filipino and Indonesian staff members who are generally gracious and friendly without being cloying.

On one occasion, one of our contributors somehow managed to get his baggage onboard a Holland America ship in Vancouver, B.C.—while the keys to the bags were lying on the bedside table at home 1,000 miles away! The cabin steward refused to let him break the locks and ruin the rather expensive (and brand-new) luggage. Instead, he called an engineer and together they toiled patiently with a variety of tools—and a huge ring of keys—until, about a half-hour after boarding, they managed to free the offending locks. Luggage saved—and score one for the HAL service spirit!

Onboard services on every ship in the fleet include laundry and dry cleaning.

CRUISETOURS & ADD-ON PROGRAMS As might be expected of a company that owns its own tour company (Royal Caribbean and Princess also own tour companies in the Alaska market), HAL offers a variety of land arrangements in combination with its cruises, and they are extensive. Cruisetours range from 10 to 20 days in length, including a 3- or 7-day cruise, and vary widely in price. It depends entirely on what category of cabin, and in some cases, hotel accommodations you choose. One sample itinerary includes a rail ride through the Denali Corridor with 2 nights in the park, an overnight in Tok, a cruise on the Yukon River from Eagle, overnights in Dawson and Whitehorse, in the Yukon Territory, and ending with a 4-day cruise from Skagway. The per diems for this comprehensive land tour range between $200 and $490 a day, the former for an inside cabin on the ship, the latter for the best suite. (This tour, incidentally, although grueling—there's a lot of early rising in the land portion—is one of the all-time favorites.) All land transportation is, of course, included. Overnight hotel stays are also available in Fairbanks, Vancouver, Seattle, and Anchorage—again, with a wide price range. (Staying at an airport hotel in Vancouver, for example, will cost you less than bunking at the Pan Pacific, next to the Canada Place Passenger Pier—a lot less.) This year again, the cruisetour brochure includes tours featuring Tombstone Territorial Park, 90 minutes' drive from Dawson City in the heart of Canada's Yukon Territory, and to the Yukon Territory's Kluane National Park (a HAL exclusive), which has been designated by UNESCO as a World Heritage Site. The opening up of these two vast, hitherto untouched wilderness areas several years ago reflects HAL's preeminent position in the Yukon tourism market. Whereas other lines (in particular, Princess and Celebrity/Royal Caribbean) have tended to concentrate their investment focus in the Denali Corridor, the Interior, and the Kenai Peninsula, HAL has built instead in the Yukon Territory. Its entry into Kluane and Tombstone allows it to offer, in conjunction with Parks Canada, fixed-wing flightseeing over Kathleen Lake, a Tatshenshini River whitewater rafting outing, a hike though the King's Throne region (all in Kluane), and a motorcoach tour from Dawson City to Tombstone for wildlife viewing and hiking.

Statendam

The Verdict

The smallest of Holland America's ships in Alaska, this vessel is a good choice for cruisers looking for a more intimate, less crowded experience than found on many mass-market lines.

Statendam *(photo: Holland America Line)*

Specifications

Size (in Tons)	55,819	Crew	580
Passengers (Double Occ.)	1,258	Passenger/Crew Ratio	2.2 to 1
Space/Passenger Ratio	43 ft. to 1	Year Launched	1993
Total Cabins/Veranda Cabins	630/149	Last Major Refurbishment	2010

Frommer's Ratings (Scale of 1–5) ★★★★

Cabin Comfort & Amenities	4	Dining Options	3.5
Ship Cleanliness & Maintenance	4	Gym, Spa & Sports Facilities	4
Public Comfort/Space	4	Children's Facilities	4
Decor	4	Enjoyment Factor	4

THE SHIP IN GENERAL This ship is part of Holland America's Statendam class of vessels built between 1993 and 1996. While among the oldest in the line's fleet, it remains a wonderful ship that, at under 60,000 tons, offers a decidedly more intimate experience than the 100,000-ton megaships of, say, Princess Cruises. Moreover, in 2009, Holland America began a massive overhaul of the entire Statendam class that included a complete renovation of rooms; the addition of new, more open and contemporary public lounges and bars; the addition of innovative "Lanai cabins" with sliding doors that open onto the Promenade Deck; and other big changes. The *Statendam* received its $40-million revamp in April 2010. The overhauls are bringing a decidedly more contemporary vibe to the vessels while maintaining many of the classical touches for which Holland America is known. Public areas still feature a healthy sprinkling of the antique furniture, Delft pottery, seafaring-themed artwork, and historic textiles that are a hallmark of the line, but they now also boast a more stylish feel than in the past. In one of the biggest changes, several walls have been knocked out on Deck 7 to create a more contemporary lounge and bar area called Mix, which includes a martini bar, champagne bar, and spirits-and-ales bar. In addition, on the *Veendam,* the renovation brought a stylish new decktop area called The Retreat that features a refreshing 3-inch wading pool filled with lounge chairs (yes, they're placed right in the water), a pool bar, a fresh pizza counter, and giant LED screen for evening movies. (The *Statendam* and *Ryndam* also are slated to get the new area, but not until further dry-docks over the next 2 years.)

CABINS All the cabins have at least a small sitting area, plus lots of closet and drawer space. The outside doubles have either picture windows, verandas, or a sliding door that opens onto the Promenade Deck (the so-called Lanai cabins that the line began adding to the ships in 2009). ***Note:*** Like most ships built more than a decade ago, Holland America's Statendam-class vessels have relatively few cabins with verandas—at least compared to the line's newer ships. If a balcony is something you won't sail without (and many travelers to scenic Alaska demand a balcony), be sure to book early. The least expensive inside cabins run almost 190 square feet (quite large by industry standards) and have many of the amenities of their higher-deck counterparts—sofas, chairs, desks-cum-dressers, stools, hair dryers, safes, and coffee tables. The overhaul that we mentioned earlier in this section has made the rooms much more welcoming—and functional. All cabins have TVs and telephones, and some have bathtubs (including some whirlpool tubs), DVD players, and minibars. Penthouses (one only on each ship) are huge—almost 1,200 square feet. Six cabins on each ship are wheelchair-accessible.

Cabins & Rates

Cabin	Per Diem Rates	Sq. Ft.	Fridge	Hair Dryer	Sitting Area	TV
Statendam						
Inside	$128–$150	182	no	yes	some	yes
Outside	$157–$204	197	no	yes	yes	yes
Suites	$365–$764	292–1,159	yes	yes	yes	yes

PUBLIC AREAS The striking dining rooms and the two-tiered showrooms are among these ships' best features; the latter are comfortable and have great views of the stage area from all seats. It helps, of course, that Holland America has made huge strides in upgrading its entertainment package.

The lobby area on each ship is not just the place to board the ship, but a place to hang out in as well. The *Statendam*'s lobby houses a magnificent three-story fountain.

Other public rooms include a recently redesigned Explorations coffee bar/library/game area, a casino, a children's playroom, a cinema, and conference facilities. We especially like the forward-facing Crow's Nest bar and lounge up on the top deck of the ship, an inviting place from which to view the spectacular Alaska scenery for an hour or three.

DINING OPTIONS The overhaul in the works for these ships is bringing a new alternative eatery, Italian-themed Canaletto, available to passengers at no extra charge (reservations recommended). In addition, as on other Holland America vessels, the ships have the line's signature, reservations-only Pinnacle Grill ($20-a-head charge for dinner, $10 for lunch) and the casual Lido buffet, which is open in the evenings as well as for breakfast and lunch.

POOL, FITNESS, SPA & SPORTS FACILITIES The *Statendam* has a sprawling expanse of teak-covered aft deck surrounding a swimming pool. The ship also has a main swimming pool plus a wading pool, with a spacious deck area, bar, and two hot tubs in the middle of the top deck (all of which can be sheltered from inclement weather with a sliding-glass roof—a godsend in sometimes chilly Alaska). Both areas are well planned and wide open. There's a practice tennis court and an unobstructed track on the Lower Promenade Deck for walking or jogging. The ships' roomy, windowed gyms have a couple dozen exercise machines, a large separate aerobics area, steam rooms, and saunas. The spas lack pizzazz, but provide the typical treatments.

Amsterdam • Volendam • Zaandam

Volendam *(photo: Holland America Line)*

The Verdict

A decade after debuting, these three markedly similar vessels remain an attractive choice for cruisers looking for a midsize vessel in the Alaska market. At 62,000 tons, they are just a tad bigger than the Statendam class mentioned above.

Specifications

Size (in Tons)	62,000	Crew	615
Passengers (Double Occ.)	1,440	Passenger/Crew Ratio	2.2 to 1
Space/Passenger Ratio	43 ft. to 1	Year Launched	2000/1999/2000
Total Cabins/Veranda Cabins	716/197	Last Major Refurbishment	N/A

Frommer's Ratings (Scale of 1–5) ★★★★

Cabin Comfort & Amenities	4	Dining Options	3.5
Ship Cleanliness & Maintenance	4.5	Gym, Spa & Sports Facilities	4
Public Comfort/Space	4	Children's Facilities	4
Decor	4	Enjoyment Factor	4

THE SHIPS IN GENERAL Holland America pulled out all the stops on these ships. The centerpiece of the striking, triple-decked, oval atrium on the *Volendam,* for instance, is a glass sculpture by Luciano Vistosi, one of Italy's leading practitioners of the art—and that's just part of the ship's $2-million art collection, which reflects a flower theme. On the *Zaandam,* the focal point of the atrium is a 22-foot-tall pipe organ that is representative of the ship's music theme, which is filled out by a collection of guitars signed by rock musicians, including the Rolling Stones, Iggy Pop, David Bowie, and Queen (an attempt to attract a younger, baby boomer clientele?). Apart from the artwork and overall decorating motifs, there aren't many differences among these magnificent vessels; they really are virtually indistinguishable from one another. The *Zaandam* may look just the teeniest bit brighter than the *Volendam* and the *Amsterdam,* but hardly enough to make a real difference.

CABINS The 197 suites and deluxe staterooms on each ship have private verandas, and the smallest of the remaining 523 cabins is a comfortable 182 square feet. All cabins come complete with sofa seating areas, hair dryers, telephones, and TVs. The suites and deluxe rooms also have VCRs, whirlpool tubs, and minibars. The ships have more balcony cabins than other HAL vessels. Twenty-three of the cabins on each are equipped to accommodate wheelchairs.

Cabins & Rates

Cabins	Per Diem Rates	Sq. Ft.	Fridge	Hair Dryer	Sitting Area	TV
Amsterdam						
Inside	$157–$186	182	no	yes	yes	yes
Outside	$186–$230	197	no	yes	yes	yes
Suites	$307–$778	292–1,159	yes	yes	yes	yes
Volendam						
Inside	$157–$193	182	no	yes	yes	yes
Outside	$193–$241	197	no	yes	yes	yes
Suites	$307–$943	292–1,159	yes	yes	yes	yes
Zaandam						
Inside	$143–$171	182	no	yes	yes	yes
Outside	$171–$216	197	no	yes	yes	yes
Suites	$286–$943	292–1,159	yes	yes	yes	yes

PUBLIC AREAS Each ship has five entertainment lounges, including the main two-tiered showroom. The Crow's Nest, a combination nightclub and observation lounge, is a good place to watch the passing Alaska scenery during the day. Each ship also has a casino, a children's playroom, a cinema, a library, an arcade, and an Internet center where you can surf for 75¢ a minute, with a 5-minute minimum.

DINING OPTIONS All three ships have an alternative restaurant, the Pinnacle Grill (a staple on all HAL ships), which features steak and seafood, available on a reservations-only basis ($20 per-person supplement for dinner; $10 per person for lunch). Designed to inspire an artsy bistro vibe, these restaurants also have a display of drawings and etchings on the walls.

POOL, FITNESS, SPA & SPORTS FACILITIES The gym is downright palatial on these ships, with dozens of state-of-the-art machines surrounded by floor-to-ceiling windows. There is an adjacent aerobics room. The spa and hair salon are not quite as striking. Three pools are on the Lido Deck, with a main pool and a wading pool under a retractable glass roof that also encloses the café-like Dolphin Bar. A smaller and quieter aft pool is on the other side of the Lido buffet restaurant. On the Sports Deck is a pair of paddle-tennis courts as well as a shuffleboard court. Joggers can use the uninterrupted Lower Promenade Deck for a good workout.

Westerdam • Zuiderdam • Oosterdam

Westerdam *(photo: Holland America Line)*

The Verdict

The biggest of the HAL ships in Alaska, these three are nevertheless intimate, and certainly well equipped to support HAL's position as a force in the Alaska market.

Specifications

Size (in Tons)	82,300	Crew	817
Passengers (Double Occ.)	1,916	Passenger/Crew Ratio	2.2 to 1
Space/Passenger Ratio	44 ft. to 1	Year Launched	2004/2002/2003
Total Cabins/Veranda Cabins	958/640	Last Major Refurbishment	N/A

Frommer's Ratings (Scale of 1–5) ★★★★

Cabin Comfort & Amenities	4	Dining Options	3.5
Ship Cleanliness & Maintenance	5	Gym, Spa & Sports Facilities	4
Public Comfort/Space	4	Children's Facilities	4
Decor	4	Enjoyment Factor	4

THE SHIPS IN GENERAL The *Zuiderdam* comes back to Alaska this year after spending last summer in Europe. The *Westerdam* is in its second season in the North Country. The ships' thoughtful layout prevents bottlenecks at key points—outside the dining room, for instance, and at the buffet and pool area. Art worth about $2 million, according to HAL, is well displayed throughout each of the vessels, and the decor reflects Holland's (and Holland America's) contribution to the development of cruising and, indeed, of ships as a trade and transportation medium. The nautical pieces on display are plentiful, but never overwhelming.

CABINS Nearly 85% of the ships' cabins have ocean views, 67% of them with verandas. The smallest of the inside cabins is just 170 square feet, and the standard outside rooms start at 185 square feet. Suites here go up to 1,318 square feet, making them some of the biggest in the HAL fleet. All rooms have Internet/e-mail dataports. All of the rooms—even the smallest—have ample drawer and closet space, are tastefully decorated in quiet colors, and have quality bathroom fittings. All have DVD players and minibars. On each ship, 28 cabins, in several categories, are wheelchair-accessible.

Cabins & Rates

Cabins	Per Diem Rates	Sq. Ft.	Fridge	Hair Dryer	Sitting Area	TV
Westerdam						
Inside	$157–$193	154–185	no	no	no	yes
Outside	$186–$300	171–249	yes	yes	yes	yes
Suites	$328–$500	389–1,318	yes	yes	yes	yes

Cabins	Per Diem Rates	Sq. Ft.	Fridge	Hair Dryer	Sitting Area	TV
Zuiderdam						
Inside	$171–$207	154–185	no	no	no	yes
Outside	$207–$321	171–185	yes	yes	yes	yes
Suites	$357–$536	398–1,318	yes	yes	yes	yes
Oosterdam						
Inside	$171–$207	154–185	no	no	no	yes
Outside	$207–$321	171–185	yes	yes	yes	yes
Suites	$357–$536	398–1,318	yes	yes	yes	yes

PUBLIC AREAS The ships include a disco; a two-level main dining room; a library; a 24-hour cafe; an alternative, reservations-requested restaurant; and seven lounges/bars, including HAL's signature splendid Crow's Nest observation lounge/nightclub. And each ship has not one, but two showrooms—a spectacular three-level main showroom and a more intimate "cabaret-style" venue for smaller-scale performances.

The Club HAL children's facilities are extensive and have both indoor and outdoor components. The ships have two interior Promenade Decks, affording walkers protection against the elements—these decks can prove very useful in Alaska!

Wheelchair users are well catered to on these vessels. Besides the 28 cabins specially designed for them, they have wheelchair elevators dedicated for use in boarding the tenders in port, two tenders equipped with special wheelchair-accessible platforms, and accessible areas at virtually all public desks, bars, and lounges.

The ships have well-equipped casinos, offering passengers the chance to try their luck at stud poker, slots, craps, and roulette. Dozens of original works of art, with combined values ranking in the millions, dot the public areas. Each of the ships also features Explorations Café, a coffee house environment in which passengers can browse the Internet, check e-mail, or just read that day's *New York Times*—transmitted electronically to the ships daily.

DINING OPTIONS All three of these ships have HAL's signature Pinnacle Grill (for a supplemental charge) and a more casual, 24-hour cafe. There is also 24-hour room service for those who prefer in-cabin dining.

POOL, FITNESS, SPA & SPORTS FACILITIES The main pool on the Lido Deck has a retractable dome—a feature that has proven popular on other ships in Alaskan waters. A couple of hot tubs and a smaller pool complement the main pool. A huge spa, complete with the usual array of treatments and services (reserve in advance), occupies part of the topmost deck.

7 Norwegian Cruise Line

7665 Corporate Center Dr., Miami, FL 33126. © **866/234-7350** or 305/436-4000. Fax 305/436-4120. www.ncl.com.

THE LINE IN A NUTSHELL The very contemporary Norwegian Cruise Line (Norwegian) offers an informal and upbeat Alaska program on two large ships, including one of the newest in its fleet: the 5-year-old *Norwegian Pearl.* This year, both the *Pearl* and the older *Norwegian Star* will remain in Seattle for the summer's Inside Passage schedule, and the line no longer will offer Alaska sailings out of Vancouver, B.C.

(something it did up until 2 years ago, when it still had three ships in the region). Both the *Pearl* and *Star* are in 7-night rotations.

THE EXPERIENCE Norwegian excels in activities, lack of regimentation, and alternative dining. Recreational and fitness programs are among the best in the industry. The line's children's program is also top-notch. The company offers what it calls "Freestyle Cruising," which makes life a whole lot easier for passengers. Norwegian was, in fact, the pioneers of the concept in the North American cruise market. One of the main components of Freestyle Cruising is freedom in when, where, and with whom passengers dine. Guests can eat in their choice of a variety of restaurants pretty much any time between 5:30pm and midnight (you must be seated by 10pm), with no prearranged table assignment or dining time. Other features of Freestyle Cruising are that tips are automatically charged to room accounts, dress codes are more relaxed (resort casual) at all times, and at the end of the voyage, passengers can remain in their cabins until their time comes to disembark, rather than huddling in lounges or squatting on luggage in stairwells until their lucky color comes up. Freestyle Cruising has since been copied, to whatever extent possible, by other lines operating in the U.S. Naturally, with each new ship in a line's fleet, there usually comes innovation. In this case, one special addition was added on the *Norwegian Pearl:* a four-lane bowling alley tied in with an ultrachic South Beach–like lounge.

In 2008, Norwegian decided to take Freestyle Cruising a step further and underwent a multimillion-dollar enhancement program called Freestyle 2.0. Among the additions: cabin improvements, including new linens, pillows, mattresses, toiletries (by Elemis), and enhanced room service menus. There are also all sorts of new benefits for those booking balcony (and higher category) cabins, which vary by category but include priority restaurant reservations, pillow menus, special Bliss Beds, daily food treats, and bathrobes. Top cabins also get butler service.

As part of Freestyle 2.0, Norwegian has also enhanced its pool decks, creating quiet areas for adults, where they can enjoy cold towels and Evian spritzes.

Pros

- **Flexible dining.** Norwegian's dining policy lets you sit where and with whom you want, dress as you want (within reason), and dine when you want (dinner is served 5:30pm–midnight; guests must be seated by 10pm) at a wide variety of restaurants, including one that's open 24 hours. Room service is also available.
- **Sports orientation.** Sports fans will be happy to find that ESPN Domestic or International is broadcast (depending on the location of the ship) into cabins and at the sports bars.
- **Smoke-free zones.** Norwegian promotes a smoke-free environment for those who want it, and all dining rooms are smoke-free. Smoke-free tables in the casino can be requested.

Cons

- **Not all Freestyle.** Shows and activities have specific start and end times; it's not up to the passenger.
- **Few quiet spots.** Other than the library, there's not a quiet room to be found indoors, but Norwegian has added adult quiet zones at its pool decks.
- **Crowded dining areas.** The most popular of the alternative restaurants can get booked up early; best to make reservations as quickly as one can.

THE FLEET The *Norwegian Star* joined the fleet in 2001 and is a tad smaller than the newer *Norwegian Pearl.* Both ships have lots of windows for great viewing. Though these ships are relatively large and have a lot of public areas, some of the cabins are on the small side and some have insufficient closet space.

PASSENGER PROFILE In Alaska, the overall demographic tends more toward older, affluent retirees than on the line's warmer climate sailings, but you'll find an increasing number of younger couples and families as well, attracted by the line's flexible dining policy and relaxed dress code. Generally, passengers are not seeking high-voltage activities or 'round-the-clock action. The disco is seldom the most frequented room on a Norwegian ship, the exception being the Bliss Lounge on *Norwegian Pearl.* There is a good mix of first-timers and veteran cruisers (many of whom have cruised with this line before).

DINING The cruise line handles the business of dining in an innovative way, with its extensive number of alternative restaurants as well as smallish main dining rooms. And you can dress pretty much however you like, too—guests are allowed to wear blue jeans, shorts, and T-shirts in the evenings at the buffets, outdoor barbecues, and 24-hour venues. There is one optional formal night for those who want to dress up. On this night, some of the dining outlets are dressier, while others remain casual. As on all ships, breakfast and lunch are available either in the dining room, on an open-seating basis, or in the buffet up top, where passengers can help themselves, dress pretty much as they please (many of them have come straight from the pool), and enjoy a more relaxed meal—chefs manning cooking stations at the buffet prepare food in front of your eyes. In addition to the main dining rooms, the ships both have a variety of other food options. *Norwegian Pearl* has 13 dining options; *Norwegian Star* has 14. Included in the mix, depending on the ship, are French; sushi, sashimi, and teppanyaki; Italian eateries; and an a la carte Californian/Hawaiian/Asian outlet for which reservations are strongly recommended. As part of the Freestyle 2.0 upgrade, there are now delicious signature dishes in all specialty restaurants. A chocolate buffet, presented once during each cruise, was an industry first, and it's probably still the best.

ACTIVITIES In Alaska, the line has a destination lecturer or two on the history, landscape, and culture of the state; wine-tasting demonstrations; art auctions; dance classes and a fitness program; daily quizzes; crafts; board games; and bingo, among other activities. Passengers also tend to spend time at sports activities, which include basketball and minisoccer. The ships all have Internet cafes that cost 75¢ a minute a la carte, with package rates available. In addition, Alaska sailings feature over 130 options for exciting shore excursions, including the Great Canadian Rafting Adventure, Whale Watching and Wildlife Quest, and the Historic Gold Mine & Pan for Gold. Norwegian Alaskan voyages also feature one-of-a-kind Freestyle Private Tours on all cruises calling in Juneau and Ketchikan. Freestyle Private Touring is a completely personalized experience comprised of carefully chosen tours created exclusively for Norwegian guests, encouraging them to customize their time ashore and discover Alaska at their own pace. Tours include a personal guide, giving guests an exclusive insider's perspective.

CHILDREN'S PROGRAM Norwegian ships tend to be very family friendly: There's at least one full-time youth coordinator per age group, a kids' activity room, video games, an ice-cream stand, and group babysitting for ages 2 and up, plus a Polar Bear Pajama Party and a visit from a park ranger for the ships that sail to Glacier Bay

Norwegian Fleet Itineraries

Ship	Itineraries
Norwegian Pearl	**7-night Inside Passage/Glacier Bay:** Round-trip from Seattle, visiting Juneau, Skagway, Ketchikan, and Victoria, B.C. (May–Sept).
Norwegian Star	**7-night Inside Passage/Sawyer Glacier:** Round-trip from Seattle, visiting Ketchikan, Juneau, Skagway, and Prince Rupert, B.C. (May–Sept).

National Park. The line is constantly upgrading its kids' program. More family features aboard ships include a splash pool on the *Star,* a bowling alley and a jungle gym with ball pit and tunnels on the *Pearl,* and arcades on all Norwegian ships.

ENTERTAINMENT Entertainment is a Norwegian hallmark, with Vegas-style productions that are surprisingly lavish and artistically ambitious; the gymnasts are superb. On some nights, the showrooms also feature magic, comedians, and juggling acts. The two ships boast the Norwegian fleet's big splashy casinos, and all have intimate lounges that present pianists and cabaret acts. Music for dancing—usually by a smallish band and invariably the kind of dancing that mature passengers can engage in (that is, not a lot of rock 'n' roll)—is popular and takes place before or after shows. Each ship also has a late-night disco, for those who prefer a more frenetic beat. In 2008, Norwegian rolled out a new ultrahip theme party—"White Hot Night"—that really keeps the ship lively into the wee hours.

SERVICE Generally, room service and bar service fleetwide are speedy and efficient, and the waitstaff is attentive and accommodating. In the alternative dining rooms, service can be somewhat slow if it's a large group at one table, but at least on the *Norwegian Pearl,* they have made great strides in improving this. With the introduction of the line's flexible dining program, additional crew members, mostly waiters and kitchen staff, have been added to each ship. To eliminate tipping confusion, the line automatically adds a charge of $12 per passenger per day to shipboard accounts, which also can be pre-paid at the time of booking (you are free to adjust the amount up or down as you see fit based on the service you received). Full-service laundry and dry cleaning are available.

CRUISETOURS & ADD-ON PROGRAMS Norwegian offers a 4-night pre-cruise Discover Denali land package, starting from $1,349 per person. The package includes hotel accommodations, transfers, and airfare from Anchorage to Seattle at the end of the tour.

Norwegian Pearl

The Verdict

Norwegian's newest ship in Alaska is an evolutionary step forward with such features as bowling. It's the perfect ship for those who like lots of things to do and places to eat without much regimentation.

Norwegian Pearl *(photo: NCL)*

Specifications

Size (in Tons)	93,530	Crew	1,084
Passengers (Double Occ.)	2,394	Passenger/Crew Ratio	2.4 to 1
Space/Passenger Ratio	37 ft. to 1	Year Launched	2006
Total Cabins/Veranda Cabins	1,197/360	Last Major Refurbishment	N/A

Frommer's Ratings (Scale of 1–5) ★★★★½

Cabin Comfort & Amenities	4	Dining Options	5
Ship Cleanliness & Maintenance	5	Gym, Spa & Sports Facilities	5
Public Comfort/Space	4.5	Children's Facilities	5
Decor	4	Enjoyment Factor	4.5

THE SHIP IN GENERAL Launched in December 2006, *Norwegian Pearl* is Norwegian's newest ship in Alaska.

CABINS *Norwegian Pearl* has 1,197 cabins, 360 of which have balconies. The smallest of the rooms is about 142 square feet, average for this new breed of ship—not big, but not cramped, either. The ship's biggest accommodations—the spectacular, three-bedroom Garden Villa—runs to a staggering 4,252 square feet. One oft-voiced complaint in some of the lower-end cabins is an age-old Norwegian bugbear—not enough closet and drawer space. (That doesn't apply, of course, to the suites—and most assuredly not to the Garden Villa.) This should not be an issue for a 1-week Alaska cruise when there are two to a cabin. Freestyle 2.0 improvements have been added as noted above.

Cabins & Rates

Cabins	Per Diem Rates	Sq. Ft.	Fridge	Hair Dryer	Sitting Area	TV
Inside	$114–$164	143	no	yes	no	yes
Outside	$136–$271	161	no	yes	yes	yes
Suites	$271–$2,857	285–4,390	some	yes	yes	yes

PUBLIC AREAS Public areas are bright and airy, if just a tad too colorful and varied; the casino's red and yellow pillars, for instance, and the nightclub's lilac and blue chairs and carpeting are definitely a bit overheated. The Library, on the other hand, is a tastefully decorated, relaxing room and the only quiet room on the ship. As part of the "Freestyle" concept, *Pearl* has a vast array of eating and drinking spots. Other spaces include a huge casino, offering blackjack, roulette, craps (with wonderfully fair, Las Vegas–type odds), Caribbean Stud Poker—plus more than 200 slot machines—and a Texas Hold 'em table. The main showroom, the two-story Stardust Theater, holds about 1,100 in comfy seating, with good sightlines from either floor (and an air-conditioning flow from the back of each chair, helping to keep the room nice and cool). With its massive stage and loads of technological bells and whistles, the Stardust pulls off some pretty ambitious Broadway-style revues. The Internet cafe isn't a cafe at all (no coffee or pastries here), but it can keep you in e-touch with the outside world for 75¢ a minute. Packages lowering the per-minute cost are available. The Aqua Kids Club and Metro Center, for ages 2 through 17, has trained supervisors and is fully equipped with a cinema, a nursery and sleep/rest area, a computer area, an arts and crafts area, and a dance floor.

DINING OPTIONS In addition to its two main dining rooms (Indigo and the Summer Palace), the ship houses several other eateries in keeping with Norwegian's promise of providing maximum dining flexibility. Guests choose from two main dining rooms; a French bistro; an Italian trattoria; a steakhouse; eateries for teppanyaki, sushi, tapas/Tex-Mex, and more; and Blue Lagoon, open 24 hours a day. Supplemental fees ($10–$25 per person) are added for some of the restaurants. Colorful electronic signage around the ship lets guests know which restaurants are full and which ones have space. Even late in the afternoons, it's often possible to book a table in any restaurant for prime or near-prime dining times.

POOL, FITNESS, SPA & SPORTS FACILITIES The *Pearl* has an adult pool, six hot tubs, a kiddie pool, a spa with exceptional thermal offerings highlighted by the large thalassotherapy pool, and a salon. The pool deck experience was enhanced last year with quiet zones for adults. Active types should check out the Body Waves fitness center, the jogging/walking track, the rock-climbing wall, bowling alley, and the court used for basketball, volleyball, minisoccer, and tennis. Also nice in this day and age is the Deck 7 promenade, which goes around the entire ship (2⅔ laps to a mile).

Norwegian Star

The Verdict

As the first ship introduced after Star Cruises bought Norwegian, this ship firmly established Norwegian Cruise Line as a revitalized player in the cruise game. It's big and handsome—inside and out—and has a great choice of dining rooms.

Norwegian Star *(photo: NCL)*

Specifications

Size (in Tons)	91,740	Crew	1,065
Passengers (Double Occ.)	2,348	Passenger/Crew Ratio	2 to 1
Space/Passenger Ratio	40 ft. to 1	Year Launched	2001
Total Cabins/Veranda Cabins	1,120/515	Last Major Refurbishment	2010

Frommer's Ratings (Scale of 1–5) ★★★★

Cabin Comfort & Amenities	4	Dining Options	4.5
Ship Cleanliness & Maintenance	4	Gym, Spa & Sports Facilities	4
Public Comfort/Space	4	Children's Facilities	3.5
Decor	4	Enjoyment Factor	4.5

THE SHIP IN GENERAL The *Norwegian Star* looks a lot like its fleetmate, the *Norwegian Pearl,* particularly from behind, with that blunt rear end so favored by ship designers these days. Its real strength is the quality of the interior. The decor is modern, but not jarringly so, with muted but not washed-out colors. There are lots of pastel shades of green and blue, some gold (on drapes and bed-top covers, for instance), and a lot of blond wood. The overall effect is a pleasing meld of functionality and aesthetics.

CABINS Almost 800 of the *Star*'s accommodations are outside, and about two-thirds of those have verandas. The inside cabins are smallish, ranging from 142 to 150 square feet. Suites have floor-to-ceiling windows, refrigerators, and private balconies. All cabins are equipped with TVs, telephones, small dressing tables, soundproof doors, individual climate control, and sitting areas that are actually big enough to stretch out in. Freestyle 2.0 enhancements are as noted above. Closet and drawer space is quite limited, so pack lightly. Twenty cabins are suitable for wheelchair access.

Cabins & Rates

Cabins	Per Diem Rates	Sq. Ft.	Fridge	Hair Dryer	Sitting Area	TV
Inside	$100–$143	142–150	yes	yes	no	yes
Outside	$189–$257	160–204	yes	yes	some	yes
Suites	$200–$2,857	284–5,750	yes	yes	yes	yes

PUBLIC AREAS The *Star* has 14 eateries, for everything from snacks on up to full meals. Its two main dining rooms (Versailles and Aqua) offer traditional (that is to say, multi-course) meals and a range of lighter fare. Dining doesn't involve the traditional assigned seating ("If it's 8pm, it must be dinnertime"), but instead is on a no-reservations, come-as-you-please basis in a wide variety of restaurants. Public rooms include a casino, conference center, disco, library, karaoke bar, wine-tasting cellar, English pub, ice-cream counter, and three-level show lounge. For kids, there's a children's playroom (Planet Kids) and a video arcade.

DINING OPTIONS You won't go hungry on the *Star:* Choose from Le Bistro, a French/Mediterranean restaurant; Ginza, serving Japanese/Chinese cuisine; the SoHo Room, specializing in Pacific Rim/Hawaiian/Californian fusion dishes; and La Cucina, the Italian trattoria; and much, much more. Most of the specialty restaurants have a per person service charge. As if that weren't enough, the Blue Lagoon serves hamburgers, hot dogs, soups, salads, and pizza 24 hours a day.

POOL, FITNESS, SPA & SPORTS FACILITIES The *Star* is well equipped for the sports-minded and active vacationer. In addition to the fitness center, there are heated pools (a main pool and a children's pool), a jogging/walking track (3½ laps is 1 mile), and an array of sports facilities, including Ping-Pong tables and two golf driving ranges. Adults now can experience quiet zones poolside. The Fitness Center, on Deck 12, and the Barong Spa and Beauty Salon, on Deck 11, are well stocked with Jacuzzis, hydrotherapy baths, and saunas. The spa has facilities for couples to take their treatments together.

8 Oceania Cruises

8300 NW 33rd St., Ste. 308, Miami, FL 33122. ✆ **800/531-5658.** www.oceaniacruises.com.

THE LINE IN A NUTSHELL Oceania Cruises entered the cruise industry in late 2003 when it launched *Regatta,* formerly the *R Two* from Renaissance, which went belly-up after the September 11, 2001, terrorist attacks. It was an interesting beginning for *Regatta,* along with its sister ship, *Insignia,* formerly the *R One,* as the ships were being positioned above the premium lines and below the luxury lines. It was essentially a new category they called "deluxe" and it's been very successful, with Oceania adding a third ship to the fleet in 2005 (*Nautica,* formerly the *R Five*) and a new build, *Marina,* scheduled for January 2011. Oceania and Regent Seven Seas make up Prestige Cruise Holdings, a cruise division of the Apollo Management investment firm, which also owns a big portion of Norwegian Cruise Line.

THE EXPERIENCE Oceania truly offers a deluxe, or said another way, upscale, experience. There's little glitz or hoopla onboard and the hallmarks are dining, service, and itineraries. The two no-charge alternative restaurants are way above the norm. But, to be sure, one of the biggest strengths is the size of their first three vessels. At 30,277 tons and carrying 684 guests, they are really small-to-midsize by today's standards. It's an informal setting (Oceania calls it country club-casual) without crowds and lines. 2011 will be the first time Oceania will be in Alaska, so it's a completely new experience for the ship and the cruise line. They will likely draw upon the experience of the Regent Seven Seas ships which have been in the 49th state for over ten years. And the ship size allows for docking right in downtown Anchorage, a very big convenience.

Pros

- Dining is excellent, whether it be the main dining room or the two alternative restaurants.
- The size of the ships makes for an intimate, warm experience without masses of people.
- Itineraries are longer than the industry norm. In the case of Alaska, they're 10-, 12-, and 14-day cruises, giving plenty of time to experience the destination.
- Many public rooms, including the library, the Grand Bar, and the main atrium, are as pretty as there is at sea.

Cons

- Cabins are relatively small.
- In some areas, the ship's low ceilings make for a somewhat cramped feeling, or, in the case of the main dining room, it gets quite noisy.

THE FLEET This will be *Regatta*'s first year in Alaska but the line's sister company Regent Seven Seas has more than a decade's experience for them to draw from. The ship's size is excellent for the destination, making it easier for navigation closer to the highlights. Carrying only 684 passengers, *Regatta* offers a midsize alternative compared to the much larger premium ships and provides lots of really upscale features at way lower cruise fares than the luxury lines. At press time, *Regatta* is scheduled for major refurbishment in January 2011. All staterooms and suites will be redone as well as the two alternative restaurants. There will be new carpeting and artwork throughout the ship.

PASSENGER PROFILE The basic profile is one of couples in their 40s and 50s, but it's a very comfortable ship for both younger and older cruisers. It's very appropriate for those looking for a somewhat informal cruise, where dining and excellent service take a higher priority than glitz, glamour, and non-stop activity. Historically, the line's itineraries have been very port intensive, with very few sea days, so a busy shipboard agenda has never been a priority to passengers.

DINING *Regatta* has four main places to dine. The Grand Dining Room has about 340 seats and meals are all open seating. While there are plenty of tables for two, many

Oceania Fleet Itineraries

Ship	Itineraries
Regatta	**14-day round-trip San Francisco:** Victoria, Vancouver, B.C., Sitka, Hoonah, Skagway, Juneau, and Astoria; scenic cruising: Inside Passage, Hubbard Glacier, Tracy Arm (May and Aug).
	12-days between San Francisco and Vancouver, B.C.: Victoria, Astoria, Wrangell, Juneau, Hoonah, Sitka, and Ketchikan; scenic cruising: Inside Passage, Hubbard Glacier (May and Aug).
	10-days round-trip from Vancouver, B.C.: Sitka, Hoonah, Kodiak, Wrangell, and Ketchikan; scenic cruising: Inside Passage and Hubbard Glacier (June and Aug).
	12-days between Vancouver, B.C. and Anchorage: Ketchikan, Wrangell, Juneau, Hoonah, Skagway, Seward, and Homer; scenic cruising: Inside Passage, Hubbard Glacier, and College Fjord (June and July).

of them are side-by-side with other tables for two; it's best to try and get the tables along the windows or the walls. The center section is raised and noisy. But the food is terrific, with a range of international dishes. And, a nice aspect during the line's longer sailings, entrees and featured items are not repeated, allowing the galley staff to show off their skills with great variety. The two excellent alternative restaurants, Toscana for Italian dining and Polo Grill, the steakhouse, are both no-charge and reservations are really necessary. The Terrace Café offers up buffets (with some custom made items) for breakfast and lunch and converts to a really nice alternative for evenings, with tapas, pasta, sushi, and various other dishes. The aft section is outdoors with plenty of seating, which will be great for the evenings in Alaska when it stays light so late. Famed chef Jacques Pepin is the line's Executive Culinary Director, working with Oceania's chefs to develop exciting and exotic dishes as well as the more traditional ones. For those who want more, there's afternoon pizza, an ice-cream and sundae bar, 24-hour complimentary room service, and afternoon tea. Alternatives also include Canyon Ranch Spa Cuisine and vegetarian and kosher meals upon request.

ACTIVITIES Oceania does not go out of its way to provide an extensive list of things for passengers to do, and this is very appropriate for its informal style and port-intensive sailings. There will be lectures, mostly about the destination, including the ports of call. The spa makes working out a possibility, and the beautiful library has lots of reading selections. Weather permitting, the private cabanas are a great place to hang out and watch the scenery unfold. Dance classes and cooking lessons are part of a sea-day's agenda. And there's plenty of live music around the ship to enjoy.

CHILDREN'S PROGRAM While there may be kids on board, it's going to be up to their parents to entertain them. The ship does not have any facilities specifically for kids, and it really doesn't cater to them.

ENTERTAINMENT *Regatta*'s show lounge is relatively small, so it limits what performers can do. But there's an eight-piece orchestra for shows and musical entertainment, a small team of performers, and cabaret acts. Depending on the cruise, there may be a string quartet, flamenco guitarist, concert pianist, jazz combos, local and regional folk ensembles, and the occasional headline entertainers. In Alaska it's likely that most passengers will not be up late since the days themselves are so full of scenery and shore excursions.

SERVICE The crew complement of 400 (European officers and international crew) does a great job and the passenger-to-crew ratio of 1.7 is right there with the top luxury lines. Service is warm and friendly without being overbearing. In the dining room and bars, staff gets to know passenger names quite well (an amazing skill to be sure). In the main dining room, service can be a bit rushed since they do need to turn the tables. Also, many of the tables are a bit close to each other, so service can be a bit informal. It's a much more relaxed experience in the alternative restaurants. Cabin service is excellent and, of course, those rooms that come with butler service get extra pampering.

CRUISETOURS & ADD-ON PROGRAMS For those who have never been to Alaska before, a land trip before or after the cruise is virtually a must. The line's brochure includes 3- and 5-day and pre- and post-cruise tour packages from Anchorage. They both include a combination of rail and bus travel. There are also tram rides and floatplane trips depending on the package chosen. All transfers and hotels as well as most meals are included in the pricing. Brochure prices for 3- and 5-day packages are $1,699 and $2,299 per person, double occupancy, respectively. Oceania also offers hotel packages in San Francisco, Vancouver, and Anchorage for pre/post stays. Prices depend on number of days booked.

Oceania Regatta

The Verdict

Regatta is a terrific mid-size ship carrying 684 passengers in a decidedly deluxe/upscale informal atmosphere. Dining and service are key elements in this non-glitzy ship with very classy decor and features. The ship, scheduled at press time for a major refurbishment in January 2011, is a great midpoint between the more heavily populated premium ships and the more expensive luxury ships.

Regatta *(photo: Oceania Cruises)*

Specifications

Size (in Tons)	30,277	Crew	400
Passengers (Double Occ.)	684	Passenger/Crew Ratio	1.7 to 1
Space/Passenger Ratio	44 ft. to 1	Year Launched	1998
Total Cabins/Veranda Cabins	342/232	Last Major Refurbishment	2011

Frommer's Ratings (Scale of 1–5) ★★★★

Cabin Comfort & Amenities	4	Dining Options	5
Appearance & Upkeep	5	Gym, Spa & Sports Facilities	4.5
Public Comfort/Space	4.5	Children's Facilities	N/A
Decor	5	Enjoyment Factor	4.5

THE SHIP IN GENERAL *Regatta,* a midsize 30,277-ton vessel, is a deluxe vessel, offering a great compromise between the bigger premium ships and the more expensive luxury ships. The space ratio (the industry measure that tells you how spacious a ship is going to be based on the amount of inside room per person) is 44, a nice midpoint in today's market. It's a calm experience where passengers mostly fend for themselves without relying on the ship to keep them active every minute of every day. It's mostly a couples experience that is decidedly not for kids. The decor of the ship is old-world country club classy with a mix of styles. Some rooms, such as the library, Grand Bar, and the atrium/staircase, are just gorgeous. The refurbishment scheduled for January 2011 should really make a big difference, with the alternative restaurants redone and all suites and staterooms going through a makeover. New carpeting and artwork throughout the vessel will be a nice feature as well.

CABINS The 342 rooms break down into 16 different pricing categories but, realistically, there are eight types of rooms. At the top end of the spectrum are the six Owner's Suites and four Vista Suites, located fore and aft on decks 6, 7, and 8. Including their verandas, these rooms range from 786 to nearly 1,000 square feet. The 52 Penthouse Suites are all on Deck 8 and measure 322 square feet including veranda. These categories come with butler service.

The three categories of Concierge Level Veranda Staterooms on Deck 7 and the two categories of Veranda Staterooms on Deck 6 all measure 216 square feet including the veranda. The four categories of Deluxe Ocean View Staterooms on decks 4, 6, and 7 are 165 or 143 square feet. The 24 Inside Staterooms measure 160 square feet.

Naturally, the larger rooms come with the most amenities. For example, butler service comes with penthouses on up; Jacuzzis, 42-inch plasma TVs, a laptop computer, and more are in the Owner's and Vista suites; living room area and bathtubs in the Penthouse Suites; and large flatscreen TVs and premier services (such as priority restaurant reservations and debarkation) in the concierge level rooms. But all rooms are being redone in January 2011, so the furnishings and fittings all will be upgraded. The new decor will include custom-crafted fabric headboards, new lighting and wenge walnut paneling that adds to such existing amenities as queen or twin Tranquility Beds, vanity desk, breakfast table, 20-inch flatscreen TVs with DVD player, security safe, goose-down pillows, Egyptian-cotton linens, plush towels, Grohe handheld shower head, full length mirror, and more.

Cabins & Rates

Cabins	Per Diem Rates	Sq. Ft.	Fridge	Hair Dryer	Sitting Area	TV
Inside	$350	160	yes	yes	yes	yes
Outside	$400	165	yes	yes	yes	yes
Outside w/Veranda	$460	215	yes	yes	yes	yes
Penthouses/ Suites	$600–850	322–1,000	yes	yes	yes	yes

PUBLIC AREAS Beyond the very attractive reception area on Deck 4 with the reception desk, concierge, and shore excursion desk, the rest of the public areas cover Deck 5 and decks 9 through 11. Deck 5 starts with the Lounge at one end, where all performances and most activities take place, including cooking demos, dance classes, lectures, and more. At the other end is the Grand Dining Room. Midship has the casino, shops, and two great bars. First is the martini bar and lounge with an extensive list of beverage options and, often, live music before and after dinner. The second is the lovely Grand Bar, adjacent to the main dining room. Comfy seating and excellent service makes this a great spot before meals. Deck 9 has the Canyon Ranch Spa-Club at one end with salon, fitness center, treatment rooms, and steam rooms/lockers. Tucked in nearby are the Internet facility and the card room. At the other end is the Terrace Café. In between, naturally, is the pool area. It's not a huge pool, but there are two whirlpools, plenty of seating areas, and comfy loungers. On the side opposite the Grill is the Patio, a wonderful relaxing space. Deck 10 offers up the forward looking Horizons Bar at one end and Toscana/Polo Grill at the other. Just outside the alternative restaurants is the library, perhaps the most beautiful room of its kind to be found anywhere at sea. Forward on Deck 11 is the sun deck; at the very front end are the private cabanas. They're a bit pricey, but for scenic days in Alaska, they're a sure bet to be booked early.

DINING OPTIONS *Regatta* features four primary places to dine. First is the Grand Dining Room on Deck 5. It holds about 340 passengers, all open seating, for breakfast, lunch, and dinner. While there are plenty of tables for two, some of them are side by side so there's not much privacy. For more intimacy, try and get a table along the wall or window. Table settings include Versace bone china, Riedel crystal, and Christofle silverware. Menus, all prepared under the auspices of famed chef Jacques Pepin, are a delight; none of the nightly international-cuisine entrees and specialties are repeated during a cruise. In addition to the regular menu, Canyon Ranch Spa Cuisine as well as vegetarian and kosher options are available. The two alternative restaurants—Polo Grill offering steaks, chops, and seafood (98 seats) and Tuscany (96 seats) for Italian dining—are terrific. There's no additional charge, but reservations are strongly recommended. Casual dining is available for all meals in The Terrace, which has 154 seats inside and 186 seats outside. Weather permitting, this outside seating will be great for Alaska, where it stays light so late. In the evening, The Terrace has a variety of options including tapas, sushi, pasta, and more; it's a great alternative to the other three rooms. In addition, there's 24-hour room service at no charge, sunrise continental breakfast in Horizon lounge, pizza, ice cream, and poolside dining (with burgers, hot dogs, and sandwiches).

POOL, FITNESS, SPA & SPORTS FACILITIES The Canyon Ranch SpaClub, a nautical branch of Arizona's famous Canyon Ranch, offers up a wide range of spa and salon services including their signature Canyon Stone Massage, Thai Massage, and Total Elegance Facial. Special treatments for men are also on the menu. In addition, there are wellness lectures and lifestyle analysis, holistic sessions, a thalassotherapy pool, steam rooms, private spa deck with day beds, personal fitness training, yoga and Pilates, aerobics, step, and strength training classes. The smallish pool is ship-center on Deck 9 while the short jogging track goes around part of Deck 10.

9 Princess Cruises

24305 Town Center Dr., Santa Clarita, CA 91355. ✆ **800/PRINCESS** [774-6237] or 661/753-0000. Fax 661/753-1535. www.princess.com.

THE LINE IN A NUTSHELL The company strives, successfully, to please a wide variety of passengers. It offers more choices in terms of accommodations, dining, and entertainment than nearly any other line.

THE EXPERIENCE If you were to put Carnival, Royal Caribbean, Celebrity, and Holland America in a big bowl and mix them all together, you'd come up with Princess Cruises' megaships. The *Coral, Island, Diamond,* and *Sapphire Princess* are less glitzy and frenzied than the ships of, say, Carnival and Royal Caribbean; not quite as cutting-edge as Celebrity's *Infinity* and *Summit;* and more exciting, youthful, and entertaining than Holland America's near-megas. The Princess fleet appeals to a wider cross-section of cruisers by offering loads of choices and activities, plus touches of big-ship glamour, along with plenty of the private balconies, quiet nooks, and calm spaces that characterize smaller, more intimate-size vessels. Aboard Princess, you get a lot of bang for your buck, attractively packaged and well executed.

Although its ships serve every corner of the globe, nowhere is the Princess presence more visible than in Alaska. Through its affiliate, Princess Tours, the company owns wilderness lodges, motorcoaches, and railcars in the 49th state, making it one of the major players in the Alaska cruise market, alongside Holland America and, increasingly, Royal Caribbean Cruises' two brands, Celebrity and Royal Caribbean International. Princess also operates spectacular wilderness lodges, including the Copper River Lodge at Cooper Landing near Wrangell–St. Elias National Park.

In 2004, Princess became the first line to use the rather nondescript Whittier as the northern terminus for its Gulf cruises instead of the more commonly used Seward, and it has done so ever since. Whittier's primary advantage over Seward is that it's about 60 miles closer to Anchorage. Passengers bound for rail tours of Denali National Park are able to board their trains right on the pier instead of taking a bus to Anchorage and then embarking on their rail carriages. The inauguration of the service was yet another effort by a cruise line to gain a competitive edge over its Alaska rivals. The battle for the minds and wallets of the public is being fought as much on land as at sea these days. With so many ship lines striving to attract new passengers or persuade old ones to come back, every little bit helps. The competition goes on, to the benefit of the traveling public. Princess Cruises is now a member of the same group that owns Holland America and Carnival, both of them highly visible in the Alaska cruise market. That gives the parent, Miami-based Carnival Corp., control of no fewer than 15 ships in Alaska in 2011.

Pros

- **Good service.** The warm-hearted Italian, British, and Filipino service crew does a great job. On a Princess cruise a few years ago, one barman with a glorious cockney accent (which we noted he could mute or emphasize at will) was a huge hit with our group, dispensing one-liners, simple magic tricks, and drinks with equal facility. We've met others on Princess ships with the same gift for making passengers feel welcome without being overly familiar.
- **Private verandas.** Virtually all of the line's Alaska ships have scads and scads of verandas, some of them in as many as 75% of the cabins.

Cons

- **Average food.** The ships' cuisine is perfectly fine if you're not a gourmet, but if you are, you'll find that it's pretty banquet hall–esque.

THE FLEET Princess' diverse fleet in Alaska comprises six ships, five of which have entered service since the start of the millennium. The fleet includes the *Diamond* and *Sapphire,* which were completed in 2004; the *Coral* and *Island,* of 2002/2003 vintage;

and the *Golden* (2001). The *Sea Princess* (1998) completes Princess' Alaska fleet this year. The ships generally are pretty but not stunning, bright but not gaudy, spacious but not overwhelmingly so, and decorated in a comfortable, restrained style that's a combination of classic and modern. They're a great choice when you want a step up from Carnival, Royal Caribbean, and Norwegian, but aren't interested in (or can't afford) the luxury of Regent Seven Seas or Silversea.

Like Holland America and Carnival, Princess is owned by Carnival Corp.

PASSENGER PROFILE Typical Princess passengers are likely to be between about 50 to 65 and are often experienced cruisers who know what they want and are prepared to pay for it. The line's recent additional emphasis on its youth and children's facilities has begun to attract a bigger share of the family market, resulting in the passenger list becoming more diverse overall.

DINING In general, Princess serves meals that are good, if hardly gourmet. But you've got to give it points for at least trying to be flexible: A few years ago, Princess implemented a new fleetwide dining option known as Personal Choice. Basically, this plan allows passengers to sign up for the traditional first or second seating for dinner, or for a come-as-you-please restaurant-style dining option. The latter allows you to eat dinner anytime between 5:30pm and midnight, though you must be seated by 10pm. Passengers who choose the restaurant-style option may request a cozy table for two or bring along a half-dozen shipmates, depending on their mood that evening. A $10.50-a-day hotel and dining charge ($11 in suites and minisuites) will be automatically added to your bill for both the restaurant service and tips for your room steward. If you want to raise or lower that amount, you can do so at the passenger services desk. It's also possible to eat all your meals in the 24-hour Horizon Court cafe on all Princess ships in Alaska. If you don't go to the main dining room, though, you may miss one of Princess' best features: its pastas. The newest ships also have several alternative-dining restaurant options, including a steakhouse, and it's our experience that meals at these restaurants are well worth the price of admission, ranging from $15 to $20 per person.

ACTIVITIES Princess passengers can expect enough onboard activity to keep them going from morning to night if they've a mind to, and enough hideaways to let them do absolutely nothing, if that's their thing. The line doesn't go out of its way to make passengers feel that they're spoilsports if they don't participate in the amateur night tomfoolery or learn to fold napkins. These activities are usually there, along with the inevitable bingo, shuffleboard, and the rest, but they're low-key. Internet access is provided on all the ships for 75¢ per minute. Various packages that bring the cost down are also available for those who use the Net more—for instance, $55 for 100 minutes, $75 for 150 minutes, and $100 for 250 minutes. The line's ScholarShip@Sea program, which allows passengers to take classes in subjects as diverse as photography, computers, cooking, and even pottery, has been hugely popular since it was pioneered by Princess in 2003. All of the Princess ships in Alaska also are equipped with Nintendo Wii Fit game systems, projected on a wide screen.

Specifically in Alaska, the line has naturalists and park rangers onboard to offer commentary.

CHILDREN'S PROGRAM Supervised activities are held year-round for ages 3 to 17, clustered in three groups: Princess Pelicans for ages 3 to 7, Shockwaves for ages 8 to 12, and Remix for ages 13 to 17. Princess is seeking to broaden its appeal and

Princess Fleet Itineraries

Ship	Itineraries
Coral/Diamond/Island	**7-night Gulf of Alaska:** North- and southbound between Vancouver, B.C. and Whittier/Anchorage, visiting Ketchikan, Juneau, and Skagway, and cruising Glacier Bay and College Fjord (or Hubbard Glacier; May–Sept).
Golden/Sapphire	**7-night Inside Passage:** Round-trip from Seattle, visiting Ketchikan, Juneau, Skagway, Tracy Arm, and Victoria, B.C. (May–Sept).
Sea	**10-night Inside Passage:** Round-trip from San Francisco, visiting Victoria, B.C., Juneau, and two other ports (either Ketchikan, Sitka, Skagway or Ice Strait Point), plus Tracy Arm (May–Sept).

distance itself from its old image as a staid, adults-only line, and all of the ships are now well equipped for children and clearly intended to cater to families. Each ship has a spacious children's playroom and a sizable area of fenced-in outside deck for kids only, with a shallow pool and tricycles. Teen centers have computers, video games, and a sound system. Wisely, these areas are placed as far away as possible from the adult passengers.

ENTERTAINMENT From glittering Vegas-style shows, to New York cabaret-singer performances, to a rocking disco, this line provides a terrific blend of musical delights, and you'll always find a cozy spot where some soft piano or jazz music is being performed. You'll also find entertainers such as hypnotists, puppeteers, and comedians, plus karaoke for you audience-participation types. In the afternoons, there are always a couple of sessions of that ubiquitous cruise favorite, the Newlywed and Not-So-Newlywed Game. Each of the ships also has a wine bar selling caviar by the ounce and vintage wine, champagne, and iced vodka by the glass. The Princess casinos are sprawling and exciting places, too, and are bound to excite gamblers with their lights and action. Good-quality piano-bar music and strolling musicians, along with dance music in the lounge, are part of the pre- and post-dinner entertainment.

For years, Princess has had a connection to Hollywood—this is the *Love Boat* line, after all. It's the only line we know of where you can watch yesterday's and today's television shows on your in-room TV. Also shown are A&E, Biography, E! Entertainment TV, Nickelodeon, Discovery Channel, BBC, and National Geographic productions, as well as recently released movies.

SERVICE Throughout the fleet, the service in all areas—dining room, lounge, cabin maintenance, and so on—tends to be of consistently high quality. An area in which Princess particularly shines is the efficiency of its shore-excursion staff. Getting 2,600-plus people off a ship and onto motorcoaches, trains, and helicopters—all staples of any Alaska cruise program—isn't as easy as this company makes it look. And a real benefit of the Princess shore-excursions program is that passengers are sent the options about 60 days before the sailing and can book their choices on an advanced-reservations basis before the trip (tickets are issued onboard), either by mail or on the Internet at www.princess.com. The program improves your chances of getting your first choice of tours before they sell out. All of the Princess vessels in Alaska have laundry and dry-cleaning services and have their own self-service laundromats.

CRUISETOURS & ADD-ON PROGRAMS Princess has an array of land packages this year in Alaska in conjunction with its Gulf of Alaska and Inside Passage voyages.

Virtually every part of the state is covered—from the Kenai Peninsula to the Interior to the Far North. The land portions come in 3- to 8-night segments, all combinable with a 7-night cruise. Four types of land itineraries are offered in conjunction with Princess' five wilderness lodges—Denali Explorer, On Your Own, Off the Beaten Path, and Connoisseur (escorted).

Coral Princess • Island Princess

Coral Princess *(photo: Matt Hannafin)*

The Verdict

These two are plenty big, but such is the sophistication of marine architecture nowadays that passengers don't have the feeling of living with a couple of thousand others: There are lots of places to get away from it all.

Specifications

Size (in Tons)	92,000	Crew	900
Passengers (Double Occ.)	1,974	Passenger/Crew Ratio	2.2 to 1
Space/Passenger Ratio	44 ft. to 1	Year Launched	2003/2003
Total Cabins/Veranda Cabins	987/727	Last Major Refurbishment	2009/2010

Frommer's Ratings (Scale of 1–5) ★★★★

Cabin Comfort & Amenities	4	Dining Options	4.5
Ship Cleanliness & Maintenance	4	Gym, Spa & Sports Facilities	5
Public Comfort/Space	4	Children's Facilities	4.5
Decor	4	Enjoyment Factor	4

THE SHIPS IN GENERAL These two ships are essentially twins, with the same amenities and services, and nothing but relatively minor cosmetic differences between them. Roominess is the key here. The ships carry around the same number of passengers as, say, the *Sea Princess,* but have about 20% more public space—a noticeable difference.

The ships reflect the marine design inventiveness that is becoming more obvious with the arrival of every new ship. Each has a 9-hole putting green, a world-class art collection, a spacious kids' and teens' center, a wedding chapel, a cigar lounge, a martini bar (the last two features have become almost standard on new ships), and much more. Decor is tasteful and rich, with a lot of teak decking, stainless-steel and marble fittings, and prominent use of light shades of gray, blue, and brown in the soft furnishings.

CABINS The two ships have a remarkable number of outside rooms (almost 90%) and a huge number of private balconies—727, or more than 7 out of 10 of the outside units. The smallest accommodations on either of the ships are about 160 square feet, and the largest, the 16 top suites, stretch to 470 square feet, including the veranda. In between, the *Coral* and *Island* offer rooms with square footage ranging from 217 to 248. Don't assume when making a reservation that a minisuite will necessarily come with a veranda; each of the ships has eight minisuites without that amenity, so if you want one, be sure to specify that when you make your reservation. Twenty of the cabins (16 outside, 4 inside) are configured for wheelchair use. They are very spacious—between 217 square feet and 248 square feet.

Cabins & Rates

Cabins	Per Diem Rates	Sq. Ft.	Fridge	Hair Dryer	Sitting Area	TV
Inside	$109–$129	156–166	yes	yes	no	yes
Outside	$139–$169	217–248	yes	yes	no	yes
Suites	$185–$428	280–470	yes	yes	yes	yes

PUBLIC AREAS In keeping with the trend these days, the *Coral* and *Island* each have a comfy cigar bar and a martini lounge—the Churchill Lounge and the Rat Pack Bar, respectively. Their nautical-themed Wheelhouse Bars are warm, inviting places to spend time after-hours. Also appealing but more frenetic is the Explorers Lounge, which functions as the disco after dinner. The huge casinos on the *Coral* and *Island* are London- and Paris-themed rooms, respectively. An Internet cafe, a wedding chapel, children's and teens' centers, a golf putting green, and a golf simulator are located on the top deck.

DINING OPTIONS The ships have two main dining rooms and four smaller alternative dining areas—Sabatini's, an elegant Italian eatery found on most recent vintage Princess ships for which there is a $20-per-head charge (well worth the price); a Creole restaurant called The Bayou Café and Steakhouse ($15 per head); the poolside hamburger grill; and the poolside pizza bar. In combination, they allow passengers to eat pretty much when they want, and to be as formal or as relaxed as they wish.

POOL, FITNESS, SPA & SPORTS FACILITIES There are three pools and five whirlpool tubs. The fitness center is a large, well-stocked, airy room with absolutely the last word in equipment. The Lotus Spa has one of the widest arrays of massage and beauty treatments afloat, including oxygenating facials, an "aromaflex" package that combines the ancient healing therapies of massage and reflexology, and a treatment that involves the placing of heated, oiled volcanic stones on key energy points of the body to release muscular tension and promote relaxation.

Diamond Princess • Sapphire Princess

The Verdict

If the aim in the ship-designing business nowadays is "keeping up with the Joneses," these two succeed completely. Classy interiors, for sure. But let's face it—there's no way to hide from 2,669 other passengers.

Diamond Princess *(photo: Princess Cruises)*

Specifications

Size (in Tons)	116,000	Crew	1,100
Passengers (Double Occ.)	2,670	Passenger/Crew Ratio	2.4 to 1
Space/Passenger Ratio	43 ft. to 1	Year Launched	2004
Total Cabins/Veranda Cabins	1,337/746	Last Major Refurbishment	2010/2011

Frommer's Ratings (Scale of 1–5) ★★★★½

Cabin Comfort & Amenities	4	Dining Options	4.5
Ship Cleanliness & Maintenance	5	Gym, Spa & Sports Facilities	4
Public Comfort/Space	4.5	Children's Facilities	4
Decor	4.5	Enjoyment Factor	4

THE SHIPS IN GENERAL For all practical purposes, these two giants are also virtual twins, offering only the inevitable cosmetic (no structural) differences. Built in Nagasaki, Japan, they are the youngest ships in Princess' Alaska fleet.

CABINS Almost 60% of these ships' accommodations come with private balconies (78% of all the outside rooms)—a lot, though not as high a percentage as on some other ships in the market, including some of their own fleetmates. These are very much mass-market vessels. That requires ample space for people who want less pricey inside and standard outside (nonbalcony) cabins. The rooms range from 168 square feet in the low-end inside units to between 354 and 1,329 square feet (including the veranda) in the suite category. Twenty-seven cabins (16 outside, 11 inside) are wheelchair-accessible.

Cabins & Rates

Cabins	Per Diem Rates	Sq. Ft.	Fridge	Hair Dryer	Sitting Area	TV
Inside	\$109–\$156	168	yes	yes	no	yes
Outside	\$164–\$224	197–277	yes	yes	yes	yes
Suites	\$260–\$442	354–1,329	yes	yes	yes	yes

PUBLIC AREAS As in the case of other ships in the fleet, these two vessels cater to a range of tastes. There is, for example, the high-tech Club Fusion, a lounge with flashing lights and modernistic furnishings. At the other end of the spectrum, for those with a more traditional bent, there is the classic Wheelhouse Bar, with dark wood and a cozy feeling.

You wanna dance? Take your pick. For those whose taste runs to the more frenzied, there's Skywalkers, a lounge/disco in the sky with a balcony where you can cool off, and the Explorers Lounge, a cabaret-style lounge lower on the ship that serves as a venue for comedians and jugglers as well as singers. For those who prefer more sedate venues, the numerous lounges and bars throughout the ships afford more traditional, less hectic dance opportunities. There's also a cozy well-stocked library, a large casino, an Internet cafe, children's and teens' centers, a wedding chapel, and an art gallery. Up top, there's a Sports Deck with a jogging track, basketball/paddle tennis courts, a golf putting course, and a golf simulator.

DINING OPTIONS The *Sapphire* and *Diamond* each have multiple dining venues. The main dining room is a handsome, somewhat traditional large room with two seatings for dinner; four small dining venues (on decks 5 and 6; no cover charge) have "theme" decor and specialty dishes. For a great Italian meal, worth every cent of its $20 cover, try the upscale Sabatini's, perhaps the finest—and surely the most filling—Italian restaurant at sea.

During strategic times of the day, hamburgers, hot dogs, and sandwiches are available at the Trident Grill, located poolside, and ice cream is served at Sundae's, also on the Pool Deck, along with a pizza counter. And, of course, 24-hour room service is also available.

POOL, FITNESS, SPA & SPORTS FACILITIES There are three major outdoor pool areas and a generously supplied spa and fitness center on each ship, each with the expected (and demanded) full range of treatments, facials, herbal wraps, and massages. Trainers are present to conduct stretching, meditation, and aerobics classes.

Golden Princess

The Verdict

This ship, one of three 109,000-ton Grand Class vessels in the Princess fleet (the others are the *Star* and the *Grand*) is a real winner. Despite its size and megacapacity (2,590 passengers!), you won't usually feel the crush of all those other guests, thanks to plenty of opportunities to "get away from it all."

Golden Princess *(photo: Princess Cruises)*

Specifications

Size (in Tons)	109,000	Crew	1,200
Passengers (Double Occ.)	2,600	Passenger/Crew Ratio	2.1 to 1
Space/Passenger Ratio	42 ft. to 1	Year Launched	2001
Total Cabins/Veranda Cabins	1,301/710	Last Major Refurbishment	2009

Frommer's Ratings (Scale of 1–5) ★★★★½

Cabin Comfort & Amenities	4	Dining Options	5
Ship Cleanliness & Maintenance	4	Gym, Spa & Sports Facilities	4
Public Comfort/Space	5	Children's Facilities	4
Decor	5	Enjoyment Factor	4.5

THE SHIP IN GENERAL With 15 towering decks, the *Golden* is taller than the Statue of Liberty (from pedestal to torch). In fact, it's so big that the *Pacific Princess* (take your pick: either the now-departed ship that inspired the original *Love Boat* series or the one of the same name that the company introduced into service recently) could easily fit inside the hull of the ship and still have lots of room to spare.

Inside and out, the vessel is a marvel of size and design. Its massive white, boxy body, with its spoilerlike aft poking up into the air, cuts a slightly bizarre, space-age profile. But the ship's interior design is well laid out and easy to navigate. Amazingly, it seldom feels crowded—a characteristic, we've found, of the bigger, newer ships of Princess and many other lines—a tribute to the growing sophistication and creativity of the marine architecture community.

The ship provides an amazing variety of entertainment, dining options, and recreational activities. It has five restaurants (plus a pizzeria and outdoor grill), four swimming pools, and three show lounges, as well as expansive deck space.

Even the ship's medical center is grand, boasting high-tech "teleradiology" equipment that enables doctors to transmit x-rays to land-based experts.

CABINS Even the smallest of the *Golden*'s inside cabins is quite adequate, at about 160 square feet; standard outside units, sans balcony, go from 165 to 210 square feet; and larger oceanview rooms run between 215 and 255 square feet, including balcony. All of the rooms have twin beds that easily convert to queens, along with refrigerators, televisions, spacious closets, robes, safes, and plenty of drawer space. The larger of the outside rooms comes with a small writing desk. Minisuites give you 325 square feet (including balcony), and the suites range from 515 to about 800 square feet—again, including the balcony—and feature a tub and shower. (Nonbalcony staterooms have only shower stalls.) The rooms are tastefully decorated with subdued, hidden lighting; soft furnishings in quiet colors; and eye-catching, though not gallery-quality art. The ship has 28 wheelchair-accessible cabins. (The Skywalkers disco has a wheelchair lift up to the elevated dance floor, too.)

Nearly two-thirds of the ship's 992 cabins have balconies. But be forewarned: The verandas are tiered, as they are on so many new ships these days, so passengers in levels above may be able to look down on you. While they might be said to be private, they're really rather exposed. Don't do anything out there you wouldn't want the neighbors to see! TV stations available (geography permitting) include CNN, ESPN, Nickelodeon, BBC programming, and TNT (as well as the inevitable *Love Boat* reruns).

Cabins & Rates

Cabins	Per Diem Rates	Sq. Ft.	Fridge	Hair Dryer	Sitting Area	TV
Inside	$114–$135	160	yes	yes	no	yes
Outside	$149–$182	170–274	yes	yes	no	yes
Suites	$235–$422	323–800	yes	yes	yes	yes

PUBLIC AREAS Hey, where'd everyone go? Thanks to the smart layout of the vessel, with lots of small rooms rather than a few large rooms, passengers are dispersed rather than concentrated into one or two main areas; you'll have no problem finding a quiet retreat.

The public areas have a contemporary and upscale appeal, thanks to pleasing color schemes and the well-designed use of wood, marble, and brass. Two full-time florists create and care for impressive flower arrangements and a large variety of live plants.

A major overhaul of the ship in 2009 brought a new piazza-style atrium that serves as a central meeting point on the ship and is home to casual, cafe-like seating. It's ringed by the International Café, where you can pick up a specialty coffee, a pastry, and more; and a wine bar called Vines.

Besides the three—count 'em—main dining rooms, there are two principal alternative eateries: Sabatini's, a fine Italian staple found on every new Princess ship, and the Crown Grill, for steaks and seafood. Other options include the casual 24-hour

Horizon Court and two spaces—the Trident Grill (poolside) and a pizza counter—both with limited hours and serving snacks and light meals. The ship's restaurants are on the small side, designed that way so you don't feel like you're dining with a crowd and in order to maintain good acoustics (although you may also feel like the ceiling is closing in on you a bit).

Gamblers will love the sprawling and dazzling 13,500-square-foot casino, among the largest at sea. Near the casino, two lounge areas are ideal for whiling away a few moments before attacking the gaming tables.

The ship's most striking design feature (part of the Grand Class design) is its disco, which juts out over the stern and is suspended—scarily, in our opinion—some 155 feet above the water. It's really quite spectacular. If you're scared of heights, of course, don't even think of looking down; you're so far above the water that it's (literally!) breathtaking. Smoke machines and other high-tech gizmos add to the spooky effect at night. During the day, its banquettes make a particularly cozy spot to snuggle up with a good book.

The *Golden* also has a library and an Internet cafe.

DINING OPTIONS The principal alternative eating areas are Sabatini's and the Crown Grill. At Sabatini's, the $20 cover charge gets you the finest Italian food at sea—and gobs of it. The $25-a-head Crown Grill is a traditional steakhouse with steaks and seafood.

POOL, FITNESS & SPA FACILITIES The ship has something like 1.7 acres of open deck space, so it's not hard to find a quiet place to soak in the sun. It has four great swimming pools, including one with a retractable glass roof so it can double as a sort of solarium (of special importance in Alaska), another touted as a swim-against-the-current pool (although, truth be told, there really isn't enough room to do laps if others are in the water with you), and a third, aft under the disco, that feels miles from the rest of the ship (and is usually the least crowded). There are also nine whirlpool tubs up front.

On the forward Sun Deck, surrounding the lap pool and its tiered, amphitheater-style wooden benches, is the large Lotus Spa, which almost appears to be separate from the rest of the ship. Personally, we find the layout to be a bit weird: For instance, there are no showers in the dressing area. The complex includes a very large oceanview salon and an oceanview gym, which is surprisingly small and cramped for a ship of this size (although there is an unusually large aerobics floor).

Other active diversions include basketball, paddle tennis, a 9-hole putting green, and computerized simulated golf.

Sea Princess

The Verdict

It wasn't so long ago that this ship was one of the huge ships in the fleet. Not anymore. Now some of its fleetmates outweigh it by almost 40,000 tons—about the weight of a good midsize ship!

Sea Princess *(photo: Princess Cruises)*

Specifications

Size (in Tons)	77,000	Crew	900
Passengers (Double Occ.)	1,990	Passenger/Crew Ratio	2.2 to 1
Space/Passenger Ratio	39 ft. to 1	Year Launched	1998
Total Cabins/Veranda Cabins	975/410	Last Major Refurbishment	2009

Frommer's Ratings (Scale of 1–5)

★★★★

Cabin Comfort & Amenities	4	Dining Options	3.5
Ship Cleanliness & Maintenance	4.5	Gym, Spa & Sports Facilities	4
Public Comfort/Space	4	Children's Facilities	3.5
Decor	3.5	Enjoyment Factor	4

THE SHIP IN GENERAL On paper, passengers on the *Sea Princess* might expect to be a little cramped for space. Not so. Despite the ship's size and passenger complement, you'll probably never feel crowded: There always seems to be lots of space on deck, in the buffet dining areas, and in the lounges.

CABINS More than 400 of the ship's 975 cabins and suites have private balconies, including many in the midprice range, such as those on Baja Deck. All cabins, including the 408 inside units, come equipped with minibars, TVs, and twin beds that easily convert to a queen. Closet space is adequate, although it's a little tight in the lower-end cabins. The smallest cabins are 135 square feet, and the six suites measure up at 695 square feet, offering a large living room, separate bedroom/dining area, stall shower and bathtub with whirlpool, two TVs, refrigerator, and safe. The 32 minisuites are somewhat less lavish, though they're still highly desirable. The ship has 19 wheelchair-accessible cabins located on several decks and in several different categories.

Cabins & Rates

Cabins	Per Diem Rates	Sq. Ft.	Fridge	Hair Dryer	Sitting Area	TV
Inside	\$109–\$131	135–148	yes	yes	no	yes
Outside	\$149–\$175	155–179	yes	yes	no	yes
Suites	\$269–\$458	370–695	yes	yes	yes	yes

PUBLIC AREAS This ship shines when it comes to communal areas. It has a decidedly unglitzy decor that relies on lavish amounts of wood, glass, and marble. Collections of original paintings and lithographs worth \$2.5 million are featured onboard. The one-story showroom allows unobstructed viewing from every seat, and several seats in the back are reserved for passengers with mobility problems. The smaller Vista Lounge also has shows with good sightlines and comfortable cabaret-style seating. The twin dining rooms are broken up by dividers topped with frosted glass. The elegant Wheelhouse Bar is the perfect spot for pre- or post-dinner drinks; done in warm, dark-wood tones, it has live entertainment (a pianist or a duo mostly). More spaces include a dark and sensuous disco; a bright, spacious casino; a card room; a cinema; and a show lounge. Other lounges, scattered throughout the ship, provide opportunities for an intimate rendezvous (check out the Premier Cru) or a bigger bash (try the popular Atrium Lounge, the setting for the captain's opening cocktail party). Another striking feature on this ship is the library, with leather easy chairs equipped with built-in headphone sound systems. They absolutely cry out, "Sit here!"

The ship has an extensive children's playroom with a ball drop, castles, computer games, a puppet theater, and more.

DINING OPTIONS If you'd like a break from the main dining rooms and buffet, check out the bistro-style restaurant, where you can get a full dinner until 4am, or the Sterling Steakhouse (carved out of Horizon Court in the evening and coming with a $15-a-person charge). Italian dishes are available at the pizzeria.

POOL, FITNESS, SPA & SPORTS FACILITIES The *Sea Princess* has four pools (one of which is the kids' wading pool), plus hot tubs scattered around the Riviera Deck. The ship boasts a well-designed and appealing health club—one of the best on any of Princess' vessels. The spa provides all of the requisite massages and spa treatments. A teakwood deck encircles the ship for joggers, walkers, and shuffleboard players, and a computerized golf center called Princess Links simulates the trickiest aspects of some of the world's most legendary golf courses.

Fitness classes are available throughout the day in a spacious aerobics room, where stretching and meditation classes are also held.

10 Regent Seven Seas Cruises

1000 Corporate Dr., Ste. 500, Fort Lauderdale, FL 33334. ✆ **800/285-1835.** www.rssc.com.

THE LINE IN A NUTSHELL Regent's guests travel in style and extreme comfort. Its brand of luxury is casually elegant and subtle, its cuisine among the best in the industry. The line operates three midsize ships geared toward affluent and worldly travelers. This year marks the line's 12th full season in Alaska, and it'll be deploying the refurbished, all-suite, 490-passenger *Seven Seas Navigator* to the region for the second year in a row.

THE EXPERIENCE The Regent Seven Seas experience means outstanding food, service, and accommodations in an environment that's a little more casual than some of its luxury competitors; there is, for instance, no formal dress night during its 7-night Alaska program. The line also moved to being ultra-all-inclusive in 2009, with most shore excursions included in the cruise fare (excluding the more exclusive Regent Choice tours). The *Navigator*—no stranger to Alaska, as it was deployed there in 2000, 2002, and again in 2010—is one of the most intimate and comfortable ships at sea, providing its passengers with mostly large outside suites and spacious public areas.

Pros

- **Overall excellence.** The line has a no-tipping policy, excellent food, open seating for meals, generally fine service, great accommodations, and creative shore excursions. *Navigator*'s recent refurbishment really brought the ship up to date.
- **Great room service.** It's about the best we've found on a ship, with the food served promptly, fresh, and course-by-course or all at once—your choice (okay, so the room service pizza isn't so great).
- **Liquor included in the price.** Regent has a fleetwide liquor-inclusive policy on all departures.

Cons

- **Sedate nightlife.** Although the line recently upgraded its evening entertainment, many guests, exhausted after a full day in port, retire early, perhaps to watch a movie on their in-suite DVD player, leaving only a few night owls in the disco and other lounges. The ship does have some late-night fun, though, for those with the energy to stay up that long.

THE FLEET *Seven Seas Navigator* is not new to the Alaska market, having returned in 2010 after an 8-year absence. It is the smaller ship in the Regent fleet, with an elegant yet comfortable modern design and a graceful yet casual onboard atmosphere. Nearly nine out of ten cabins on the ship have balconies, an advantage in stunning view-laden Alaska.

PASSENGER PROFILE Regent tends to attract travelers from their 40s to their 70s, (sometimes even in their 20s and 30s), who have a high household income, but don't like to flaunt their wealth. The typical guest profile is that of an admirably well-educated, well-traveled, and inquisitive person. The travelers may also be a mixed bunch. On a recent cruise, passengers included an economist for an international financial institution, a man who opens banks for a living, a retired auto parts engineer, and an environmental lobbyist.

DINING Regent's cuisine would gain high marks even if it were on land. Service by professional waiters adds to the experience, as do little touches such as fine china and fresh flowers on the tables. The complimentary wines served with meals are generally quite good; there's very little reason to want to trade up (however, the wines available by paying extra are actually fairly priced). The attractive Compass Rose room's new table settings, window decor, and comfy chairs make dining a pleasure. It serves lavish breakfasts, lunches, and dinners. Its dinner menu has such yummy starter items as chilled kiwi and mango with apricot liqueur; napoleon of crabmeat, avocado, and black sesame crisp; and grilled calamari marinated with herbs. For entrees, choices include a fabulous grilled rib-eye steak, couscous Casablanca, baked fresh turbot fillet Viennoise, and much more. The ship also has a new Prime 7 steakhouse/grill and another eatery called La Veranda (in the style of the *Seven Seas Voyager* and *Mariner*). Prime 7 has an extensive list of main courses including beef cuts, chops, Alaska king crab, lobster, and more. Meals also come with a vast range of appetizers, side dishes, and desserts (there's no charge, but reservations are a must). Buffets in La Veranda are not as lavish as they are on *Voyager* and *Mariner* but diners definitely will not go hungry.

ACTIVITIES The line assumes that, for the most part, guests want to entertain themselves onboard, but that doesn't mean there isn't plenty to do, considering the relatively small size of the *Navigator.* There are lectures by local Alaska experts and golf instruction. There are card and board games, art auctions, blackjack and Ping-Pong tournaments, bingo, and big-screen movies with popcorn. Bridge instructors are onboard for select sailings; check when you make a reservation. The ship has Wi-Fi throughout and has great deals on Internet packages. Regent Seven Seas has a deal with Jean-Michel Cousteau's Ocean Futures Society, one of the world's leading maritime environmental organizations, and will have a destination expert/naturalist onboard its 2011 Alaska cruises.

CHILDREN'S PROGRAM The line in general is adult-oriented, and the smaller *Navigator,* in any case, is not the perfect vehicle for kids. But the ship does have Club Mariner on Alaska cruises, where you might find a handful of youngsters on any given

Regent Seven Seas Fleet Itineraries

Ship	Itineraries
Seven Seas Navigator	**7-night Gulf of Alaska:** North- and southbound between Vancouver, B.C. and Seward/Anchorage, visiting Ketchikan, Juneau, Skagway, Sitka, and cruising Tracy Arm and Hubbard Glacier (late May–Aug).
	12-night Inside Passage: North- and southbound between San Francisco and Vancouver, B.C., visiting Astoria, Ketchikan, Juneau, Skagway, Sitka, and Victoria, plus cruising Hubbard Glacier and Glacier Bay (northbound) or Tracy Arm (southbound). (May and September)

sailing. Activities, held in borrowed spaces such as the nightclub, stairway landings, or card room (there is no dedicated children's facility), include games, tournaments, Alaska-oriented crafts projects, and storytelling. There are also a limited number of special kids' shore excursions.

ENTERTAINMENT The *Navigator*'s smaller size limits its ability to provide entertainment as lavish as some of its bigger competitors; however, the program in the two-tiered showroom, the South Seas Lounge, includes well-presented, medium-scale production shows with high-quality performers, cabaret acts, and headliners including comedians and magicians, and sometimes members of symphony orchestras and other musical groups. On a recent cruise there was a Beatles review in Galileo's Lounge that really drew a big crowd. The library stocks books and movies, which guests can play on their in-suite DVD player.

SERVICE The senior dining room staff generally has had experience at fine hotels as well as on ships. (They provide service so good that you don't really notice it.) A small point about bar service: During a cruise last year, just about all the staff members in the public lounges remembered our favorite drinks after just one meeting. Excellent room stewards and butlers do a great job in the suites and bar service is outstanding. The *Navigator* also provides dry cleaning and full-service and self-service laundry.

CRUISETOURS & ADD-ON PROGRAMS The Denali Corridor features prominently in Regent Seven Seas' land packages. The company's brochure includes 3-, 4-, and 5-night packages originating in Anchorage. The rates start at under $2,000 depending on the itinerary chosen. A 2-night "Tea at the Empress" package in Victoria, B.C., also costs around $2,000.

Seven Seas Navigator

The Verdict

Seven Seas Navigator is the true luxury leader among the medium-size ships in Alaska. All rooms are outside-facing and 85% have balconies; the spacious public and deck areas make viewing easy and supremely comfortable. A recent $31-million refurbishment really spiffed up the ship nicely.

Seven Seas Navigator *(photo: Regent Seven Seas)*

Specifications

Size (in Tons)	28,550	Crew	345
Passengers (Double Occ.)	490	Passenger/Crew Ratio	1.4 to 1
Space/Passenger Ratio	58 to 1	Year Launched	1999
Total Cabins/Veranda Cabins	245/208	Last Major Refurbishment	2009

Frommer's Ratings (Scale 1–5) ★★★★½

Cabin Comfort & Amenities	5	Dining Options	4.5
Ship Cleanliness & Maintenance	5	Gym, Spa & Sports Facilities	4.5
Public Comfort/Space	4.5	Children's Facilities	N/A
Decor	4.5	Enjoyment Factor	4.5

THE SHIP IN GENERAL The *Seven Seas Navigator* is a luxurious vessel that carries its 490 guests in extreme comfort. The amount of public space per person is enormous for a ship this size, and its roomy, all-outside accommodations design gives everyone lots of private space as well. The three dining rooms plus poolside options make sure nobody on the *Navigator* goes hungry. Daytime activities are not extensive, but that seems to suit the clientele just fine. The company has made enormous strides in service and entertainment in recent years, putting this ship in the upper echelon of luxury cruises. It is arguably one of the most luxurious ships in Alaska this year.

CABINS All rooms are oceanview suites, more than 85% of them with private verandas, the remainder with huge picture windows. Even the smallest of the suites is a very large 301 square feet. The largest of the suites is a whopping 1,173 square feet, including a 106-square-foot balcony. All suites—even nonveranda units—have separate living room areas, and top levels of suites have dining areas as well. Every suite comes with queen-size beds that convert to twins, walk-in closets, tons of drawer space, marble-appointed bathrooms with shower and separate tubs (some have large shower stalls instead), TVs and DVD players, refrigerators stocked with complimentary bottled water and soft drinks, safes, phones, and 24-hour room service. You can order full meals from the dining room menu, served in-suite. The larger suites come with butler service and upgraded amenities, including such things as iPod players/speakers. Four of the suites are wheelchair-accessible.

Cabins & Rates

Cabins	Per Diem Rates	Sq. Ft.	Fridge	Hair Dryer	Sitting Area	TV
Suites	$575–$2,250*/ $475–$1,300**	301–1,067	yes	yes	yes	yes

**Rates based on 7-night cruise.*
***Rates based on 12-night cruise.*

PUBLIC AREAS Italian-designed and -built, the *Navigator* has an eclectic interior that's elegant yet comfortable. *Navigator* guests may relax in a number of intimate evening bar/lounges (all of which were refurbished in late 2009), including Galileo's, with its live piano music; the Stars Lounge, with DJ-chosen dance tunes; the Navigator Lounge, popular all day long now that it's also a coffee bar; and the Connoisseur Bar, a haven for cigar smokers. The casino has blackjack, roulette, Caribbean stud poker, minicraps, and slots. Shoppers can indulge at a few small, classy boutiques selling clothes, jewelry, and your usual array of cruise-line logo items (but no alcohol). The library/computer area has books, games, and DVDs, as well as nine new computer terminals. Guests only pay for transmission time and can use word-processing software free of charge (a very nice feature).

DINING OPTIONS The design of the main dining room, the Compass Rose, has a great open feeling so that passengers can see out both sides of the ship without straining, but it still gives one the impression of eating in a much smaller, more intimate facility. The addition of the magnificent steakhouse Prime 7 and the more casual La Veranda has added a whole new dimension to the dining experience on the *Navigator.* Room service is also readily available (if only the pizza were better). An enlarged and enhanced pool grill and bar serves a very nice range of lunch fare such as hot dogs, custom-made hamburgers, paninis, and salads.

POOL, FITNESS, SPA & SPORTS FACILITIES When the ship was refurbished in late 2009, the spa was changed into a Canyon Ranch SpaClub. It's a classy operation and there's virtually no product push either during or after treatments. The smallish gym and aerobics area do not seem to get crowded despite their size. The five treatment rooms and beauty salon offer the normal range of services (treatments aren't cheap though). The pool is flanked by heated whirlpools and surrounded by an enormous amount of open deck space (the pool area was actually reduced in favor of more comfy seats). Recreational facilities beyond the gym include a golf driving cage, a paddle tennis court, a jogging track, table tennis, and shuffleboard.

11 Royal Caribbean International

1050 Caribbean Way, Miami, FL 33132. ✆ **866/562-7625** or 305/379-2601. www.royalcaribbean.com.

THE LINE IN A NUTSHELL This bold, brash, innovative company has the largest passenger capacity in the industry on the biggest ships. Royal Caribbean introduced the concept of the megaship with its *Sovereign of the Seas* in 1988, and the industry hasn't been the same since. The mass-market style of cruising that Royal Caribbean sells aboard its megaships is reasonably priced and has nearly every diversion imaginable.

THE EXPERIENCE The ships are more informal than formal and are well run, with a large team of friendly service employees paying close attention to day-to-day details. Dress is generally casual during the day and informal most evenings, with 2 formal nights on a typical 7-night cruise. The contemporary decor on Royal Caribbean vessels doesn't bang you over the head with glitz like, say, Carnival. It's more subdued, classy, and witty, with lots of glass, greenery, and art. All the Royal Caribbean vessels feature the line's trademark Viking Crown Lounge, an observation area located in a circular glass structure on the upper deck (in some cases, encircling the smokestack), which looks like a Martian spacecraft atop the vessels. Another popular trademark feature is the ships' nautically themed Schooner bars. The range of what's available on different Royal Caribbean ships does vary somewhat depending on the age, size, and design.

Pros

- **Great spas and recreation facilities.** Royal Caribbean's Alaska ships for 2011 all have elaborate health-club and spa facilities, a covered swimming pool, and large, open sun-deck areas.

- **Great observation areas.** The Viking Crown Lounge and other glassed-in areas make excellent observation rooms for gazing at the Alaska sights.
- **Quality entertainment.** Royal Caribbean spends big bucks on entertainment, which includes high-tech show productions. Headliners are often featured.

Cons

- **Crowds.** As with some other big ships, you almost need a map to get around, and you'll likely experience the inevitable lines for buffets, debarkation, and boarding of buses during shore excursions.

THE FLEET Royal Caribbean owns most of the largest ships in the world, including the recently introduced *Oasis of the Seas* and sister ship *Allure of the Seas*—the world's largest vessels at 225,282 gross registered tons. But don't expect to see the line's biggest vessels in Alaska. While *Oasis* and *Allure* have room for 5,400 passengers at double occupancy and several other Royal Caribbean ships can hold nearly 4,000, the largest vessel the line sends to Alaska is the 2,112-passenger *Radiance of the Seas.* Introduced in 2001 as a new category of ship for the line, the vessel has many innovations, including a billiards room with self-leveling pool tables. The *Radiance* is in Gulf of Alaska service between Vancouver, B.C. and Seward, Alaska. It's joined in Alaska in 2011 by a second ship (one less than in 2009)—the 1,998-passenger *Rhapsody of the Seas.* The *Rhapsody* is sailing round-trip out of Seattle.

PASSENGER PROFILE The crowd on Royal Caribbean ships, like the decor, tends to be a notch down on the flashy scale from what you'll find on Carnival and perhaps a notch up from those on, say, Princess or the Holland America Line. Guests represent an age mix from 30 to 60, and an increasing number of families are attracted by the line's well-established and fine-tuned kids' programs.

DINING Food on Royal Caribbean has been upgraded and improved in recent years, and occasionally a dish will knock your socks off. The dining rooms have two seatings with assigned tables at dinner, as well as the more flexible My Time Dining program for dinner, and open seating at breakfast and lunch. Every menu contains selections designed for low-fat, low-cholesterol, and low-salt dining, as well as vegetarian and children's dishes. On the *Radiance,* you also have the option of dining on a reservations-only basis at Chops Grille, a classy steakhouse, or Portofino, an upscale Italian eatery. The line levies a cover charge of $20 per person at Portofino and $25 per person at Chops, but in our experience, the food soars above what's served in the dining room. Casual table-service dining is enjoyed at the Seaview Café for dinner as an alternative for those who don't want to sit in the dining room (no extra charge). Buffet-style breakfast, lunch, and dinner are available in the Windjammer Café, on Deck 11. In addition to a poolside midnight buffet on one evening, sandwiches are served nightly throughout public lounges. A basic menu is available from room service 24 hours a day, and during normal dinner hours, a cabin steward can bring you anything being served in the dining room that night. Royal Caribbean bans smoking in the dining rooms on all its vessels.

ACTIVITIES On the activity front, Royal Caribbean has plenty of the standard cruise-line fare (crafts classes, horse racing, bingo, shuffleboard, deck games, line-dancing lessons, wine-and-cheese tastings, cooking demonstrations, and art auctions). But if you want to take it easy and watch the world go by or scan for wildlife, nobody

Royal Caribbean Fleet Itineraries

Ship	Itineraries
Radiance of the Seas	**7-night Gulf of Alaska:** North- and southbound between Vancouver, B.C. and Seward, visiting Ketchikan, Juneau, Skagway, Icy Strait Point, and Hubbard Glacier (May–Sept).
Rhapsody of the Seas	**7-night Inside Passage:** Round-trip from Seattle, visiting Juneau, Tracy Arm, Skagway, and Victoria, B.C. (May–Sept).

will bother you or cajole you into joining an activity. Port lectures are given on topics such as Alaska wildlife, history, and culture. The ships also have an extensive fitness program called Vitality.

CHILDREN'S PROGRAM Children's activities are some of the most extensive afloat and include a teen disco, children's play areas, and the Adventure Ocean and teen programs, which have a full schedule of scavenger hunts, arts-and-crafts sessions, and science presentations—so many activities, in fact, that kids get their own daily activities programs delivered to their cabins. Royal Caribbean also provides teen-only spaces onboard every ship in its fleet.

ENTERTAINMENT Royal Caribbean's entertainment package, which incorporates sprawling, high-tech cabaret stages into each of its ship's showrooms, some with a wall of video monitors to augment live performances, is as good as any other mainstream line. It begins before dinner and continues late, late into the night. There are musical acts, comedy acts, sock hops, toga parties, talent shows, and that great cruise favorite, karaoke. The Vegas-style shows are filled with all the razzle-dazzle guests have come to expect, and these large-cast revues are among the best you'll find on any ship. Royal Caribbean uses 10-piece bands in its main showroom. Show bands and other lounge acts keep the music playing all over the ship.

SERVICE Overall, service in the restaurants and cabins is friendly, accommodating, and efficient. You're likely to be greeted with a smile by someone polishing the brass in a stairwell. That said, big, bustling ships like Royal Caribbean's are no strangers to crowds and lines, and harried servers may not be able to get to you exactly when you'd like them to. Considering the vast armies of personnel required to maintain a line as large as Royal Caribbean, it's a miracle that staffers appear as motivated and enthusiastic as they do. Laundry and dry-cleaning services are available on all the ships, but none has a self-service laundromat.

CRUISETOURS & ADD-ON PROGRAMS Royal Caribbean International offers 10- to 14-night Alaska cruisetours combining a 7-night cruise with a 3- to 7-night land package in the Denali Corridor, in conjunction with the Northbound/Southbound Inside Passage sailings onboard *Radiance of the Seas.* The 10-night Alaska cruisetour prices start at $1,240 per person, with package prices varying depending on the stateroom category, land package, and departure date. Additionally, Royal Caribbean offers pre- and post-cruise hotel stays in Anchorage (from $228 per person, double, including transfers) and Vancouver (from $194 per person, double, including transfers).

Radiance of the Seas

The Verdict

So what if you need a map to find your way around these large vessels? It's worth it if the map leads you to the superb spa, the self-leveling billiards tables, or the revolving bar in the disco.

Radiance of the Seas *(photo: Royal Caribbean International)*

Specifications

Size (in Tons)	90,090	Crew	857
Passengers (Double Occ.)	2,112	Passengers/Crew Ratio	2.5 to 1
Space/Passenger Ratio	43 ft. to 1	Year Launched	2001
Total Cabins/Veranda Cabins	1,056/577	Last Major Refurbishment	N/A

Frommer's Ratings (Scale of 1–5) ★★★★

Cabin Comfort & Amenities	3.5	Dining Options	4.5
Ship Cleanliness & Maintenance	5	Gym, Spa & Sports Facilities	4.5
Public Comfort/Space	4	Children's Facilities	4
Decor	4	Enjoyment Factor	4

THE SHIP IN GENERAL *Radiance of the Seas* was one of Royal Caribbean's first ships of the 21st century, as well as being one of the first vessels in a new class, and the class continues the line's tradition of being an innovator in the industry. Highlights include a billiards room with custom-made, self-leveling tables (in case there are big waves) and a revolving bar in the disco. The ships are designed to remind guests that they are at sea. With that goal in mind, they feature huge expanses of glass (adding up to over 3 acres) in some rooms through which to view the passing Alaska scenery. You won't even miss the views when you are in the 12-story lobby elevators because they, too, are made of glass and face the ocean. Even the Internet cafe has an ocean view! These ships are slightly more upscale than the line's other vessels—Royal Caribbean seems to have borrowed a page from sister company Celebrity. They feature wood, marble, and lots of nice fabrics and artwork, adding up to a pretty, low-key decor that lets the views provide most of the visual drama.

CABINS Staterooms on *Radiance* are larger than on the *Rhapsody*—the smallest is 165 square feet—and more come with verandas than on the earlier vessels. All rooms are equipped with an interactive TV, telephone, computer jack, vanity table, refrigerator/minibar, and hair dryer. Suites also come with a veranda, sitting area with a sofa bed, dry bar, stereo and VCR, and bathtub and double sinks. The Royal Suite on each ship has a separate bedroom (with a king-size bed) and living room, a whirlpool bathtub, and a baby grand piano. Family staterooms and suites can accommodate five. Fourteen rooms are wheelchair-accessible.

Cabins & Rates

Cabins	Per Diem Rates	Sq. Ft.	Fridge	Hair Dryer	Sitting Area	TV
Inside	$78	170	yes	no	no	yes
Outside	$157–$214*	185	yes	yes	yes	yes
Suites	$264–$1,107	293–1,001	yes	yes	yes	yes

**with balcony*

PUBLIC AREAS The ship is full of little surprises. There's that billiards room we mentioned and a card club with five tables dedicated to poker. Of course, you can also find more gaming options in the ship's massive French Art Nouveau–inspired Casino Royale (although dice-players will be disappointed by the less-than-friendly odds). Bookworms will want to check out the combo bookstore and coffee shop.

The numerous cushy bars and lounges include champagne and piano bars. If you tire of the ocean views, you can gaze into the atrium, eight decks below, from a portholelike window in the floor of the Crown and Anchor Lounge. The ship's Viking Crown Lounge holds the disco and its revolving bar, as well as an intimate cabaret area. The three-level theater recalls the glacial landscapes of not only Alaska, but the North Pole as well.

Other public rooms include a show lounge, conference center, library, shopping mall, and business center. For kids, there's a children's center equipped with computer and crafts stations. Teens get their own hangout space. There's also a video arcade.

DINING OPTIONS The elegant two-level main dining room features a grand staircase, but is a rather noisy space. Casual buffet breakfasts and lunches are provided in the Windjammer Café, while casual dinners, with waiter service, are enjoyed in the Windjammer Café and the Seaview Café. The ship also features two reservations-only restaurants that come with a cover charge: Chops Grill, serving steaks and chops for $25 per person, and Portofino, serving Italian cuisine for $20 per person. Both are a big step beyond the regular dining. Pizza and an assortment of other fast food selections are served in the solarium.

POOL, FITNESS, SPA & SPORTS FACILITIES For the active sort, there's a rock-climbing wall and a 9-hole mini–golf course designed as a baroque garden, of all things. There is a nice spa (including a sauna and steam rooms), an oceanview fitness center with dozens of machines (including 18 Stairmaster treadmills), a jogging track, a sports court (including basketball), golf simulators (for those who like to play virtual golf), and three swimming pools—one outside, one enclosed (the indoor pool has an African theme complete with 17-ft.-high stone elephants and cascading waterfalls), and the third a teen/kiddie pool with slide. Whirlpools can be found in the solarium and near the outdoor pool.

Rhapsody of the Seas

Rhapsody of the Seas *(photo: Royal Caribbean International)*

The Verdict

This ship has it all—a great spa, good shopping, and lots of glass for premium viewing of the passing Alaska scenery.

Specifications

Size (in Tons)	78,491	Crew	765
Passengers (Double Occ.)	1,998	Passenger/Crew Ratio	2.6 to 1
Space/Passenger Ratio	39 ft. to 1	Year Launched	1998
Total Cabins/Veranda Cabins	999/229	Last Major Refurbishment	2000

Frommer's Ratings (Scale of 1–5)

★★★½

Cabin Comfort & Amenities	3.5	Dining Options	3.5
Ship Cleanliness & Maintenance	4	Gym, Spa & Sports Facilities	4
Public Comfort/Space	3.5	Children's Facilities	4
Decor	3.5	Enjoyment Factor	3.5

THE SHIP IN GENERAL The *Rhapsody* is a true floating city, with trappings from multimillion-dollar art collections to a wide range of onboard facilities. Plenty of nice touches—a sumptuous, big-windowed health club/spa with lots of health and beauty treatments, and loads of fine shopping, dining, and entertainment options—give the *Rhapsody* the feel of a top-flight shore resort. But also like a popular resort, the ship sometimes feels crowded.

CABINS Staterooms are not large—inside rooms measure 138 square feet and outside ones 153 square feet—but do have small sitting areas. All staterooms have TVs, phones, twin beds that convert to queens, ample storage space, and well-lit, moderately sized bathrooms. TVs feature movies, news, and information channels, and excursion and debarkation talks are rebroadcast in-room just in case you missed any information. Nearly a quarter of the staterooms have private verandas, and about a third of the rooms are designed to accommodate third and fourth guests. For bigger digs, check out the Royal Suite—it measures a mammoth 1,150 square feet and even has a grand piano. Fourteen rooms on the ship are wheelchair-accessible.

Cabins & Rates

Cabins	Per Diem Rates	Sq. Ft.	Fridge	Hair Dryer	Sitting Area	TV
Inside	$75	138	no	no	yes	yes
Outside	$104–$168*	153	some	no	yes	yes
Suites	$185–$857	1,150	yes	no	yes	yes

**with balcony*

PUBLIC AREAS The *Rhapsody* soars 11 stories above the waterline and features a seven-story glass-walled atrium with glass elevators (a la Hyatt Regency) and a winding brass-trimmed staircase. At the top of the staircase, the Viking Crown Lounge affords a 360-degree view of the passing scenery. You'll also appreciate the view through the glass walls of the bi-level dining room, although the dining room has no stern views (the galley is placed behind the dining room). Actually, other than in the windowless casino and show lounge, there are great views to be found virtually everywhere on this ship—perfect for scoping glaciers.

A playroom, teen center, and video arcade provide plenty to keep kids happily occupied while parents relax, gamble, attend one of the many activities (there are dozens to select from each week, including informative nature lectures), take in a show, or dance the night away in the disco or one of numerous lounges and bars, which include a champagne/caviar bar and piano bar. Other rooms include a card room, a library, several shops, and a conference room.

DINING OPTIONS Meals are served both in the windowed, two-story dining room and in the casual, open-seating Windjammer Café (an indoor/outdoor facility open for breakfast and lunch); so there's freedom as to when you dine and, since the menus in each venue are different, choices as to what you'll eat. Pizza and other treats are served in the solarium.

POOL, FITNESS, SPA & SPORTS FACILITIES The spa on the ship is a soothing respite from the hubbub of ship life. It offers a wide selection of treatments, as well as the standard steam rooms and saunas. Adjacent to the spa, the spacious solarium has a pool, lounge chairs, floor-to-ceiling windows, and a retractable glass ceiling. This is a peaceful place for repose before or after a spa treatment, or anytime at all. Surprisingly, the gym is small for the ship's size—and in comparison to those on the megaliners of Carnival, Holland America Line, and Celebrity—but it's well equipped.

The main pool area has four whirlpools, and there are two more in the solarium. The observatory on deck (complete with stargazing equipment) is protected from wind by glass windbreaks. The *Rhapsody* also has a cushioned jogging track and a basketball half-court.

12 Silversea

110 E. Broward Blvd., Fort Lauderdale, FL 33301. ✆ **800/722-9955**. Fax 954/522-4477. www.silversea.com.

THE LINE IN A NUTSHELL There's no argument. Silversea is a very worthy member of the small number of operators of truly luxurious small to midsize ships. The only rival to its *Silver Shadow* in that category in Alaska this year is Regent's *Seven Seas Navigator*. Silversea isn't in Alaska every year, though this will mark its fourth year in a row in the market. It likes to give past passengers as much variety as possible, so some years it chooses to move from the 49th State to deploy its ships in more exotic trades—Southeast Asia, South America, and the like. And by adding in its newest ship to the deployment mix even more options become available.

THE EXPERIENCE Silversea represents the last word in elegance and service. Spacious accommodations, all oceanview suites, no tipping expected, free beverages (alcoholic and otherwise), swift and caring baggage handling—these are the hallmarks of the Silversea product.

Pros

- **All-around excellence.** A no-tipping policy is always a hit and the cuisine, open seating for meals, exemplary service, and great accommodations make Silversea well worth the money for those who want something special.
- **Surprisingly little formality.** Considering the economic status of most of the passengers, there's very little stuffiness.
- **A huge number of private verandas.** More than 80% of the suites on the *Silver Shadow* have this desirable feature.

Cons

- **Not a great deal of nightlife.** Although the ship has a show lounge, it's not really big enough for anything overly lavish. The line keeps changing its program relative to production shows or cabaret acts. On a recent cruise there were three full shows. By summer of 2011, that may have changed again.

THE FLEET The *Silver Shadow,* which joined the fleet in 2000, is one of six Silversea ships and it's the only one that cruises to Alaska. Its twin, the *Silver Whisper,* entered service the following year. The others are the smaller and virtually identical *Silver Cloud* (1994) and *Silver Wind* (1995), as well as *Prince Albert II,* the company's expedition ship (2008). Launched in late 2009 was the line's newest ship, the *Silver Spirit.*

PASSENGER PROFILE Guests tend to be in their 50s and up. They are generally well educated, with definite ideas on just what luxury means in accommodations, cuisine, and service. And they have the means to pay for it!

DINING Food is one of Silversea's strengths—both in preparation and in presentation—not only in the main dining room (known simply as The Restaurant), but also in the breakfast/lunch buffets in La Terrazza as well. That room doubles as a low-capacity candle-lit Italian restaurant in the evening.

Silversea serves very acceptable complimentary wine with dinner (and at other meals), but if you must upgrade to something really, really expensive (Opus One and Dom Perignon are a couple of tipples that come to mind) you should expect to pay the going rate. But there are many mid-priced options by the bottle as well.

ACTIVITIES In the last couple of years, Silversea has significantly enhanced its onboard enrichment program. Naturalists, historians, well-known authors, award-winning chefs, and wine experts host excellent sessions, often targeted for the specific cruising location. The line has also introduced a Cooking School with state-of-the-art cooking theaters that allow chefs to present a variety of specialized cooking classes and demonstrations on every cruise.

CHILDREN'S PROGRAM Silversea normally does not have a children's program but was putting one in place for Alaska 2011 at press time. There will be youth counselors based on the number of children on board and activities will be defined accordingly.

ENTERTAINMENT It's just not possible to stage extravagant song-and-dance presentations on a ship—and a stage—as small as this one, but the vessel's team of seven singers and dancers does an excellent job nonetheless as they put on three production shows every week. On other nights there may be cabaret acts or movies in the main theater. Outside the main show room, there's usually a small combo for dancing (no disco, please!). The library has an ample supply of books.

Silversea Fleet Itineraries

Ship	Itineraries
Silver Shadow	**7- to 10-night Inside Passage:** North- and southbound between Vancouver, B.C. and Anchorage and Seward, visiting Ketchikan, Sitka, Sawyer Glacier, Hubbard Glacier, Juneau, and Skagway (May–Sept).

SERVICE This is uniformly of the highest order. These people could take their places in the finest restaurants and hotels ashore—from where, in fact, many of them came. The finest compliment that anybody can pay the Silversea staff is that they provide the kind of service that you just don't notice. There is a self-service laundry and remarkably speedy valet service, including laundry and dry cleaning.

CRUISETOURS & ADD-ON PROGRAMS Silversea offers a small number of pre- and post-cruise land packages ranging from 3 to 6 nights. The shortest, least expensive one is a 3-night trip to Denali National Park, which starts at $1,699 per person. The most elaborate outing: a 6-night trip that includes a visit to the Eskimo settlement of Barrow above the Arctic Circle, which starts at $3,169 per person.

Silver Shadow

The Verdict

If this ship had a movie equivalent, it would have to be Jack Nicholson's *As Good as It Gets.*

Silver Shadow *(photo: Silversea Cruises)*

Specifications

Size (in Tons)	28,258	Crew	295
Passengers (Double Occ.)	382	Passenger/Crew Ratio	1.3 to 1
Space/Passenger Ratio	74 ft. to 1	Year Launched	2000
Total Cabins/Veranda Cabins	194/168	Last Major Refurbishment	2006

Frommer's Ratings (Scale of 1–5) ★★★★½

Cabin Comfort & Amenities	5	Dining Options	5
Ship Cleanliness & Maintenance	4.5	Gym, Spa & Sports Facilities	4
Public Comfort/Space	4.5	Children's Facilities	N/A
Decor	4.5	Enjoyment Factor	5

THE SHIP IN GENERAL This ship has one of the highest passenger/space ratios in the industry—technically determined as 74. That's a rather esoteric measurement that's arrived at by dividing the ship's gross tonnage (the volume of its interior space) by the lower berth capacity. It's complicated, but take our word for it—this ship is plenty spacious. The *Silver Shadow* takes Silversea's concept of luxury cruising to exceptional heights: walk-in closets, dressing table with hair dryer close at hand, real marble, double-vanity basin, bathtubs and separate showers, and DVD units in every stateroom. Butler service is provided for all suites (in other words, in all rooms). Wi-Fi access is available throughout the ship.

Cabins All outside, all suites. All but a few of them have private verandas. The smallest of the units—there are only a handful—have none. But they're a roomy 287 square feet, with picture windows. From there, the sizes go up and up, ranging from 345 square feet all the way up to 1,435 square feet. Every suite comes with convertible twin-to-queen beds, a minibar (stocked), and safes.

Two of the suites are wheelchair-accessible.

Cabins & Rates

Cabins	Per Diem Rates	Sq. Ft.	Fridge	Hair Dryer	Sitting Area	TV
Suites	$508–$1,725	287–1,435	yes	yes	yes	yes

PUBLIC AREAS The *Silver Shadow*'s two-level showroom is not the biggest we've ever seen, but it has good sightlines and it's a good place to while away an hour after dinner. There is a small cigar bar, known as the Humidor. The casino provides the usual array of money-speculating ventures—roulette, blackjack, and a few slots. You can have a drink in the casino, or in a bigger room simply called The Bar that is a great gathering spot with live music in the evening. The best place for a drink may well be the really small Lampadina just off the casino. The rear-facing Panorama Lounge has dancing to a range of musical styles, from ballroom and dinner dancing to rock-'n'-roll favorites to the latest club mixes. The ship's forward-facing Observation Lounge on the top deck is a quiet sanctuary for a game of chess or backgammon, conversation, reading, or watching the scenery. There's also a fully equipped eight-computer Internet center, card room, an upscale boutique, and an H. Stern jewelry store.

DINING OPTIONS Thanks to recent changes, there are now four dining venues on *Silver Shadow.* The Restaurant, the main dining room, serves breakfast, lunch, and dinner in elegant style. A more casual, buffet-style breakfast and lunch are served at the indoor/outdoor La Terrazza—and in the evening, this spot becomes a lovely specialty Italian restaurant. The menus no longer rotate among different regions; rather there's one menu with a very extensive list of offerings (reservations required, no cover charge). The third location, Le Champagne, has special Relais & Châteaux wine-pairing menus—an extravagant experience for connoisseurs at $200 per person—in an intimate setting on Deck 7 next to La Terrazza (reservations are absolutely necessary). But passengers now can just enjoy the meal for $30 per person with no wines included. The fourth dining venue is the outside poolside cafe for burgers, sandwiches, and salads at lunchtime; it turns into a wonderful outside grill restaurant at night. Of course, there's 24-hour room service and meals can be served course-by-course if so desired.

POOL, FITNESS, SPA & SPORTS FACILITIES The redesigned spa is, like most of the other public rooms, small when measured alongside its megaship competition. But, even with just four treatment rooms, it provides the same range of hydrotherapy, massage and beauty treatments, men's and women's saunas, and more. The line recently introduced a Wellness Program that combines daily activities, including yoga, Pilates, and meditation classes, with suggestions from its light and low-carb lunch and dinner menus. For fitness buffs, there is a newly expanded fitness center and a small jogging track. The beauty shop provides pedicures, manicures, and facials as well as hair styling. The one pool and two hot tubs are just right for a ship this size, and they are surrounded on two levels by lots of lounge chairs.

6

The Cruise Lines, Part 2: The Small Ships

Big ships show you Alaska while immersed in a vibrant, resortlike atmosphere; small ships let you see it from the waterline, with no distraction from anything un-Alaskan—no glitzy interiors, no big shows or loud music, no casinos, no spas, no crowds. On the small ships, you're immersed in the 49th state from the minute you wake up to the minute you fall asleep, and for the most part, you're left alone to form your own opinions, although there invariably will be a naturalist, a historian, or some such expert along to provide a running commentary en route.

The vessels listed in this chapter allow you to visit more isolated parts of the coast. Thanks to their smaller size and shallow draft (the amount of hull below the waterline), they can go places larger ships can't, and they have the flexibility to change their itineraries as opportunities arise—say, to go where whales have been sighted or to watch black bears on the shore. (Keep in mind, though, that ships are prohibited from "stalking" wildlife for too long: They must keep their distance and break off after a relatively short while.) Depending on the itinerary, small-ship ports of call might include popular stops such as Juneau, Sitka, or Ketchikan; lesser visited areas such as Elfin Cove or Warm Springs Harbor; or a Tlingit Native village such as Kake. The one thing you can be confident of is that all itineraries will include **glacier viewing** and **whale-watching.** Most of the itineraries also have time built in for passengers to explore the wilder parts of Alaska and for ferrying passengers ashore for hikes in wilderness areas. In some cases, the ships also carry **sea kayaks** and **Zodiac** inflatable boats for passenger use—allowing a type of exploration not available on big ships in Alaska.

Rather than glitzy entertainment, you'll likely get informal and informative **lectures** and sometimes video presentations on Alaskan wildlife, history, and Native culture. In most cases, at least some shore excursions are included in your cruise fare. Meals are served in open seatings, so you can sit where and with whom you like; and time spent huddled on the outside decks scanning for whales fosters great camaraderie among passengers. It must be noted, though, that the size of the ships precludes any kind of spacious dining rooms. Generally, they're quite small—some would say cramped. And on most of the smaller ships, room service is not an option—unless you are sick, of course.

Cabins on these ships don't always have TVs or telephones, and they tend to be tiny and sometimes spartan. (See individual reviews below for exceptions.) Most don't have e-mail access. There are no stabilizers on most small ships, so the ride can be bumpy in rough seas. Because the vessels tend to spend most of their time in the somewhat protected waters of the Inside Passage, this is not usually a major concern. But it can be a problem when the vessels ply open seas.

A Note on Ship Ratings

Because the small-ship experience is so completely different from the megaship experience, we've had to adjust our ratings. For instance, because all but a tiny fraction of these ships have just one dining room for all meals, we can't judge them by the same standard we use for ships with 5 or 10 different restaurants. So we've set the default **Dining Options** rating for these ships at 3, or "good," with points deducted if a restaurant is particularly uncomfortable and points added for any options above and beyond. Similarly, we've changed the "Gym, Spa & Sports Facilities" rating to **Adventure & Fitness Options** to reflect the fact that on small ships the focus is what's outside, not inside. Options covered in this category include kayaks, trips by inflatable Zodiac, and frequent hiking trips.

When reading the reviews in this chapter, bear in mind, too, that small-ship lines often measure their ships' gross register tonnage, or GRT (a measure of internal space, not actual weight), differently than the large lines. There's not even a definite standard within the small-ship market, so to compare ship sizes, it's best to just look at the number of passengers aboard. Also note that where GRT measures are nonstandard, passenger/space measurements are impossible or meaningless.

Another drawback of small ships is that they generally are not wheelchair-friendly; small ships are not a good choice for travelers with mobility issues. Small ships also may not be the best choice for families with children, unless those kids are avid nature buffs and are able to keep themselves entertained without a lot of outside stimuli.

READING THE REVIEWS

In this chapter, you'll also see the following terms used to describe the various small-ship experiences:

- **Soft adventure:** These ships don't provide onboard grandeur, organized activities, or entertainment, but instead give you a really close-up Alaska experience. These ships often avoid large ports.
- **Active adventure:** These ships function less like cruise ships than like base camps. Passengers use them only to sleep and eat, getting off the ship for hiking and kayaking excursions every day.
- **Port-to-port:** These ships are for people who want to visit the popular Alaska ports (and some lesser known ones), but also want the flexible schedules and maneuverability of a small ship and a more homey experience than you would find aboard a glitzy big ship.

RATES

Cruise rates in these reviews are brochure rates. Some discounts may apply, including early booking and last-minute offers (see more in chapter 3), although small-ship lines do not traditionally discount their fares as much as bigger ship lines. As in chapter 5, all rates have been calculated by nights spent on ship, based on 7-night sailings, unless otherwise indicated. Note that, in general, small ships are more expensive—often significantly so—than the large ships operating in Alaska. It costs more to provide the more intimate experience of small ships and that extra cost is passed on to passengers.

TIPPING

Tipping on small ships is not exactly standardized, as it tends to be on the big ships. It varies quite wildly from company to company. Gratuities on the following lines are pooled among the crew. Below is a rundown of suggested tips per passenger, for a 1-week cruise:

- **American Safari Cruises:** 5% to 10% of the cost of the cruise.
- **Lindblad Expeditions:** $56 to $70 ($8–$10 per day).

DRESS CODE

The word is *casual.* You're fine with polo shirts, jeans, khakis, shorts, and a fleece pullover and Gore-Tex shell. Having a pair of rubber sandals or old sneakers is handy as going ashore in rubber landing crafts might require you to step out into the surf. Hiking boots are also recommended.

1 American Safari Cruises

3826 18th Ave. W., Seattle, WA 98119. © **888/862-8881**. Fax 206/283-9322. www.AmericanSafariCruises.com.

THE LINE IN A NUTSHELL Directed toward the slightly jaded high-end traveler, American Safari Cruises (ASC) sails luxury soft-adventure cruises aboard three full-fledged luxury yachts.

THE EXPERIENCE American Safari Cruises promises an intimate, all-inclusive yacht cruise to more out-of-the-way stretches of the Inside Passage—and it succeeds admirably. The price is considerable—but so is the pampering. The company's three vessels carry between 12 and 36 guests, guaranteeing unparalleled flexibility, intimacy, and privacy. Once passenger interests become apparent, the expedition leader shapes the cruise around them. Black-bear aficionados can chug off in a Zodiac boat for a better look, active adventurers can explore the shoreline in one of the yacht's kayaks, and slacker travelers can relax aboard ship. A crew-to-passenger ratio of about one to two ensures that a cold drink, a good meal, or a sharp eagle-spotting eye is always nearby on the line's comfortable yachts, which range in length from 105 to 145 feet.

Pros

- **Near-private experience.** With only a handful of fellow passengers, it's like having a yacht to yourself. In fact, if you have the money and the inclination, you can literally have the yacht to yourself: Whole charters are available, for a stiff price. A 7-night charter of, say, the *Safari Quest* (capacity 22 passengers) could set you back a cool $160,000 or so midseason in 2010.
- **Built-in shore excursions.** All off-ship excursions and activities are included in the cruise fare, as are premium drinks.
- **Night anchorages.** A great boon to light sleepers is that the route taken allows time for the vessels to anchor overnight, making for quieter sleeping than aboard most ships, which travel through the night.
- **More time to explore.** In 2010, all three yachts will operate 7-night round-trip Juneau cruises that include an unusual 2 days for exploration in Glacier Bay National park—allowing time for hiking with a park ranger on a glacier or into the rainforest, or even kayaking.

American Safari Cruises Fleet

Ship	Itineraries
Safari Explorer	**7-night Discoverers' Glacier Bay:** Round-trip from Juneau, with an extended, 2-day visit to Glacier Bay, plus Icy Strait, Frederick Sound, Endicott Arm/Dawes Glacier, and Admiralty Island (May–Sept).
Safari Quest	**7-night Glacier Bay:** Same as *Safari Explorer.*
Safari Spirit	**7-night Glacier Bay:** Same as *Safari Explorer.*

**In addition to the itineraries above, all three yachts offer 14-night repositioning cruises between Seattle and Juneau.*

Cons

- **The price.** Shore excursions and drinks are included, but even when you remove these costs, the price is still high (the least expensive accommodations start at about $710 a head per night). At a recommended 5% to 10% of the tariff, gratuities can add mightily to the outlay. You pay for all the luxury you get.

THE FLEET The line's newest yacht, the 36-passenger *Safari Explorer,* entered service just in time for the cruise season in 2008, after a 10-month refurbishment costing $3.5 million. The 22-passenger *Safari Quest* (1992) and the 12-passenger *Safari Spirit* (1991) are the closest things you'll find to private yachts in the Alaska cruise business. They're sleek, they're stylish, and they're as far as you can get from the megaship experience without owning your own boat.

PASSENGER PROFILE Passengers—almost always couples—tend to be more than comfortably wealthy and range from about 45 to 65 years of age. Most hope to get close to nature without sacrificing luxury. (You know the old saying: "Some people will go to the ends of the air-conditioned earth in search of adventure.") They've paid handsomely for food, drink, and service, all of which American Safari delivers—and then some. Dress is always casual, in a Saks Fifth Avenue sort of way, with comfort being the prime goal.

DINING Shipboard chefs assail guests with multiple course meals and clever snacks (wild mushroom cups, rack of lamb, thyme-infused king salmon, amaretto cheesecake, fresh-baked bread). They barter with nearby fishing boats for the catch of the day, and raid local markets for the freshest fruits and vegetables—say, strawberries the size of a cub's paw and potent strains of basil and cilantro. Between meals, snacks such as Gorgonzola and brie with pears, walnuts, and table crackers are set out. Guests may always serve themselves from the ludicrously well-stocked bar, which during our recent visit had two kinds of sherry and four brands of gin alone, all of them premium.

ACTIVITIES When passengers aren't eating or drinking, an expedition leader is helping them into Zodiac boats or kayaks to investigate black bears along the shoreline or prancing river otters, or to navigate fjords packed with ice floes and lolling seals. Expeditions include trips to cannery towns and remote villages with boardwalks, where local people receive the yachts more personally and gracefully than they might a larger ship. Activities throughout the day are well spaced, with many opportunities to see wildlife.

From time to time, local bush pilots may swoop down for a landing beside the ships and take two or three passengers for a whirl over a glacier or a nearby fjord. Because these are private operations, they're not included in the cruise fare.

CHILDREN'S PROGRAM There is none of any consequence, although kids are welcome. A selected few of the sailings are designated "Kids in Nature" outings on which an expedition guide tailors educational programs for the younger set.

ENTERTAINMENT A big-screen TV in the main lounge forms a natural center for listening to impromptu lectures during the day and watching a movie at night. Guests may choose from a library of 300-plus DVDs (all cabins have flatscreen TV/DVDs) or opt for a casual game of cards or Scrabble in the yacht's Wine Library or Observation Lounge.

Given that these vessels spend a huge percentage of their time at sea—far more than other ships—land visits are kept to a minimum. The amount of time exploring back bays and narrow waterways results in extreme encounters with whales that sometimes can be seen lunging out of the water (during feeding), dolphins, bears on the beach, sea lions, sea otters, mountain goats, eagles, and even moose and wolves inside Glacier Bay.

SERVICE Crew members cosset passengers cheerfully and discreetly, fussing over such details as the level of cilantro in lunchtime dishes or making elaborate cocktails from the fully stocked open bar. They've even been known to call ahead to upcoming anchorages to arrange for a passenger's favorite brand of beer to be brought aboard. Laundry service is not available onboard except in "emergency situations." (The company recommends, by the way, a crew gratuity of 5%–10% at the end of each voyage; a hefty sum when you're paying, say, $4,500 for a cruise.)

CRUISETOURS & ADD-ON PROGRAMS American Safari offers add-on trips to lodges in the interior of Alaska at Winterlake and Redoubt Bay. Transportation to the lodges is by floatplane, and the stays include gourmet meals, animal watching, and more. The line also sells pre- and post-stopover packages in Juneau at the Goldbelt Hotel.

Safari Explorer • Safari Quest • Safari Spirit

Safari Quest *(photo: American Safari Cruises)*

The Verdict

Aah—the good life!

Specifications

Size (in Tons)	698/345/231	Crew	15/9/6
Passengers (Double Occ.)	36/22/12	Passenger/Crew Ratio	2 to 1 (approx.)
Passenger/Space Ratio	N/A*	Year Launched	2000/1992/1991
Total Cabins/Veranda Cabins		Last Major Refurbishment	
Safari Explorer	18/2	*Safari Explorer*	2007
Safari Quest	11/4	*Safari Spirit*	2005
Safari Spirit	6/2	*Safari Quest*	2006

**These ships' sizes were measured using a different scale than the others in this book, so comparison is not possible.*

Frommer's Ratings (Scale of 1–5) ★★★★ ½

Cabin Comfort & Amenities	5	Dining Options	3
Ship Cleanliness & Maintenance	4	Adventure & Fitness Options	4
Public Comfort/Space	5	Children's Facilities	N/A
Decor	4.5	Enjoyment Factor	5

THE SHIPS IN GENERAL More private yacht than cruise ship, these three vessels are an oddity in the cruise community, and as far from the Alaska cruising norm as it's possible to get. Some ships in Alaska are so big, you sort of feel they should have their own zip code, maybe a couple of time zones. The biggest of these three, the *Safari Explorer,* is just 145 feet long. The ASC ships have sleek, contoured, Ferrari-looking exteriors. Inside, virtually no area is out of bounds, including the captain's work space: He'll welcome your visit, provided he's not involved in some critical nautical maneuver at the time. It all leads to the feeling that you're vacationing on an impossibly rich friend's space-age yacht.

CABINS Sleeping quarters are comfortable and clean, with large beds outfitted with memory foam Tempur-Pedic® mattresses, adequate light, and art (of varying quality, if hardly museum-standard) on the walls. Bathrooms are roomy, even in the standard cabins; cabins on the *Safari Quest* have showers only. The showers shoot a steady but not spectacular stream of reliably hot water. On the *Safari Explorer* there are six premium cabins that have a combination Jacuzzi tub/shower (a feature also standard with all six cabins on the *Safari Spirit*). The top category cabins have sliding glass doors and a step-out balcony, a small sitting area, and even a separate living room. Down below, deluxe rooms are tidy, filled with a surprising amount of natural light, and fairly spacious. All staterooms have iPod docking stations, binoculars, hair dryers, heated tile floors in the bathrooms, robes, slippers, and flatscreen TV/DVDs. There are no special facilities for travelers with disabilities. The *Safari Explorer* and *Safari Quest* have cabins designed specifically for single occupancy and are priced accordingly.

Cabins & Rates

Cabins	Per Diem Rates	Sq. Ft.	Fridge	Hair Dryer	Sitting Area	TV
Safari Quest						
Outside	\$785–\$970*/ \$592–\$728**	125–168	no	yes	some	yes
Safari Spirit						
Outside	\$870–\$1,242*/ \$714–\$857**	172–266	no	yes	some	yes
Safari Explorer						
Outside	\$699–\$999*/ \$578–\$864**	133–275	some	yes	some	yes

**Rates are per day, based on 7-night cruises.*
***Rates are per day, based on 14-night cruises.*

PUBLIC AREAS Sitting rooms are intimate and luxurious, almost as if they've been transported intact from a spacious suburban home. Four or five prime vantage points for spotting wildlife (one is a hot tub!) ensure as little or as much privacy as you desire. All public rooms have generous panoramic windows for gazing out when you can't be on deck because of cold or inclement weather. Meals are served fully plated at one seating in a casual room, usually when the yacht is anchored in some quiet cove or off some incredibly beautiful shoreline or mountain range. Expect paper napkins at lunch, cloth at dinner—and gourmet cuisine. There are 24-hour espresso/coffee/tea facilities, a fully stocked open bar, and a small book/DVD library.

POOL, FITNESS, SPA & SPORTS FACILITIES There are stair-steppers and elliptical machines on all three yachts, and sea kayaks for passenger use (15 on *Safari Explorer,* eight on *Safari Quest,* and four on *Safari Spirit*). All three yachts have hot tubs on the top deck. The *Safari Explorer* and *Safari Spirit* also have saunas. The best equipped of all is the *Explorer,* which also has a small dedicated fitness area. The Wellness Director/licensed masseuse on the *Safari Explorer* leads yoga classes in the early mornings and provides each passenger with a complimentary massage.

2 InnerSea Discoveries

3826 18th Ave. W., Seattle, WA 98119. ✆ **877/901-1009.** Fax 206/283-9322. www.InnerSeaDiscoveries.com.

THE LINE IN A NUTSHELL Looking for an off-the-beaten-path adventure in Alaska? That's what it's all about at InnerSea Discoveries, a new line for 2011.

THE EXPERIENCE As this book went to press, InnerSea Discoveries had yet to sail its first cruise (scheduled for May 2011). But the line comes with a strong pedigree, and its focus—getting adventure-minded vacationers into the most beautiful and wildlife-filled corners of Southeast Alaska's Inside Passage—has many Alaska tourism-watchers excited. The two-vessel outfit is the brainchild of Dan Blanchard and Tim Jacox, who revolutionized luxury cruising in Alaska in 1997 with the launch of American Safari Cruises. This time around, the duo aims to offer a more affordable way for adventurers to explore the region. Operating as a sister brand to American Safari, InnerSea Discoveries will cost less than half as much as its sibling, with pricing starting around $300 per person per day (American Safari trips often start at $850 per person per day or more). The ships are a bit bigger than at American Safari, with room for 49 passengers (as compared to 12 to 36), not everything is included in the price, and the crew-to-passenger ratio of about one to three is not quite as impressive. But in many ways, the concept is similar. By forgoing calls in Southeast Alaskan towns such as Skagway and Haines, InnerSea's ships will have more time to explore the many remote (and little visited) bays, fjords, and glaciers of the region. Getting off the ship and interacting with the landscape in a meaningful way will be a focus, and the company says the voyages should appeal to adventurers who thrive on new experiences and want to push themselves physically, mentally, and emotionally. Still, the cruises are being designed so passengers who don't want to participate in the most active adventure activities won't be left out.

Pros

- **Intimate experience.** With barely two dozen cabins, these aren't ships that are overrun with tourists. It's almost like having your own private vessel to take you into the wilderness.
- **More time outdoors.** If it's nature and wildlife you love, this line could be hard to beat. Eschewing port towns, InnerSea's two vessels will pretty much spend their entire weeks exploring the more remote tree-lined fjords and inlets of the mountainous Southeast region in search of wildlife and natural beauty.

Cons

- **The price.** Sure, it's a lot less than its sister line American Safari Cruises. But at $300 and up per person, per day, it's still not inexpensive.

THE FLEET While the line is new, its ships aren't. InnerSea Discoveries is launching with two vessels that have been out of commission for several years, the 49-passenger *Wilderness Discoverer* and the 49-passenger *Wilderness Adventurer.* Parent company American Safari purchased the vessels in 2009 from a bank that had held them since the bankruptcy of Glacier Bay Cruise Lines in 2006. The two ships, originally built for 80- and 66-passengers, respectively, have gone through a top-to-bottom overhaul over the past year. InnerSea has given the main salon areas of the ships a new look and feel aimed at making them hubs for passengers to share their experiences of the day. The line has re-shaped the bar areas to extend into the salon and added flatscreen TVs that drop from the ceiling so passengers can pop in videos shot during the day. Cabins have been updated with cabinetry designed to be more suitable for outdoor gear storage; reading lamps above the beds and softer lighting overall; flatscreen TVs/DVDs; iPod docks in each cabin; Tempur-Pedic® mattresses (pretty much unheard of on expedition vessels); upgraded linens/bedspreads; artwork; and some other nice touches such as new sink fixtures.

PASSENGER PROFILE The company is anticipating a relatively young, outdoorsy type of customer—the kind of people who shop at outdoor store REI, says one manager. Most passengers will be in their mid-30s to mid-60s in age, with a smattering younger and older. Multi-generational families will be a solid market as the line won't have the age restrictions imposed at sister American Safari Cruises. The size and number of passengers and the environment onboard the small ships will be conducive to families with teens or younger children to travel on any departure. InnerSea managers are calling the experience an "un-cruise," as they expect to attract a number of people who have not cruised before and who would not be interested in a big ship experience. The idea is that this is a vacation to the outdoors of Southeast Alaska that only is on a ship because that's the easiest way to get people into the region's remote back bays and hidden areas. It's not about cruising but about getting out into the wilderness.

DINING The company is promising the same sort of highly-trained kitchen staff as on its upscale American Safari ships. Breakfast and lunches will be served mostly buffet style, with dinner at a single seating in ship dining rooms. The ships will feature fresh Alaska-caught seafood (some purchased along the way from wilderness-based families who make their living fishing or running their own oyster farms); pastries, breads, and desserts baked from scratch; and local flavors/specialties. Coffee and espresso will be available 24 hours. Lunches will be provided from the galley for extended hikes and kayaking excursions (some of which will be all-day, 6- to 8-hr. affairs).

ACTIVITIES Getting outdoors is what it's all about at InnerSea Discoveries. When passengers aren't eating or drinking, an expedition leader is helping them into Zodiac boats or kayaks to explore glaciers and icebergs and to look for wildlife such as whales, bears, and sea lions. Outings also will include landings for hikes through remote forests, paddle boarding, snorkeling, "polar bear club swims," fishing, birding, and glacier walks. The line even plans optional overnight backpacking and kayaking trips from the ship.

By forgoing calls in Southeastern Alaska towns such as Skagway and Haines, InnerSea's ships promise much more time to explore rarely visited and sparsely populated

InnerSea Discoveries Fleet

Ship	Itineraries
Wilderness Discoverer	**7-night Alaska Inside Passage: Eastern Coves:** One-way from Juneau to Ketchikan with a stop in Wrangell and visits to Windham Bay, Thomas Bay, Ideal Cove, LeConte Bay, Yes Bay, and Misty Fjords National Monument (May–Sept).
Wilderness Discoverer	**7-night Alaska Inside Passage: Western Coves:** One-way from Ketchikan to Juneau with a stop in Klawoch and visits to El Capitan Passage and Cave, Devilfish Bay, Trocadero Bay, Little Port Walter, Bay of Pillars, Frederick Sound, and Endicott Arm (May–Sept).
Wilderness Adventurer	**7-night Alaska Inside Passage: Eastern Coves:** Same as *Wilderness Discoverer.*
Wilderness Adventurer	**7-night Alaska Inside Passage: Western Coves:** Same as *Wilderness Discoverer.*
Wilderness Discoverer	**14-night Alaskan Inside Passage: Ultimate Adventure:** A two-week trip that combines the *Discoverer's* Eastern Coves and Western Coves itineraries above.
Wilderness Adventurer	**14-night Alaskan Inside Passage: Ultimate Adventure:** Same as *Wilderness Discoverer.*
Wilderness Discoverer	**14-night Wilderness Passages of Discovery:** One-way trips from Seattle to Juneau (on May 7) and Juneau to Seattle (on Sept 10).

parts of the region. Caving will be offered on the northbound itinerary on Prince of Wales Island (Forest Service guides will lead passengers into El Capitan cave, the largest mapped cave in North America). On the southbound Eastern Coves voyage, another adventure offering will be a river boat trip up the Stikine River to search for wildlife such as moose and to visit Shakes Lake and possibly Shakes Glacier. Several optional full-fledged fishing trips also will be available (at an extra charge) for interested passengers on each itinerary. Fully-outfitted boats will take fishermen to backcountry fishing sites for king salmon, halibut or, in one case, fly fishing and also crabbing.

The ships also will be stopping (anchoring) close to Wrangell on the southbound itinerary and the native community of Klawock going northbound. Billed as non-traditional port calls, these won't be the typical cruise stop where a bus awaits to take people around the town, says the line. Instead, in the case of Klawock, passengers can kayak to a landing area near the totem carving shed just outside of Klawock where elders will be instructing native teens on how to carve and restore ancient totem poles; others may choose to stroll over to the totem park; others to make their way through town; or, some may choose to continue to take advantage of the daily activities from the ships such as kayaking or exploring by skiff. In Wrangell, passengers similarly can experience the native tribal house on Chief Shakes Island by skiff; elders will be there to interpret the totems. Or they can visit town, explore the petroglyphs, or fish.

The line notes it will carry high-quality equipment to use during outings, including top-of-the-line sea kayaks; trekking poles; some backpacks and day packs; binoculars; rain pants and slickers; mud boots; paddle boards; and dry suits (some, but not for all guests) for water activities.

CHILDREN'S PROGRAM There is no formal children's program, but the line's outdoorsy focus makes it a natural for animal-loving kids, and the line says activities such as kayaking and hiking will be tailored for all ages. Children ages 12 and under receive discounted rates on all departures, and three 2011 departures on the Wilderness Adventurer (June 25, July 23, and August 13) are being aimed specifically at families. Designated "Alaska Family Discovery" voyages, the two family voyages are being sold with even higher discounts for children.

ENTERTAINMENT In the evenings after dinner, passengers will have opportunities to share discoveries made during the day in the main salon. The bar area will be arranged to invite socializing and discussion, with a setting conducive to conversation, with 10 to 12 microbrews to choose from at the full bar. Flatscreen TVs will drop from overhead for passengers to connect video devices to show off shots from the day's adventures. Educational presentations also will be provided by onboard naturalists on select nights, with topics such as whales, glaciers, and native cultures. Passengers also can relax in the evening under the Alaska night sky in the top-deck hot tub or saunas (added during the line's refurbishment of the ships). Some may choose to schedule a massage with the onboard wellness director/licensed masseuse (extra charge). Passengers and crew also will be encouraged to show off their singing or musical talents in the main salon, and there will be a night or two on every voyage where Alaskans who live in the wilderness will come aboard to have dinner with passengers and stay afterwards to talk about their unique and rugged lifestyle. DVDs also will be available for passengers to watch in their cabins.

SERVICE The line is promising the same sort of top-notch service found on sister American Safari Cruises. Naturalists and other English-speaking crew members will facilitate all off-ship and onboard activities as well as serve meals and perform housekeeping duties.

CRUISETOURS & ADD-ON PROGRAMS The line says it plans to add interior land tours, which were under development at press time. The line also will offer pre- and post-cruise stopover packages in Ketchikan and Juneau.

Wilderness Discoverer • Wilderness Adventurer

The Verdict

Looking for a way to get off-the-beaten-path in Alaska's Inside Passage? These two small ships will bring you right into the wilderness where bears and eagles outnumber humans.

Wilderness Adventurer *(photo: InnerSea Discoveries)*

Specifications

Size (in Tons)	99/89	Crew	16
Passengers (Double Occ.)	49	Passenger/Crew Ratio	3 to 1
Passenger/Space Ratio	N/A*	Year Launched	1992/1984
Total Cabins/Veranda Cabins	26/0	Last Major Refurbishment	2011/2010

**These ships' sizes were measured using a different scale than the others in this book, so comparison is not possible.*

Frommer's Ratings (Scale of 1–5) **NR**

Cabin Comfort & Amenities	NR	Dining Options	NR
Ship Cleanliness & Maintenance	NR	Adventure & Fitness Options	NR
Public Comfort/Space	NR	Children's Facilities	NR
Decor	NR	Enjoyment Factor	NR

THE SHIPS IN GENERAL Built as expedition ships, the similar sized *Wilderness Discoverer* and *Wilderness Adventurer* (the *Discoverer* is slightly longer) are capable of nimble exploration through nature's most dramatic hideaways. The shallow draft and hull design allow easy access to Southeast Alaska's wildlife-rich shores and glacially-fed inlets and serve as ideal "launching pads" for an array of daily adventure excursions. Fully-equipped small boats carried on the ships provide wilderness fishing several times on each voyage (for an extra charge). The interior spaces offer contemporary colors and a unique decor that mixes pub and National Park Service influences.

CABINS While not luxurious, cabins aren't spartan, either. All face outward and have view windows except for the lead-in Seafarer category (two cabins on each ship). Four large cabins added to the top deck of the *Discoverer* (labeled the Explorer category) offer a premium location for wildlife viewing and privacy, full bathrooms with full-sized shower, sitting area, and a full sofa that can be made out into a bed for a triple. The company has updated the decor and functionality of all cabins with softer lighting overhead as well as reading lamps above each bed; additional storage areas for adventure gear; new sink fixtures; a fresh color palette; new carpets; upgraded linens, bedspreads, and pillows; and new Tempur-Pedic® mattresses. Binoculars, alarm clocks, hair dryers, iPod docks, and flatscreen TVs/DVDs round out the amenities. With the exception of the Explorer category, cabins have bathroom facilities that are the expedition ship style: smaller in size with a shower curtain, with the sink and vanity outside the shower and bathroom.

Cabins & Rates

Cabins	Per Diem Rates	Sq. Ft.	Fridge	Hair Dryer	Sitting Area	TV
Wilderness Discoverer						
Outside	$255–$855*	90–180	no	yes	some	yes
Wilderness Adventurer						
Outside	$255–$570*	90–100	no	yes	no	yes

**Rates are per day, based on 7-night cruises.*

PUBLIC AREAS The main public area that passengers will congregate in during the evening is the main salon and, on the same deck, the dining room (the two areas essentially blend into each other, though they are delineated).

POOL, FITNESS, SPA & SPORTS FACILITIES There are hot tubs and two saunas on the top deck of each ship as well as exercise equipment such as elliptical cross trainers and exercise bikes. The ships also will offer complimentary yoga classes, with yoga mats onboard.

3 Lindblad Expeditions

96 Morton St., 9th Floor, New York, NY 10014. ✆ **800/397-3348** or 212/765-7740. Fax 212/265-3770. www.expeditions.com.

THE LINE IN A NUTSHELL In 1979, Sven-Olof Lindblad, son of adventure-travel pioneer Lars-Eric Lindblad, followed in his father's footsteps by forming Lindblad Expeditions, which specializes in providing environmentally sensitive, soft-adventure/educational cruises to remote places in the world, with visits to a few large ports. In 2004, Lindblad Expeditions entered into a mission-driven alliance with National Geographic. As pioneers of global exploration, the organizations work in tandem to produce innovative marine expedition programs and to promote conservation and sustainable tourism around the world. The venture lifts Lindblad's educational offerings out of the commonplace.

THE EXPERIENCE Lindblad's expedition cruises are explorative and informal, designed to appeal to the intellectually curious traveler seeking a vacation that's educational as well as relaxing. Passengers' time is spent learning about the life above and below the sea (from National Geographic experts and high-caliber expedition leaders and naturalists trained in botany, anthropology, biology, and geology) and observing the world either from the ship or on shore excursions, which are included in the cruise package. Lindblad Expeditions' crew and staff emphasize respect for the local ecosystem—the company's literature calls it "Responsible Travel"—and the company has won many awards for its commitment to conservation. Flexibility and spontaneity are keys to the Lindblad experience, as the route may be altered anytime to follow a pod of whales or school of dolphins. Depending on weather and sea conditions, there are usually two or three excursions every day.

Pros

- **Great expedition feeling.** Lindblad's programs have innovative, flexible itineraries; outstanding lecturers/guides; and a friendly, accommodating staff.
- **Built-in shore excursions.** Rather than relying on outside concessionaires for their shore excursions (which is the case with most other lines, big and small), Lindblad Expeditions runs its own. These excursions are an integral part of its cruises and are included in the cost of the cruise fare.
- **Highly knowledgeable experts onboard.** The partnership with National Geographic has resulted in many top National Geographic–affiliated photographers, explorers, scientists, and researchers joining the line's voyages. There are five naturalists on board every expedition, for a 12-to-1 passenger to naturalist ratio.

Cons

- **Cost.** Cruise fares tend to be a little higher than the line's small-ship competition.

THE FLEET The 62-passenger *National Geographic Sea Lion* and *National Geographic Sea Bird* (built in 1981 and 1982, respectively) are nearly identical in every respect. Both are basic vessels built to get you to beautiful spots and have a minimum of public rooms and conveniences: one dining room, one bar/lounge, and lots of deck space for wildlife and glacier viewing. There are no inside cabins or suites.

PASSENGER PROFILE Lindblad Expeditions tends to attract well-traveled and well-educated, professional, 55-plus couples who have "been there, done that" and are looking for something completely different in a cruise experience. The passenger mix

Lindblad Expeditions Fleet Itineraries

Ship	Itineraries
Sea Bird/Sea Lion	**11-night Alaska, British Columbia, San Juan Islands:** North- and southbound between Juneau and Seattle, visiting Point Adolphus, Chichagof Island, Glacier Bay, Sitka, Frederick Sound, Misty Fjords, Alert Bay, and Johnstone Strait, B.C., and the San Juan Islands, Washington (Apr and Sept). **7-night Coastal Wilderness:** North- and southbound between Juneau and Sitka, visiting Tracy Arm, Petersburg, Frederick Sound, Chatham Strait, Glacier Bay, Point Adolphus, and Inian Pass (May–Aug).

may also include some singles and a smattering of younger couples. Although not necessarily frequent cruisers, many passengers are likely to have been on other Lindblad Expeditions programs, and share a common interest in history and wildlife.

DINING Hearty buffet breakfasts and lunches and sit-down dinners include a good variety of both hot and cold dishes with plenty of fresh fruits and vegetables. Many of the fresh ingredients are obtained from ports along the way, and meals may reflect regional tastes. (In Alaska, Lindblad chefs will search out sustainably caught local fish as part of an overall commitment to promoting sustainable cuisine.) Although far from haute cuisine, dinners are well prepared and presented, and are served at single open seatings that allow passengers to get to know each other by moving around to different tables. Lecturers and other staff members dine with passengers.

ACTIVITIES During the day, most activity takes place off the ship, aboard Zodiac boats or kayaks and/or on land excursions. While onboard, passengers entertain themselves with the usual small-ship activities: wildlife watching, gazing off into the wilderness, reading, and chatting. Shore excursions are included in the cruise fare. Lindblad also has an open-bridge policy—rare in the cruise industry—that gives travelers the opportunity to spend time on the bridge to observe and interact with the captain and staff.

CHILDREN'S PROGRAM Family cruising to Alaska is big business and Lindblad has stepped up to the plate and now has special family activities on all sailings led by specially-trained staff. Activities have a nature slant, such as exploring an Alaskan rainforest. Don't expect such big-ship features as a video arcade or playroom for the little ones, however.

ENTERTAINMENT Lectures and slide presentations are scheduled throughout the cruise, and documentaries or movies may be screened in the evening in the main lounge. Books about Alaska are found in each ship's small library. Many voyages have a special photo element that provides opportunities for travelers to learn from National Geographic photographers onboard.

SERVICE Dining room staff and room stewards are affable and efficient, and seem to enjoy their work. As with other small ships, there's no room service unless you're ill and unable to make it to the dining room.

CRUISETOURS & ADD-ON PROGRAMS The company offers no land packages in 2011.

Sea Bird • Sea Lion

The Verdict

Get up close and personal in Alaska on these comfortable small ships, and expect excellent commentary from knowledgeable naturalists along the way.

Sea Lion *(photo: Lindblad Expeditions)*

Specifications

Size (in Tons)	100	Crew	22
Passengers (Double Occ.)	62	Passenger/Crew Ratio	3.2 to 1
Passenger/Space Ratio	N/A*	Year Launched	1982/1981
Total Cabins/Veranda Cabins	31/0	Last Major Refurbishment	N/A

**These ships' sizes were measured using a different scale than the others in this book, so comparison is not possible.*

Frommer's Ratings (Scale of 1–5) ★★★½

Cabin Comfort & Amenities	3	Dining Options	3
Ship Cleanliness & Maintenance	4	Adventure & Fitness Options	5
Public Comfort/Space	3	Children's Facilities	N/A
Decor	3.5	Enjoyment Factor	4

THE SHIPS IN GENERAL The shallow-draft *National Geographic Sea Lion* and *National Geographic Sea Bird* are identical twins, right down to their decor schemes and furniture. Not flashy at all, they have just two public rooms and utilitarian but comfortable cabins.

CABINS Postage-stamp cabins are tight and functional rather than fancy. Each has twin or double beds, a closet (there are also drawers under the bed for extra storage), and a sink and mirror in the main room. Behind a folding door lies a Lilliputian bathroom with a head-style shower (toilet opposite the shower nozzle, all in one compact unit). All cabins are located outside and have picture windows that open to fresh breezes. The vessels have no wheelchair-accessible cabins.

Cabins & Rates

Cabins	Per Diem Rates	Sq. Ft.	Fridge	Hair Dryer	Sitting Area	TV
Outside	$706–$933*/ $640–$824**	118–152	no	no	no	no

**Rates are based on 7-night cruises.*
***Rates are per day based on an 11-night cruise; includes shore excursions.*

PUBLIC AREAS Public space is limited to the open sun deck and bow areas, the dining room, and an observation lounge that serves as the nerve center for activities. In the lounge, you'll find a bar; a library of atlases and books on Alaska's culture, geology, history, plants, and wildlife; a gift shop tucked into a closet; and audiovisual aids for the many naturalists' presentations.

DINING OPTIONS None.

POOL, FITNESS, SPA & SPORTS FACILITIES While there is no formal gym space, there are two outdoor exercise machines (bicycle and treadmill) and a 30-minute stretching class every morning on the top deck led by the wellness specialist. In addition, Lindblad's style of soft-adventure travel means you'll be taking frequent walks/hikes in wilderness areas, usually accessed via Zodiac landing craft. The ships offer a full line of wellness treatments through the LEXspa.

4 Alaska Marine Highway System

7559 N. Tongass Hwy., Ketchikan, AK 99901. ✆ **800/642-0066** or 907/465-3941. Fax 907/465-8824. www.ferryalaska.com.

In Alaska, which has fewer paved roads than virtually any other state, getting around can be a problem. There are local airlines, of course, and small private planes—lots and lots of small private planes, some with wheels, some with skis, some with floats for landing on water. (In fact, there are more private planes per capita in Alaska than in any other state in the union.) But given the weather conditions in many northland areas for large parts of the year, airplanes are not always the most reliable way of getting from Point A to Point B.

That's why the Alaska Marine Highway System (aka the Alaska Ferry, or AMHS) is so important. Sometimes in inclement weather, even the state capital, Juneau, cannot be reached by air (there are no roads of any consequence linking it with the rest of the state) and relies heavily on the ferryboats of the AMHS to bring in visitors, vehicles, supplies, and even, now and then, the legislators who run the state. (Although the AMHS relocated its administrative headquarters to Ketchikan in 2005, its reservations center remains in Juneau.)

Although the ferry system was originally created with the aim of providing Alaska's far-flung, often inaccessible smaller communities with essential transportation links with the rest of the state and with the Lower 48, the boats have developed a following in the tourism business as well. Each year, thousands of visitors eschew luxury cruise ships in favor of the more basic services of the 11 vessels of the AMHS. The service is of particular value to independent travelers, enabling visitors to come and go as they please among Alaska's outposts. All of the AMHS ferries carry both passengers and vehicles.

In 2005, AMHS was officially designated an "All American Road" by the U.S. Department of Transportation. To qualify for such recognition, according to federal rules, a road must have qualities that are nationally significant and contain features that do not exist elsewhere—it must be "a destination unto itself." AMHS definitely fits the bill.

The AMHS's southernmost port is Bellingham, Washington. Its network stretches throughout Southeast and Southcentral Alaska and out to the Aleutian island chain to the west of Anchorage.

THE LINE IN A NUTSHELL The ferries operate in three distinct areas—year-round in the Southeast or the Inside Passage (from Bellingham to Skagway/Haines); in Southcentral, which includes Prince William Sound, the Kenai Peninsula, and

Kodiak Island; and, in the summer months, the Southwest region, which includes the Aleutian chain. The Aleutian's service is not offered during the winter due to the extreme weather of the region. The seas become too rough, the fog too thick, and the cold too intense for the ferries to operate safely or profitably in the winter. See the website (www.ferryalaska.com) for details on the many routes that the AMHS operates and the ports that it services.

THE EXPERIENCE It must be stressed that ferry-riding vacations are different from cruise vacations, to say the least. Don't even think about one if you're looking for a lot of creature comforts—fancy accommodations, gourmet food, spa treatments, Broadway-style shows, and the rest. You won't find any of the above on the sturdy vessels of the AMHS. In fact, not all ferry passengers get sleeping berths—5 of the 11 ferries in the fleet have no bedroom accommodations.

It's in the lounges or on deck that riders may encounter the only entertainment onboard, all created by passengers on a strictly impromptu basis. It might be a backpacker strumming a guitar and singing folk songs or a father keeping his children occupied by performing magic tricks. Occasionally, spirited discussion groups will form in which all are welcome to participate. The subject might be the environment (always a hot, hot topic in Alaska, especially now with talk of opening up the Alaska Wildlife Preserve for oil exploration), politics (Alaskan or federal), the effect of tourism on wildlife (as much a hot-button issue as the environment), or any of a thousand other topics. (It's tempting to suggest—tongue slightly in cheek—that the entertainment on many Alaska Ferry boats is better than on some cruise ships we've been on, but that wouldn't be kind!) Occasionally, sports will be discussed—but don't look for the locals to want to talk about anything as much as dog sledding. It's almost a religion in the 49th State—their World Series, their Super Bowl, and their Stanley Cup rolled into one.

Pros

- **Unique way to travel.** The ferry system allows the chance for adventuresome travel that is not too taxing.
- **Lots of flexibility.** Passengers can combine the various journeys that the ferry system has scheduled to customize their vacation package.

Cons

- **No doctor onboard.** None of the vessels carries a doctor, so this may not be a good way to travel if you have health concerns.
- **Space books up quickly.** The only way you will be able to find a space on most of the ferries is by booking promptly. Don't call in May and expect to get what you want in June. It ain't gonna happen! If you're serious about experiencing Alaska by ferry, book now. Call the company at ✆ **800/642-0066** or book electronically through the website at www.ferryalaska.com.
- **Spartan cabins.** Sleeping accommodations, when available, are basic, to say the least—no fridge, no telephone, and so on. (One traveler was overheard to say, "I've known Trappist monks with more luxurious quarters!")

THE FLEET All nine of the traditional AMHS boats are designated M/V, as in motor vessel. The two newer, catamaran-style vessels are designated FVF, for fast vehicle ferries. Below is a thumbnail description of each one:

- One of the newest and fastest in the fleet is the *Fairweather,* which operates in the North Lynn Canal in Southeast, mostly between Juneau and Sitka, and Juneau and Haines. It is a 235-foot, 250-passenger catamaran. The vessel has no sleeping quarters; it is designed purely to provide fast access to and from the capital. Its value to locals is immense; they can now be in the grocery and clothing stores of Juneau, or in the offices of the Legislature, twice as fast as they once were. Its value to tourists is that it enables them to spend less time in transit.
- A sister high-speed vessel, the *Chenega* (pronounced Che-*nee*-ga), is entering its third year of providing service to the communities of Prince William Sound. It also has no sleeping accommodations.
- The *Lituya,* the smallest and slowest of the ferry company's boats, joined the fleet in 2004. Carrying just 149 passengers, the *Lituya* operates between Ketchikan and the Indian village of Metlakatla. Although built with a specific local market in mind, it has the advantage also of allowing tourists to visit the quaint Native community 17 miles from Ketchikan.
- The *Kennicott* (in service since 1998) was built in Gulfport, Mississippi. It is 382 feet long (about one-third as long as the biggest of today's cruise ships), has a service speed of just under 17 knots, and carries 499 passengers. Five of its 109 cabins are wheelchair-accessible.
- The *Taku* was built in 1981 in Seattle. It is 352 feet long and carries 370 passengers. Two of its 44 cabins are wheelchair-accessible. The boat has a cocktail lounge and cafeteria.
- The Wisconsin-built *Aurora,* which is used as a day boat, has room for 300 riders. Although it has no sleeping berths, it has a cafeteria.
- The *Columbia* is the largest of the AMHS vessels. The ferry, built in Seattle in 1974, is 418 feet long and holds 600 passengers and 134 vehicles. Of its 103 sleeping rooms, three are suitable for wheelchair users. The vessel has a cafeteria, dining room for fine dining, and cocktail lounge.
- The 300-passenger *Le Conte,* built in Wisconsin in 1973, is a no-sleeper day boat ferry with cafeteria food service.
- The *Matanuska* entered service in 1963 after leaving the builder's yard in Seattle. In 1972, the boat was lengthened and renovated in Portland, bringing it to its current capacity of 499. It has 108 cabins, one of which can accommodate a wheelchair user. The vessel has a cafeteria and a cocktail lounge.
- Another Wisconsin product, the *Tustumena,* began in Alaska waters in 1964 and was extensively renovated in San Francisco 5 years later. It has 26 sleeping rooms, one adapted for wheelchair use. It carries 174 passengers. The *Tustumena* has a cafeteria and a cocktail lounge.
- The 499-passenger *Malaspina,* another ship built in Seattle, has 73 cabins. One is suitable for a wheelchair user. The *Malaspina* has a cafeteria and a cocktail lounge.

PASSENGER PROFILE The travelers who use the ferries are looking for a laid-back, totally casual Alaska experience. Jeans and climbing boots (sometimes not removed for days), anoraks and backpacks—these are the basic accessories of ferry travelers in the 49th state. Ferry passengers who are on vacation (the AMHS is also heavily used as basic transportation by Alaska locals) often are young and don't often bring their families. They are definitely not looking for luxury.

The ferries also have become extremely popular with RVers who use the ferries to move their vehicles into and out of the state, saving thousands of miles of driving.

CABINS Booking your passage on the AMHS can be a complicated affair. First, there's the basic cost of a cabin for the trip if, indeed, you want a cabin. The journey between, say, Bellingham, Washington, the southernmost port in the system, and Skagway (a trip that takes about 60 hours, depending on the route), costs $580 one-way in a three-person cabin. From Ketchikan to Prince Rupert, B.C., a journey of less than 8 hours, the fare is just $88 one-way. (In winter, the ferries drop some lesser visited ports from their itineraries.) Children between the ages of 6 and 11 are charged roughly half the adult fare throughout the system, and children 5 and under travel free. Once you've booked passage and paid for the sleeping cabin, you'll then have to account for what you're taking along. A kayak? A motor vehicle? A motorcycle? An inflatable boat? All of that, and more, are extra to the cost. Only in Alaska! Pricing is complicated, so be careful when you make a reservation that there are "no ups, no extras" when you get to the boat.

The great majority of the cabins are small and spartan to say the least, coming in two- and four-bunk configurations, and either inside (without windows) or outside (with windows). For a premium, you can reserve a more comfortable sitting-room unit on some vessels. Most cabins have tiny private bathrooms with showers. Cabins can be stuffy, and the windowless units can be claustrophobic as well, so try to get an outside one. (If you're used to a veranda cabin, forget about traveling on the AMHS!)

Travelers who do not book their ferry passage in time to snag a cabin must spend their time curled up in chairs in the lounges if it's cold, or out on deck in a tent when the days lengthen and the sun stays high until late into the night. The patio-furniture lounge chairs on the covered outdoor solarium, on the top deck, are the best public sleeping spot onboard, in part because the noise of the ship covers other sounds. If you're tenting, the best place is behind the solarium, where it's likely to be less windy. On the *Columbia,* that space is small, so grab it early. Bring duct tape to secure your tent to the deck in case you can't find a sheltered spot, as the wind blows like an endless gale over the deck of a ship in motion. The recliner lounges are comfortable, too, but can be stuffy. If the ship looks crowded, grab your spot fast to get a choice location. Showers are available, although there may be lines. Lock valuables in the coin-operated lockers.

DINING Only one of the 11 AMHS ferries *(Columbia),* has a full-service, sit-down dining room. The others have cafeteria-style facilities that serve hot meals and beverages. There are also vending machines on all of the boats, which dispense snacks and drinks. Food prices—ranging from $2 for a vending machine snack to $10 for a hot meal in the dining room—are not included in the fares.

ACTIVITIES There are no organized activities, but lots of scenic viewing—and good listening on most sailings. Mainline sailings have interpretive talks from U.S. Forest Service and Fish and Wildlife personnel who educate passengers on the surrounding flora and fauna, and Native history.

CHILDREN'S PROGRAM None.

ENTERTAINMENT None.

SERVICE Service is not one of the things for which the AMHS is noted. The small American staff on each vessel works enthusiastically, but without a great deal of distinction.

CRUISETOURS & ADD-ON PROGRAMS None. However, those seeking a change from the more popular and frequently congested, larger Inside Passage and Gulf ports find that the ferries are an ideal way to get around the less-visited parts of Alaska, where paved roads are in short supply and reliable air connections—especially when the weather turns ugly—are nonexistent. A trip on one of the ferries can deposit you in, say, Pelican, on Chichagof Island, where you can enjoy fishing and scenery and join in the banter of the local fisherfolk in Rosie's Bar, the center of activity in town. A trip on another ferry will transport you to Tenakee Springs, a popular spa as far back as the gold-rush days, where you can "take the waters" and take advantage of saltwater fishing opportunities. The ferry will get you to Port Lions, which is on the northeast coast of Kodiak Island at the eastern end of the Aleutian Chain; to other areas of the Aleutians—False Pass and King Cove, for instance; to Chenega Bay, in Prince William Sound; to the Indian settlements at Kake, on Kupreanof Island; and to Metlakatla on Annette Island, among many other destinations. These are not, and never will be, ports with mass appeal. No luxury liner will ever unload 2,600 cruise passengers in any of them. But those who seek a taste of down-home spirit, Alaskan style, find these ports to be attractive destinations. In short, the AMHS can get you to places where cruise ships just don't go. Of course, the ferry system can also get you to big-ship cruise ports such as Ketchikan, Juneau, Whittier, and the rest, but much of the system's appeal, to many visitors, is its ability to transport travelers to lesser known outposts.

PUBLIC AREAS All of the ferries have warm, if somewhat sparse, interiors, with room for all when the weather is foul. They have solariums with high windows for viewing the passing scenery.

POOL, FITNESS, SPA & SPORTS FACILITIES Are you kidding?

7

The Ports of Embarkation

Most Alaska cruises operate either round-trip from Vancouver or Seattle, or one-way northbound or southbound between Vancouver or Seattle and Seward/ Anchorage. Whittier, an unprepossessing little place that has the advantage of being 60 miles closer to Anchorage, has become the northern turnaround port for Princess' cruises in the Gulf of Alaska. In 2011, six lines—Carnival, Celebrity, Holland America, Norwegian, Princess, and Royal Caribbean—will have ships sailing out of Seattle, with 10 ships in total operating out of the city. And another U.S. city, San Francisco, also is growing as a home port for voyages to Alaska, with new round-trip and one-way sailings in 2011 from Crystal Cruises and Oceania Cruises adding to existing options from Princess, Holland America, and Regent Seven Seas. The small adventure-type vessels sail from popular Alaska ports of call such as Juneau, Ketchikan, and Sitka (as well as Whittier and Seattle). In this chapter, we'll cover the most common of these home ports: Anchorage, Seward, Vancouver, Seattle, Juneau, and Whittier.

Consider traveling to your city of embarkation at least a day or two before your cruise departure date. You can check out local attractions, and if you're traveling from afar, give yourself time to overcome jet lag.

Use the port-city information provided here; in addition, you may want to refer to *Frommer's Alaska, Frommer's Vancouver & Victoria, Frommer's Seattle,* or *Frommer's San Francisco* for more details, particularly if you're planning to spend a few days in the port.

1 Anchorage

Anchorage, which started as a tent camp for workers building the Alaska Railroad in 1914, stands between the Chugach Mountains and the waters of upper Cook Inlet. It was a remote, sleepy railroad town until World War II, when a couple of military bases were located here and livened things up a bit. Even with that, though, Anchorage did not start becoming a city in earnest until the late 1950s, when oil was discovered on the Kenai Peninsula, to the south.

Fortunes came fast and development was haphazard, but the city seems at this point to have settled into its success. It now boasts good restaurants, fine museums, and a nice little zoo. In addition, the **Alaska Native Heritage Center,** a 26-acre re-creation of the villages of Alaska's five Native groups, welcomes visitors. Anchorage is, without argument, Alaska's only cosmopolitan city, but surrounded as it is by wilderness, moose regularly annoy gardeners in the town, and even bears occasionally show up in the streets. It's unlikely, though, that you'll run into such critters in the height of the cruise season.

Anchorage's downtown area, near Ship Creek, is about 8 by 20 blocks wide, but the rest of the city spreads some 5 miles east and 15 miles south. Most visitors, whether heading off on a cruise ship or not, spend a day or two in town before going somewhere more remote. The city center is pleasant, but we recommend you try to see more than just the streets of tourist-oriented shops. Check out the **coastal trail** and the **museums,** and if you have time, plan a day trip about 50 miles south along **Turnagain Arm** to explore the receding **Portage Glacier** and visit the mountains.

GETTING TO ANCHORAGE & THE PORT

Cruise ships, with the exception of Holland America's *Amsterdam,* dock in Seward or Whittier on the east coast of the Kenai Peninsula, to avoid the extra day that cruising around the peninsula to Anchorage adds to Gulf of Alaska itineraries. It's quicker to transport passengers between the towns in motorcoaches or by train than it is to sail all the way around the peninsula. The *Amsterdam* docks in Anchorage proper—last year it became the first major cruise ship to do so in 25 years, and it repeats visits this year. Most visitors will use Anchorage as a hub because, thanks to the international airport, it's where Alaska connects to the rest of the world. We recommend spending a day or two in Anchorage before or after your cruise.

BY PLANE If you're arriving or leaving by plane, you'll land at the **Ted Stevens Anchorage International Airport.** The facility is located within the city limits, a 15-minute drive from downtown. Taxis run about $27 for the trip downtown; many hotels also have free shuttles.

BY CAR By car, there is only one road into Anchorage from the rest of the world: the Glenn Highway. The other road out of town, the Seward Highway, leads to the Kenai Peninsula.

EXPLORING ANCHORAGE

INFORMATION The **Anchorage Convention and Visitor Bureau** (**© 907/276-4118;** www.anchorage.net) maintains five information locations. The main one is the **Log Cabin Visitor Information Center** at 4th Avenue and F Street (**© 907/274-3531**). It's open daily from 7:30am to 7pm from June through August, and from 8am to 6pm in May and September. Visit the bureau's website for everything you need to know before you go.

GETTING AROUND Most car-rental companies maintain a counter at the airport. A compact car costs about $50 a day, with unlimited mileage. (There aren't many of those $30-a-day specials that you see advertised in some other states!) Advanced bookings are strongly recommended in midsummer. Anchorage's bus system, People Mover (www.peoplemover.org), is an effective way of moving to and from the top attractions and activities. The buses operate between around 6:30am and 9pm daily, with limited service on weekends and holidays, and passage costs $1.75 for adults and $1 for ages 5 to 18 (4 and under free). In the 20-block downtown area, which consists of 5th and 6th avenues between Denali and K streets, the bus operates as a free People Mover.

ATTRACTIONS WITHIN WALKING DISTANCE

With its old-fashioned grid of streets, Anchorage's downtown area is pleasant, if a bit touristy. The 1936 **Old City Hall,** at 4th Avenue and E Street, has an interesting display on city history in its lobby, including dioramas of the early streetscape. For a better sense of what Alaska's all about, though, you'll want to check out the heritage museums or take a ride outside the city to the Chugach Mountains. You can also take

Anchorage

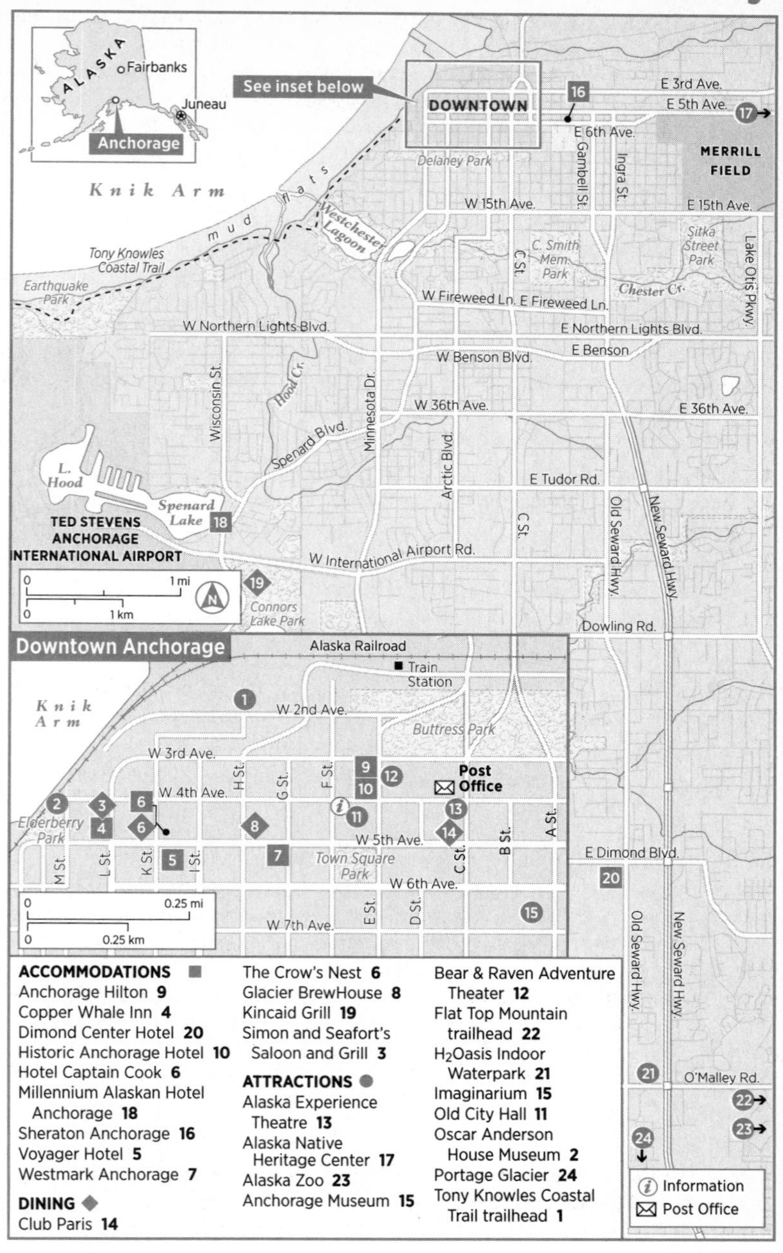

ALASKA
Fairbanks
Juneau
Anchorage
See inset below
DOWNTOWN
Knik Arm
mud flats
Westchester Lagoon
Tony Knowles Coastal Trail
Earthquake Park
Delaney Park
E 3rd Ave.
E 5th Ave.
E 6th Ave.
Gambell St.
Ingra St.
MERRILL FIELD
W 15th Ave.
E 15th Ave.
C. Smith Mem. Park
C St.
Sitka Street Park
Lake Otis Pkwy.
Chester Cr.
W Fireweed Ln.
E Fireweed Ln.
W Northern Lights Blvd.
E Northern Lights Blvd.
W Benson Blvd.
E Benson
Wisconsin St.
Hood Cr.
Minnesota Dr.
W 36th Ave.
E 36th Ave.
Spenard Blvd.
Arctic Blvd.
L. Hood
Spenard Lake
E Tudor Rd.
TED STEVENS ANCHORAGE INTERNATIONAL AIRPORT
W International Airport Rd.
Old Seward Hwy.
New Seward Hwy.
0 1 mi
0 1 km
N
Connors Lake Park
Dowling Rd.
Downtown Anchorage
Alaska Railroad
Train Station
Knik Arm
W 2nd Ave.
Buttress Park
W 3rd Ave.
W 4th Ave.
H St.
G St.
F St.
Post Office
Elderberry Park
W 5th Ave.
M St.
L St.
K St.
I St.
Town Square Park
C St.
B St.
A St.
W 6th Ave.
E Dimond Blvd.
0 0.25 mi
0 0.25 km
W 7th Ave.
E St.
D St.
O'Malley Rd.
ACCOMMODATIONS
Anchorage Hilton 9
Copper Whale Inn 4
Dimond Center Hotel 20
Historic Anchorage Hotel 10
Hotel Captain Cook 6
Millennium Alaskan Hotel Anchorage 18
Sheraton Anchorage 16
Voyager Hotel 5
Westmark Anchorage 7
DINING
Club Paris 14
The Crow's Nest 6
Glacier BrewHouse 8
Kincaid Grill 19
Simon and Seafort's Saloon and Grill 3
ATTRACTIONS
Alaska Experience Theatre 13
Alaska Native Heritage Center 17
Alaska Zoo 23
Anchorage Museum 15
Bear & Raven Adventure Theater 12
Flat Top Mountain trailhead 22
H2Oasis Indoor Waterpark 21
Imaginarium 15
Old City Hall 11
Oscar Anderson House Museum 2
Portage Glacier 24
Tony Knowles Coastal Trail trailhead 1
Information
Post Office

a walk on the **Tony Knowles Coastal Trail,** which comes through downtown and runs along the water for about 11 miles, from the western end of 2nd Avenue to Kincaid Park. You can hop onto the trail at several points, including Elderberry Park, at the western end of 5th Avenue. And if you're in the mood for some music, local musical acts perform at Peratrovich Park on 4th Avenue every Monday, Wednesday, Thursday, and Friday during the summer as part of the Music in the Park program.

The Alaska Experience Theatre Think Alaska, think big. This popular attraction features Alaska-themed Omnivision presentations shown in a newly renovated domed theater with a wraparound, planetarium-style screen that stands nearly three stories high. It is a cool introduction to some of the places you'll be touring, but be aware Omnivision (like IMAX) may cause motion sickness in some people. There is also a smaller Earthquake Video Theatre with a video about the 1964 Alaska earthquake and seating that shakes to simulate an earthquake. The Alaska Salmon Bake Dinner Theatre package includes dinner, a native dance performance, and film admission, and is available seven days a week.

333 W. 4th Ave., at C St. ✆ **907/272-9076.** Mon–Sat 9am–6pm; Sun 11am–6pm.

Anchorage Museum In the Alaska Gallery, you can enjoy an informative walk through the history and anthropology of the state, and in the art galleries you can see what's happening in Alaska art today. But it's a $106-million expansion, completed last year, that makes this museum a must on your list of places to visit. The new Smithsonian Arctic Studies Center displays Native Alaska artifacts—including clothing, baskets, masks, weapons, utensils, drums, and games—all on loan from the Smithsonian and most never on display before. The new space also includes the Thomas Planetarium and the Imaginarium Discovery Center, recently relocated from downtown. The Imaginarium is geared towards kids, with lots of fun learning experiences including a bubble space and saltwater touch tank that re-creates a tide pool indoors. Check out the museum's lovely new lunch spot, Muse, with its modern decor and cuisine. You can eat outside in the new 2-acre outdoor common area filled with young birch trees, and view "Habitat," a permanent steel installation of a seated human figure by English artist Antony Gormley which occupies the northwest corner of the space. Special exhibits are frequent.

625 C St., at the corner of 7th Ave. ✆ **907/929-9200.** www.anchoragemuseum.org. Admission $10 adults, $8 seniors and students, $7 for children 3–12. May 10–Sept 12 Fri–Wed 9am–6pm, Thurs 9am–9pm; Sept 14–May 9 Tues–Sat 10am–6pm, Sun noon–6pm, closed Mon.

Bear & Raven Adventure Theater This 35-seat theater screens two locally produced movies about Alaska while providing visitors with state-of-the-art virtual experiences, including full sensory effects and surround sound. Learn about the Iditarod Trail while the lights of the aurora borealis dance on the ceiling and snow falls over the audience, or brush up on some bear smarts while your seat rumbles right along with the on-screen grizzlies. After the show, hook some virtual fish or take a virtual hot-air balloon ride in the lobby. The theater is located in Bear Square, which also features a restaurant, used bookstore, and panning for gold attraction.

315 E. St. ✆ **907/277-4545.** www.bearsquare.net. Admission $18 adults, $16 children (both movies plus lobby experience) and $13 adults, $11 children (one movie).

The Oscar Anderson House Museum This house museum, which is listed on the National Register of Historic Places, shows how an early Swedish butcher lived. It's a quaint dwelling built in 1915 and surrounded by a lovely little garden. The 45-minute house tour provides a good explanation of the city's short history. Furnishings include a working 1909 player piano.

420 M St., in Elderberry Park. ✆ **907/274-2336.** Admission $3 adults (13 and up), $1 children 5–12. Summer Mon–Fri noon–5pm; closed in winter.

ATTRACTIONS OUTSIDE THE DOWNTOWN AREA

The Alaska Native Heritage Center Don't miss this 26-acre center that introduces visitors to the lives and cultures of the state's major Alaska Native groupings: the Southeast (Inside Passage) region's Tlingits, Eyaks, Haida, and Tsimshians; the Athabascans of the Interior; the Iñupiat and St. Lawrence Island Yup'ik Natives of the far north; the Aleuts and Alutiiqs of the Aleutian Islands; and the Yup'ik and Cup'ik tribes of the extreme west. A central Welcome House holds a small museum, a theater, a workshop where Native craftspeople demonstrate techniques, and a rotunda where storytelling, dance, and music performances are presented throughout the day. Outside, spaced along a walking trail around a small lake, five traditional dwellings represent the five regional Native groupings, each hosted by a member of that group. You can catch a complimentary shuttle to the Center from the Anchorage Museum and other Anchorage locations, or it's about a 10-minute walk from the dock.

From the Glenn Hwy., take the North Muldoon exit. ✆ **800/315-6608** or 907/330-8000. www.alaskanative.net. Admission $25 adults, $21 seniors and military, $17 children 7–16, free for children 6 and under. Family rate (2 adults, 2 children) $71.50. A combined Anchorage Museum/Native Heritage Center admission ticket is $27. Summer daily 9am–5pm. Closed in winter.

The Alaska Zoo Don't expect a big city zoo. Instead, come to experience a little Eden complete with Alaskan bears, seals, otters, musk oxen, mountain goats, moose, caribou, and waterfowl. There are also decidedly non-Alaskan elephants, tigers, and the like here.

4731 O'Malley Rd. ✆ **907/346-2133.** www.alaskazoo.org. Admission $12 adults, $9 seniors, $6 children 3–17, free for children 2 and under. Daily 9am–6pm. New Seward Hwy. to O'Malley Rd., then turn left and go 2 miles; it's 20 min. from downtown, without traffic.

Flat Top Mountain Rising right behind Anchorage, this mountain is a great and easy climb, and perfect for an afternoon hike. The parking area at Glen Alps, above the tree line, is a good starting point.

In the Chugach Mountains. From the New Seward Hwy., drive east on O'Malley Rd., turn right on Hillside Dr. and left on Upper Huffman Rd., then right on the narrow, twisting Toilsome Hill Dr.

The H_2Oasis Indoor Waterpark This aquatic attraction features a 575-foot lazy river perfect for idling away an hour, a wave pool that can generate 4-foot rollers, a water coaster more than 40 feet high and 500 feet long, a 150-foot-long enclosed slide, and a children's lagoon with a pirate ship and water cannons.

The Castle on O'Malley, 1520 O'Malley Rd. (about 5 miles from downtown). ✆ **907/522-4420.** www.h2oasis waterpark.com. Day pass $24 adults (13 and up), $19 children 3–12, free for children 2 and under. Summer daily (beginning June 1) 9am–9pm; winter Mon, Wed 3–8pm, Fri 3–9pm, Sat–Sun 10am–9pm. Take the New Seward Hwy. from downtown past O'Malley Rd. Park is btw. O'Malley and Huffman rds.

Portage Glacier In 1985, the National Forest Service spent $8 million building the Begich-Boggs Visitor Center at Portage. Imagine its chagrin when the glacier then started receding, moving away from the center so fast that at this point, you can't even see one from the other. You must now board a tour boat to get close to the glacier face.

Portage is not the best glacier in Alaska—it's relatively small—but if you haven't had enough of them after your cruise (or want a preview beforehand), it's well worth a stop. The visitor center itself is worth a stop; it's a sort of glacier museum and an excellent place to learn about what you'll be seeing (or saw) on your cruise. Many bus tours are offered (your cruise line may give one, too), including a 7-hour **Gray Line of Alaska** (© **907/277-5581;** www.graylinealaska.com) trip from Anchorage, which involves a motorcoach ride to the glacier and a 1-hour cruise across Portage Lake. On the way back, stop for lunch at Hotel Alyeska and take an optional tram ride to the top of Mount Alyeska. The cost is $79 adults, $39 children, and the trip is offered twice daily (at 9am and noon) in the summer.

About 50 miles south of the city on the Seward Hwy. (toward Seward). Free admission. Visitor Center Memorial Day–Labor Day daily 9am–6pm; Labor Day–Memorial Day Sat–Sun 10am–4pm.

BEST CRUISE-LINE SHORE EXCURSIONS

See the "Anchorage City Tour," on p. 169.

Discovery McKinley/Denali National Park Flightseeing (4 hr.; $449): Head off to view some of Alaska's most spectacular views and wild settings. The bush pilot will follow the spine of the Alaska Range, with its walls of rock and ice, to the awesome sight of the south face of Mount McKinley, where climbers summit.

Anchorage Flightseeing Safari (1½ hr.; $149): See Anchorage surroundings by air as a bush pilot takes you on an exciting seaplane ride to explore the Chugach Mountain Range, where views include secluded valleys and slopes with Dall sheep, and over the Cook Inlet in search of beluga whales.

Portage Cruise and Alaska Wildlife Conservation Center (5½ hr.; $99): Travel by bus on the Seward Highway to visit the Conservation Center, a refuge for wildlife including moose, bears, and caribou. Then board the Mv Ptarmigan for a cruise across Portage Lake to the Portage Glacier, narrated by a U.S. Forest Service representative.

EXCURSIONS OFFERED BY LOCAL AGENCIES

Anchorage Historic Properties This 2-hour guided walking tour covers 2 miles and 27 different locations, including the historic City Hall, the Anchorage Museum, and the Imaginarium. The volunteer guides are both fun and knowledgeable. Meet at the Log Cabin Visitor Information Center (p. 158).

645 W. 3rd Ave. © **907/274-3600.** Admission $5 adults, $1 children 5–12, children 4 and under free. Combination ticket for $6.50 ($2 kids) with the Oscar Anderson House Museum (p. 160). June–Aug Mon–Fri 1pm.

Scenic City Tour Locally owned and operated Salmonberry Tours offers a variety of different excursions including a 2-hour scenic drive through the city and up Flat Top Mountain for stunning photo opportunities of the Chugach Mountains as well as Anchorage itself. Other tours include the Chocolate City Circuit, during which you'll check out local chocolate boutiques as well as the world's largest chocolate waterfall, and the Big Rig Experience, highlighting the Ice Road Truckers of Alaska which includes a visit to Anchorage's trucking terminal and the chance to try out a truck-driving simulator.

527 W. 3rd Ave. © **907/278-3572.** www.salmonberrytours.com. 2-hr scenic city tour $49. April–Oct.

WHERE TO STAY

Rooms can be hard to come by in Anchorage during summer, so be sure to arrange lodging as far in advance of your trip as possible, whether through your cruise line or

The Iditarod

Few things fire up Alaska's residents like the **Iditarod Trail Sled Dog Race,** a 1,000-mile run from Anchorage to Nome that takes place in mid-March. Winners cover the distance in 9 or 10 days, which includes mandatory stopovers of up to 24 hours to rest the dogs. (The 2010 victor, Lance Mackey, completed the course in 8 days, 23 hr., and 59 min., becoming the only musher to win the race for the fourth time in as many years.) The race is big news—TV anchors speculate on the mushers' strategies at the top of the evening news, and school children plot the progress of their favorite teams on maps. Its start, in downtown Anchorage, has been covered repeatedly by ABC's *Wide World of Sports.* When the event hits Nome, the town overflows with visitors kept busy by the many local events and activities that coincide with the race. Even if the first team crosses the finish line at 3am in –30°F (–34°C) weather, a huge crowd turns out to congratulate the musher.

This is Alaska's Super Bowl, its World Series. The victors are feted and admired throughout the state as much as any sports star ever is in the Lower 48. They're not compensated quite as well, mind you. First prize in the grueling event varies, but Mackey took home $50,000 and a new Dodge truck last year. The cruise lines long ago recognized the significance of the Iditarod, even to non-Alaskans. Princess, for instance, has a contract with Libby Riddles, the first woman to win the race, in 1985. She comes aboard in Juneau with a slide show to talk about her mushing experience. The *Riverboat Discovery* is a popular day cruise on the Chena River in Fairbanks, an outing cruise lines include in their cruisetour itinerary if they have programs in the Denali Corridor. The boat stops for awhile on each of its sailings at the dog yard where the late Susan Butcher—an Alaska legend who won the Iditarod four times (1986, 1987, 1988, and 1990)—kept some of her champion dogs. The Iditarod Trail Sled Dog Race headquarters is located in Wasilla, a city near Anchorage made famous by its former mayor, Sarah Palin, and is also a part of the shore-excursion schedule of virtually all Gulf of Alaska cruise operators.

Cruise aficionados may never be in the state to see the race itself, as it takes place off season—*way* off season. But they are likely to see and hear plenty about it during their summer vacations.

Visitors interested in learning more should check out the touristy but fun **WildRide Sled Dog Rodeo** located at 185 E. Ship Creek Ave. (✆ **907/561-MUSH** [6874] or 888/221-6874; www.iditarodexperience.com). The Seavey family will guide you through the history of sled dogs in this hour-long family-oriented show featuring Dallas Seavey, the youngest musher ever to ride the Iditarod, and a 16-dog Iditarod team. Afterwards, meet the dogs and mushers, along with some fluffy husky puppies and Hugo, one of the stars of Disney's *Snow Buddies.* Matinee tickets are $24 for adults and $12 for ages 2 to 11 (kids under 2 free), with performances held at 3pm daily. Evening and dinner shows are also offered for a higher price.

on your own. In addition to the listings below, you can try the luxurious **Anchorage Hilton,** 500 W. 3rd Ave. (✆ **800/245-2527** or 907/272-7411; www.hilton.com); the **Hotel Captain Cook,** 939 W. 5th Ave. (✆ **800/843-1950** or 907/276-6000; www.captaincook.com); the **Westmark Anchorage,** 720 W. 5th Ave. (✆ **800/544-0970** or 907/276-7676; www.westmarkhotels.com); the **Sheraton Anchorage,** 401 E. 6th Ave. (✆ **866/716-8145** or 907/276-8700; www.sheratonanchoragehotel.com); the small and charming **Historic Anchorage Hotel** at 330 E. St., right next door to the Hilton (✆ **800/544-0988** or 907/272-4553; www.historicanchoragehotel.com); the **Dimond Center Hotel,** 700 E. Dimond Blvd. (✆ **866/770-5002** or 907/770-5000; www.dimondcenterhotel.com); or the **Millennium Alaskan Hotel Anchorage,** 4800 Spenard Rd. (✆ **800/544-0553** or 907/243-2300; www.millenniumhotels.com/millenniumanchorage). It's not a cheap city: Room rates in Anchorage, before discounts, range upward of $200. Hotels accept all major credit cards. The hotels mentioned above are among the city's more upscale. The following are some lower priced alternatives.

Copper Whale Inn There's a wonderfully casual feeling to this bed-and-breakfast place. A pair of clapboard houses overlooks the water and Elderberry Park right on the coastal trail downtown, with charming rooms of every shape and size. The rooms in the newer building, lower on the hill, are preferable, with cherry-wood furniture and high ceilings. All rooms are wired for TV, phone, and Wi-Fi—you just have to ask for the actual instrument to be connected. Bikes are available for about $30 a day through Lifetime Adventures (www.lifetimeadventures.net), and a full breakfast is included in the price.

440 L St., Anchorage, AK 99501. ✆ **866/258-7999** or 907/258-7999. Fax 907/258-6213. www.copperwhale.com. 14 units, 12 with bathroom. $185 double without bathroom; $210 double with bathroom. Extra person $20. Lower rates in winter and shoulder seasons. Special packages available. Rates include continental breakfast. AE, DC, DISC, MC, V. Parking $15. *In-room:* TV, hair dryer, Wi-Fi (free).

The Voyager Hotel The Voyager is just about right. The size is small, the location central, the rooms large and light (all with kitchens), and the housekeeping exceptional. The desks have modem ports and extra electrical outlets, and the hospitality is warm, yet highly professional. There's nothing ostentatious or outwardly remarkable about this boutique hotel, yet the most experienced travelers rave about it the loudest. There's no smoking.

501 K St. (at W. 5th Ave.), Anchorage, AK 99501. ✆ **800/247-9070** or 907/277-9501. Fax 907/274-0333. 40 units. $145–$209 double. Lower rates in winter and shoulder seasons. Rates include continental breakfast. AE, DC, DISC, MC, V. Limited free parking. **Amenities:** Restaurant, access to nearby pool and steam room. *In-room:* A/C, TV, hair dryer, kitchenette, Wi-Fi (free).

WHERE TO DINE

Club Paris STEAK/SEAFOOD Walking from a bright spring afternoon under a neon Eiffel Tower into midnight darkness, past a smoke-enshrouded bar, and sitting down at a secretive booth for two, we felt as if we should have been plotting a shady 1950s oil deal. We probably have not been the first diners to feel that way. Smoky Club Paris may be too authentic for some, but it's the essence of the old Anchorage boomtown years, when the streets were dusty and an oilman needed a classy joint in which to do business. Beef, of course, is what to order, and it'll be done right. Club Paris has a full liquor license.

417 W. 5th Ave. ✆ **907/277-6332.** www.clubparisrestaurant.com. Reservations recommended. Lunch $7–$29; dinner $20–$59. AE, DC, DISC, MC, V. Mon–Sat 11:30am–2:30pm and 5pm–midnight; Sun 4pm–midnight.

The Crow's Nest FRENCH/NEW AMERICAN Known for its fine cuisine and 10,000-bottle wine cellar, the Crow's Nest is the best in town. Perched atop the Hotel Captain Cook, it boasts breathtaking views of the city, the Cook Inlet, and the Chugach Mountains. Chef Gary Murphy, Jr., prepares a mix of French and New American cuisine, with some Alaskan favorites thrown in.

939 W. 5th Ave. © **907/276-6000.** www.captaincook.com/dining/crows-nest. Dinner $28–55. AE, DC, DISC, MC, V. Tues–Sat 5–9pm.

Glacier BrewHouse GRILL/SEAFOOD The tasty, eclectic, and ever-changing cuisine is served in a large dining room with lodge decor, where the pleasant scent of the wood-fired grill hangs in the air. This place brews five hearty beers behind a glass wall. It's noisy and active, with lots of agreeable if trendy touches, such as the bread—made from spent brewery grain—that's set out on the tables with olive oil. An advantage for travelers is the wide price range—all of the pizzas are under $11.

737 W. 5th Ave. © **907/274-BREW** (2739). www.glacierbrewhouse.com. Reservations recommended for dinner. Lunch $9–$19; dinner $9–$37. AE, DC, DISC, MC, V. Mon 11am–9:30pm, Tues–Thurs 11am–10pm, Fri–Sat 11am–11pm, Sun noon–9:30pm.

Kincaid Grill REGIONAL/SEAFOOD Just a 5-minute drive from Ted Stevens International Airport, Kincaid Grill is known for its "inflight menu," in particular the hot breakfasts, but the dinner menu is also a foodie favorite. Chef Al Levinsohn, well-known in town for his "What's Cookin'?" segment on a local morning TV show, opened the restaurant in 2003 and has been serving up everything from lobster risotto to pumpkin cheesecake ever since.

6700 Jewel Lake Rd. © **907/243-0507.** www.kincaidgrill.com. Dinner $16–38. AE, MC, V. Tues–Sat 5–10pm.

Simon and Seafort's Saloon and Grill STEAK/SEAFOOD This is one of the city's great dinner houses, with turn-of-the-century decor, a cheerful atmosphere, warm service, and fabulous sunset views of Cook Inlet. Prime rib and seafood are the specialties. Light meals are served in the bar.

420 L St. © **907/274-3502.** www.simonandseaforts.com. Reservations recommended (days in advance in summer). Lunch $10–$18; dinner $16–$49. AE, MC, V. Lunch Mon–Fri 11am–2:30pm; dinner Mon–Thurs 5pm–9:30pm, Fri 5pm–10pm, Sat 4:30pm–10pm, Sun 4:30pm–9:30pm.

SHOPPING

Anchorage is truly an international city, but when all is said and done, it's a part of Alaska; for that reason, if no other, visitors should shop for genuine products of the 49th state. The **4th Avenue Market,** 333 W. 4th Ave. (© **907/278-3263**) in the heart of downtown, has a number of stores, some quite touristy, some more upscale, with similar kinds of goods, but less expensive. The 4th Avenue Market used to be known as the Ship Creek Center.

DIY (do-it-yourself) clothing makers may enjoy **The Quilt Tree,** 341 E. Benson Blvd. (© **907/561-4115;** www.quiltree.com), with its wide selection of Alaska-pattern fabrics, while wine aficionados should check out **Grape Expectations,** 510 W. 6th St. (© **907/258-9463**). Run by friendly owner/wine enthusiast Terri Potter, this boutique wine store also offers demos by craftspeople and performance artists.

Those with a sweet tooth have a couple of options. The **Cake Studio Bakery & Boutique,** 608 W. 4th Ave. (© **907/272-3995;** www.alaskacakestudio.com) offers amazing cupcakes among other fresh baked goods. A Boston Cream cupcake is worth the $3. Lattes ($2.75) and other coffee drinks are available as well.

Shopping Smart for Native Art

If you're interested in Native Alaskan art, know that there is a large market in fakes: More than one shopkeeper's assistant has been spotted removing MADE IN TAIWAN stickers from supposedly Native art objects.

Before you buy a piece of Native art, ask the dealer for a biography of the artist and ask whether the artist actually carved the piece (rather than just lending his or her name to knockoffs). Most dealers will tell you where a work really comes from—you just have to ask.

Price should also be a tip-off to fakes, as real Native art is pricey. An elaborate mask, for instance, should be priced at $3,000, not $300. Be particularly wary of soapstone carvings, as most are not made in Alaska.

There are two marks used for Alaska products: a MADE-IN-ALASKA polar bear sticker, which means the item was at least mostly made in the state, and a silver hand sticker, which indicates authentic Native art. An absence of the label, however, does not mean the item is not authentic; it may just mean the artist doesn't like labels. So just ask if you're curious about a piece of artwork that doesn't have a sticker.

There's also **Modern Dwellers Chocolate Lounge,** 423 G St. and 751 E. 36th Ave. (**© 907/868-1818** and **907/677-9985;** www.moderndwellers.com), which describes itself as a chocolate and espresso experience. Its chocolate-colored walls are covered with contemporary works of art (some for sale, some just on display), and jewelry and gifts are sold too. Remnants from carnivals and old factories complete the offbeat decor. Be sure to try the hand-crafted artisan truffles and what may be the best hot chocolate anywhere, made from actual melted chocolate.

And if you're on G Street, check out the eco-friendly **Octopus Ink Clothing** (**© 907/333-3657;** www.octopusinkclothing.com) and **ShuzyQ** shoe store (**© 907/586-1055;** www.shuzyq.com), located in the same building as Ristorante Orso and Glacier BrewHouse.

During the height of cruise season, expect these and other stores to be open from 9am to 7pm, but in the early and late weeks of the season (early May or mid-Sept), they tend to close a little earlier.

2 Seward

Since Seward is the northern embarkation and debarkation port for many Gulf of Alaska cruise operators, passengers can almost be forgiven if they sometimes think the correct name of this Resurrection Bay community is "Seward-the-port-for-Anchorage." Although the majority of 7-day Gulf cruises are advertised as "Vancouver to Anchorage" (or the reverse), the ships don't actually sail to Anchorage. Instead, they dock in Seward and guests are carried by motorcoach (or, more recently, by rail) to or from Anchorage. Why? Because Seward—and Whittier—lie on the south side of the Kenai Peninsula, while Anchorage is on the north. Sailing around the peninsula would add another day to the cruise.

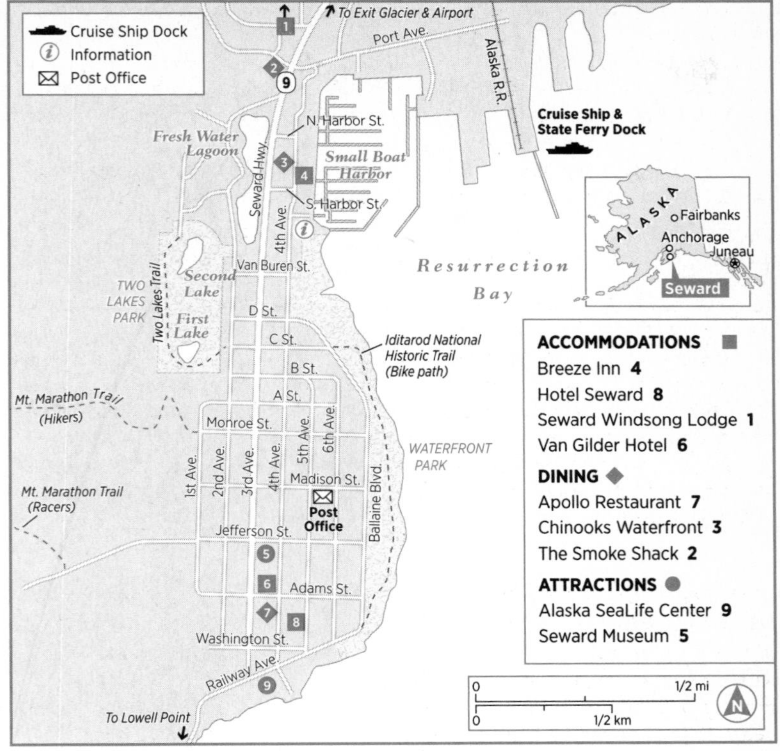

As such, most people pass through Seward on their way to or from their ship, but never really see much of the town. And that's a pity. Seward, which traces its history back to 1793 when the Russian Pooh-Bah, Alexander Baranof, first visited, is an attractive little town rimmed by mountains and ocean, with streets lined with old wood-frame houses and fishermen's residences. It's also home to the spectacular **Alaska SeaLife Center** (a marine research, rehabilitation, and public education center where visitors can watch scientists uncovering the secrets of nearby **Prince William Sound**). Seward is an ideal spot from which to take wildlife-watching day trips by boat into the sound or to begin one of a variety of road and rail trips through the beautiful **Kenai Peninsula.**

Seward was hit hard on Good Friday 1964 when a massive earthquake rattled Anchorage, the peninsula, and everything in between. The villagers (there were only about 2,500 of them) watched the water in the harbor drain away after the shaking stopped and realized immediately what was about to happen: a tidal wave. Because they were smart enough to read the signs and run for high ground, loss of life was miraculously slight when the towering 100-foot wall of water struck. The town itself, however, was heavily damaged, so many of the buildings that visitors see today are of a more recent vintage than might be expected. However, care has been taken to rebuild them in the style of the town's earlier days.

GETTING TO SEWARD

Most cruise passengers will arrive at Seward either by ship (at the end of their cruise) or by bus.

BY PLANE The nearest major airport, Ted Stevens Anchorage International Airport, is 130 miles away.

BY BUS The bus trip from the airport takes about 3 hours, passing through the beautiful Chugach National Forest. If you haven't made transportation arrangements through your cruise line, **Seward Bus Line** (✆ **907/224-3608;** www.sewardbuslines.net) has one trip a day (9am check-in) from Anchorage for $50 one-way.

BY CAR For those arriving by car, Seward and the Kenai Peninsula are served by a single major road, the Seward Highway.

BY TRAIN The train ride to or from Anchorage with a stop at Seward goes through some truly beautiful scenery; it costs $75 one-way adults ($119 round-trip) and $38 one-way for kids ($59 round-trip) on the **Alaska Railroad** (✆ **800/321-6518** or 907/265-2494; www.alaskarailroad.com). The route is prettier than going by road; you'll see gorges, rushing rivers, and tunnels cut through mountains.

EXPLORING SEWARD

INFORMATION The **Seward Chamber of Commerce** (✆ **907/224-8051;** www.seward.com) operates an information booth right on the cruise-ship dock; it's open from 8am to noon and 3 to 7pm daily. If you have time, stop by **Kenai Fjords National Park Visitor Center,** near the waterfront at 500 Adams St. (✆ **907/224-7500**), to learn about what's in the area, including nearby hiking trails. It's open daily from May through Labor Day 9am to 6pm, off season Monday through Friday from 9am to 5pm.

GETTING AROUND The downtown area is within walking distance of the cruise-ship dock, and you can easily cover downtown Seward on foot. If it's not raining, consider a bike ride through town. **Seward Bike Shop** (✆ **907/224-2448**), 411 Port Ave., in a railcar near the depot at the harbor, rents high-performance mountain bikes that are good for getting around town and into the surrounding hills, plus other equipment. A cruiser is $27 for a full day. For motorized transport, a little bus known as the **Seward Trolley** (✆ **907/224-4378;** www.sewardtrolley.com) will carry you between the downtown area and the waterfront. An all-day pass costs $15 for adults ($8 for children 12 and under), and $5 for a one-way trip ($3 for children). The trip isn't much more than a mile, though, so it's a pleasant walk if the weather cooperates.

ATTRACTIONS WITHIN WALKING DISTANCE

Downtown Seward can be explored with the help of a **walking-tour map,** available from the Chamber of Commerce visitor center near the cruise-ship docks and at establishments throughout town.

The Alaska SeaLife Center Opened in 1998, this nonprofit facility allows scientists to study, in their natural habitat, Steller sea lions, porpoises, sea otters, harbor seals, fish, and other forms of marine life that abound in the area, as well as the umpteen species of local seabirds—colorful rock puffins, cormorants, and more. The important thing, of course, is that you can study them, too—through windows that show you the undersea world (watch a 2,000-pound Steller sea lion glide past, for instance). The center itself is something of a phoenix, rising from the metaphorical ashes of the 1989 *Exxon Valdez* disaster that so drastically affected the area's marine ecology and the creatures that inhabit the sound. Much of the $60 million needed to create the center came from an oil-spill reparation fund established by Exxon Corporation. The SeaLife Center should be on everybody's must-see list.

301 Railway Ave. ✆ **800/224-2525** or 907/224-6300. www.alaskasealife.org. Admission $20 adults, $15 children 12–17, $10 children 4–11, free for children 3 and under. May 15–Sept 14 Mon–Thurs 9am–6:30pm, Fri–Sun 8am–6:30pm; Sept 15–May 13 daily 10am–5pm.

The Seward Museum This is a charming grandma's attic of a place, with clippings, memorabilia, and curiosities recalling town history, painter Rockwell Kent, and the ways of the past. An interesting exhibit revolves around the Russian ships built here in the 18th century.

Corner of 3rd Ave. and Jefferson St. ✆ **907/224-3902.** Admission $2 adults, 50¢ children 5–18, free for children 4 and under. May–Sept daily 10am–5pm. Open by appointment other times of year.

ATTRACTIONS BEYOND THE PORT AREA

Caines Head State Recreation Area Parts of this 7-mile coastal trail, south of town, are accessible only at low tide, so it's best done with someone picking you up and/or dropping you off by boat beyond the beach portion; **Miller's Landing water taxi** (✆ **866/541-5739** or 907/224-5739; **www.millerslandingak.com**) offers this service for $38 per person one-way, $48 round-trip. The trail has some gorgeous views, rocky shores, and the concrete remains of Fort McGilvray, a World War II defensive emplacement. Take flashlights and you can poke around in the spooky underground corridors and rooms. For an easy 2-mile hike to Fort McGilvray, start with a boat ride to North Beach. The main trail head is on Lowell Point Road. Stop at the Kenai Fjords National Park Visitor Center at the boat harbor for tide conditions and advice. Check out **www.alaskastateparks.org** for more about these local trails.

BEST CRUISE-LINE SHORE EXCURSIONS

Anchorage City Tour (3 hr.; $99 adults, $69 children): A restroom-equipped motorcoach takes you on a 3-hour drive from Seward through the Chugach National Forest and along Turnagain Arm between Seward and Anchorage. Once you hit Anchorage, the bus makes a circuit through the downtown area, pointing out sights of interest, good shops, and popular restaurants. You'll then be free for a few hours to shop, eat, or visit the Anchorage Museum. The tour is either an all-day round-trip affair from Seward or a half-day trip that ends in Anchorage (either downtown at Egan Center or at the Anchorage Airport).

Resurrection Bay Wildlife Cruise (4 hr.; $99 adults, $50 children): Board a dayboat for a cruise past Bear Glacier and the hanging glaciers of Thumb Cove as you search for wildlife, including puffins and bald eagles, whales and Dall's porpoises.

Resurrection River Kayaking (3 hr.; $109 adults and children): Kayak in beautiful Resurrection Bay, enjoying the marine life and glacial vistas. You'll explore the shoreline of Tonsina Creek, where you may encounter sea otters, bald eagles, porpoises, sea lions, leaping salmon, and other wildlife inhabitants. (Minimum age is 8).

Horseback Trail Ride (2½ hr.; $119): A must-do for horse lovers, ride through historic sections of Seward to Resurrection Bay where you'll view bald eagles where they nest and watch them feed. Then, still on horseback, cross a river where spawning salmon may be swimming through the horse's legs.

Resurrection River Float Trip (3 hr.; $115 adults, $89 children 5–12): Take a relaxing trip on an inflatable raft along the Resurrection River, with an expert oarsman as your pilot. Sights include Exit Glacier and expansive views of the Resurrection Valley.

EXCURSIONS OFFERED BY LOCAL AGENCIES

Alaska Railroad (✆ **800/544-0552;** www.alaskarailroad.com) has a variety of day tours from Seward, including a 5-hour cruise (offered with Major Marine Tours) that explores Resurrection Bay. The cruise is narrated by a park ranger and costs $216 per person; advance reservations are suggested.

Kenai Fjords Tours (✆ **877/777-4051;** www.kenaifjords.com) has a variety of land excursions and day cruises in Resurrection Bay and the Kenai Fjords National Park. A 6-hour cruise is priced at $139 for adults and $70 for children, while an 8½-hour, 150-mile cruise, including an all-you-can-eat wild Alaska salmon and prime rib dinner, is priced at $159 for adults, $80 for children 12 and under. The company also offers full- or half-day kayaking packages at Fox Island for $179 or $129, respectively, for adults and children 12 and older.

IdidaRide dog-sled tours, Old Exit Glacier Road, 3¾ miles off the Seward Highway (✆ **800/478-3139** or 907/224-8607), has dog-sled demonstrations and rides on a wheeled dog sled. IdidaRide is also offering a summer glacier dog-sledding adventure. After your 15-minute scenic flight to the top of Punch Bowl Glacier, you'll meet your musher and an enthusiastic team of huskies ready to let you take the reins or simply sit back and enjoy the ride. Each 2-hour tour costs $459 for adults and $429 for children, with flights leaving from Girdwood Airport every hour and 45 minutes between 8:30am and 5:15pm.

In addition to these tours, **fishing charters** are available from various operators in the harbor.

WHERE TO STAY

The Breeze Inn Located right at the boat harbor, this large, three-story motel-style building has good standard accommodations with the most convenient location for a fishing or Kenai Fjords boat trip. Twenty new rooms located in the "deluxe annex" at the upper end of the price range are especially nice. Some rooms have Jacuzzi tubs.

303 North Harbor Dr., Seward, AK 99664. ✆ **907/224-5237** or 888/224-5237. Fax 907/224-7024. www.breezeinn.com. 100 units. $139–$279 double. AE, DC, DISC, MC, V. Free parking. **Amenities:** Restaurant; bar. *In-room:* A/C, TV, fridge (in some), hair dryer, Wi-Fi (free).

Hotel Seward The rooms here are large, fresh, and attractively decorated. Many rooms have big bay windows, and all have TV/VCRs, refrigerators, and coffeemakers. Rooms with a view of Resurrection Bay go for a premium. Avoid the south-facing rooms, with views of the back of another hotel. The cheaper economy rooms are smaller, but have the same amenities as the standard rooms.

221 5th Ave. (P.O. Box 2288), Seward, AK 99664. ✆ **800/440-2444** or 907/224-8001. Fax 907/224-3112. www.hotelsewardalaska.com. 62 units. $229–$370 double; economy rooms $129–$149. Extra person $10. Special packages available. AE, MC, V. Free parking. **Amenities:** Restaurant; lounge. *In-room:* TV, hair dryer, kitchenette, Wi-Fi (free).

The Seward Windsong Lodge This hotel is the only one near Kenai Fjords National Park with a national park atmosphere. The location is out of town, among spruce trees in the broad, unspoiled valley of the Resurrection River, but still a mere

10 minutes from downtown Seward. The collection of buildings goes on and on, with rooms set in separate lodges and entry from exterior porches. All accommodations have a crisp feel and feature two queen beds, rustic-style furniture, and good amenities. The Jacuzzi suites are perfect for families with children.

Mailing address: P.O. Box 2301 or 31772 Herman Leirer Rd., Seward, AK 99664. (Mile .5 exit Glacier/Herman Leirer Rd. Continue for ½ mile.) ✆ **877/777-4079** or 907/777-2888. www.sewardwindsong.com. 180 units. $149–$279 double. Extra person (12 or older) $15. Special packages available. AE, DC, MC, V. Free parking. **Amenities:** Restaurant; bar/grill. *In-room:* TV/DVD, hair dryer, Wi-Fi (free).

The Van Gilder Hotel This charming if creaky old place was founded in 1916 and is listed on the National Register of Historic Places. Some rooms have a lot of charm, but authenticity means they tend to be small and unique, so choose carefully. The bathrooms are small and some are shared—one bathroom per two bedrooms. Know what you're signing on for when booking here.

308 Adams St. (P.O. Box 609), Seward, AK 99664. ✆ **800/478-0400** or 907/224-3079. Fax 907/224-3689. www.vangilderhotel.com. 24 units. $134 double with shared bathroom; $159–$189 double with private bathroom. Extra person $10. AE, DC, MC, V. *In-room:* TV, Wi-Fi (free).

WHERE TO DINE

Apollo Restaurant MEDITERRANEAN/SEAFOOD The atmosphere is Greek and a number of Greek dishes are on the menu, along with fresh local seafood, pizza, pastas, and more.

229 4th Ave. ✆ **907/224-3092.** www.apollorestaurantak.com. Main courses $13–$26. MC, V. Daily 11am–11pm.

Chinooks Waterfront STEAK/SEAFOOD Formerly known as Ray's Waterfront, the lively, noisy, and newly expanded dining room here has big windows that look out across the small-boat harbor. This is where the locals will send you, and for good reason: The food is just right, and the atmosphere is fun. The specialty is salmon served on a cedar plank. To eat well and less expensively, order the delicious fish chowder and a small Caesar salad. Don't count on speedy seating or service.

1316 4th Ave. ✆ **907/224-2207.** www.chinookswaterfront.com. Lunch $9–$15; dinner $16–$25. AE, DISC, MC, V. Mid-Mar to Sept daily noon–10pm. Closed Oct to mid-Mar.

The Smoke Shack AMERICAN Located in an old railcar, this new, little place has only six tables (located both inside and outside), but has quickly become a local favorite. The menu includes home-smoked meats—ribs, chicken, and pulled pork—and burgers, served with beans and slaw. At breakfast, the eggs Benedict come with yummy, fresh-smoked ham. All desserts, including pies and bread pudding, are made in-house.

411 Port Ave. (at the Small Boat Harbor). ✆ **907/224-7427.** Breakfast $4–$12; lunch $7–$17. MC, V. Wed–Sun 7am–3pm.

SHOPPING

Seward isn't exactly a shopping mecca. But given the arty nature of the place, there are some local products to be found. One of the more interesting facilities is the **Resurrect Coffee House Art Gallery** (✆ **907/224-7161;** www.resurrectart.com), located in a converted church at 320 3rd Ave. It's a neat place to buy art or just schmooze with the residents over a cup of java. **Softly Silk,** at 416 4th Ave. (✆ **907/224-6088;** www.softlysilk.com), is another worthy art stop.

3 Vancouver

Located in the extreme southwestern corner of British Columbia, Vancouver has the good fortune to be surrounded by both mountains and ocean. The city has been expanding and growing rapidly, thanks to an influx of foreign money (especially from Hong Kong), and has undergone a major construction boom. But the development has not diminished the quality of life in Vancouver, which has a rich cultural heritage that includes Northwest Coast Native tribes and a flourishing Asian community. As part of the push for the 2010 Winter Olympics and Paralympic Games, Vancouver saw a host of developments, including a new 12-mile line connecting the Vancouver National Airport to downtown and the opening of the luxury Shangri-La Hotel Vancouver, part of a 62-story mixed-use skyscraper that debuted last year as the tallest building in the city.

The city has a thriving **arts** scene, including numerous summertime festivals focusing on various forms of entertainment such as folk music, jazz, comedy, and even the art of fireworks display. Residents and visitors alike relish the proximity to **outdoor activities:** You can sailboard, rock-climb, mountain-bike, wilderness-hike, kayak, and ski on a world-class mountain here. For day-trippers, the city offers easily accessible attractions, including the historic **Gastown district,** with its shops and cafes, and a bustling **Chinatown.**

Rates are in U.S. dollars. Shopping on Robson Street and Granville Island is not the bargain it once was, but the shops are still enticing. You'll likely visit Vancouver at the beginning or end of your Alaska cruise, as it's the major southern transit point. We recommend that you try to visit for at least a day before or after your cruise so you have time to explore.

Note: Rates below are in Canadian dollars. At press time, the conversion was C$1 = US96¢ and may change based on the exchange rate at the time of your trip.

GETTING TO VANCOUVER

Most cruise ships dock at **Canada Place** (**✆ 604/666-7200**) at the end of Burrard Street. A landmark in the city, the pier terminal is noted for its five-sail structure, which reaches into the harbor. It's located at the edge of the downtown district and is just a quick stroll from the **Gastown** area (see below), filled with cafes, art galleries, and souvenir shops, and Robson Street, a mecca for trendy clothing stores. Right near the pier are hotels, restaurants, and shops, as well as the **Tourism Vancouver Infocentre.** Ships also sometimes dock at the **Ballantyne** cruise terminal, a 5-minute cab ride from Canada Place.

BY PLANE **Vancouver International Airport** is 13km (8 miles) south of downtown Vancouver. The average taxi fare from the airport to downtown is about $30. **Limo Jet Gold** (**✆ 604/273-1331;** www.limojetgold.com) offers flat-rate limousine service at $80 total for up to six passengers. British Columbia Rapid Transit (**✆ 604/953-3333;** www.skytrain.info) offers service to the waterfront between 5am and 1am.

BY CAR Take Granville Street in and hope that the traffic's light.

EXPLORING VANCOUVER

INFORMATION The **Tourism Vancouver Infocentre,** 200 Burrard St. (**✆ 604/683-2000;** www.tourismvancouver.com), is open from 8:30am to 6pm.

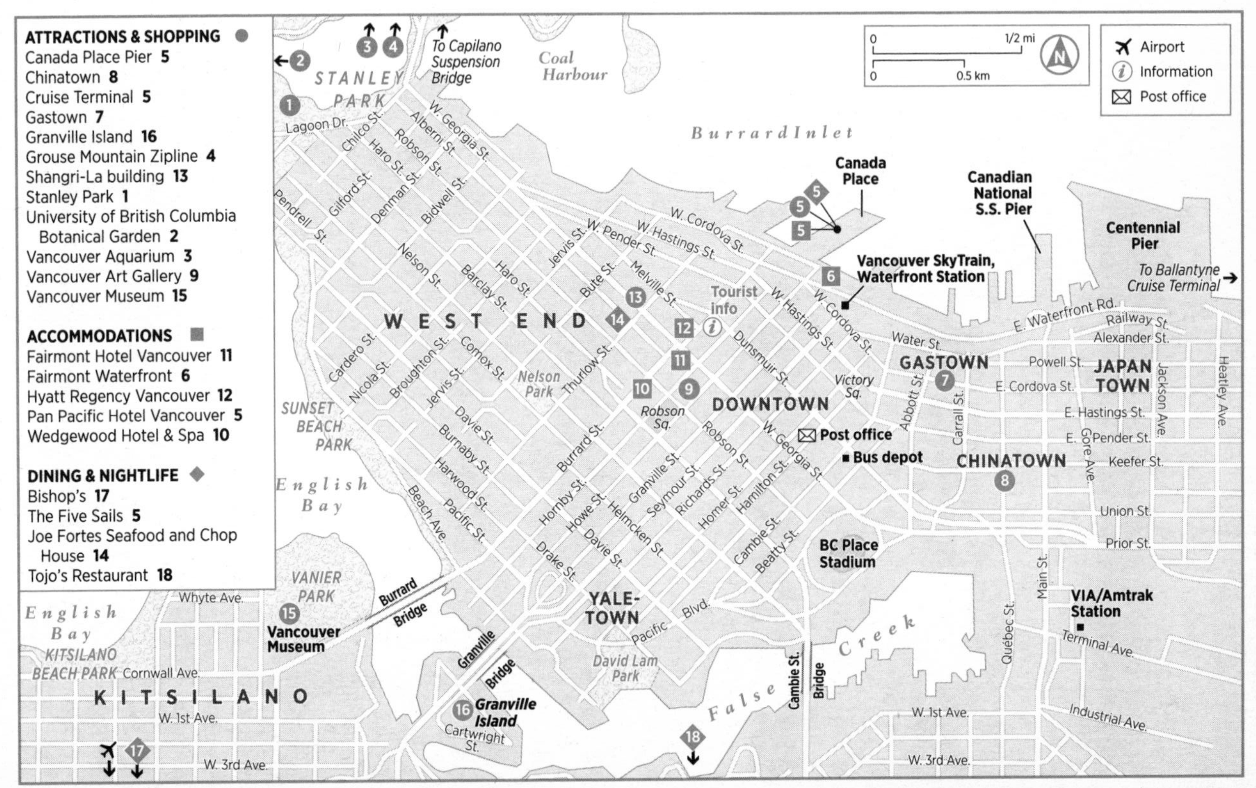

ATTRACTIONS & SHOPPING
Canada Place Pier 5
Chinatown 8
Cruise Terminal 5
Gastown 7
Granville Island 16
Grouse Mountain Zipline 4
Shangri-La building 13
Stanley Park 1
University of British Columbia Botanical Garden 2
Vancouver Aquarium 3
Vancouver Art Gallery 9
Vancouver Museum 15
ACCOMMODATIONS
Fairmont Hotel Vancouver 11
Fairmont Waterfront 6
Hyatt Regency Vancouver 12
Pan Pacific Hotel Vancouver 5
Wedgewood Hotel & Spa 10
DINING & NIGHTLIFE
Bishop's 17
The Five Sails 5
Joe Fortes Seafood and Chop House 14
Tojo's Restaurant 18
0 1/2 mi
0 0.5 km
N
Airport
Information
Post office
STANLEY PARK
To Capilano Suspension Bridge
Coal Harbour
Burrard Inlet
Canada Place
Canadian National S.S. Pier
Centennial Pier
To Ballantyne Cruise Terminal
Vancouver SkyTrain, Waterfront Station
Tourist info
WEST END
DOWNTOWN
GASTOWN
JAPAN TOWN
CHINATOWN
Victory Sq.
Robson Sq.
Nelson Park
Post office
Bus depot
SUNSET BEACH PARK
English Bay
BC Place Stadium
VIA/Amtrak Station
VANIER PARK
Vancouver Museum
Burrard Bridge
Granville Bridge
Granville Island
YALE-TOWN
David Lam Park
False Creek
Cambie St. Bridge
KITSILANO BEACH PARK
KITSILANO
Lagoon Dr.
Chilco St.
Alberni St.
W. Georgia St.
Robson St.
Haro St.
Pendrell St.
Gilford St.
Denman St.
Bidwell St.
Nelson St.
Barclay St.
Jervis St.
W. Pender St.
W. Hastings St.
W. Cordova St.
Bute St.
Melville St.
Dunsmuir St.
Cardero St.
Nicola St.
Broughton St.
Comox St.
Thurlow St.
Davie St.
Burnaby St.
Harwood St.
Pacific St.
Beach Ave.
Burrard St.
Hornby St.
Howe St.
Granville St.
Seymour St.
Richards St.
Homer St.
Hamilton St.
Helmcken St.
Drake St.
Cambie St.
Beatty St.
Pacific Blvd.
Cartwright St.
Water St.
E. Waterfront Rd.
Railway St.
Alexander St.
Powell St.
E. Cordova St.
E. Hastings St.
E. Pender St.
Keefer St.
Abbott St.
Carrall St.
Gore Ave.
Jackson Ave.
Heatley Ave.
Union St.
Prior St.
Main St.
Québec St.
Terminal Ave.
Industrial Ave.
W. 1st Ave.
W. 3rd Ave.
Whyte Ave.
Cornwall Ave.

Twilight Mania

Recently, Vancouver has become known as the place where the teen cult movie *Twilight* and sequels *New Moon* and *Eclipse* were filmed, so "Twi-hard" fans will be in their element. The cast, headed by teen heartthrobs Rob Pattinson and Kristen Stewart, have been seen eating, shopping, and partying all over the city. In case you're traveling with teens: Pattinson seemed to favor the **Glowbal Grill & Satay Bar** in Yaletown (1079 Mainland St.; ✆ **604/602-0835;** www.glowbalgrill.com), where he was seen dining two to three times a week during filming, even celebrating his birthday there. The **Blue Water Café & Raw Bar** (1095 Hamilton St.; ✆ **606/688-8078;** www.bluewatercafe.net) is another Twi-hard must-see as it hosted the entire cast for both the *New Moon* wrap party and the *Eclipse* kick-off. A Yaletown institution, the restaurant is known for its wooden interiors and expansive patio. Pattinson was also seen having a drink at the **Yaletown Brewing Company** (1111 Mainland St.; ✆ **604/681-2739**), while Kristen Stewart and co-star Nikki Reed were seen shopping on Robson Street. Elsewhere, Kellan Lutz sampled sushi at Miku Restaurant (1055 W. Hastings St.; ✆ **604/568-3900**) and Jamie Campbell Bower Twittered about his visit to the **Vancouver Art Gallery** (p. 176). When not sightseeing and sampling local cuisine, the actors spent their days filming at various locations around town, including David Thompson Secondary School (Forks High in the movie) and the Ridge Theatre in the Kerrisdale neighborhood.

GETTING AROUND Because of its shape and setting, Vancouver has lots of bridges—Burrard Bridge, Granville Bridge, Cambie Street Bridge, and, of course, Lions Gate Bridge. Cruise ships pass under the Lions Gate Bridge on their way to and from Canada Place. The bridges sometimes make driving in Vancouver a slow endeavor. The **Aquabus ferries** shuttle visitors from Granville Island and elsewhere. Fares are $3 to $6 for adults (depending on destination), $1.50 to $3 for seniors and children (✆ **604/689-5858;** www.theaquabus.com). A water taxi service called the **Bowen Island Express** launched in 2009 and runs between Granville Island and Bowen Island. There are six sailings per weekday from 6am to 6:45pm, and 9am to 7pm on weekends, and the trip takes 35 minutes. Bowen Island makes for a perfect Vancouver day trip, with opportunities for hiking, kayaking, golf, dining, and shopping. Fares are $20 for adults, $10 for children; reservations are recommended (✆ **604/484-8497;** www.englishbaylaunch.ca).

Car-rental agencies with local branches include Avis, Budget, Hertz Canada, and Thrifty. You can easily walk the downtown area of Vancouver, but if you want transportation, you've got a few options. The **Translink system** (schedules and trip info ✆ **604/953-3333** [6:30am–11:30pm daily]; www.translink.bc.ca) includes electric buses, ferries, and the magnetic-rail SkyTrain. On the main routes, it runs from 5am to 2am daily. Schedules are available at many hotels and online. **Taxis** are available through **Black Top** (✆ **604/731-1111;** www.blacktopcheckercabs.supersites.ca), **Yellow Cab** (✆ **604/681-1111;** www.yellowcabonline.com), and **MacLure's** (✆ **604/683-6666;** www.maclurescabs.ca); call them by phone or look for them around the major hotels.

You can rent a bicycle from **Bayshore Bicycle Rentals** (which also rents in-line skates), 745 Denman St. (✆ **604/688-BIKE** [2453]; www.bayshorebikerentals.com), or **Spokes Bicycle Rentals,** 1798 W. Georgia St. (✆ **604/688-5141;** www.vancouverbikerental.com); rates start at about $6 per hour, $20 for a half-day, and $28 for a full day. Helmets (required by law) and locks are included in the rate. The city has several great bicycle runs, including Stanley Park, the Seawall Promenade on the park's north end, and Pacific Spirit Park.

ATTRACTIONS WITHIN WALKING DISTANCE

Canada Place Pier Vancouver's most distinctive landmark is Canada Place Pier, with five gleaming white Teflon sails that recall a giant sailing vessel. The pier houses the Vancouver Convention and Exhibition Centre as well as the Alaska cruise-ship terminal. Check out Canada's Storyboard, a 14×25 foot LED high definition video screen featuring iconic Canadian content, as well as the Canadian Trail, a unique walk across Canada involving the use of surface tiles and colored glass, that opened last year. At foot of Howe and Burrard sts., next to the Waterfront SkyTrain Station. www.canadaplace.ca.

Chinatown Vancouver's Chinatown is one of the largest in North America (though it doesn't hold a candle to those in New York and San Francisco), and, like Gastown, it's also a historic district. Chinese architecture and the **Dr. Sun Yat-Sen Garden,** 578 Carrall St. (✆ **604/662-3207;** www.vancouverchinesegarden.com; admission $10 adults, $9 seniors, $8 students, free for children 5 and under; daily 10am–6pm May 1–June 14, 9:30am–7pm June 15–Aug 31, 10am–6pm Sept 1–30; closed Mon Nov–May), are among the attractions, along with great food and shops selling Chinese wares. In addition to photogenic Chinese gates, bright red buildings, and open-air markets, you'll find the amazing 6-foot-wide **Sam Kee Building** at 8 W. Pender St., which holds the record for being the narrowest commercial building in the world. In the area bordered by E. Pender and Keefer sts., from Carrall St. to Gore Ave.

Gastown Gastown is named for "Gassy" Jack Deighton, who in 1867 built a saloon in Maple Tree Square (at the intersection of Water, Alexander, and Carrall sts.) to serve the area's loggers and trappers. The Gastown of today has cobblestone streets, historic buildings, gaslights, a steam-powered clock (near the corner of Water and Cambie sts.), street musicians, and a touch of bohemia. It's so close to the ship pier that it's a must-see. Boutiques, antiques stores, and art galleries stand beside lots of touristy shops, restaurants, clubs, and cafes. In the area bordered by Water and Alexander sts., from Richard St., east to Columbia St.

Stanley Park Just a few miles from downtown and the green-space pride of the city, this is also Canada's largest urban park and attracts 8 million visitors a year. Stanley Park was damaged by high winds in December 2006, with some 3,000 of its 150,000 trees toppled or otherwise destroyed and parts of the seawall damaged (forcing the seawall promenade to be closed). Millions of dollars were committed to a repair effort, and the park is now completely restored. Its 405 hectares (1,000 acres) contain rose gardens, totem poles, a yacht club, a kids' water park, miles of wooded hiking trails, great views of Lions Gate Bridge, and the outstanding **Vancouver Aquarium** (✆ **604/659-FISH** [3474]; www.vanaqua.org; admission $30 adults, $23 seniors/students, $19 children 4–12, free for children 3 and under; open summer daily 9:30am–7pm, winter daily 9:30am–5pm). Check out the 15-minute 4-D movie

"Planet Earth: Shallow Seas 4-D Experience," feed archerfish and frogs, and catch one of the three daily dolphin shows. The aquarium also boasts a baby beluga, named Nala, born in June 2009.

Downtown Vancouver, northwest of the cruise-ship terminal. http://vancouver.ca/parks/parks/stanley. Park daily sunrise–sunset; in summer, a shuttle bus operates throughout the park 10am–6:30pm.

University of British Columbia Botanical Garden Canada's oldest continuously operating university botanical garden has more than 8,000 different plants spread over an area spanning 110 acres. The Garden's new "eco-adventure," the Greenheart Canopy Walkway, is a 1,010-foot aerial trail system suspended 57 feet in the air. It allows visitors to experience the west coast forest canopy close up in a 45-minute fully guided tour.

6804 SW Marine Dr. ✆ **888/755-3227.** www.greenheartcanopywalkway.com. Admission $20 adults, $16 seniors, $14 youth (13–17), $6 children (5–12), kids under 5 are free (rates include entry to the botanical garden). There is a family rate of $36. Daily 9am–5pm. Open-toed shoes are not permitted on the walkway, and visitors must have both hands free to hold onto the railing. Children should be able to walk on their own or be securely carried in an approved child backpack (no walkers).

Vancouver Art Gallery Located within easy walking distance of the pier, the gallery is housed in a building constructed in 1906 as the provincial courthouse. It contains an impressive collection that includes works by British Columbia artist Emily Carr and the Canadian Group of Seven. Also on display are international and other regional paintings, sculptures, graphics, photography, and video ranging from classic to contemporary. The Annex Gallery features rotating educational exhibits geared toward younger audiences. The gallery began construction of a new building in 2010, to be completed in 2014.

750 Hornby St. ✆ **604/662-4719.** www.vanartgallery.bc.ca. Admission $21 adults, $16 seniors, $15 students, $7 for children 5–12, free for children 4 and under. Daily 10am–5pm; Tues 10am–9pm.

Vancouver Museum This museum offers a history of the city, from the Coast Salish Indian settlement to the arrival of early pioneers, to European settlement, to 20th-century expansion. Exhibits allow visitors to walk through the steerage deck of a 19th-century immigrant ship, peek into a Hudson Bay Company trading post, and sit in an 1880s Canadian-Pacific passenger car. Re-creations of Victorian and Edwardian rooms show how early Vancouverites decorated their homes. The "You Say You Want A Revolution" permanent exhibit showcases Vancouver's hippie culture during the 1960s, while the Gateway to the Pacific exhibit focuses on life in Vancouver in the early 1900s right up to the impact of World War II (including the government's registering of all Canadians of Japanese descent); objects displayed include a 1906 Oldsmobile, Vancouver's first gas station, and ashes from Hiroshima.

1100 Chestnut St. ✆ **604/736-4431.** www.museumofvancouver.ca. Admission $12 adults, $10 seniors and students 18 and older, $8 ages 6–17, children 5 and under free. Family rate $35. Tues–Sun 10am–5pm (till 8pm Thurs in summer); closed on Mondays.

ATTRACTIONS BEYOND THE PORT AREA

Capilano Suspension Bridge Sure, it's touristy, but it's still a kick to cross this narrow, historic, 137m (449-ft.) walking bridge, located 70m (230 ft.) above the Capilano River in North Vancouver (about a 10-min. drive, or a $17 cab ride, from downtown). From this vantage point, even the towering evergreens below look tiny (this attraction is not for those with a fear of heights). The adjacent park has hiking trails, history and forestry exhibits, a carving center, and Native American dance performances (only in summer), as well as restaurants and a gift shop. A new Treetops Adventure (included in admission price) lets you walk across 197m (646 ft.) of cable bridges high in the forest.

3735 Capilano Rd., North Vancouver. ✆ **604/985-7474.** www.capbridge.com. Admission $30 adults, $28 seniors, $24 students 17 and older with ID, $19 youth 13–16, $10 children 6–12, free for children 5 and under. May 1–28 9am–7pm, May 29–Sept 6 8:30am–8pm, Sept 6–Oct 2 9am–6pm, Oct 3–Dec 2 9am–5pm, Dec 3–Jan 1 10am–9pm (Canyon Lights 5–9pm), Jan 3–Mar 5 9am–5pm, Mar 6–Apr 30 9am–6pm.

Grouse Mountain Zipline Only about 15 minutes from the city, this ski and year-round mountain resort features the summertime attraction **Air Grouse,** a Zipline high above the rainforest. On the three-line adventure circuit, you whip along at more than 40 mph, and if you take a look you'll see Blue Grouse Lake and other views whizzing by. Along the 1-hour ride, guides will tell you about the indigenous flora and fauna and its significance to the First Nations people. The Grouse Mountain Skyride is a more restful way to view your surroundings, by way of North America's largest aerial tramway.

6400 Nancy Greene Way, North Vancouver. ✆ **604/980-9311.** www.grousemountain.com. General admission $40; Air Grouse mountain Zipline $105, including aerial tramway up mountain. Daily 9am–10pm (time of last departure).

BEST CRUISE-LINE SHORE EXCURSIONS

Capilano Canyon Nature Tour (4 hr.; $99 adults, $49 children 12 and under): Walk alongside the canyon and through a rainforest with 500-year-old trees, as guides describe the ecosystem and wildlife habitats. Then cross the Lions Gate Bridge, with its spectacular views of the skyline, and eat a picnic lunch before returning to the airport or your downtown hotel.

City Tour (2½–3½ hr.; $59 adults, $29 children): This bus tour covers major sights such as Gastown, Chinatown, Stanley Park, and high-end residential areas. You'll also visit Queen Elizabeth Park, the city's highest southern vantage point and home of the Bloedell Conservatory, which commands a 360-degree city view and features an enclosed tropical rainforest complete with free-flying birds; the tour may also include Granville Island.

Note: This tour is usually offered after the cruise and is available only to passengers with late-afternoon or evening flights. At the end of the tour, you are dropped off at the airport for your flight home.

EXCURSIONS OFFERED BY LOCAL AGENCIES

Stanley Park Horse-Drawn Tours (✆ **604/681-5115;** www.stanleyparktours.com) has offered tours of the 405-hectare (1,000-acre) Stanley Park by horse-drawn trolley for more than a century. The narrated 1-hour tours depart from the Coal Harbour parking lot beside the Stanley Park information booth on Park Drive. Tickets are $29 adults, $27 seniors and students, $16 children 3 to 12, free for children 2 and under. March 15-Oct 31.

The **Vancouver Trolley Company** (✆ **888/451-5581** or 604/801-5515; www.vancouvertrolley.com) has old-fashioned (engine-powered) San Francisco-style trolleys with narrated tours on a circuit that includes Gastown, Chinatown, Granville Island, Stanley Park, and other areas of interest. You can get off and on as you like. Stop number one is in Gastown. Tickets are $38 for adults, $35 for seniors and students, and $20 for children.

A Wok Around Chinatown (✆ **604/736-9508;** www.awokaround.com) is a 4-hour walking tour that takes visitors around the colorful and flavorful neighborhood. The tour is given Friday through Monday at 10am and leaves from Dr. Sun Yat-Sen Garden (see listing for "Chinatown" in "Attractions Within Walking Distance," above); the tour costs $68 and includes a dim sum lunch.

For a great day trip, take a ride on the **Whistler Mountaineer** (✆ **888/687-7245;** www.whistlermountaineer.com). You'll be picked up at your hotel around 7am and board the train at 8am, where you'll enjoy breakfast and the scenery, then have a chance to tour the charming alpine village for 3 hours as part of the Sea to Sky Climb package. En route back to Vancouver, afternoon tea and sandwiches are served. The Mountaineer departs daily from May through October; a round-trip ticket costs $199 for adults and $109 for children 2 to 11 (free for kids under 2).

If you'd prefer to stay on the water, **Prince of Whales** marine adventure company (✆ **888/383-4884;** www.princeofwhales.com) offers harbor tours, day trips to Victoria, and whale-watching from its floating offices adjacent to the Westin Bayshore Hotel. Passengers don red cruiser suits and then climb aboard for the chance to see harbor seals, sea lions, eagles, and maybe even bears, in addition to beautiful scenery. Prices range from $35 to $235, depending on the tour.

For another fast-paced way to check out the best of Vancouver's scenery and wildlife, **Sewell's Marina** (✆ **604/921-3474;** www.sewellsmarina.com) now offers a "Taste of the West Coast" tour that combines a 2-hour guided Sea Safari with a gourmet meal at the Boathouse Restaurant in Horseshoe Bay. A 20-minute scenic floatplane tour will transport you back to downtown Vancouver. The custom-designed 30-foot inflatable vessel is "fast but safe," and fetching orange waterproof outerwear is provided. The tour runs from April to October, leaves from 6409 Bay St. in West Vancouver, and costs $219 per person. Salmon fishing charters, "Sea to Tee" golf packages, and boat rentals are also available.

A more unusual way of seeing the city is urban kayaking. Paddle down False Creek (actually an inlet), which threads past up-market Yaletown condos and the bustle of Granville Island, and float under the Granville and Burrard street bridges. If you have time, take a few hours to explore the rugged coastline of Stanley Park, Vancouver's 1,000-acre nature reserve. **Ecomarine Ocean Kayak Centre** (✆ **604/689-7575;** www.ecomarine.com) is the place to go for rentals, sales, and guided tours from Granville Island and English Bay, with prices starting at $59 per person. Rainforest and nighttime paddles are also available.

WHERE TO STAY

Almost all of Vancouver's downtown hotels are within walking distance of shops, restaurants, and attractions, although you might want to avoid places around Hastings and Main after dark. Granville Street downtown is an area that has been "cleaned up" and is now home to some lower end, boutique-type hotels. The area has clubs and an active nightlife, but also lots of panhandlers.

The Fairmont Hotel Vancouver The grande dame of Vancouver's hotels is designed on a generous scale, with a copper roof, marble interiors, and massive proportions, with unparalleled luxury and spaciousness in its lobby and public areas. Afternoon high tea is a proud tradition here. Guest rooms have marble bathrooms and mahogany furnishings, and offer city, harbor, and mountain views.

900 W. Georgia St., Vancouver, BC V6C2W6. ✆ **866/540-4452** or 604/684-3131. Fax 604/662-1929. www.fairmont.com/hotelvancouver. 556 units. $389–$429 double; from $459 suite. Children 17 and under stay free in parent's room. AE, DC, DISC, MC, V. Parking $27. **Amenities:** 2 restaurants; lounge; babysitting; concierge; state-of-the-art health club & spa. *In-room:* A/C and ceiling fans, TV, hair dryer, high-speed Internet ($15/24 hr.).

The Fairmont Waterfront This ultramodern hotel with 23 stories of blue reflective glass takes advantage of its harborside location, providing spectacular waterfront and mountain views from 70% of the rooms. A concourse links the hotel to the rest of Waterfront Centre, Canada Place, and the Alaska cruise-ship terminal.

900 Canada Place Way, Vancouver, BC V6C 3L5. ✆ **866/540-4509** or 604/691-1991. Fax 604/691-1999. www.fairmont.com/waterfront. 489 units. $389–$489 double; from $509 suite. AE, DC, MC, V. Parking $27. **Amenities:** Restaurant; lounge; babysitting; concierge; health club & spa; outdoor heated pool. *In-room:* A/C, TV, VCR (in some), hair dryer, high-speed Internet ($15/24 hr.), minibar.

Hyatt Regency Vancouver The Hyatt is a modern white tower built over the Royal Centre Mall, which contains 60 specialty shops. The very large guest rooms are tastefully decorated with understated yet comfortable furnishings. Corner rooms on the north and west sides have balconies with lovely views.

655 Burrard St., Vancouver, BC V6C 2R7. ✆ **800/233-1234** or 604/683-1234. Fax 604/689-3707. www.vancouver.hyatt.com. 644 units. From $294–$369 double; $449 suite. AE, DC, DISC, MC, V. Valet parking $35; self-parking $26. **Amenities:** 2 restaurants; bar; babysitting; concierge; health club & whirlpool; heated outdoor pool; room service. *In-room:* A/C, TV, hair dryer, minibar, Wi-Fi ($15/24 hr.).

Pan Pacific Hotel Vancouver Atop the landmark Canada Place Pier and cruise-ship terminal is the spectacular 23-story Pan Pacific Hotel. This and the Fairmont Waterfront are the closest accommodations to the cruise-ship dock. All of the guest rooms are modern, spacious, and comfortably furnished. All come with such amenities as coffeemakers, irons, and ironing boards. Try to book a harborside room for the best view. The eighth floor terrace features Vancouver's only saltwater, heated outdoor hotel pool as well as a Jacuzzi, a sauna, and a poolside bar. The luxurious Spa Utopia and Salon is a Roman-inspired sanctuary with towering pillars and cascading waterfalls—an excellent place to recover from jet lag (or end-of-cruise blues).

300–999 Canada Place, Vancouver, BC V6C 3B5. ✆ **800/937-1515** or 604/662-8111. Fax 604/685-8690. www.panpacific.com/vancouver. 503 units. $269–$509 double; from $1,000 suite. AE, DC, MC, V. Valet parking $28. **Amenities:** 3 restaurants; bar/lounge; babysitting; concierge; health club; heated outdoor pool; room service. *In-room:* A/C, TV, hair dryer, high-speed Internet (free), minibar.

Wedgewood Hotel & Spa This small boutique property near the Robson Street shops has individually furnished rooms with nice amenities, and all have balconies. Penthouse suites are equipped with fireplaces, wet bars, Jacuzzis, and scenic garden terraces. Public rooms are decorated with antiques and fresh flowers. The hotel has one of the best watering holes in town, Bacchus, an upscale piano bar where you can sink into a plush chair or couch, enjoy an excellent martini, and take in the local scene. The Bacchus restaurant has also won awards for its fine cuisine.

845 Hornby St., Vancouver, BC V6Z 1V1. ✆ **800/663-0666** or 604/689-7777. Fax 604/608-5348. www.wedgewoodhotel.com. 89 units. $268–$380 double; $450–$880 suite. AE, DC, MC, V. Valet parking $21. **Amenities:** Restaurant; bar; babysitting; concierge; health club & spa; room service. *In-room:* A/C, TV/DVD, CD player, hair dryer, minibar, Wi-Fi (free).

WHERE TO DINE

Bishop's PACIFIC NORTHWEST The atmosphere is all candlelight, white linen, and soft jazz; the service is impeccable; and the food is even better. Owner John

Winter Olympics

If you want to reminisce about the 2010 Winter Olympics, check out some of the sites around town that were central to the Games. BC Place (www.bcplacestadium.com) is where the opening and closing ceremonies were held (and where the Canadian Football League's BC Lions play). Get there from the Stadium/Chinatown SkyTrain Station; it's about a 5-minute walk from the station. By bus, take downtown Vancouver's no. 15 and no. 17 buses.

Bishop greets you personally, escorts you to a table, and introduces you to an extensive catalog of fine wines and a menu he describes as "contemporary home cooking." Entrees include seared BC halibut filet with house corned beef and sunroot hash, grilled BC spotted shrimp with leeks, and braised beef and lentils. If you have only one evening to dine out in Vancouver, spend it here.

2183 W. 4th Ave. ✆ **604/738-2025.** www.bishopsonline.com. Reservations recommended. Main courses $37–$40. AE, DC, MC, V. Daily 5:30–11pm.

The Five Sails PACIFIC NORTHWEST/SEAFOOD The Five Sails' view of Coal Harbour, Stanley Park, and the Coast Mountains is pure magic, a vision of the rugged nirvana that is Vancouver. The Five Sails' excellent cuisine, inventive without being too clever, is the perfect accompaniment. The restaurant is sparkling after a major renovation, and the menu features West Coast ingredients, including local produce and lake trout. The Five Sails Seafood Tower is a special treat for two or more, literally bursting with fresh local shellfish (market price).

999 Canada Place Way, in the Pan Pacific Hotel. ✆ **604/844-2855.** www.fivesails.ca. Reservations recommended. Main courses $32–$39. AE, DC, MC, V. Daily 5:30–10pm.

Joe Fortes Seafood and Chop House SEAFOOD This place has been winning awards—for its food, its wine list, and its oysters—for years. This two-story darkwood restaurant, with an immensely popular bar, is filled with Vancouver's young and successful. The decor and atmosphere are reminiscent of an oyster bar, and the spacious covered and heated roof garden (where cigar smokers gather) is pure Vancouver. Pan-roasted oysters are a menu staple. A daily selection of up to a dozen types of oysters are offered raw or cooked in a variety of ways, along with fresh fish, Dungeness crab, and live lobsters. A rooftop patio provides outdoor seating high above the bustle of Robson Street.

777 Thurlow St. ✆ **604/669-1940.** www.joefortes.ca. Reservations recommended. Most main courses $15–$58; early-bird (4–6pm) 3-course menu $28. AE, DC, DISC, MC, V. Daily 11am–11pm.

Tojo's Restaurant JAPANESE/SUSHI Hidekazu Tojo's sushi is Vancouver's best, attracting Japanese businessmen, Hollywood celebrities, and anyone else who's willing to pay for the finest. Tell Tojo how much you want to spend, and he'll prepare an incredible meal to fit your budget.

1133 W. Broadway. ✆ **604/872-8050.** www.tojos.com. Reservations required for sushi bar. Personalized meals $55–$110 and up. A la carte menu $24–55. AE, DC, MC, V. Mon–Sat 5–10pm.

SHOPPING

Granville Island is a shopper's paradise, with its vibrant daily market and streets lined with fine art studios (it's a hearty walk from downtown, so depending on where you're staying, you may want to take a cab or a water taxi). Downtown, **Robson Street** is chockablock with boutiques, souvenir shops, coffeehouses, and bistros. The massive **Pacific Centre Mall** fills the city blocks between Robson, Dunsmuir, Howe, and Granville streets and is within easy walking distance of the pier. Our coauthor, Fran Golden, can attest to the fine offerings at **Hill's Native Art** (✆ **604/685-4249;** www.hills.ca), 165 Water St., in Gastown; she has a totem pole from this shop in her dining room. The store also sells moccasins, ceremonial masks, silkscreen prints, and jewelry.

4 Seattle

Americans now have more opportunities than ever to begin and end their Alaska-bound cruises on U.S. soil. In recent years, Americans' growing interest in the 49th state and their clear preference for American gateways and destinations has had the cruise lines falling over themselves to deploy more of their Alaska ships in Seattle. Seattle has become an attractive alternative home port to Vancouver for large ocean-going passenger liners bound for the Northland. In 2000, only one major ship was based in Seattle for the Alaska cruise season. In 2011, 10 large vessels will be based in the city. Seattle is now clearly the top port for Alaska cruises. Small ship line Lindblad has some ships cruising from here too.

As cruise ports go, Seattle doesn't have to bow to any other. Known as the Emerald City because of the abundant greenery found in every direction, it is every bit as scenically appealing as Vancouver. Its skyline is dominated by the 607-foot-high revolving Space Needle, built in 1962 for the World's Fair (known at the time as the Century 21 Exposition). It's linked to the heart of downtown by a monorail. Seattle has shopping, fine restaurants, attractions galore, good air service, culture, a wide range of accommodations, internal transportation—everything you need, in fact, to enjoy a day or two before or after your cruise.

Seattle is very much a water-oriented city, set between Puget Sound and Lake Washington, with Lake Union in the center. Practically everywhere you look, the views are of sailboats, cargo ships, ferries, windsurfers, and anglers—and trees and parklands, of course. One of our favorite pastimes on nice days in Seattle is to take one of the local ferries—to anywhere—just for the fun of it.

The **Seattle Waterfront,** along Alaskan Way from Yesler Way North to Bay Street and Myrtle Edwards Park, is one of the city's single most popular attractions, and much like San Francisco's Fisherman's Wharf area, this can be both good and bad. Yes, it's very touristy, with tacky gift shops, saltwater taffy, T-shirts galore, and lots of overpriced restaurants, but it's also home to the Seattle Aquarium and the Pike Place Market. Your ship will dock right along this strip. There are companies located here that offer sailboat and sea-kayak tours.

At Pier 54, you'll find companies for sea-kayak tours, sport-fishing trips, jet-boat tours, and bicycle rentals. At Pier 55, boats leave for 1½-hour harbor cruises, as well as the **Tillicum Village** excursions to Blake Island (see "Attractions Beyond the Port Area," below). At Pier 57, you'll find the **Bay Pavilion,** which has a vintage carousel and a video arcade to keep the kids busy. At Pier 59, you'll find the **Seattle Aquarium** and a waterfront park. Meanwhile, Pier 69 is the dock for the ferries that ply the waters between Seattle and Victoria. Sunset and jazz cruises leave from this pier.

If you are in the city for a day or two you may want to venture 20 minutes from downtown (by car, cab, or bus) to Ballard, a waterfront area that has moved from blue collar to trendy with a variety of boutiques, hip eateries, and nighttime spots.

GETTING TO SEATTLE

BY PLANE **Seattle-Tacoma International Airport** (© **800/544-1965** or 206/787-5388; www.portseattle.org/seatac/), also known as **Sea-Tac,** is located about 14 miles south of Seattle. It's connected to the city by I-5. Generally, allow 30 minutes for the trip between the airport and downtown. Because the Bell Street passenger ship pier, where Norwegian Cruise Line and Celebrity ships depart, is superbly located a few minutes' walk from the heart of downtown, airport taxis will drop you at the terminal for about the same price as they would charge to go to any of the major Seattle hotels. Other lines depart from the new Smith Cove Cruise Terminal at Terminal 91, opened in 2009, just north of downtown but not within walking distance. (The cruise ships previously docked at Terminal 30, but that's been returned to cargo container use).

A **taxi** between the airport and downtown will cost you between $35 and $40. **Gray Line Airport Express** (© **800/426-7532** or 206/626-6088; http://graylineseattle.com/airportexpress1.cfm) provides service between all the airport terminals and seven downtown hotels, with the first hotel pickup at 5am and then every half-hour through the day until the last pickup at 9:30pm. The fares are $15 one-way, $25 round-trip; children ages 2 to 12 pay $11 one-way, $18 round-trip. **Shuttle Express** (© **425/981-7000;** www.shuttleexpress.com) also gets you between Sea-Tac and downtown. The company's check-in desk is on the third floor of the parking garage at the airport, and a one-way fare for up to two people is $36 ($6 for the third rider) to most downtown areas. The public **Seattle Metro** (© **800/542-7876** or 206/553-3000; http://metro.kingcounty.gov) operates service from the airport to downtown for as little as $2 in the off-peak hours, clearly the least expensive transportation. But the bus drops passengers only at the Seattle Convention Center, not at the hotel of their choice, so it's not necessarily the most convenient.

BY CAR The major freeway running through Seattle is I-5. Follow it south from downtown to Sea-Tac. I-5 runs north to the Canadian border, which leads, ultimately, to the road to Vancouver. Alaskan Way, a busy street, runs along the waterfront and past the Bell Street cruise-ship terminal. For Terminal 91, you'll head towards the Magnolia Bridge. It's only a very short car or cab ride from any city hotel to the cruise terminals, which are not more than 10 minutes from even the most distant of the hotels listed here.

EXPLORING SEATTLE

INFORMATION The **Seattle-King County Convention and Visitors Bureau** operates a visitor information center in the Washington State Convention and Trade Center, 800 Convention Place, Galleria Level, at the corner of 8th Avenue and Pike Street (© **206/461-5840;** www.visitseattle.org). It's open 9am to 5pm Monday through Friday.

GETTING AROUND Nearly every major car rental company has an outlet at Sea-Tac, and many companies also have offices in downtown hotels. Prices will depend on the season and even on the day of the week (rentals on Fri, for example, when cruise passengers are likely to arrive in large numbers, will probably cost more than on, say, Wed). **Seattle Metro** (© **800/542-7876** or 206/553-3000; http://metro.kingcounty.gov) operates buses in the downtown area and throughout King County. The standard

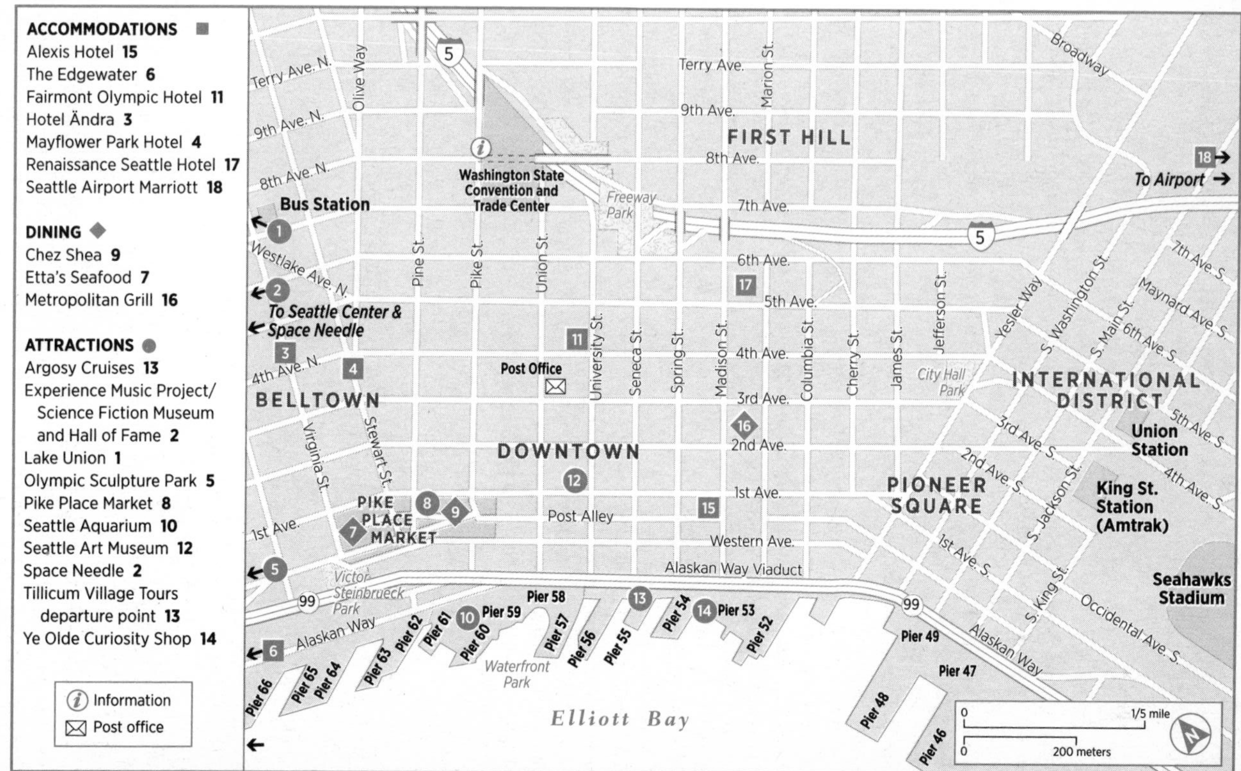
ACCOMMODATIONS
Alexis Hotel 15
The Edgewater 6
Fairmont Olympic Hotel 11
Hotel Ändra 3
Mayflower Park Hotel 4
Renaissance Seattle Hotel 17
Seattle Airport Marriott 18
DINING
Chez Shea 9
Etta's Seafood 7
Metropolitan Grill 16
ATTRACTIONS
Argosy Cruises 13
Experience Music Project/ Science Fiction Museum and Hall of Fame 2
Lake Union 1
Olympic Sculpture Park 5
Pike Place Market 8
Seattle Aquarium 10
Seattle Art Museum 12
Space Needle 2
Tillicum Village Tours departure point 13
Ye Olde Curiosity Shop 14
Information
Post office
FIRST HILL
BELLTOWN
DOWNTOWN
PIKE PLACE MARKET
PIONEER SQUARE
INTERNATIONAL DISTRICT
Bus Station
To Seattle Center & Space Needle
Washington State Convention and Trade Center
Freeway Park
Post Office
City Hall Park
Union Station
King St. Station (Amtrak)
Seahawks Stadium
To Airport
Victor Steinbrueck Park
Waterfront Park
Elliott Bay
Terry Ave. N.
9th Ave. N.
8th Ave. N.
Westlake Ave. N.
4th Ave. N.
1st Ave.
Olive Way
Pine St.
Pike St.
Union St.
University St.
Seneca St.
Spring St.
Madison St.
Marion St.
Columbia St.
Cherry St.
James St.
Jefferson St.
Yesler Way
S. Washington St.
S. Main St.
S. Jackson St.
S. King St.
Terry Ave.
9th Ave.
8th Ave.
7th Ave.
6th Ave.
5th Ave.
4th Ave.
3rd Ave.
2nd Ave.
1st Ave.
Post Alley
Western Ave.
Alaskan Way Viaduct
Alaskan Way
Virginia St.
Stewart St.
Broadway
7th Ave. S.
Maynard Ave. S.
6th Ave. S.
5th Ave. S.
4th Ave. S.
3rd Ave. S.
2nd Ave. S.
1st Ave. S.
Occidental Ave. S.
Pier 46
Pier 47
Pier 48
Pier 49
Pier 52
Pier 53
Pier 54
Pier 55
Pier 56
Pier 57
Pier 58
Pier 59
Pier 60
Pier 61
Pier 62
Pier 63
Pier 64
Pier 65
Pier 66
0
1/5 mile
0
200 meters

fare is $2 to $2.75 for adults, 75¢ for seniors. Seattle Metro also operates a free downtown waterfront service using buses painted to look like old-fashioned streetcars. The Route 99 buses operate every 20 to 30 minutes during the day and evenings too in summer.

ATTRACTIONS WITHIN WALKING DISTANCE

Pike Place Market City officials have worked overtime to ensure that the Pike Place Market, begun in 1907 and one of Seattle's most enduring institutions, remains true to its roots. Just a few blocks from the passenger pier, the city made a big push a few years ago to add more tourist-friendly T-shirt and souvenir shops, but the market vendors fought to keep the emphasis on food and flowers and were at least partly successful. The market remains the single best place in the city to find fresh produce and such seasonal specialties as Rainier cherries, Washington asparagus, fresh king salmon, and Northwest hazelnuts. Go hungry: The grazing opportunities here are unsurpassed. We strongly recommend that you don't leave without trying a Dungeness crab cocktail, a fresh-baked cinnamon roll or *piroshki* (Russian meat pie), and, of course, coffee from any number of vendors, including the *original* Starbucks. Go underground to explore wonderful specialty shops, including one of the best stores devoted to magic and old magic posters in the country, a fragrant store dedicated to spices, and an exotic bird store where the parrots squawk in your face. A 90-minute **Market Heritage Tour,** beginning at the Market's Information Booth, located at 1st Avenue and Pike Street, is offered Wednesday through Friday at 11am ($10 adults; $7 seniors/children 18 and under); make reservations at **www.pikeplacemarket.org**, or call © **206/774-5249.** The area is in the middle of renovations, but disruption to the public is minimal. A free map of the complex is also available at the information booth. At night, the vendors clear out, but several excellent restaurants, bars, and theaters in the market keep hopping.

Btw. Pike and Pine sts., at 1st Ave. © **206/682-7453.** Mon–Sat 10am–6pm; Sun 11am–5pm.

The Seattle Aquarium The Seattle Aquarium presents well-designed exhibits dealing with the watery worlds of the Puget Sound region. One of the aquarium's most popular exhibits is an interactive tide pool and discovery lab that re-creates Washington's wave-swept intertidal zone. From the underwater viewing dome, you get a fish's view of life beneath the waves. Each September, you can watch salmon return up a fish ladder to spawn.

1483 Alaskan Way, Pier 59, Waterfront Park. © **206/386-4300.** www.seattleaquarium.org. Admission $17 adults, $11 ages 4–12, free for children 3 and under. Daily 9:30am–6pm. Last entry is at 5pm.

Seattle Art Museum and Olympic Sculpture Park Following a major expansion, the art museum reopened in spring 2007 with nearly double its original museum space. The updated design features two floors of public space, 70% more gallery space, a new restaurant, and a store. The museum is a repository for everything from African masks, old masters, and Andy Warhol to one of the nation's premier collections of Northwest Coast Native art. In addition, the new, free outdoor Olympic Sculpture Park (2901 Western Ave.; open 30 min. before sunrise to 30 min. after sunset) opened as part of the relaunch. Transforming an industrial site on downtown Seattle's waterfront, the 9-acre Olympic Sculpture Park has paths that zigzag down to the bay through four ecosystems. Works and special commissions by artists Louise Bourgeois,

Richard Serra, Alexander Calder, Teresita Fernandez, Roy McMakin, Mark Dion, and other leading contemporary artists are on display. Admission to the park is free.

1300 1st Ave. ✆ **206/654-3137.** www.seattleartmuseum.org. Admission is a suggested donation of $15 adults, $12 seniors, $9 students and youths 13–17, free for children 12 and under; free to all 1st Thurs of month. Sat–Sun, Wed 10am–5pm; Thurs–Fri 10am–9pm. Closed Mon and Tues.

The Space Needle From a distance, this structure resembles a flying saucer on top of a tripod. When it was built for the World's Fair, it was meant to suggest future architectural trends; today, the soaring structure is the quintessential symbol of Seattle. At 518 feet above ground level, the views from the observation deck are stunning. High-powered telescopes let you zoom in on distant sights, and there's a lounge and two very expensive restaurants inside.

Intersection of 6th Ave. and Broad St. ✆ **206/905-2100.** www.spaceneedle.com. Admission $17 adults, $15 seniors, $9 children 4–13, free for children 3 and under. Mon–Thurs 9:30am–11pm, Fri–Sat 9am–11:30pm, Sun 9am–11pm.

Experience Music Project Located in the shadow of the Space Needle, this impressive museum was designed by Frank Gehry. Planned as a memorial to Seattle native Jimi Hendrix, it's grown to encompass all of the Northwest rock scene as well as the general history of American popular music. The EMP houses a guitar gallery, music memorabilia, and interactive rooms where you can play different instruments. In the same building (admission covers both museums) is the **Science Fiction Museum and Hall of Fame** (✆ **206/724-3428;** www.empsfm.org), the world's first. Notable permanent exhibits feature artistic representations of aliens, famous science fiction characters, and an armory of intergalactic weaponry, including Klingon daggers.

325 5th Ave. N. ✆ **206/770-2700.** www.empsfm.org. $15 adults, $12 seniors, students and children 5–17, free for children 4 and under; free to all 1st Thurs of month 5–8pm. Summer daily 10am–7pm; winter daily 10am–5pm.

Ye Olde Curiosity Shop It's weird! It's tacky! It's always packed! A cross between a souvenir store and Ripley's Believe It or Not!, Ye Olde Curiosity Shop features an oddball collection started in 1899 by Joe Standley. It's the place (the only place, probably) to see Siamese-twin calves, a natural mummy, the Lord's Prayer on a grain of rice, a narwhal tusk, shrunken heads, a 67-pound snail, fleas in dresses, and walrus and whale *oosiks* (the bone of the male reproductive organ).

1001 Alaskan Way, on Pier 54. ✆ **206/682-5844.** www.yeoldecuriosityshop.com. Free admission. 10am–6pm daily.

ATTRACTIONS BEYOND THE PORT AREA

Lake Union A $12 cab ride from the port, glacially carved Lake Union, in the central part of Seattle, is worth a visit. It's pretty and is home to hundreds of pleasure craft and houseboats and some naval vessels. While the lake is big, it's becoming smaller as city planners, in the name of "progress," fill in parts of it for construction.

Tillicum Village/Tillicum Village Tours Located at Blake Island State Marine Park across Puget Sound from Seattle, and accessible only by tour boat or private boat, **Tillicum Village** was built in conjunction with the 1962 Seattle World's Fair. The "village" is actually a large restaurant and performance hall fashioned after a traditional Northwest Coast Indian longhouse. With totem poles standing vigil out front, the forest encircling the longhouse, and the waters of Puget Sound stretching out into the distance, it's a beautiful spot. **Tillicum Village Tours** operates trips that include the scenic boat ride to and from the island, a lunch or dinner of alder-smoked salmon, and a performance by traditional masked dancers—members of 11 Northwest tribes.

After the meal and the dance performance, you can strike out on forest trails to explore the island.

Pier 55. ✆ **206/623-1445.** www.tillicumvillage.com. 4-hr. tour $78 adults, $71 seniors, $30 children 5–12, free for children 4 and under.

BEST CRUISE-LINE SHORE EXCURSIONS

Seattle City Tour (2–3½ hr.; $59 adults, $32 children): A basic spin around Pike Place Market, the World's Fair site, downtown Seattle, Lake Union, and more, offered by virtually all cruise lines. May include a stop at the Space Needle.

Seattle Boats, Buildings & Billionaires (3½ hr.; $75 adults, $40 children): Take a narrated bus drive to Lake Union and board a sightseeing boat for a 1½-hour cruise of Lake Union and Lake Washington. See the historic houseboat and floating home communities, including the home featured in the movie *Sleepless in Seattle.* You'll also see the world's longest floating bridge and catch a glimpse of the residence of Bill Gates.

Woodinville Wine Country (4 hr.; $67): Visit the renowned Columbia Winery for a behind-the-scenes tour and tasting and then take a quick drive to Château Ste Michelle for a look at the winemaking process and more tasting. You'll sample both red and white selections. Minimum age for this tour is 21.

EXCURSIONS OFFERED BY LOCAL AGENCIES

Argosy Cruises (✆ **206/623-1445;** www.argosycruises.com) offers a variety of short cruises around the Seattle area, including a **Seattle harbor cruise,** a cruise through the **Hiram Chittenden Locks to Lake Union,** and cruises around **Lake Washington** (which, among other things, take you past the fabled Xanadu, built by Bill Gates on the shore of Lake Washington). Cruises depart from Pier 55. Tickets for the 1-hour Harbor Cruise are $22 for adults, $10 for children 5 to 12, and free for children 4 and under; the 2-hour Lake Cruise costs $32.50 for adults, $11.50 for children 5 to 12, and free for children 4 and under. **Gray Line of Seattle** (www.graylineseattle.com) offers a 4-hour tour that takes visitors 30 miles from downtown to the Future of Flight Aviation Center and Boeing Tour at Paine Field Airport in Everett, a cutting-edge facility with interactive aviation exhibits (you also visit the Boeing factory) for $48.

WHERE TO STAY

Alexis Hotel Unbelievable as it sounds, this elegant boutique hotel, enviably located halfway between Pike Place Market and Pioneer Square, and only 2 blocks from the waterfront, was once a parking garage. Now listed in the National Register of Historic Places, the 90-year-old building is a sparkling gem, with a pleasant mix of old and new and a friendly staff. Classic styling prevails in the guest rooms, each of which is a little different (the nicest by far are the splurge-worthy fireplace suites). ***Tip:*** Wi-Fi is free for members of Kimpton Hotels' InTouch loyalty program, and there is no charge to join.

1007 1st Ave. (at Madison St.), Seattle, WA 98104. ✆ **800/426-7033** or 206/624-4844. Fax 206/621-9009. www.alexishotel.com. 121 units. $279–$365 double; $479–$599 suite. AE, DC, MC, V. Valet parking $36. **Amenities:** Restaurant; bar; concierge; fitness center with steam room; room service; spa. *In-room:* A/C, TV (in suites), Wi-Fi ($10/day).

The Edgewater Built on a pier, Seattle's only waterfront hotel is incongruously designed to resemble a deluxe mountain lodge. Somehow, it works. A vaulted open-beamed ceiling, a deer-antler chandelier, a river-stone fireplace, and a wall of glass that looks out on busy Elliott Bay and gorgeous sunsets all combine to make the lobby a great place to hang out. Rooms feature rustic lodgepole-pine furniture. Because the least expensive rooms here overlook the parking lot (and city), you really should opt for a water-view or partial water-view room. It makes all the difference.

Pier 67, 2411 Alaskan Way, Seattle, WA 98121. ✆ **800/624-0670** or 206/728-7000. Fax 206/441-4119. www.edgewaterhotel.com. 236 units. $161–$399 double; $438–$2,000 suite. AE, DC, DISC, MC, V. Valet parking $30. **Amenities:** Restaurant; bar; concierge; fitness center; room service. *In-room:* TV, hair dryer, high-speed Internet ($4.95/hr. or $9.95/day), minibar.

Fairmont Olympic Hotel This is one of the biggest and absolutely one of the most elegant hotels in Seattle. Reminiscent of an Italian Renaissance palace, complete with crystal and gilt chandeliers, marble facings, and dark-oak walls and pillars, the hotel has a health club, shopping area (upscale, of course), concierge, complimentary overnight shoeshine, and much more. It's located on a hill in the city's financial district, affording good views all around. Not cheap, but worth it.

411 University St., Seattle, WA 98101. ✆ **800/821-8106** or 206/621-1700. Fax 206/682-9633. www.fairmont.com. 450 units. $369–$489 double; $455–$3,000 suite. AE, DC, DISC, MC, V. Valet parking $36; self-parking $26. **Amenities:** 2 restaurants; piano bar; babysitting; concierge; health club; indoor pool; room service; spa; Wi-Fi (free, in lobby). *In-room:* TV, CD player, hair dryer, high-speed Internet (free), minibar.

Hotel Ändra Part Art Deco, part Buzz Lightyear—that describes this boutique hotel located in the trendy Belltown enclave, an easy walking distance from Pike Place Market, the Seattle Art Museum, and downtown shopping. Originally built in 1926, the classic brick and terra-cotta building was thoroughly reinvented in 2004 with design elements that meld the Northwest style (extensive use of wood and stone) with high-tech toys such as flatscreen TVs, Wi-Fi, and blue-glass bedside lamps. All rooms score high for creature comforts, too, especially the Frette towels and plump goose-down pillows and comforters. One of Seattle's hottest restaurants beckons downstairs: Lola, from top chef Tom Douglas, has a menu that ranges from local seafood to Greek cuisine.

2000 4th Ave., Seattle, WA 98121. ✆ **877/448-8600** or 206/448-8600. Fax 206/441-7140. www.hotelandra.com. 119 units. $196–$320 double; $379–$1,500 suite. AE, DC, DISC, MC, V. Valet parking $37. **Amenities:** 2 restaurants; concierge; exercise room; room service. *In-room:* A/C, TV, hair dryer, minibar, Wi-Fi ($10/day).

Mayflower Park Hotel If shopping and sipping martinis are among your favorite recreational activities, there's no question of where to stay in Seattle. The Mayflower Park Hotel, built in 1927 and completely renovated a few years back, is connected to the upscale shops of Westlake Center and is flanked by Nordstrom and Bon Marché department stores. The hotel also serves up the best martinis in Seattle, at Oliver's Lounge. (It's won the annual martini contest sponsored by a local newspaper umpteen times!) Most rooms are furnished with an eclectic blend of contemporary Italian and traditional European furnishings. If you crave space, ask for one of the large corner rooms or splurge for a suite. The smallest rooms here are very cramped.

405 Olive Way, Seattle, WA 98101. ✆ **800/426-5100** or 206/623-8700. Fax 206/382-6997. www.mayflowerpark.com. 161 units. $169–$279 double; $279–$405 suite. AE, DC, DISC, MC, V. Valet parking $32. **Amenities:** Restaurant; bar; concierge; exercise room; room service; Wi-Fi (free, in lobby). *In-room:* A/C, TV, hair dryer, high-speed Internet (free).

Renaissance Seattle Hotel Despite its large size and its location a stone's throw from the freeway, this hotel manages to stay quieter and less hectic than most convention hotels. With its rooftop restaurant and swimming pool with a view, it's a good choice for leisure travelers. All rooms are larger than average and many have views of either Puget Sound or the Cascade Range. For the best views, ask for a room on the west side of the hotel.

515 Madison St., Seattle, WA 98104. ✆ **800/546-9184** or 206/583-0300. Fax 206/447-0992. www.renaissancehotels.com. 558 units. $179–$239 double; $269–550 suite. AE, DC, DISC, MC, V. Valet parking $36; self-parking $30. **Amenities:** 3 restaurants; babysitting; concierge; exercise room; indoor pool; room service; spa (nearby). *In-room:* A/C, TV, fridge, hair dryer, Wi-Fi ($13).

Seattle Airport Marriott If you want to stay near the airport, this is a fantastic bet—a resortlike hotel with a huge central atrium that has a swimming pool, dense tropical greenery, a bar, two whirlpool tubs, and a scattering of totem poles. Rooms are sizable and comfortable, some with a view (on a clear day) of Mount Rainier.

3201 S. 176th St., Seattle, WA 98188. ✆ **800/314-0925** or 206/241-2000. Fax 206/248-0789. www.marriotthotels.com/seawa. 459 units. $199–$219 double; $239–$540 suite. Children 17 and under stay free in parent's room. Discounts on Fri–Sat. AE, DC, DISC, MC, V. Valet parking $22; self-parking $18. **Amenities:** 3 restaurants; bar; free airport transfers; exercise room; indoor pool; room service. *In-room:* A/C, TV, hair dryer, Wi-Fi (free).

WHERE TO DINE

Chez Shea PACIFIC NORTHWEST Quiet, dark, and intimate, Chez Shea is one of the finest restaurants in Seattle. Its dozen candlelit tables with views across Puget Sound to the Olympic Mountains are the perfect setting for a romantic dinner. The menu changes with the season, and ingredients come primarily from Pike Place Market, conveniently located below the restaurant. There are usually five entree choices, along the lines of filet of Alaskan halibut with asparagus; or farm lamb chops with roasted fennel and fingerling potatoes. While there are equally fine restaurants in the city, few have the quintessential Seattle atmosphere of Chez Shea.

Corner Market Building, Ste. 34, 94 Pike St., Pike Place Market. ✆ **206/467-9990.** www.chezshea.com. Reservations highly recommended. Main dishes $23–$36; fixed-price 5-course tasting menu $49; add $25 for wine pairing. AE, MC, V. Tues–Sun 5–10pm.

Etta's Seafood SEAFOOD Etta's boasts the best seafood in town. Located in the Pike Place Market area, this place serves chef/owner Tom Douglas' signature crab cakes (crunchy on the outside, creamy on the inside) and more. Consider the seared ahi tuna if it's on the menu. It's almost like sushi and has a wonderful texture. If you're not a lover of seafood, fear not: Even though seafood makes up most of the menu, there are other fine dishes.

2020 Western Ave. ✆ **206/443-6000.** www.tomdouglas.com/restaurants/ettas. Reservations recommended. Main dishes $12–$18. AE, DC, DISC, MC, V. Mon–Thurs 11:30am–9:30pm; Fri 11:30am–10pm; Sat 9am–3pm, 4–10pm; Sun 9am–3pm, 4–9pm.

Metropolitan Grill STEAK The Metropolitan is dedicated to carnivores. When you walk in, you'll see various cuts of meat, from filet mignon to triple-cut lamb chops, displayed on ice. Green-velvet booths and floral-design carpets create a sophisticated atmosphere, and mirrored walls and a high ceiling trimmed with elegant plasterwork make the dining room feel larger than it actually is. Perfectly cooked steaks are the prime attraction, and a baked potato and a pile of thickly cut onion rings complete the perfect steak dinner.

820 2nd Ave. ✆ **206/624-3287.** www.themetropolitangrill.com. Reservations recommended. Main dishes lunch $18–$43, dinner $20–$120. AE, DC, DISC, MC, V. Mon–Thurs 11am–3pm, 5–10pm; Fri 11am–3pm, 4pm–10:30pm; Sat 4–11pm; Sun 4–9pm.

SHOPPING

You can't be in Seattle without visiting the **Nordstrom** department store in the heart of downtown at 500 Pine St. (✆ **206/628-2111**). Seattle is, after all, where the company originated—in 1901. (It was financed, incidentally, with money earned by founder John W. Nordstrom in the Klondike gold rush.) This Nordstrom store is the second biggest attraction for tourists in town—after Pike Place Market—and worth a visit for its historical significance, if for nothing else. There's a **Nordstrom Rack**—the discounted version of the department store—nearby at 1601 2nd Ave. (✆ **206/448-8522**).

Elliott Bay Book Company, 1521 10th Ave. (✆ **800/962-5311;** www.elliottbay book.com), in an area known as Pioneer Square, has a tremendous selection of titles and a bargain books floor of some repute. A cafe opened there last year.

Outdoor enthusiasts will also want to stop at **Recreational Equipment, Inc. (REI)** at 222 Yale Ave. N. (✆ **888/873-1938** or 206/223-1944; www.rei.com/stores/11). It's the nation's largest co-op selling outdoor gear. This is the company's flagship store and has a 64-foot climbing pinnacle and play area for kids.

5 Juneau

Because Juneau is also a major port of call, see the Juneau section in chapter 8, "Ports & Wilderness Areas Along the Inside Passage," for a map and information on attractions and tours.

GETTING TO JUNEAU

BY PLANE Juneau is served by **Alaska Airlines** (✆ **800/426-0333** or 907/789-9791; www.alaskaair.com) with daily nonstop flights from Seattle and Anchorage. Because weather can wreak havoc with landing conditions, it's especially advisable, if you're flying to Juneau, to get there a day or two before your embarkation date.

BY BOAT The vessels of the Alaska Marine Highway (www.dot.state.ak.us/amhs; commonly known as the Alaska Ferry) link Juneau with Alaska, British Columbia, and U.S. gateways as far south as Bellingham, Wash., but unless you have 2 or 3 days to spare, you probably won't use that service to get to your ship.

BY CAR You can't drive to Juneau (there are no roads to the outside world) or get there by train. That leaves you with airplanes or long boat trips, period.

EXPLORING JUNEAU

INFORMATION The main **Visitor Information Center** is in Centennial Hall at 101 Egan Dr., near the State Museum (✆ **888/581-2201** or 907/586-2201; fax 907/586-6304; www.traveljuneau.com). It's open May through September, daily from 8:30am to 5pm; October through April, Monday through Friday from 9am to 4:30pm. There is also a visitor center midway down the cruise ship pier, and it's open when ships are in.

GETTING AROUND A cab from the airport to downtown will cost about $25. The **Capital Transit city bus** (✆ **907/789-6901**) comes to the airport at 11 minutes past the hour on weekdays from 7:11am to 5:11pm and costs $1.50 for adults and $1 for children; your luggage has to fit under your seat or at your feet. Ask the driver for the stop closest to your hotel; you may need a short cab ride from there. The public bus can also get you to the city's top visitor attraction, Mendenhall Glacier (p. 225).

The passenger cruise-ship pier is right in town and an easy walk. However, with baggage it might be necessary to take a taxi, which shouldn't cost more than $8. Major car rental companies have offices at the airport.

WHERE TO STAY

Breakwater Inn Located in a residential area close to downtown, and across from the Aurora Boat Harbor, this casual motel has decent-size rooms and provides complimentary van service to downtown. The restaurant serves steak and seafood.

1711 Glacier Ave., Juneau, AK 99801. ✆ **888/586-6303** or 907/586-6303. Fax 907/463-4820. www.breakwaterinn.com. 49 units. $89–$119 double. Children 11 and under stay free with adult. AE, DISC, MC, V. Free parking. **Amenities:** Restaurant; bar; room service. *In-room:* TV, high-speed Internet (free), kitchenettes.

Goldbelt Hotel Juneau This hotel has been renovated in recent years and has large rooms favored by business travelers. The rooms in the front (which are more expensive) overlook the Gastineau Channel. The atmosphere is quiet and almost hermetic. Chinook's Restaurant, decorated with museum-quality Native American art and serving Southeast Alaska–inspired cuisine, is just off the lobby.

51 Egan Dr., Juneau, AK 99801. ✆ **888/478-6909** or 907/586-6900. Fax 907/463-3567. www.goldbelthotel.com. 105 units. $189–$199 double. Extra person in room $15. AE, DC, DISC, MC, V. Free parking. **Amenities:** Restaurant; free airport transfers; room service. *In-room:* TV, hair dryer, Wi-Fi (free).

Prospector Hotel The Prospector is a comfortable hotel right on the waterfront, with large standard rooms and suites in attractive pastel colors. More than two dozen rooms have kitchenettes, and some of the more expensive ones feel like nicely furnished apartments. Those facing the channel have good views. The lower level, called the first floor, is half-basement and somewhat dark. The hotel has a full-service restaurant and lounge called T. K. Maguire's.

375 Whittier St., Juneau, AK 99801-1781. ✆ **800/331-2711** or 907/586-3737. Fax 907/586-1204. www.prospectorhotel.com. 62 units. $139–$209 double. AE, DC, DISC, MC, V. Free parking. **Amenities:** Restaurant; bar. *In-room:* TV, hair dryer, kitchenette (in some), Wi-Fi (free).

Westmark Baranof In winter, the venerable old Baranof acts like an annex of the state capitol for legislators and lobbyists who gather to confer; in the summer, it's full of guests who come through package-tour companies. The nine-story concrete building, built in 1939, has the feel of a grand hotel, although some rooms are on the small side. The upper-floor rooms are modern and have great water views. There are many room configurations, including suites, and some rooms have kitchenettes; discuss the options with the reservationist to make sure you get what you want. The hotel has two restaurants, including the upscale Gold Room (see below).

127 N. Franklin St., Juneau, AK 99801. ✆ **800/544-0970** or 907/586-2660. Fax 907/586-8315. www.westmarkhotels.com. 195 units. $152–$249 double. AE, DC, DISC, MC, V. Free parking. **Amenities:** 2 restaurants; bar; exercise room; room service; Wi-Fi (free, in lobby). *In-room:* TV, kitchenette (in some).

WHERE TO DINE

The Gold Room AMERICAN/SEAFOOD With its polished wood, shiny brass, and etched glass, the Art Deco Gold Room is Juneau's most traditional fine-dining establishment and among its best (politicians and other movers and shakers are among the clientele here). Pacific Northwest Cuisine is featured, with the chef making good use of local ingredients, including crab (order Alaskan king crab and the legs and claws are presplit, so you don't even need a bib or cracker).

127 North Franklin St. (at the Westmark Hotel). ✆ **800/544-0970** or 907/586-2660. www.westmarkhotels.com. Dinner entrees $25–$35. AE, DC, DISC, MC, V. Daily 5–9pm.

Red Dog Saloon BREW PUB This is not an elegant eatery by any means—it's more of an experience. The Red Dog is a Juneau landmark, and its restaurant serves good pub grub and burgers in a frontier atmosphere. Just don't go looking for speedy or particularly distinguished service. Enjoy the honky-tonk piano and banjo and the emcee's constant stream of one-liners while waiting for your grub. It's noisy. It's crowded. And it's fun!

728 S. Franklin St. ✆ **907/463-3777.** www.reddogsaloon.com. Main courses $9–$16. AE, MC, V. Summer daily 11am–11pm.

Twisted Fish Company SEAFOOD/GRILL/PIZZA Right near the cruise-ship pier, but still popular with locals, this casual publike eatery serves up fish tacos (salmon or halibut), pizzas topped with salmon, salmon served on a cedar plank, burgers, pasta, and an excellent Caesar salad. Wash your meal down with some Alaskan Pale Ale. Several tables have views of Gastineau Channel and there is outdoor dining when the weather is warm. It's our new favorite in Juneau.

550 S. Franklin St. (behind Taku Smokeries). ✆ **907/463-5033.** http://twistedfish.hangaronthewharf.com. Lunch $7–$15; dinner $9–$29. AE, DISC, MC, V. Daily 11am–10pm.

6 Whittier

Unless you're getting on or off a cruise ship or are going sightseeing in Prince William Sound, there's little reason to go to Whittier—unless, that is, you're on a quest to find America's oddest towns. Most of the townspeople (about 250 at last count) live in a single 14-story concrete building, Begich Towers, which has dark, narrow hallways. A grocery store is on the first floor and the medical clinic is on the third. The rest of the people live in a second building.

Begich Towers was built during the 1940s, when Whittier's strategic location on the Alaska Railroad and at the head of a deep fjord made it a key port in the defense of Alaska. Today, with its barren gravel ground and ramshackle warehouses and boat sheds, the town maintains a stark military-industrial character. The pass above the town is a funnel for frequent whipping winds, it always seems to rain, and the glaciers above the town keep it cool even in summer. The official boosters look on the bright side: With everyone living in two buildings, it saves on snow removal in a place that gets an average of 20 feet each winter. The kids don't even have to go outside to get to school—a tunnel leads from the tower to the classroom. It's an unusual setup even for Alaska.

No matter how odd or dreary Whittier may seem, it has assumed huge importance to Princess—and vice versa. The line's Gulf ships do their turn-arounds here, exposing tens of thousands of visitors to the city. How much money any of those thousands of passengers actually spend on goods and services is open to question. But the cruise lines' docking fees alone are worth big bucks to Whittier. An **ATM** is located at the liquor store near the boat harbor, but Whittier lacks a bank and other services, so bring what you need.

GETTING TO WHITTIER

BY PLANE Fly to the **Ted Stevens International Airport** in Anchorage, then drive for about 1½ hours. You're best off booking a transfer through the cruise line to get there.

BY BUS The **Magic Bus** departs from the Anchorage Museum of History and Fine Art (at 7th and A sts.) at 3pm on Monday, Wednesday, and Saturday, and arrives in Whittier some 90 minutes later. Luggage is limited to two bags per passenger (extra luggage is allowed on a space-available basis, for an extra fee). The trip costs $65 for adults, $32.50 for kids, each way. For reservations, call © **800/208-0200,** or go to **www.alaskatravel.com/bus-lines/anchorage-whittier.html**.

BY CAR It's possible to drive to Whittier from Anchorage by way of the Portage Glacier Highway through the Anton Anderson Memorial Tunnel at Whittier. ***Be forewarned:*** Although, theoretically, Whittier is only a couple hours' drive or train ride from Anchorage, the journey can take much, much longer. That's because the tunnel on the outskirts of town is shared by both automobiles and trains, and while one is using it, the other can't. They switch every half-hour or so, but it can make for some frustrating waits. Get the schedule through the tunnel's website (go to www.dot.state.ak.us and click on "Travel Info"), through its phone recording (© **877/611-2586** or 907/566-2244), or by tuning to 1610AM in Portage or 530AM in Whittier. The toll for cars is $12. Parking in Whittier is $5 per day.

BY RAIL You can get to Whittier from Anchorage on the Alaska Railroad (© **800/544-0552** or 907/265-2494). The fare is $65 for adults and $33 for children ages 12 and under. The dock is near the mouth of Whittier Creek. Nothing in Whittier is more than a 5-minute walk away. Don't look for taxi ranks or free shuttles—you won't need them.

EXPLORING WHITTIER

INFORMATION Probably because it doesn't have much to promote, Whittier has no tourist board, per se, and there is no visitor center, but you can contact the city offices at © **907/472-2327,** ext. 101 (admin@ci.whittier.ak.us). There is a Greater Whittier Chamber of Commerce that lists "attractions" on its website (www.whittieralaskachamber.org). The people at the harbor master's office are also helpful and maintain public toilets and showers; it's the only two-story building at the harbor (© **907/472-2327,** ext. 110 or 115). Inside the cruise terminal, brochures promote area tour operators and the like.

GETTING AROUND You can walk everywhere, but there's also a cab or two in town. Look for them when you get off the boat or train.

ATTRACTIONS WITHIN WALKING DISTANCE

Everything is within walking distance; there just isn't much to see. Visit the yacht harbor and the town's apartment building, and stop by the **Prince William Sound Museum** at **The Anchor Inn** (see listing under "Where to Dine," below), for a few exhibits highlighting the city's military and civilian history. (Suggested donation $3 for adults, $1.50 for children 12 and under.)

ATTRACTIONS BEYOND THE PORT AREA

You can take the **Alaska Railroad** train (© **800/544-0552** or 907/265-2494; www.alaskarailroad.com) straight to Anchorage, a fun scenic ride, one-way for $65 adults, $33 children 2 to 11 (free for kids 1 and under).

BEST CRUISE-LINE SHORE EXCURSIONS

The following two cruises are offered only to passengers with a pre- or post-cruise stay in Anchorage or to those with departing flights after 5pm.

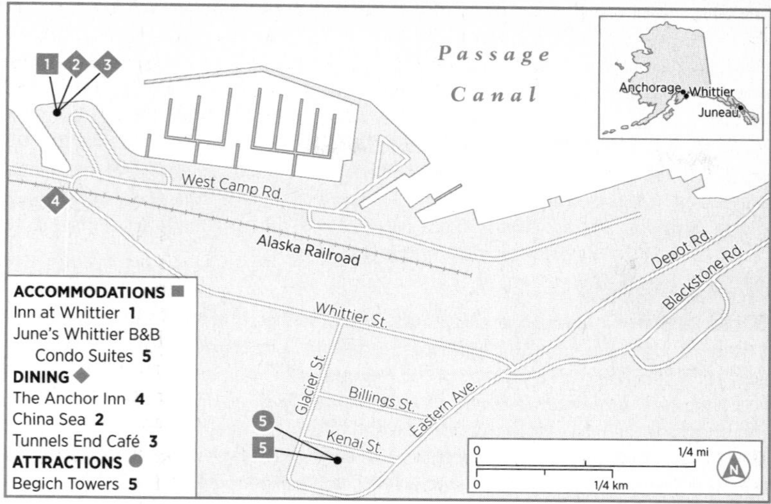

Blackstone Glacier Adventure Cruise (5½ hr.; $124 adults, $64 children): Cruise a glacier-carved fjord and view two tidewater glaciers. The vistas of the unspoiled wilderness are breathtaking. Marine science activities and a baked Alaska halibut lunch are included.

Kayaking in Prince William Sound (3 hr.; $99): Learn the basics, and then follow your guide into the pristine waters of Prince William Sound. He or she will point out the native flora, fauna, and marine life.

EXCURSIONS OFFERED BY LOCAL AGENCIES

Several companies offer day trips to Prince William Sound's western glaciers. Besides having incredible scenery, the water is calm, making seasickness unlikely—for the queasy, this is a much better choice than Kenai Fjords National Park. Departures are timed with the daily Alaska Railroad train from Anchorage, described above, which means they have up to 6 hours for the trip. Some visitors see as much as possible, while others savor the scenery and wildlife sightings. **Phillips Cruises and Tours** (✆ **800/544-0529** or 907/276-8023; www.26glaciers.com) has a 26-glacier cruise of the Sound on a fast three-deck catamaran, narrated by a U.S. Forest Service Ranger. The ride is 4½ hours and costs $139 for adults, $79 for children 12 and under.

Major Marine Tours (✆ **800/764-7300** or 907/274-7300; www.majormarine.com) operates a smaller, 149-passenger vessel at a slower pace than Phillips' catamaran—it visits merely 10 glaciers, but spends more time waiting for them to calve. The route goes up Blackstone Bay, and the boat is comfortable, with reserved table seating. Food costs extra; the all-you-can-eat salmon and prime rib buffet is $19 ($8 for children). The trip lasts 5 hours; the price is $107 adults, $53 children 12 and under.

Sound Eco Adventures (✆ **888/471-2312** or 907/472-2312; www.soundecoadventure.com) is operated by a retired wildlife biologist who spent years researching the waterfowl and ecology of Prince William Sound. The 30-foot wheelchair-accessible boat carries up to six passengers at a time on wildlife, whale, and glacier tours and does kayak drop-offs as well. Prices range from $194 per person for an 8-hour wildlife-viewing cruise to $234 per person for a whale and wildlife adventure. Occasional photography tours are also offered. Lunch and a snack are included. Open scheduling is available.

Honey Charters (✆ **888/477-2493** or 907/472-2493; www.honeycharters.com) is a family-run business with three small boats. The biggest, *Qayaq Chief,* can carry 22 visitors on a sightseeing cruise. No food is available onboard, so bring lunch and snacks with you. For a 3-hour cruise, the price is $139 per person; for a 4- to 6-hour cruise, it's $189 per person; inquire about longer trips.

WHERE TO STAY

Inn at Whittier Located at the mouth of the harbor, this new luxury property has a timber-framed design with a lighthouse structure as its centerpiece. Get a room with views of Prince William Sound or of the mountains, if you prefer. All rooms have TVs and dataports. Junior suites have Jacuzzi tubs, and both of the two-story town-house suites include Jacuzzis and fireplaces. The hotel has a 150-seat restaurant (serving three meals a day) and the chef will prepare your day's catch if you go fishing. Otherwise, the dinner menu features seafood, including Copper River king salmon as well as meat dishes such as crab-stuffed pork tenderloin; the lunch menu has crab cakes, Reuben sandwiches, and the like.

P.O. Box 773, Whittier, AK 99693. ✆ **866/472-5757** or 907/472-3200. Fax 907/472-5081. www.innatwhittier.com. 25 units. Rates $169–$239 double; $250–$329 suite. DC, MC, V. Free parking. **Amenities:** Restaurant; bar. *In-room:* TV, high-speed Internet (free).

June's Whittier Bed and Breakfast Condo Suites Nine of these condo units are in the top two floors of the Begich Towers, the concrete building that dominates Whittier. It allows guests to live as Whittier people do, with great views and hummingbirds feeding at the windows. All have full kitchens, and some have Jacuzzi tubs. The hotel provides a free shuttle service to the harbor and shares a website with fishing charter company Bread n Butter Charters.

P.O. Box 715, Whittier, AK 99693. ✆ **888/472-2396** or 907/472-2396. Fax 907/472-2503. www.breadnbutter charters.com. 10 units. $155–$275 double. Rates include continental breakfast. AE, MC, V. Free parking. *In-room:* TV/VCR, kitchen, Wi-Fi (free; some).

WHERE TO DINE

Most dining spots in Whittier are for people who just want to grab a sandwich while passing through. Several such restaurants are in the triangle at the east end of the harbor, including a Chinese place, the Korean-owned **China Sea** (✆ **907/472-2222**). It's okay. Lunch there is $8 or $9, dinner $12 to $19, and in the summer, specials are served, such as kung pao halibut. Hours are 11am to 10pm daily. The **Tunnels End Café & Espresso** (✆ **907/472-3000**), at 12 Harbor Loop Rd., serves espresso, breakfast (including egg burritos), and sandwiches ($7.95–$8.95), as well as seafood and steak. Dinner entrees range from $9 to $27. Hours are 6:30am to 10pm Wednesday through Monday. You will rub shoulders with fishermen and other locals at **The Anchor Inn** (✆ **907/472-2354** or 877/870-8787; www.anchorinnwhittier.com), 100 Whittier St., a combination restaurant, grocery store, Laundromat, and bar (with live entertainment). There are also a few rooms available. The inn houses the small Prince William Sound Museum, highlighting the history of Whittier. The restaurant is open for three meals a day—the lunch menu includes burgers ($6) and assorted seafood baskets ($12). Dinner ranges from $12 for fried chicken to $21 for steak and prawns.

SHOPPING

When the big ships started arriving a few years ago, there weren't many shops here—though if you ran out of toothpaste, the grocery store on the first floor of the Begich Building was helpful. But now, local entrepreneurs are filling the void. At the new **Port of Call Gallery & Gifts** (© **907/440-8840;** www.whittier-gallery.com) on Harbor Loop Drive, you can view the work of local artists and craftspeople. There are wildlife greeting cards, woolens, wood carvings, fish-shaped chocolates, and paintings among the items for sale.

8

Ports & Wilderness Areas Along the Inside Passage

The Inside Passage runs through an area of Alaska known as the **Southeast.** It's that narrow strip of the state—islands, mainland coastal communities, and mountains—that stretches from the Canadian border in the south to the start of the Gulf in the north, just above Glacier Bay National Park. It's also known as The Panhandle. The typical cruise itinerary on this route is to or from Seattle or begins or ends in Vancouver, B.C. (both of which are covered in chapter 7, "The Ports of Embarkation"). We've arranged the following sections on the various ports geographically, moving northward.

For ports and wilderness areas in the Gulf of Alaska, see chapter 9.

1 Victoria, British Columbia

Yes, we know it's in Canada, not Alaska, but cruises that start in Seattle or San Francisco typically include Victoria (on Vancouver Island) as a port of call while traveling northward. This lively city, the capital of British Columbia, has Victorian architecture and a very proper British atmosphere—some say it's more British than Britain itself—with main attractions that include high tea and a visit to **Butchart Gardens** with its incredible botanical displays.

A former British outpost, Victoria has a history filled with maritime lore. Whalers and trading ships once docked in the city's harbors, transporting Vancouver Island's rich bounty of coal, lumber, and furs throughout the world. One of the great sights on any visit to Victoria is its Inner Harbour, framed by the venerable (ca. 1908) Fairmont Empress Hotel and the British Columbia Parliament Building. It is, by any yardstick, a panorama of great beauty. The big ships don't dock there (see "Coming Ashore," below). The Inner Harbour is a great spot to begin a walking/shopping tour of the city, however.

Take a tour around the island and you'll see gorgeous homes and gardens, with views that include the snowcapped mountains of Washington State.

COMING ASHORE Spectacular as it would be to dock in the Inner Harbour, it's too small for major cruise ships, which park instead at the recently upgraded and expanded Ogden Point terminal on Juan De Fuca Strait. It's about a mile into town, so if you don't mind a stretch of the legs, walk west along Dallas Street from the dock and north on Oswego Street or Menzies Street, and you'll find yourself in the heart of the action—right on the Inner Harbour. Every cruise ship, of course, operates a shuttle service to the Empress Hotel, where flowers, milling crowds, and street performers—including, usually, a lone bagpiper—enliven the scene.

Victoria, British Columbia

Beautifully maintained, old wooden water taxis operated by Victoria Harbour Ferry ($5 each way, ✆ **250/708-0201;** www.victoriaharbourferry.com) ply the harbor. It's worth taking a jaunt, even if you're going nowhere! Be sure you (and your camera) are prepared to take lots of pictures: Victoria's Inner Harbour is one of the most photogenic sights on the planet.

Note: Rates below are in Canadian dollars. At press time, the conversion to U.S. dollars was C$1 = US96¢. Shore excursions are in US dollars.

INFORMATION You can pick up a map of the city at the Tourism Victoria **Visitor Information Centre** (✆ **250/953-2033;** www.tourismvictoria.com), on the waterfront at 812 Wharf St. It's open daily from 9am to 5:30pm in May and June, 9am to 6:30pm throughout the summer, and it reverts to the shorter hours in fall and winter.

BEST CRUISE-LINE SHORE EXCURSIONS

Note that shore excursion prices quoted here are representative of what's available, but may differ slightly among cruise lines.

English Tea at Butchart Gardens (4 hr.; $119 adults, $79 children 12 and under): The bus makes the 13-mile trip from the ship to world-renowned Butchart Gardens along Brentwood Bay. There you'll have time to explore the 131-acre grounds and enjoy an elegant, traditional afternoon tea with finger sandwiches, scones and cream, and all kinds of goodies, along with honest-to-goodness brewed English tea.

Victoria Pub Crawl (3½ hr.; $89 adults only): Flowers and greenery may be what most people envision when they think of Victoria, but the city also boasts some fabulous English-style pubs. The tour, mostly on foot, takes visitors to several of them to sample the local brews. ***Note:*** Minimum age 19.

Victoria by Horse-Drawn Trolley (1½ hr.; $49 adult, $30 children 12 and under): A romantic way to see the sights of the city—the Inner Harbour, Chinatown, the historic James Bay residential area, and much more.

EXCURSIONS OFFERED BY LOCAL AGENCIES

Several local operators greet passengers right at the pier, offering rides into the city and longer tours using various modes of transportation. **Classic Car Tours** (✆ **250/883-8747;** www.classiccartours.com) gives tours in classic convertibles (perfect on a sunny day), with commentary that is both colorful and delightful. Fares are $80 an hour per car; the cars seat up to four guests. A 3-hour beach route serving up views galore is $240. The bicycle rickshaws operated by **Kabuki Kabs** (✆ **250/385-4243;** www.kabukikabs.com) and competing firms are an unusual way to get around the city for about $70 an hour (for two people); from the ship pier to the downtown area, it's about $30 (for two people). For those seeking a more traditional bus tour, **Gray Line West, Victoria** (✆ **800/663-8390** or 250/388-5248; www.graylinewest.com) provides a wide variety of tours of Victoria and the surrounding area, including one to Butchart Gardens, leaving from near the Fairmont Empress Hotel, for $56 adults, $39 youth, and $19 children 5 to 12 (free for children 4 and under). Among the company's other tours are a 2½-hour Grand City Tour and Craigdarroch Castle package for $40 adults and $18 children 5 to 11. Whale-watching cruises are another popular Victoria diversion, and you can book one with Prince of Whales (✆ **888/383-4884;** www.princeofwhales.com). A 3-hour tour in an open, Zodiac-style boat is $95 adults, $85 seniors/students 13 to 17, and $75 children 8 to 12 (tour not available for kids 7 and under), with departures every half-hour in summer. Tours in a boat where you sit inside are at 9am, 12:15pm, and 3:30pm, for $95 adults, $85 students, and $75 children 5 to 12 (free for children 4 and under).

ON YOUR OWN: WITHIN WALKING DISTANCE

The Fairmont Empress Hotel Located right by the Inner Harbour, this ivy-covered 1908 landmark has a commanding view of the harbor and an opulent lobby. This is the place to go for your British-style high tea, and the Empress pulls out all the stops: fresh seasonal fruit and cream, tea sandwiches (with cucumber, B.C. salmon and cream cheese, and curry-mango chicken salad), raisin scones with Devonshire cream and strawberry preserves, pastries, truffles, tarts, shortbread cookies, and the rest of the trimmings. Tea at the Empress has become almost a status symbol and is in great demand. Call ahead for reservations. Expect to pay about $55 to $67 per person (special $18 Prince or Princess tea for children 12 and under) served from noon to 5:15pm. It's pricey, but such a treat! And please observe the dress code: no torn jeans, short shorts, jogging pants, or tank tops allowed.

721 Government St. ✆ **250/384-8111;** for tea reservations 250/389-2727. www.fairmont.com. Daily seatings noon–5:15pm.

Miniature World Museum Around the back of the Fairmont Empress Hotel, you'll find what's billed as "The Greatest Little Show on Earth," with quirky displays that include big dollhouses, the world's smallest working sawmill, and a model of London in 1670.

649 Humboldt St. ✆ **250/385-9731.** www.miniatureworld.com. $13 adults, $10 children 12–18, $8 children 5–11 (free for children 4 and under). Summer daily 9am–9pm.

Royal British Columbia Museum and National Geographic IMAX Theatre Outside the entrance to this modern, three-story, concrete-and-glass museum is a glass-enclosed display of towering totem poles and other large sculptural works by Northwest Native artists. Inside, exhibits showcase the natural history of the province, illustrate Victoria's recent past, and demonstrate how archaeologists study ancient cultures using artifacts from numerous local tribes. There's also an IMAX theater showing features on places such as the Amazon, Africa, and Mount Everest. (The schedule changes every few months.) Behind the museum is **Thunderbird Park,** with Native totem poles and a ceremonial house. **Helmecken House,** 10 Elliot St., next to the park, is one of the oldest houses in British Columbia. It was the home of a pioneer doctor, and there are enough torturous-looking medical tools to make you shudder. Admission to these exhibits is free. If you want to learn about British Columbia's past, this complex is the place to go.

675 Belleville St. ✆ **888/447-7977** or 250/356-7226. www.royalbcmuseum.bc.ca. $15 adults, $9.50 seniors and youth 6–18, free for children 5 and under, family admission (2 adults, 2 kids 18 or under) $39.50. Daily 9am–5pm; until 10pm most Fri–Sat evenings in summer. IMAX $11 adults, $8.75 seniors and youth 6–18, $5 children 5 and under, family admission $34.50. Daily 10am–8pm. Combined museum/IMAX ticket $35 adults, $26 seniors, $25 youth, $5 children, family admission $74.

Spinnakers Gastro Brewpub It's not exactly Victoria's version of Carlos 'n' Charlie's (the boisterous drink spot in the Caribbean), but this pub/restaurant is Canada's oldest brewpub, and a worthy place for brew fans to visit—the handcrafted ales are made using the finest hops and grain. The summer raspberry ale is made with locally grown berries. You can also play a game of darts here. There's a waterfront deck, and a new viewer-friendly area lets visitors watch the culinary team in action. Beer in Victoria has its roots in the early 1840s, and beer lovers may also want to visit **Canoe Brewpub & Restaurant** (✆ **250/361-1940;** www.canoebrewpub.com), about a 12-minute walk from the harbor front and **Buckerfield's Brewery** at the Swans Suite Hotel (✆ **250/361-3310;** www.swanshotel.com). Along with Spinnakers, both of these are featured on the city's self-guided Ale Trail map available around town.

308 Catherine St. ✆ **877/838-2739** or 250/386-2739. www.spinnakers.com. Daily 11am–11pm.

Victoria Bug Zoo This attraction highlights the amazing world of insects and spiders and allows visitors to view and experience live multi-legged creatures from around the world in a safe, fun, and friendly atmosphere. You'll see giant walking sticks, alien-eyed praying mantises, hairy tarantulas, and glow-in-the-dark scorpions, to name a few. The zoo also features Canada's largest ant farm. (How's that for a claim to fame?) Knowledgeable "bug guides" are also on hand.

631 Courtney St. ✆ **250/384-2847.** www.bugzoo.bc.ca. Mon–Sat 10am–5pm, Sun 11am–5pm. $9 adults, $8 seniors, $7 youth 12–18, $6 children 3–11 (free for children 2 and under).

ON YOUR OWN: BEYOND THE PORT AREA

Butchart Gardens A ride by cab, public bus, or other transportation (see "Excursions Offered by Local Agencies," above) and several free hours will be required for a visit to this world-renowned attraction. The gardens lie 13 miles north of downtown Victoria on a 131-acre estate and feature English-, Italian-, and Japanese-style plantings, as well as water gardens and rose beds. There are also restaurants and a gift shop on-site. ***Note:*** You can catch a public bus from downtown Victoria for less than $4 each way. A cab will cost you about $51 each way.

800 Benevenuto Ave., in Brentwood Bay. ✆ **250/652-5256.** www.butchartgardens.com. $28 adults/seniors, $14 children 13–17, $3 children 5–12, free for children 4 and under. Mid-June to Labor Day daily 9am–10pm; open hours vary rest of year.

Craigdarroch Castle You have to take a cab to see Craigdarroch Castle, the elaborate home of millionaire Scottish coal-mining magnate Robert Dunsmuir, who built the place in the 1880s. The four-story, 39-room Highland-style castle is topped with stone turrets and furnished in opulent Victoria splendor.

1050 Joan Crescent. ✆ **250/592-5323.** www.craigdarrochcastle.com. $13.75 adults, $12.75 seniors, $8.75 students with valid I.D., $5 children 6–12, free for children 5 and under. Mid-June to Labor Day daily 9am–7pm;10am–4:30pm rest of year.

SHOPPING

Book lovers shouldn't miss **Munro's Books,** at 1108 Government St. (✆ **250/382-2464;** www.munrobooks.com), with an impressive selection of thousands of titles in every subject, from metaphysics to mystery, biography to biology, and sports to self-help. Chocoholics should make a beeline for **Rogers' Chocolates,** 913 Government St. (✆ **250/881-8771;** www.rogerschocolates.com), with roots to 1885 when Charles W. (Candy) Rogers made confections in the back of his grocery shop in Victoria. Milk chocolate, dark chocolate, white chocolate, chocolates with creamy centers, chocolates with nuts, chocolate-covered ginger, espresso beans, and caramels can all be found at the shop. Another worthwhile stop is **Silk Road Aromatherapy & Tea Company,** 1624 Government St. (✆ **250/382-0006;** www.silkroadtea.com), a shop founded by two women who studied the Chinese tea tradition and blending techniques with Chinese tea masters and herbalists. The shop has expanded and opened a tea tasting bar (think tea version of wine bar) and also features an in-house spa and its own 100% natural body care products.

2 Canada's Inside Passage

Canada's Inside Passage is simply the part of an Inside Passage cruise that lies in British Columbia, south of the Alaskan border and running to Vancouver. On big ships, the first day out of Vancouver (or the last day going south) is usually a day at sea. Passengers get the chance to enjoy the coastal beauty of the British Columbia mainland to the east and Vancouver Island to the west, including some truly magnificent scenery in Princess Louisa Inlet and Desolation Sound.

In most cases, that's all the ships do, though: Go past the scenery—much of it at night. In their haste to get to Ketchikan, the first stop in Alaska, they invariably sail right past much of the Canadian Inside Passage.

One of the Canadian Inside Passage's loveliest stretches is **Seymour Narrows,** 5 or 6 hours north of Vancouver, just after the mouth of the Campbell River. It's so narrow that it can be passed through only at certain hours of the day, when the tide is right, which is often late in the day or in the wee small hours. On the long days of summer, it is often possible to enjoy Seymour Narrows if you're prepared to stay up late.

The U.S./Canada border lies just off the tip of the Misty Fjords National Monument, 43 sailing miles from Ketchikan (and 403 miles from Glacier Bay, for those who are keeping count).

3 Prince Rupert, British Columbia

Not long ago, this sleepy Canadian port just a few miles from the Alaska border registered just a tiny blip on the cruise industry's radar screen. Now, however, with the number and size of ships in the Alaska trade growing, the need for alternative ports of call en route has brought the place into the cruise-ship fold. The Northland Terminal, which previously hosted cargo vessels, is now exclusively welcoming cruise ships during the summer cruise season (some ships also tender ashore to the Atlin Terminal at Cow Bay). Retail stores have even been added a short walk away for the cruise-ship crowds.

Ships from Norwegian Cruise Line, Silversea, Oceania, and the small ship lines visit here, though not at all in the numbers that visit the bigger Alaska ports. The small city was named in 1670 for the first governor of the Hudson's Bay Company. He was Rupert, the son of Frederick V, king of Bohemia, and Elizabeth Stuart, daughter of James I of England. Today, many of its 13,000 inhabitants work in commercial fishing or at the newly developed container port, an important link in the trade route with Shanghai. Prince Rupert proclaims itself the "Halibut Capital of the World." There is also a flourishing artists' colony, the results of whose efforts can be seen in the Cow Bay artists' co-op, right next to the passenger ship dock. The city has two shopping malls, a number of good-quality stores, and some decent restaurants (including the noteworthy Opa Sushi in Cow Bay).

Prince Rupert's location makes it an ideal jumping-off point for visits to Southeast Alaska, the Queen Charlotte Islands, Vancouver Island, and the interior of British Columbia. The town is served year-round by both the **BC Ferries** system (✆ **888/BC-FERRY** [888/223-3779]; www.bcferries.com) and the **Alaska Marine Highway System** (✆ **800/642-0066;** www.dot.state.ak.us/amhs). Both ferry systems offer up to five departures a week during the summer to a number of Alaskan Inside Passage ports. By road, Prince Rupert is accessible via the Yellowhead Highway to Vancouver in the south, and to Dawson Creek, B.C. (not to be confused with Dawson City, the Yukon Territory gold-rush capital) and Alberta in the east. **VIA Rail Canada** (✆ **888/VIA-RAIL** [842-7245]; www.viarail.ca) operates daily between Prince Rupert and Jasper National Park, and **Air Canada** (✆ **888/247-2262;** www.aircanada.com) has two flights a day to Vancouver.

Note: Rates below are in Canadian dollars. At press time, the conversion was C$1 = US96¢. Shore excursions are in US dollars.

COMING ASHORE The passenger pier is a very short distance from town. Guests going to Cow Bay have a level walk of about 100 yards from the Northland Terminal, less from the Atlin Terminal. If heading uptown, there's a little uphill walking to be done, especially right by the pier. From there, 1st Avenue, the main thoroughfare into town, has a steepish climb of 50 yards or so.

INFORMATION An information kiosk is on the pier itself, and a walk of only a few yards will get you to the **Prince Rupert Visitor Information Center,** at 215 Cow

Prince Rupert, British Columbia

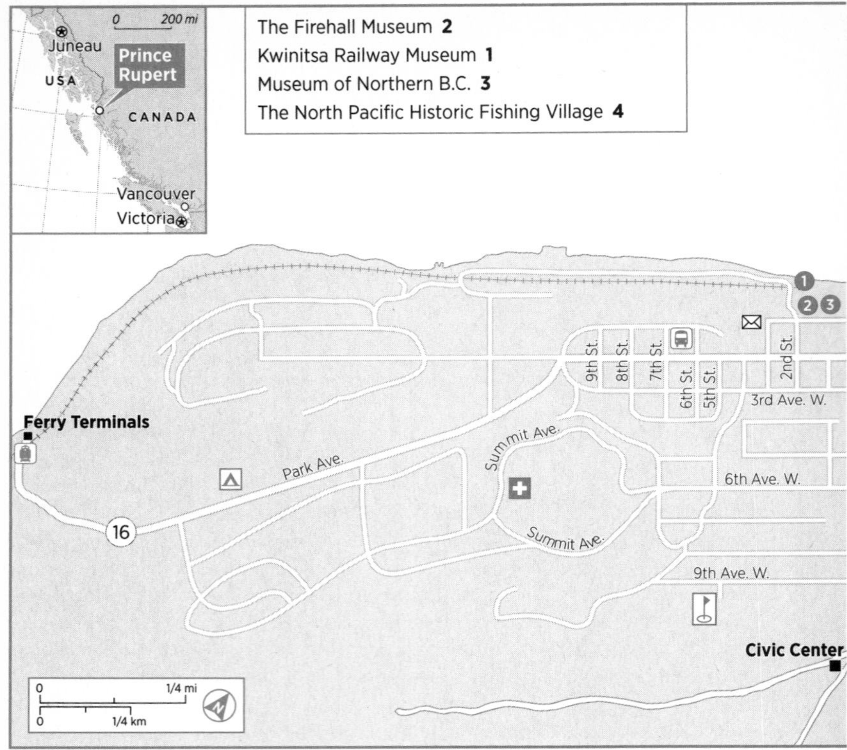

Bay Rd. (✆ **800/667-1994** or 250/624-5637; www.tourismprincerupert.com), open daily from 9am to 6pm (later if cruise ships are in town for evening stays).

BEST CRUISE-LINE SHORE EXCURSIONS

Butze Rainforest Walk Nature Walk (3 hr.; $59): Take a 2.8-mile guided walk through a temperate rainforest as you head to a viewing platform over the Butze Rapids, unusual tidal waves that reverse direction with the tides. Along the way, your guide will tell you about the use of plants in traditional Native medicine.

Canada Wilderness via Floatplane (1½ hr.; $239): See the awesome beauty of British Columbia including deep valleys, lush rainforest, rugged mountain fjords, glaciers, and glacial waterfalls. And you just may spot wildlife too including eagles, mountain goats, and whales.

Cruising with the Eagles (1¼ hr.; $65): Head off in a 50-foot catamaran to see bald eagles at a local gathering spot. If you're lucky you'll get close enough to watch them feed and hear the flap of their wings.

Whales & Marine Life Discovery Cruise (4 hr.; $125 adult, $87 child): Orcas, humpbacks, grays, and minkes inhabit the waters off Prince Rupert in their season.

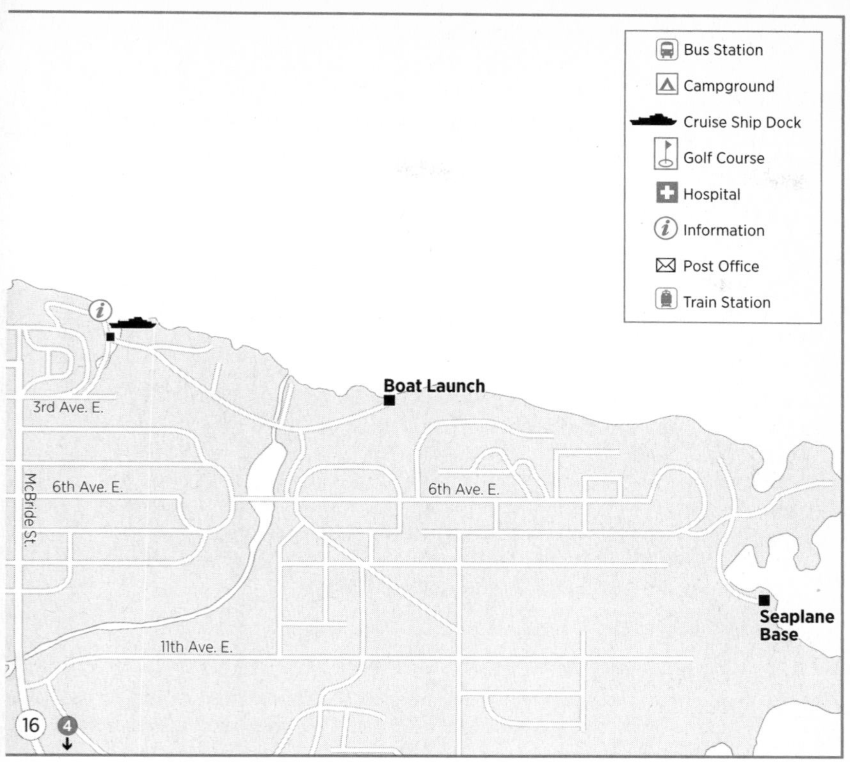

Whales are the primary object of the search, but participants are likely also to see eagles, seals, sea lions, and an abundance of other kinds of wildlife.

EXCURSIONS OFFERED BY LOCAL AGENCIES

Bear lovers can view the outskirts of the Khutzeymateen Grizzly Bear Sanctuary with **Palmerville Adventures** (✆ **888/580-2234** or 250/524-8243; www.palmerville.bc.ca). First, you take a plane or helicopter and then a boat to the sanctuary, the only grizzly bear home in Canada where you can get up close and personal (sort of) with the furry creatures. You view the bears from the boat in Khutzeymateen Inlet; rates for the 3-hour experience start at about $477 per person.

ON YOUR OWN: WITHIN WALKING DISTANCE

The Museum of Northern B.C. This well-designed facility traces the cultures and development of the Native peoples of B.C. (Tsimshian, Haida, Nisga'a, and others). The museum begins in the impressive longhouse lobby, with its cedar timbers and glass artwork. It continues through the Great Hall, the Hall of Nations, and the Treasures Gallery, which among them contain a striking collection of archaeological artifacts, ceremonial art and dress, weaponry from Indian wars, canoes, and much more.

Nanaimo

The new name in Alaska cruising is Nanaimo, British Columbia. Located on Vancouver Island, 38 nautical miles west of Vancouver, this historic port has undergone a renaissance, and Royal Caribbean, Celebrity, and Norwegian Cruise Line all have ships calling here this year, on repositioning itineraries. An extensive renovation has produced a charming boardwalk area, called Pioneer Waterfront Plaza, with floating restaurants. And on Friday's there's a down-home style outdoor farmer's market where you can sample local treats.

Nanaimo serves up plenty of shopping opportunities in the Pioneer Waterfront Plaza and nearby Old City Quarter and Art District. Local arts and crafts are the best souvenirs, and the shops will take US dollars.

Nanaimo's other big claim to fame is it's the best place on the Alaska routes where you can dive. A number of diver shops in the city (including Diver's Choice Charters, #4 1150–132 North Terminal Ave.; ✆ **866/716-8867** or 250/716-8867; http://divingbccanada.com) take divers to explore the Northwest Dodds Narrows, where there are underwater rock formations and fish, and nearby Snake Island Wall where you can explore the wreck of the navy destroyer *Saskatchewan* and Canadian Supply Ship *Cape Breton,* both sunk as part of a Canadian artificial reef project.

Television monitors in these rooms run oral histories of the area from its Indian origins right up to the modern-day commercial fishing and the creation of the city itself. At frequent intervals during the day, live performances by Indian dancers and musicians take place. The museum—a must-see for visitors to Prince Rupert—is located only a few hundred yards from the passenger terminal. But it should be noted that the first half of the road is steeply uphill. Don't miss the gift shop (see more under "Shopping" below).

100 1st Ave. W. ✆ **250/624-3207.** www.museumofnorthernbc.com. $5 adults, $2 children 6–12 (free for children 5 and under). Mon–Sat 9am–8pm; Sun 9am–5pm.

The Kwinitsa Railway Museum Located in the city's waterfront park, very close to the Museum of Northern B.C., the facility explains the evolution of Prince Rupert, from a tent town terminus for the Grand Trunk Railway, through incorporation as a city in the 1920s.

110 Bill Murray Way. ✆ **250/624-3207.** Free admission. Daily 9am–noon and 1–5pm.

The Firehall Museum This attraction features a display of a rebuilt R.E.O. Speed Wagon (ca. 1925) and illustrates the history of the Prince Rupert Fire Department through pictures and artifacts.

200 1st Ave. W ✆ **250/627-1248.** www.princerupertlibrary.ca/fire. Free admission. Mon–Sat 1–5pm.

ON YOUR OWN: BEYOND THE PORT AREA

The North Pacific Historic Fishing Village This living history museum is about 12 miles from Prince Rupert and is home to the oldest surviving salmon cannery in

British Columbia. Here, you'll learn through videos and displays what it was like to live in a company town, and discover all you need to know about fishing and canning methods. The 28 buildings date from 1889 to 1964. You can also view one of the largest model railroads on display in Western Canada. The site is operated by the nonprofit Port Edward Historical Society.

Port Edward, B.C. ✆ **250/628-3538.** www.cannery.ca. $12 adults, $9 seniors, $6 students (5–18), free for children 4 and under. May Tues–Sun 10am–5pm; Jun–Sept daily 10am–5pm, until 7pm Wed; closed to visitors rest of year.

SHOPPING

Right around Cow Bay where you come in, there are some excellent, funky little art shops with some great pieces of jewelry, pottery, and sculpture by local artists, both Native and non-Native. Best bets include the Ice House Gallery artists' co-op at Altin Terminal (190–215 Cow Bay Rd.; ✆ **250/624-4546;** www.icehousegallery.ca), Homework Gifts and Designs (145 Cow Bay Rd.; ✆ **250/624-3663;** www.home workstore.ca), and the Cow Bay Gift Gallery (24 Cow Bay Rd.; ✆ **250/627-1808**).

Uptown, try the stores of historic **Old Town Prince Rupert** (including Studio 9 Gallery, 105–515 3rd Ave. W.; ✆ **250/624-2366**), whose walkways are lined with totem poles, fountains, and flowerbeds. The area also provides easy access to a stairway from which one can enjoy spectacular views of the city and its harbor. A hidden gem for shoppers is the collection of First Nations artwork and a vast collection of regional and historical literature at the gift shop at the Museum of Northern B.C.

4 Ketchikan

Ketchikan is the southernmost port of call in Southeast Alaska, and its 14,000 residents sometimes refer to it as "the first city." That's not because it's the most important city to the region's economy, or that it's the biggest, or even that it was literally the first built. The name comes from the fact that Ketchikan is usually the first city visited by cruise ships on the Inside Passage, when ships are running northbound out of Vancouver or Seattle.

The first thing most cruise visitors encounter upon arrival at the dock is a Liquid Sunshine Gauge, which the city put up to mark the cumulative rainfall for the year, day by day. We once checked and saw that the mark showed over 36 inches—and it was only June. Even at that, the gauge had a long way to go. The average annual rainfall is about 160 inches (more than 13 ft.!) and has topped 200 inches in the rainiest years. Precipitation is so predictable here that the locals joke that if you can't see the top of nearby Deer Mountain, it's raining; if you can see it, it's going to rain!

But here's a strange thing: Through the years, we've been in Ketchikan at least once in every month of the season, and we can recall only a couple of real downpours. On one occasion, we were there in May and found sunshine and temps in the low 70s (low 20s Celsius). Go figure.

Maybe it's because the weather gods are kind to us that we have a soft spot for this place. Climate notwithstanding, this is a fun port to visit—a glorified fishing village with quaint architecture, history, salmon fishing, the great scenery found in just about every Inside Passage community, and **totem poles**—lots and lots of totem poles. However, we have to admit concern that the place has gotten touristy and overcrowded. About 70 jewelry stores and dozens of what locals call "trinket shops" cater to cruise-ship passengers. Much of the character we loved has vanished in favor of such touristy attractions as the Great Alaskan Lumberjack Show and Duck Tours (which take you on land and into the water on amphibious vehicles).

That said, from up close—say, on the sidewalk of Stedman Street—the main thoroughfare, historic Creek Street, the centerpiece of downtown, still presents a very photogenic side. It's often said (perhaps only by the Ketchikan Chamber of Commerce!) that it's the most photographed street in Alaska.

Creek Street comprises a row of historic buildings on pilings over a stream up which the salmon swim in their spawning season. Today, the narrow wooden sidewalk street is lined mostly with funky restaurants, such as the Creek Street Café, and boutiques and galleries specializing in offbeat pieces by local artists. In the early 1900s, this was Ketchikan's red-light district, with more than 30 brothels lining the waterway; a small sign at the head of the street notes that it was where both the fishermen and the fish went up the stream to spawn. The most famous of the courtesans (or, at least, the most enduring) was Dolly Arthur (born Thelma Dolly Copeland). Not the most successful—nor, according to pictures we've seen, the prettiest—working girl, she nevertheless outlived the rest. Most people can tell you who Dolly Arthur was, although she was only one of 100 girls working the area. **Dolly's House,** 24 Creek St. (**© 907/225-6329**), is now a small museum. Like the house's old clientele, you have to pay to get inside. We don't know what they used to pay, but today it'll cost you $5. It's open daily from 8am to 4pm when cruise ships are in town (sometimes earlier or later, depending on cruise-ship schedules).

Ketchikan is still a strong center of the Tlingit, Tsimshian, and Haida cultures. These proud Southeast Alaska Native peoples have preserved their traditions and kept their icons intact over the centuries. They've also re-created **clan houses** and made replicas of totem poles that were irretrievably damaged by decades of exposure to the elements. The tall hand-carved poles are everywhere—in parks, in the lobbies of buildings, in the street. It should be no surprise to anyone that there are more totems in Ketchikan than in any city in the world.

A word of caution about that: Unless you're *very* interested in the origins and the meaning of totem poles, choose your shore excursion very carefully. The **Totem Bight State Historical Park** tour (see "Best Cruise-Line Shore Excursions," below) may be led by a guide who will go into infinite detail about Alaska Native cultures and the story behind pole after pole after pole. (They're not merely decorative, and each tells the story of an incident in a tribe's life—a battle, a birth, and so on.) Those who love history will be intrigued, but others may get bored after the first five poles or so.

One of our favorite things to do in Ketchikan, besides booking a shore excursion and getting into the gorgeous surrounding natural areas, is to walk the few blocks from the ship, past Creek Street, and take the **funicular railway** ($2) to the **Westcoast Cape Fox Lodge** for lunch. The lunch is satisfying (if hardly gourmet), and the Alaskan Amber Ale is refreshing, but it's the views of the city and of the Tongass Narrows and Deer Mountain, both from the funicular and from parts of the lodge and its grounds, that make the trip worthwhile.

It's also an easy walk from here to the **Deer Mountain Tribal Hatchery and Eagle Center,** at 1158 Salmon Rd. (**© 907/228-5530;** $10 adults, $5 children 2 to 11, free for children 1 and under), a Native-run operation where you can learn where salmon come from and see some rescued and healing eagles. It's open May through September daily 8am to 4:30pm. Also nearby is the Totem Heritage Center (see below).

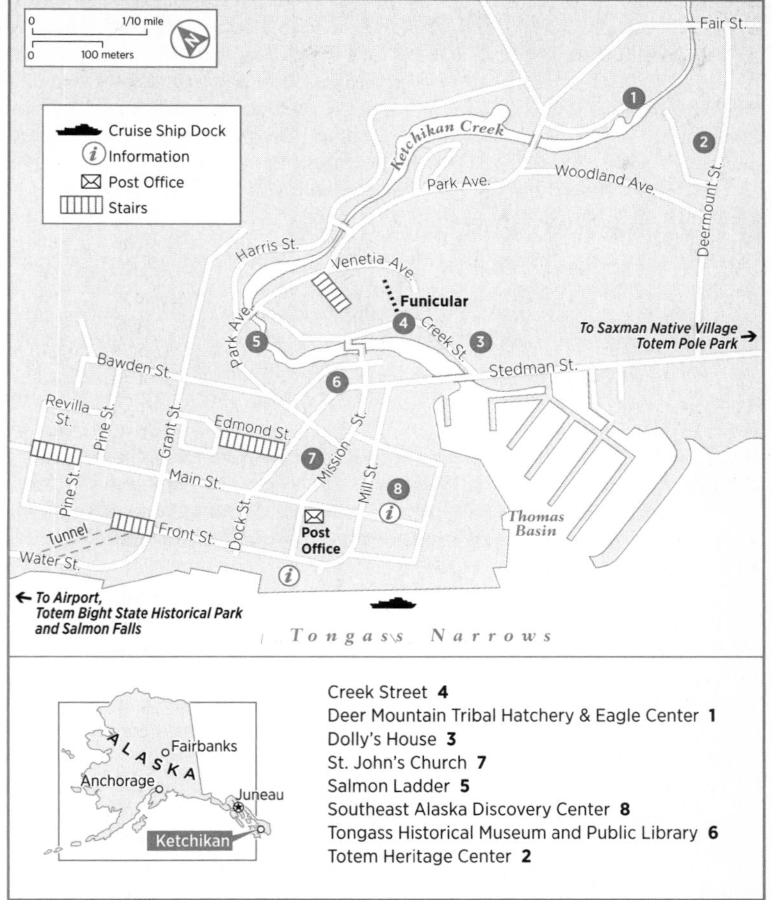

Or hang out near the pier, walking along the waterfront to see the fishing boats. Ketchikan claims to be the "Salmon Capital of the World," and in fact five species of wild Pacific salmon return from the ocean to creeks and streams near the town each year. The saltwater fishing is some of the best anywhere, and it's fun to watch the fishing boats unload their catch.

COMING ASHORE Ships dock right at the pier in Ketchikan's downtown area. Because the pier was recently expanded and there can be passengers from a half-dozen ships in at one time, guard rails have been installed and you need to cross to the town's main areas with a crossing guard.

INFORMATION Our first two stops in Ketchikan are usually the **Ketchikan Visitors Center,** right on the dock, at 131 Front St. (✆ **907/225-6166;** www.visitketchikan.com), to pick up literature and information on what's new in town (and discount coupons for attractions), and the **Southeast Alaska Discovery Center,** at nearby 50 Main St. (✆ **907/228-6220**), one of four Alaska Public Lands Information facilities in the state. The latter is more than a mere dispenser of information: It also houses a museum where a number of exhibits and dioramas depict both Native Alaskan cultures and the modern business development of Ketchikan. Admission to the exhibits is $5, free for children 15 and under. The visitor center is open whenever a cruise ship has docked. The Discovery Center is open May to October, daily from 8am to 5pm; October through April Monday to Friday 10am to 4pm.

BEST CRUISE-LINE SHORE EXCURSIONS

Alaska Duck (Amphibious) Tours (1½ hr.; $39 adults, $25 children 12 and under): See Ketchikan by both land and sea. This fun outing, in a high-riding "duck" vehicle, takes you through rustic streets (past the salmon ladder, Creek Street, and Totem Heritage Center) and into the harbor where you can eye the aquatic wildlife, check out the leisure and fishing boats, and get an up close look at the floatplanes taking off. Be forewarned that, as you hit the water, there may be splashes (which typically elicit squeals of delight).

Bear Country & Wildlife Expedition (3½ hr.; $199): This naturalist-led tour, introduced last summer, brings only 12 guests at a time to a new rainforest trail that leads to a creek frequented by black bears, who come there in search of salmon. Viewing is from elevated areas that include a suspension bridge and tree platforms. You'll likely see bald eagles too.

Bering Sea Crab Fishermen's Tour (3½ hr.; $179 adults, $119 children): This tour is a must-do for fans of the Discovery Channel's *Deadliest Catch.* Real fishermen share their tales and exploits as you travel on the F/V *Aleutian Ballard,* the same vessel featured on the show (though without the rough seas, cold conditions, and other dangers the show highlights). Plenty of crabs and other marine life are on view.

Misty Fjords Flightseeing (2 hr.; $259 adults, $199 children): Everyone gets a window seat aboard the floatplanes that run these quick flightseeing jaunts over Misty Fjords National Monument. There are no ice fields and glaciers on this trip, but Misty Fjords has another kind of majesty: You'll see sparkling fjords, cascading waterfalls, thick forests, and rugged mountains dotted with wildlife. Then, you'll come in for a landing on the fjord itself or on a nearby wilderness lake. Once you've landed, you can get out and stand—carefully—on the pontoons to take pictures.

Mountain Point Snorkeling Adventure (3 hr.; $99): Believe it or not, you can snorkel around Ketchikan, where the climate is warm for Alaska. Still, it's not the Caribbean, and insulating wetsuits are provided on this excursion, as well as hot beverages for when you get out of the water. Undersea are fish, starfish, sea urchins, sea cucumbers, and more.

Saxman Native Village and Ketchikan City Tour (2½ hr.; $59 adults, $29 children): This modern-day Native village, situated about 3 miles outside Ketchikan, is a center for the revival of Native arts and culture. The tour includes either the telling of a Native legend or a performance by the Cape Fox dancers in the park theater, plus a guided walk through the grounds to see the totem poles and learn the stories behind them. Craftspeople are sometimes on hand in the working sheds to demonstrate totem-pole carving.

Tatoosh Island Sea Kayaking (4 hr.; $149 adults, $109 children 8–12): There are typically two kayaking excursions offered in Ketchikan: this one (which requires you to take a van and motorized boat to the island before starting your 90-min. paddle) and a trip that starts from right beside the cruise-ship docks. Of the two, this one is far more enjoyable, getting you out into a wilder area rather than just sticking to the busy port waters. The scenery is incredible, and you have a good chance of spotting bald eagles, seals (whether swimming around your boat or basking on the rocks), and leaping salmon.

Totem Bight State Historical Park and City Tour (2–2½ hr.; $40 adults, $25 children 12 and under): This tour takes you by bus around Ketchikan and through the Tongass National Forest to see the historic Native fish camp, where a ceremonial clan house and totem poles sit amid the rainforest. There's a fair amount of walking involved, making the tour a poor choice for anyone with mobility problems.

Rain Forest Ropes & Zip Challenge (3 hr. 25 min.; $179): This tour allows guests to traverse a Zipline in harnesses between trees before rappelling to the ground. It's a new way to appreciate the Alaskan rainforest. This is real ziplining (unlike the offering in Icy Strait Point which is more of a ride than lining). Instruction will be given, and only minimal skill is required. A similar option is available in Juneau.

Great Alaskan Lumberjack Show (1 hr. 10 min.; $35 adults, $19 children 2–10): Chopping, sawing, speed climbing, log rolling, and more. And all within a short walk of the cruise-ship pier. The performers are in the open air, but the spectator seats are covered and the area heated.

Ketchikan Motorcycle Tour (3½ hr.; $269 drive, $142 passenger): This is your chance to ride a Harley in Alaska. You'll need a motorcycle license to drive, but you may also be able to go as a passenger on the back of a guided motorcycle. The tour covers about 50 miles on new bikes, and you get plenty of scenic views along the way.

EXCURSIONS OFFERED BY LOCAL AGENCIES

A bevy of tour operators sell their excursions at the **Ketchikan Visitors Center,** on 131 Front St. (© **907/225-6166**), right at the dock. Schoolteacher Lois Munch of **Classic Tours** (© **907/225-3091;** www.classictours.com) makes her tours fun: She wears a poodle skirt to drive visitors around in her '55 Chevy, accompanied by '50s mood music. A 2-hour tour to the Saxman totem poles is $109; a 3-hour tour adds a natural-history stop and costs $139. Rates are per person and include admission to Saxman. The maximum group size is five. Lois is also happy to customize a tour (price based on itinerary) for you, if you call in advance and tell her what you want. **Allen Marine Tours** (© **877/686-8100** or 907/225-8100; www.allenmarinetours.com) has cruises from Ketchikan to Misty Fjords National Monument on a high-speed catamaran built at the company's own boatyard in Sitka. A 4½-hour tour is $159 for adults, $109 for children 3 to 12. Other locals offer tours, too; check at the town visitor center (see above) for many more choices. **Alaska Travel Adventures** (© **800/323-5757** or 907/247-5295; www.bestofalaskatravel.com) operates several tours including a Rain Forest & Canoe Adventure (3½ hr.; $89 adults, $59 children) where you board a 37-foot, 20-passenger canoe and paddle under the direction of an experienced guide on a secluded mountain lake, surrounded by Tongass National Forest. The tour also includes a nature walk highlighting flora and fauna. **Southeast Sea Kayaks,** at 1430 Millar St. (© **800/287-1607** or 907/225-1258; www.kayakketchikan.com), has guided paddle excursions (2½ hr.; $94 adults, $64 children) as well as rentals.

ON YOUR OWN: WITHIN WALKING DISTANCE

Creek Street This former red-light district is now arguably Ketchikan's number-one tourist attraction, jewelry stores and tourist shops aside. The view of Creek Street from the bridge over the stream on Stedman Street (the main thoroughfare) is striking, to say the least. It lays claim to the title "Most photographed street in the world" and, even allowing for a little chamber of commerce hyperbole, it just might be!

Off Stedman St., along Ketchikan Creek.

St. John's Church St. John's Church is the oldest place of worship in town. Both the church (Episcopal, by the way) and its adjacent Seaman's Center—built in 1904 as a hospital and now a commercial building—are interesting examples of local architecture in the early 1900s.

On Bawden St., at Mission St.

The Salmon Ladder We could spend hours on the observation deck at the artificial salmon ladder just off Park Avenue, watching these determined fish make their way from the sea up to the spawning grounds at the top of Ketchikan Creek. How these creatures can keep throwing their exhausted bodies up the ladder at the end of their long journey from the ocean, never giving up though they fail in three out of four leaps, is one of those mysteries of nature that we will never understand—and never tire of observing.

Off Park Ave., in Ketchikan Creek.

Tongass Historical Museum and Public Library This museum has Native cultural displays and other fine exhibits. It also contains one of the city's grizzlier relics: the bullet-riddled skull of Old Groaner, a brown bear that took to attacking humans and was shot for its troubles. In the same building, the attractive Ketchikan Public Library is a great place to recharge, especially in the children's section downstairs, where big windows look out on Ketchikan Creek's falls.

In the Centennial Building, 629 Dock St. ✆ **907/225-5600.** Admission $2. Summer daily 8am–5pm.

Totem Heritage Center The Totem Heritage Center, built by the city of Ketchikan in 1976, has the virtue of being indoors, so weather isn't a factor. The museum houses a fine collection of 33 original totem poles from the 19th century, retrieved from the Tlingit Indian villages on Tongass and Village islands and the Haida village of Old Kasaan. The Tsimshian people are also represented in some exhibits. There's a nice nature path outdoors. Be aware: It's a long walk to the museum unless you take the funicular, which allows you to avoid some of the uphill hike.

601 Deermount St. ✆ **907/225-5900.** Admission $5. May–Sept daily 8am–5pm; Oct–Apr Mon–Fri 1–5pm.

ON YOUR OWN: BEYOND THE PORT AREA

In Ketchikan, we strongly recommend that you leave the out-of-port tours to either the cruise lines or tour operators in town.

SHOPPING

Ketchikan, much to our dismay, has become a tourist shopping spot. Most of the shops are owned by folks who come here just for the summer to cater to cruise passengers. But there are still some hidden gems, our favorite being a friendly hole-in-the-wall called **Salmon, Etc.** (✆ **800/354-7256;** www.salmonetc.com), a few blocks from the ship pier at 322 Mission St., where you can buy cans of yummy smoked salmon. The shop has been in town since the early 1980s and is locally owned. Its smoked-fish products are so good that, on our last visit, we bought a 24-can case of smoked salmon (for $139) and hauled it home (you can also have it shipped). That price was about $40 cheaper than at the shops at Salmon Landing, a mini mall closer to the ship pier. Ketchikan has a decent arts scene, and a good place to check out what's new is the Mainstay Gallery of the **Ketchikan Arts and Humanities Council,** near Creek Street at 716 Totem Way (© **907/225-2211;** www.ketchikanarts.org). Shows change monthly. Most local galleries are owned and operated by resident artists, including **Crazy Wolf Studio** (607 Mission St., across from Whale Park © **907/225-9653;** www.crazywolfstudio.com), co-owned by Ken Decker (and his wife, Monica), a Tsimshian artist from Ketchikan (and a member of the Wolf clan). Fish art aficionados should go directly to Ray Troll's **Soho Coho,** at 5 Creek St. (© **800/888-4070;** www.trollart.com); his SPAWN TILL YOU DIE T-shirts have become classics.

5 Misty Fjords National Monument

The 2.3-million-acre, Connecticut-size area of Misty Fjords starts at the Canadian border in the south and runs along the eastern side of the Behm Canal. Revillagigedo Island, where Ketchikan is located, is on the western side of the canal. It is topography, not wildlife, that makes a visit to Misty Fjords worthwhile. Among the prime features of Misty Fjords are New Eddystone Rock, jutting 237 feet out of the canal, and the Walker Cove/Rudyerd Bay area, a prime viewing spot for marine life, eagles, and other wildlife. Volcanic cliffs (up to 3,150 ft. high), coves (some as deep as 900 ft.), and peace and serenity are the stock in trade of the place.

Only passengers on small ships will see Misty Fjords close up, as its waterway is too narrow in most places for big ships. The bigger ships pass the southern tip of the Misty Fjords National Monument and then veer away northwest to dock at Ketchikan. Unfortunately, this means that large-ship passengers miss one of the least spoiled of all wilderness areas, unless, that is, you book a flightseeing trip to see the place (see the section on Ketchikan excursions above).

Archaeologists believe local Indian tribes (Haida, Tlingit, and Tsimshian primarily) lived here as far back as 10,000 years ago. The only way you're likely to see any trace of their existence now, though, is from a kayak or small boat that can get close enough to the rock face so you can discern the few remaining pictographs etched into the stone along the shore.

Anglers in Misty Fjords are liable to think they've died and gone to heaven. The pristine waters yield a rich harvest of enormous Dolly Varden, grayling, and lake trout. It is possible to walk in the park, but only the hardy and the experienced are advised to do that. And it is necessary to follow some simple rules. Let somebody know where you are going and when you expect to return. Keep to the trails. (The wildlife—especially bears—doesn't always appreciate intruders.) And carry out everything you carried in; that's the law.

By the way, the name Misty Fjords comes from the climatic conditions. Precipitation tends to leave the place looking as if it were under a steady mist much of the time. It also gives the waterway an almost spooky look. President Jimmy Carter protected it and named it a national treasure in 1978.

6 Admiralty Island National Monument

About 15 miles due west of Juneau, this monument comprises almost 1 million acres and covers about 90% of Admiralty Island. It's another of those Alaska areas that cruise passengers on the bigger ships will never see. The villages here, some of them Native, have recently begun to attract some small-ship operators. The Tlingit village of **Angoon,** for example, welcomes small groups of visitors off ships. Small ships may also ferry passengers ashore in a more remote area of the island for a hike.

Admiralty Island is said to have the highest concentration of **bears** on earth. Naturalists estimate that there may be as many as four of these creatures per square mile. Bears, though, don't have a monopoly on the island. Also plentiful are **Sitka black-tailed deer** and **bald eagles,** and the waters around teem with sea lions, harbor seals, and whales. One of the largest concentrations of bald eagles in Southeast Alaska (second, perhaps, only to that in Haines in the fall) is to be found in the bays and inlets on the east side of the island. An estimated 4,000 eagles congregate there because the food supply is more abundant and is easier to access.

A 25-mile-long canoe trail system links the major lakes on the island, with some overland portions where visitors must carry their canoes. Travelers who are willing to work are rewarded by magnificent scenery and quiet.

Angoon itself is not particularly close to the natural wonders of Admiralty Island. There's not much to do there except walk along the beach to an old cemetery that houses some interesting headstones.

7 Tracy Arm & Endicott Arm

Located about 50 miles due south of Juneau, these long, deep, and almost claustrophobically narrow fjords are a striking feature of a pristine forest and mountain expanse with a sinister name: **Tracy Arm–Ford's Terror Wilderness.** The place came by its name honestly after an 1889 incident in which a crewman from a U.S. naval vessel (name: Ford; rank: unknown) rowed into an inlet off Endicott Arm and found himself trapped for 6 hours in a heaving sea as huge ice floes bumped and ground around and against his flimsy craft. He survived, but the finger of water in which he endured his ordeal was forever after known as Ford's Terror.

The Tracy and Endicott arms, which reach back from Stephens Passage into the Coastal Mountain Range, are steep-sided waterways, each with an active glacier at its head—the **Sawyer Glacier** in Tracy Arm and **Dawes Glacier** in Endicott. These calve constantly, sometimes discarding ice blocks of such size that they clog the narrow fjord passages, making navigation difficult. When the passage is not clogged, ships can get close enough for amazing sights and sounds of calving glaciers (the sound of white thunder is amazing!). On a Regent Seven Seas cruise, we were thrilled when the captain ordered the tenders out at Sawyer Glacier for a great photo op.

A passage up either fjord allows eye-catching views of high cascading waterfalls, tree- and snow-covered mountain valleys, and wildlife that might include **Sitka black-tailed deer, bald eagles,** and possibly even the odd **black bear.** Around the ship, the animals you're most likely to see are whales, sea lions, and harbor seals.

8 Baranof Island

Named after the Russian trader Alexander Baranof, Russian America's first appointed honcho, the island's main claim to fame is **Sitka,** on the western coast, the center of Russian-era culture and the seat of the Russian Orthodox Church in Alaska. (The island name, by the way, is often spelled Baranov, which some people contend is the way Alexander himself spelled it.) **Peril Straits,** off the northern end of the island, separating Baranof from Chichagof Island, is a scenic passageway too narrow for big cruise ships, but some of the smaller ones can get through.

9 Sitka

Sitka differs from most ports of call on the Inside Passage cruises in that, geographically speaking, it's not on the Inside Passage at all. Rather, it stands on the outside (or western) coast of Baranof Island. Its name, in fact, comes from the Tlingit Indian *Shee Atika,* which means "people on the outside." For the relatively short time it takes ships to get to Sitka, they must leave the protected waters of the passage and sail with nothing between them and Japan but the sometimes turbulent Pacific Ocean. If you're going to run into heavy seas at any point on an Inside Passage cruise, this is where you'll most likely find them. This is also one of the ports in Alaska where you're more likely to have to tender to shore (in small boats) rather than dock at the harbor. Be that as it may, the idea of missing this delightful port of call is unthinkable to many people.

Proof it's a must-do? The town was declared one of the 2010 Dozen Distinctive Destinations by the National Trust for Historic Preservation, in recognition of its historical architecture, cultural diversity, and commitment to historic preservation. Sadly, the town was among the most hard-hit in 2010's downturn, greeting 80,000 fewer passengers then in the previous year.

Step off your cruise ship here, and you step into the Russian Alaska of yesteryear. This is where, in 1799, trader Alexander Baranof established a fort in what became known as New Archangel. Today, **St. Michael's Cathedral,** with its striking onion-shaped dome and ornate gilt interior, reflects that heritage, as does the all-female troupe the **New Archangel Dancers,** who perform during the cruise season in **Harrigan Centennial Hall.** The colorfully costumed, 30-strong troupe performs a program of energetic Russian folk dances several times a day. Once a week, the New Archangel Dancers get together with a Tlingit dance troupe for a joint performance in the Sheet'ka Kwaan Naa Kahidi Community House on Katlian Street.

Most attractions in Sitka are within walking distance of the passenger docks. The **Sitka National Historical Park,** a must-do attraction with its impressive (mostly reproduction) totem poles and excellent views, is about a 10-minute walk from the passenger docks. One attraction that's too far to walk to, but ought not to be missed, is the **Alaska Raptor Rehabilitation Center.** A nonprofit venture supported by tour companies, cruise lines, and public donations, the center was opened in 1980 to treat sick or injured birds of prey (primarily eagles) and to provide an educational experience for visitors. We don't mind admitting that the sight of our majestic national bird close up, with its snowy white head and curved beak, gives us goose bumps. Go as part of a shore excursion or take a taxi for about $22.

Every year in June, this town of 8,835 year-round residents hosts a celebration of chamber music, performed by world-class practitioners of the art in various halls throughout the town. The **Sitka Summer Music Festival** has been held every year since 1972 under the guidance of renowned violinist Paul Rosenthal. Performances are Tuesday and Friday evenings; admission prices vary. We recommend it as a perfect complement to the more frenzied, more modern entertainment found on cruise ships. All this culture is particularly impressive when you consider Sitka has more boats than people.

Despite visits by cruise ships several times a week, Sitka somehow manages to keep a quaint, small-town ambience. Walking along the harbor filled with fishing boats (and pleasure boats too), our coauthor Fran overheard this endearing conversation: "What's the fish count like this week?" "I don't know, let's ask Joe."

If you get the munchies, stop by **Ludwig's** street cart and crab-boil stand in the parking lot behind Lincoln Street (follow the signs). The fantastic clam chowder uses spicy sausage as the "secret" ingredient, and the boiled crabs are served with plenty of drawn butter. **Harry Race Pharmacy,** 106 Lincoln St., has a cool 1950s-style soda fountain (and also serves ice cream). At the **Westmark Sitka,** at 330 Seward St., you can get a fancier restaurant meal at the **Raven Dining Room,** which affords a sea view and fine service (thanks to a bunch of energetic and friendly young people). **Highliner Coffee,** in the backside of Seward Square Mall (327 Seward St.), has lattes, other coffee drinks, and excellent baked goods (try the giant oatmeal cookies); it also has computers you can use (for a fee) to e-mail your friends back home.

COMING ASHORE Most passengers will arrive by tender because the harbor is too small to accommodate large ships. Tenders drop you within walking distance of the downtown area, but shuttle buses (an all-day pass is $10) are also available to ferry you to local sights. But unless you have a very specific, distant destination in mind (the Raptor Center, for instance), we don't recommend taking a taxi or bus. Sitka is so small and the heart of town so close to the passenger pier that it's ideal for exploring on foot.

INFORMATION A kiosk in the city-operated **Harrigan Centennial Hall Visitor Center,** next to the Crescent Boat Harbor at 330 Harbor Dr. (© **907/747-3225**), is the only walk-in information stop. It is staffed by volunteers only when cruise ships are in town. The hall is open Monday through Friday 8am to 10pm, Saturday 8am to 5pm, and sometimes Sunday.

BEST CRUISE-LINE SHORE EXCURSIONS

Russian Sitka and New Archangels Dance Performance (3½ hr.; $49 adults, $34 children): This motorcoach excursion hits all the historic sites, including St. Michael's Cathedral, the Russian Cemetery, Castle Hill, and Sitka's National Historical Park, with its totem poles and forest trails, and returns for the dance extravaganza at Harrigan Centennial Hall.

4×4 Wilderness Adventure (4½ hr.; $243): Board a boat for a ride through the islands of Sitka Sound, and then, on Kruzof Island, drive yourself off-road (following a guide) on a 2-person Yamaha RHINO. You'll explore temperate rainforest and may spot brown bears.

Sea Otter & Wildlife Quest (3 hr.; $128 adults, $87 children 12 and under): A naturalist accompanies passengers on this jet-boat tour to point out the various animals you'll encounter and explain the delicate balance of the region's marine ecosystem.

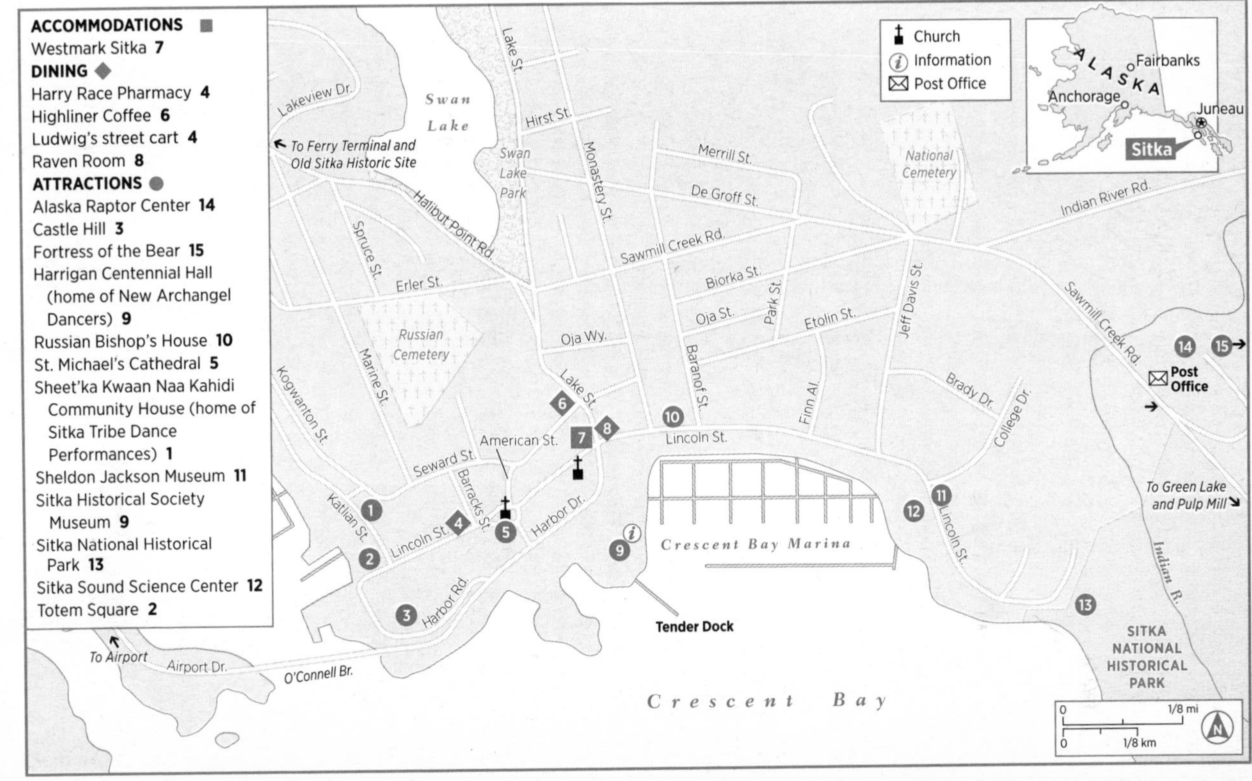
ACCOMMODATIONS
Westmark Sitka 7
DINING
Harry Race Pharmacy 4
Highliner Coffee 6
Ludwig's street cart 4
Raven Room 8
ATTRACTIONS
Alaska Raptor Center 14
Castle Hill 3
Fortress of the Bear 15
Harrigan Centennial Hall (home of New Archangel Dancers) 9
Russian Bishop's House 10
St. Michael's Cathedral 5
Sheet'ka Kwaan Naa Kahidi Community House (home of Sitka Tribe Dance Performances) 1
Sheldon Jackson Museum 11
Sitka Historical Society Museum 9
Sitka National Historical Park 13
Sitka Sound Science Center 12
Totem Square 2
Church
Information
Post Office
ALASKA
Fairbanks
Anchorage
Juneau
Sitka
Lakeview Dr.
Swan Lake
To Ferry Terminal and Old Sitka Historic Site
Lake St.
Hirst St.
Swan Lake Park
Monastery St.
Merrill St.
De Groff St.
National Cemetery
Indian River Rd.
Halibut Point Rd.
Spruce St.
Erler St.
Sawmill Creek Rd.
Biorka St.
Park St.
Oja St.
Etolin St.
Jeff Davis St.
Sawmill Creek Rd.
Russian Cemetery
Oja Wy.
Kogwanton St.
Marine St.
Lake St.
Baranof St.
Finn Al.
Brady Dr.
College Dr.
Post Office
American St.
Lincoln St.
Seward St.
Barracks St.
Katlian St.
Lincoln St.
Harbor Dr.
Crescent Bay Marina
Lincoln St.
To Green Lake and Pulp Mill
Indian R.
Harbor Rd.
Tender Dock
SITKA NATIONAL HISTORICAL PARK
To Airport
Airport Dr.
O'Connell Br.
Crescent Bay
0
1/8 mi
0
1/8 km

They're so sure you'll see a whale, bear, or otter that they offer partial cash refunds if you don't. A 4½-hr. version of the tour adds a visit to the Alaska Raptor Center ($142 adults, $103 children).

Sitka Photography Tour (3 hr.; $99): Get tips on photographing wild flowers, spawning salmon, sights in the Tongass National Forest, eagles, and more. The trip is led by a professional Southeast Alaska photographer.

Silver Bay Nature Cruise and Hatchery Tour (2 hr.; $59 adults, $37 children 12 and under): An excursion vessel takes you through beautiful Silver Bay to view wildlife, scenery, the ruins of the Liberty Prospect Gold Mine, and a salmon hatchery.

Salmon or Halibut Fishing (4 hr.; $230): An experienced captain will guide your fully equipped boat to a good spot for halibut and salmon; the rest is up to you. Your catch can be frozen or smoked and shipped to your home if you wish. ***Note:*** A $10 fishing license and a $10 king salmon tag are extra.

EXCURSIONS OFFERED BY LOCAL OPERATORS

Owned by the Sitka Tribe of Alaska, **Tribal Tours** (✆ **907/747-7290;** www.sitkatours.com) offers a cultural tour program that relates the history of Sitka, with an emphasis on Native history and culture. Tickets can be purchased at the **Sheet'ka Kwaan Naa Kahidi Community House,** at 200 Katlian St. (near the tender docks). A 2½-hour comprehensive tour, priced at $53 adults, $42 children, includes a 45-minute narrative drive, a half-hour stop at the Sheldon Jackson Museum, a stop at the Sitka National Historical Park, and a performance by the Tlingit Indian Dance Troupe (not to be confused with the New Archangel Dancers).

Sitka Sound Ocean Adventures (✆ **907/747-6375;** www.ssoceanadventures.com) provides kayak rentals ($45 single or $65 double, for a half-day) and tours ($69 adults, $49 children (6 to 12) for a 2½-hr. tour, 2 person minimum), and they'll pick you up at the pier.

ON YOUR OWN: WITHIN WALKING DISTANCE

Castle Hill At first, we found the prospect of a climb up to the top of the hill—by way of a lengthy flight of stairs from the western end of Lincoln Street—a little daunting, but after climbing to the top, we have two words of advice: Do it. The reward is panoramic views of downtown Sitka. This is where the first post–Alaska Purchase U.S. flag was raised, in 1867. The place is steeped in history. It was on this site, in the 1830s, that the marauding Russians drove off the resident Kiksadi clan of Tlingit Indians and built a stronghold from which to conduct their fur-trading business. The last of the buildings within the walls of the stronghold was used by the first Russian American governor and was called Baranof's Castle (hence: Castle Hill). The structure burned some 60 years later, and its remains can still be seen, along with a lot of other reminders of those pre-Purchase days. Castle Hill is a National Historic Landmark, managed by the Alaska State Parks Department.

Climb stairs near intersection of Lincoln and Katlian sts.

New Archangel Dancers Just watching the way these Russian folk dancers throw themselves around the stage makes us tired. Where do they get the energy? The dancers are all women—they even play the men's parts, complete with false beards if the dance requires it. When the troupe was organized in 1969, the men of the town pooh-poohed the idea. It'll never work, they said. Later, when the original handful of women proved that it could work, some of the men expressed the feeling that they might not mind joining in. Too late, guys. The founders decided to keep the show all-female. The 30-minute show is presented at least twice a day and sometimes as often as four times most days in the summer, largely determined by the number of cruise ships in town.

In Harrigan Centennial Hall, 330 Harbor Dr., near the tender docks. © **907/747-5516.** www.newarchangeldancers.com. Admission $10. Call for performance times, which change daily. Tickets must be purchased at least a half-hour before the show.

Russian Bishop's House Bishop Innocent Veniaminov, born in 1797, translated scriptures into Tlingit and trained deacons to carry Russian Orthodoxy back to their Native villages. Unlike most of the later Protestant missionaries led by Sitka's other historic religious figure, Sheldon Jackson, Veniaminov and his followers allowed parishioners to use their own language, a key element to saving Native cultures. The house was built in 1842 for Veniaminov and is now owned and operated by the National Parks Service. Ranger-led tours include the bishop's furnished quarters and an impressive chapel. Exhibits downstairs trace the development of New Archangel into Sitka.

Lincoln and Monastery sts. No phone; call Sitka National Historical Park Visitor Center (© **907/747-0110;** www.nps.gov/sitk). Admission $4 per person or $15 per family. Mid-May–Sept daily 9am–5pm; Oct–mid-May by appointment only.

St. Michael's Cathedral Even if you're not a fan of religious shrines, you'll probably be impressed by the architecture and the finery of this rather small place of worship. One of the 49th state's most striking and photogenic structures, the current church is actually a replica; the original burned to the ground in 1966. So revered was the cathedral that Sitkans, whether Russian Orthodox or not, formed a human chain and carried many of the cathedral's precious icons, paintings, vestments, and jeweled crowns from the flames. Later, with contributions of cash and labor from throughout the land, St. Michael's was lovingly re-created on the same site and rededicated in 1976. A knowledgeable guide is on hand to answer questions or give talks when large groups congregate. Sunday services are sung in English, Slavonic, Tlingit, Aleut, and Yup'ik.

At Lincoln and Cathedral sts. © **907/747-8120.** Suggested donation $2. May–Sept Mon–Fri 9am–4pm, Sat–Sun varies (call in advance). Call ahead for hours other times of year.

The Sheldon Jackson Museum This museum is operated by the state, but located on the grounds of a college founded in 1878 by Presbyterian missionary Sheldon Jackson as a vocational school for young Tlingits (it was the first educational institution in Alaska). The college suddenly closed its doors in 2007 (there was talk last year of reopening in a proposed partnership with Iowa's University of Dubuque). But the museum is still open and contains a fine collection of Native artifacts—not just those of the Tlingits, but also those of the Aleut, Athabascan, Haida, and Tsimshian peoples, as well as the Native peoples of the Arctic. The museum has a decent gift shop.

104 College Dr. (at Lincoln St.). © **907/747-8981.** www.museums.state.ak.us. Admission $4 to museum, free for youth 18 and under. Mid-May to mid-Sept daily 9am–5pm; mid-Sept to mid-May Tues–Sat 10am–4pm.

Sitka Sound Science Center In a rustic building across the street from the Sheldon Jackson Museum, the Sitka Sound Science Center (formerly the Sheldon Jackson Aquarium & Hatchery) has an 800-gallon "wall of water" and touch tanks with local marine creatures, including bright anemone and starfish. Outside is a hatchery for king salmon.

801 Lincoln St. © **907/747-8878.** www.sitkasoundsciencecenter.org. Suggested donation $2. Daily 8am–5pm.

Sitka Historical Society Museum Sharing the Harrigan Centennial Building with the New Archangel Dancers (see above), this museum (formerly the Isabel Miller Museum), operated by the Sitka Historical Society, illustrates the city's history with art and artifacts. There's a large diorama of Sitka as it was in 1867, the year the Alaska Purchase took place and the land was transferred from Russia to the United States.

In the Harrigan Centennial Building, 330 Harbor Dr., near the tender docks. ✆ **907/747-6455.** www.sitkahistory.org. Admission $2. May–Sept Sun–Fri 9am–5pm, Sat 11am–3pm; off-season Tues–Sat 10am–4pm.

Sitka National Historical Park At just 107 acres, this is the smallest national park in Alaska, but don't let that discourage you—the place breathes history. In fact, the park celebrated its 100th anniversary last year. This is where the Russians and the Tlingits fought a fierce battle in 1804. Within the park are a beautiful totem-pole trail (which you can visit on a ranger-led tour or on your own) and a visitor center, where exhibits explain the art of totem carving and a 12-minute film talks about Sitkans past and present. Native artisans from the Southeast Alaska Indian Cultural Center are frequently on hand creating totems, beadwork, weavings, and more. Totem carvers work in a studio behind the museum (last year, Tlingit carver Tommy Joseph was creating a totem pole commissioned to honor a Japanese photographer killed in a bear attack). The park is about a 20-minute walk from the farthest tender pier.

106 Metlakatla St. ✆ **907/747-6281.** www.nps.gov/sitk. Admission $4 for visitor center, free for park grounds. Visitor center mid-May–Sept daily 8am–5pm; Oct–mid-May Mon–Sat 8am–5pm. Park trails mid-May–Sept daily 6am–10pm; Oct–mid-May daily 7am–8pm.

Sitka Tribe Dance Performances The Sheet'ka Kwaan Naa Kahidi, Sitka's Community House, stands on the north side of the downtown parade ground. It is a modern version of a Tlingit clan house, with an air-handling system that pulls smoke from the central fire pit straight up to the chimney. The magnificent house screen at the front of the hall, installed in 2000, is the largest in the Pacific Northwest. Performances last 30 minutes and include three dances and a story. It's entirely traditional and put on by members of the tribe. You can also sign up for tours and activities in the lobby.

200 Katlian St. ✆ **888/270-8687** or 907/747-7290. $8 adults, $5 children. Call for times.

Totem Square This area was originally underwater. It served as the Russian shipyard, which was reclaimed from the sea from 1940 to 1941. It now contains Russian cannons, huge anchors believed to have come from ships lost in Sitka Harbor in the 1700s, and other historical memorabilia.

Katlian St., at the west end of Lincoln St. Free admission. Open 24 hr.

ON YOUR OWN: BEYOND THE PORT AREA

Alaska Raptor Center Local informational literature claims that the center is 20 minutes on foot from town, but these must be special chamber-of-commerce minutes, because it seems to take at least that long by bus. However you get there, though (and every cruise line offers it as a shore excursion), the center is well worth seeing. It's not a performing-animal show with stunts and flying action, but a place where injured raptors (birds of prey) are brought and, with luck, healed to the point whereby they can be returned to the wild. Some eventually can; those that cannot are housed permanently at the center—last year, there were 24 bald and golden eagles in residence—or sent to zoos. Very few are euthanized. A flight-training center comprises a little rainforest in an aviary where recuperating birds learn to fly again. Visitors walk through in a tube with one-way glass so they can watch the birds without disturbing them. The tour through the center and on a wheelchair-accessible nature trail in the surrounding rainforest takes about an hour.

1101 Sawmill Creek Rd. (milepost 0.9), just across Indian River. ✆ **800/643-9425** or 907/747-8662. www.alaskaraptor.org. Admission $12 adults, $6 children 3–12. May–Sept daily 8am–4pm; Oct–Apr call for hours of operation.

Fortress of the Bear This new, one-of-a-kind sanctuary for orphaned Southeast Alaska Brown Bears—also known as grizzlies—provides visitors with a chance to view the creatures up close, in a ¾-acre re-created natural habitat. The organization is nonprofit, with an education and protection mission. But it has been a controversial project in the community—some see it as an unsightly concrete zoo. Future plans call for a museum and interpretive center. The first residents are two cubs found in a residential neighborhood picking through trash. Research at the facility has been conducted by the Alaska Department of Fish and Game. The philosophy of project officials: Studying the bears in captivity can help wild grizzlies. For visitors, it's your best shot at seeing a grizzly in Alaska.

Sawmill Cove Industrial Park. ✆ **907/747-3032.** www.fortressofthebear.org. Admission $11 adults, $4 children 6–12, free for children 5 and under. May–Sept daily 9am–6pm; Oct–Apr Wed–Sun 10am–4pm.

SHOPPING

Until a few years ago, nearly all the shops in Sitka were locally owned, or at least owned by Alaskans. But then a chain shop, Del Sol, snuck in, much to the consternation of locals who vowed no more would be allowed. One of coauthor Fran's favorite shops on the whole Southeast route is the locally owned **Sitka Rose Gallery** (✆ **888/236-1536;** www.sitkarosegallery.com), in a pretty Victorian house at 419 Lincoln St. The gallery features the works of more than 100 Alaskan artists (no MADE IN TAIWAN merchandise here) at prices that are more reasonable than at bigger ports such as Ketchikan. Fran's daughter, Erin, snagged a lovely pair of antique walrus-tusk earrings for only $29. On another visit, Fran bought a fossilized whale-bone sculpture. On her recent trips, however, Fran has been most obsessed with the **Winter Song Soap Company** shop (✆ **907/747-8949** or 888/819-8949; www.wintersongsoap.com), now in the back of the gallery. Their homemade soaps come in such fragrances as Alaskan Herbs & Flowers, and they also sell nice wooden soap dishes (if you like what you buy here, you can replenish your supplies online).

10 Juneau

Quick quiz: Can you name a state capital that cannot be reached by road from anywhere else in the state? Juneau it is! Fronted by the bustling Gastineau Channel and backed by Mount Juneau (elevation 3,819 ft.) and Mount Roberts (elevation 3,576 ft.), the city is on the mainland of Alaska, but is cut off by the Juneau Icefield to the east and wilderness to the north and south. To be sure, there are roads—150 miles of them, in fact—but they all dead-end against an impenetrable forest or ice wall.

In 1900, Congress moved the territorial capital to Juneau from Sitka, which had fallen behind in the flurry of gold-rush development. Not all Alaskans believe Juneau is the right and logical place for a legislative center. Its inaccessibility, some argue, disenfranchises many voters, and every few years somebody puts a "move the capital" initiative on the ballot. So far, all of the proposals have been defeated, which is good news for Juneau's 12,500 civil servants. In Juneau, government is the city's biggest industry. However, tourism is not far behind: Besides the thousands of independent visitors who arrive by air and ferry, many thousands more come ashore during the 500 or so passenger ship port calls made here each summer.

On any given day, four or five cruise ships might be in port, ranging from the biggest in the fleets of Princess, Celebrity, Holland America, and the rest, to the small ships. The small ships and most of the large ships usually find a dock, but depending on how many large ships are in port that day, some might have to anchor in the channel and tender their guests ashore.

While the city is dependent on tourism, not everyone loves the crowds and it's easier to grasp the residents' unhappiness when you think of the number of cruise passengers who pour into the city. We were in Juneau once on a day when there were so many ships in port—four of the biggest, plus two smaller vessels, as we recall—that there might have been as many as 10,000 cruise visitors in town. That's more than a quarter of the permanent population of Juneau!

Juneau is a product of Alaska's golden past. It was no more than a fishing outpost for local Tlingit Indians until 1880, when gold was discovered in a creek off the Gastineau Channel by two prospectors, Joe Juneau and Richard (Dick) Harris. To be accurate, the gold was discovered first by Chief Kowee of the Auk Tlingit clan, who, in return for 100 warm blankets (more important to him than gold), passed on the information to a German engineer named George Pilz. Surveying sites around the Inside Passage for mineral deposits, Pilz gave the hitherto unsuccessful Juneau and Harris directions to the spot described by Chief Kowee—and they couldn't find it! Only when Kowee accompanied them on a second expedition did they succeed in pinpointing the source of the precious metal—and the rush was on. Mines sprang up on both sides of the channel. So rich was the area's gold yield that mines continued to open for the next 3 decades, including the most successful of them all, the **Alaska-Juneau Mine** (aka the A-J), which produced a whopping 3.5 million ounces of gold before it closed in 1944.

The town, incidentally, was originally called Harrisburg, until Harris fell out with his neighbors and the citizens opted to name it instead for his partner, who was better liked.

Today, Juneau is arguably the most handsome of the 50 state capitals, despite a glut of souvenir shops near the pier (where you can buy anything from "I Love Alaska" backscratchers to fur coats). The city runs with a mix of quiet business efficiency and easygoing informality. It has a good deal more sophistication to it than any city in Alaska outside of Anchorage, and yet it also has a frontier-style saloon. The newest popular attractions in town? The State Capitol and Governor's House, both haunts of the former governor and vice presidential candidate Sarah Palin.

Red Dog Saloon, 278 S. Franklin St., with its sawdust floor and swing doors, is a memorabilia-filled pub (serving food and drink) whose old-time raucousness may be tempered by its pursuit of the tourist buck (and by its location adjacent to the Juneau Police headquarters), but whose appeal is undeniable. Another place to enjoy a not-so-quiet drink is the bar of the **Alaskan Hotel,** nearby at 167 S. Franklin St., built in 1913. On the National Register of Historic Sites, the Alaskan is Juneau's oldest operating hotel.

For those who can tear themselves away from that cool drink, Juneau has another major attraction: the **Mendenhall Glacier,** at the head of a valley a dozen miles away. The glacier is one of Alaska's most accessible and most photographed ice faces. If your tummy is growling after a glacier hike, check out **Twisted Fish Company,** right near the ship pier behind **Taku Smokeries** (see "Shopping," below) and have some fish tacos or pizza topped with smoked salmon. Yummy. For something more casual, check out the bevy of outdoor stands in the pier-side parking lot near the public library. Here, **Tracy's King Crab Shack** is the place to try giant boiled crab legs and Tracy's famous crab bisque (which has become so popular that she now provides ship-home service).

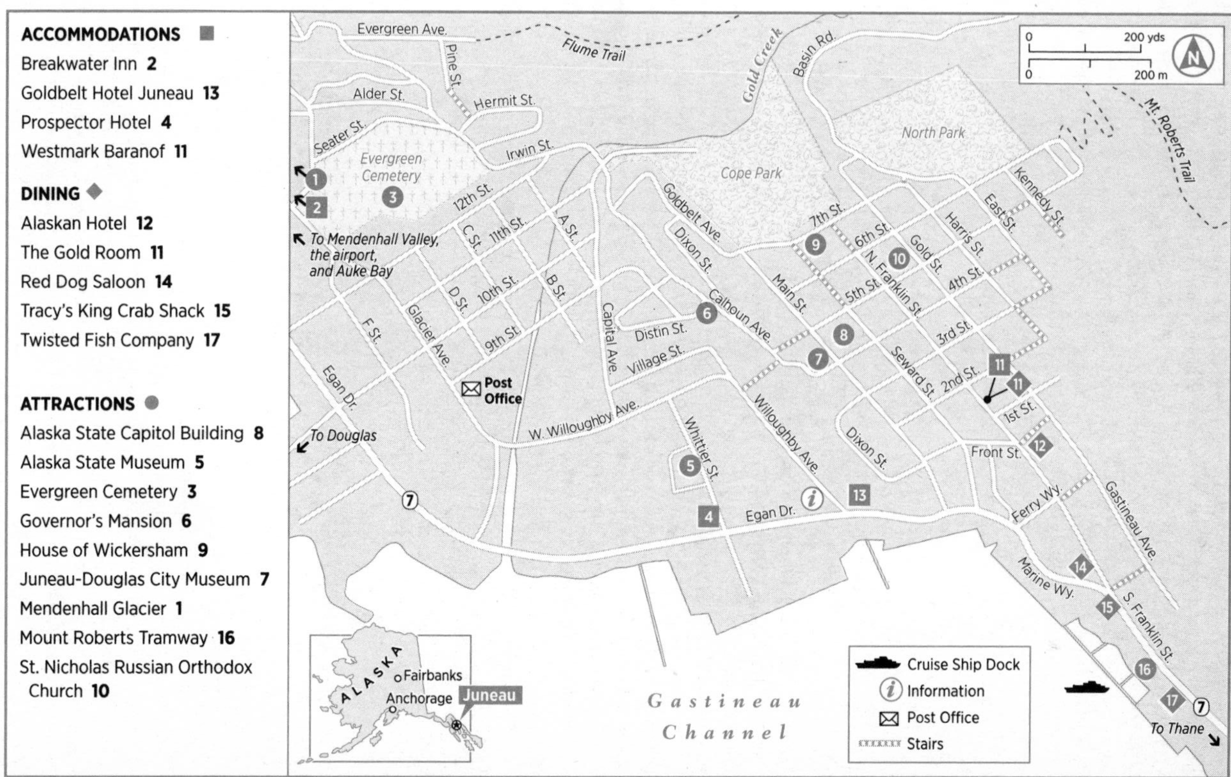
ACCOMMODATIONS
Breakwater Inn 2
Goldbelt Hotel Juneau 13
Prospector Hotel 4
Westmark Baranof 11
DINING
Alaskan Hotel 12
The Gold Room 11
Red Dog Saloon 14
Tracy's King Crab Shack 15
Twisted Fish Company 17
ATTRACTIONS
Alaska State Capitol Building 8
Alaska State Museum 5
Evergreen Cemetery 3
Governor's Mansion 6
House of Wickersham 9
Juneau-Douglas City Museum 7
Mendenhall Glacier 1
Mount Roberts Tramway 16
St. Nicholas Russian Orthodox Church 10
Cruise Ship Dock
Information
Post Office
Stairs
0 200 yds
0 200 m
Mt. Roberts Trail
Flume Trail
Gold Creek
Basin Rd.
North Park
Cope Park
Evergreen Cemetery
Gastineau Channel
To Mendenhall Valley, the airport, and Auke Bay
To Douglas
To Thane
Post Office
Juneau
Fairbanks
Anchorage
ALASKA

Note: Web addicts have free public Internet access at the Juneau Public Library, the big concrete building on the left past the ship pier, but before you get to the Red Dog.

COMING ASHORE Unless you arrive on one of the busiest days of the year, your ship will dock right in the downtown area, along Marine Way. The pier is directly adjacent to the downtown area, but there is also shuttle bus service available that travels back and forth along the waterfront road. If you are at the far end of the pier, it is about a 20-minute walk to downtown; but you may find yourself even closer.

INFORMATION Midway down the cruise-ship wharf, a blue building houses the visitor information facility; stop in to pick up a walking tour map and visitor's guide before striking out to see the sights. Another **Visitor Information Center** is in Centennial Hall, at 101 Egan Dr., near the State Museum (✆ **888/581-2201** or 907/586-2201; fax 907/586-6304; www.traveljuneau.com). It's open May through September daily from 8:30am to 5pm; and October through April Monday through Friday from 9am to 4:30pm. The visitor center at the cruise-ship dock is open during the summer when the ships come in.

BEST CRUISE-LINE SHORE EXCURSIONS

Deluxe Mendenhall Glacier & City Highlights Tour (4 hr; $99 adults, $59 children 12 and under): Twelve miles long and 1½ miles wide, Mendenhall is the most visited glacier in the world and the most popular sight in Juneau. This trip will take you by bus to the U.S. Forest Service Observatory, from which you can walk up a trail to within a half-mile of the glacier (which feels a lot closer), or take one of the nature trails, if time allows. After this, you will visit Juneau's historic highlights and, on some tours, you might also visit the Macaulay Salmon Hatchery, the Alaska State Museum, and other local attractions.

Four Glacier Helicopter (3½ hr.; $369): This thrilling trip is definitely not for those who are faint of heart or out of shape. The excursion involves a flight to the Juneau Icefield and to four glaciers found there. There is some walking involved (always in the company of a trained mountain guide). Accommodations may be made in advance for wheelchair-bound passengers, but generally a certain level of fitness is recommended—check with your cruise line for advice. An even more amazing version of the tour includes a dog-sled ride on the Icefield and costs $549.

Glacier Flightseeing by Floatplane (1¼ hr.; $215 adults, $179 children): Seeing the grand glaciers of Alaska is a thrill, and so is taking off and landing in the water in a floatplane. On this once-in-a-lifetime flight, you'll see five majestic glaciers of the Juneau Icefield. From your window seat, you'll also catch views of waterfalls and lush green rainforests. Expanded floatplane tours visit a remote, log cabin–style lodge for lunch (3½ hr.; $299 adult, $255 child) or take fishing fans to a remote creek for fly-fishing (5 hr.; $429).

Gold Mine History Tour (4 hr.; $59 adults, $35 children 12 and under): Juneau's gold-rush history comes to life (especially for kids) as you visit the ruins of the Alaska Gastineau mine. You don a hard hat for a walk along a 360-foot tunnel and a demonstration of early-20th-century mining equipment and methods.

Whales & Glaciers Citizen Science Adventure (5 hr.; $199 adult, $149 children): One of the coolest new offerings, particularly for science geeks, on this tour you get to see what it's like to be a research scientist in the wilds of Alaska. You participate in a GPS time-lapse photo project documenting climate change at Mendenhall Glacier and then board a marine observation vessel to help record humpback whale and other marine life behavior (whale sighting guaranteed; tour limited to 16 participants).

Mendenhall River Float Trip (3½ hr.; $129 adults, $99 children 12 and under): Board a 10-person raft on the shore of Mendenhall Lake, and an experienced oarsman will guide you out past icebergs and into the Mendenhall River. You'll encounter moderate rapids and stunning views, and be treated to a snack of smoked salmon and reindeer sausage somewhere along the way.

Evening Whale-watching Quest (3½ hr.; $169 adults, $129 children): Combine whale-watching from a jet-powered catamaran in Stephen's Passage with an evening buffet and a chance to enjoy Alaska's summer twilight. You are guaranteed to see whales or you get your money back. Humpbacks are likely—this is a known breeding area—and orcas are possible.

Golf in Juneau (5 hr.; $70): Newly introduced for cruise passengers is golf at the private Mendenhall Golf Course, a 9-hole course designed by Tom File (and opened in 1986). The course serves up views of Mendenhall Glacier. Wildflowers add color in summer, and you can spot spawning salmon in a stream that runs through the course. Deer sometimes stroll across the green and it's not unusual to spot eagles overhead. There are challenges and bragging rights—you can say you golfed in Alaska.

EXCURSIONS OFFERED BY LOCAL OPERATORS

The **Juneau Trolley Car Company** (**© 907/789-4342;** www.juneautrolley.com) provides narrated tours around the downtown area. Pickup is at the Tram Center at the pier. You can get off and on as you like at various sites, including the Alaska State Capitol and the Alaska State Museum. Fares are $19 for adults, $12 for children 12 and under. Also at the pier, you'll find booths operated by various independent tour operators selling city and glacier tours starting at about $30 per person.

Ziplining in Juneau is provided through locally owned **Alaska Zipline Adventure** (**© 907/321-0947;** www.alaskazip.com), which will harness you up to fly above the treetops for $139 for adults, $99 for children 10 and 11 (minimum age 10) for a 3½-hour excursion, including the ride. The company also offers combo Zipline and mountain-bike tours and ziplining combined with an Alaskan feast.

ON YOUR OWN: WITHIN WALKING DISTANCE

Alaska State Capitol Building We've often wondered how so lovely a capital city could come up with such an unprepossessing legislative home (ca. 1931). The interior is worth a visit, though, to see the old-fashioned woodwork and interesting decorative details, especially in the lobby and legislative chambers. On the third floor are the governor's offices.

4th St., btw. Main and Seward sts. **© 907/465-3800.** Free admission. Tours during summer every half-hour Mon–Fri 9am–4:30pm.

Alaska State Museum This place opened as a territorial museum in 1900, and has a wildlife exhibit, a first-class collection of artifacts reflecting the state's Russian history and Native cultures, and exhibits about the history of the city's mining and fishery industries.

395 Whittier St. **© 907/465-2901.** www.museums.state.ak.us/asm/asmhome.html. Admission $5 adults mid-May–mid-Sept, $3 rest of year, free for children 18 and under. Mid-May–mid-Sept daily 8:30am–5:30pm; mid-Sept–mid-May Tues–Sat 10am–4pm.

Governor's Mansion The six-pillar, 35-room mansion, also referred to as Governor's House, is located near the State Office Building, about 2 blocks from the State Capitol. The mansion was built and furnished in 1912 (at a cost of $40,000). The design is an interpretation of the New England style. The totem pole outside was carved in 1940 by Tlingit Indians, and tells the story of the origin of the mosquito. The mansion is not open to the public; you can only drive past it. Local residents complain about bus tour traffic near the mansion, which increased after Gov. Sarah Palin ran for vice president in 2008.

716 Calhoun Ave.

Evergreen Cemetery At this beautiful cemetery, which slopes toward the ocean, you can view the gravesites of Joe Juneau, Richard Harris, and other pioneers. The old Alaska Native graves are located in the wooded area on the far side of the cemetery.

12th St., just west of the downtown area.

House of Wickersham This house was built in 1899, and bought in 1928 by Judge James Wickersham, who did much to shape the face of Alaska. Wickersham was the first territorial delegate to the U.S. Congress, was in the vanguard of the fight for statehood, and founded the University of Alaska. The house was in the family from 1928 until the state bought it in 1984, so it still contains Wickersham's belongings. Highlights include an Edison cylinder gramophone that he took to Fairbanks, and his assignment to go to Alaska, signed by Theodore Roosevelt. ***Note:*** The house is at the top of a very steep hill.

213 7th St. © **907/586-9001.** Admission by $2 donation. Daily mid-May to late Sept 10am–noon and 1–5pm. Late Sept–mid-May by appointment only.

Juneau-Douglas City Museum This museum highlights the development of the city from its golden beginnings to statehood, and it also has exhibits on Tlingit culture. The facility specializes in programs and displays geared toward youngsters.

Corner of 4th and Main sts. © **907/586-3572.** Admission $4 adults, free for children 18 and under. Mid-May–Sept Mon–Fri 9am–5pm; Sat–Sun 10am–5pm. Oct–mid-May Fri–Sat noon–4pm & by appointment.

Mount Roberts Tramway The best place to take in Juneau's lovely position on the Gastineau Channel is from high up on Mount Roberts. The ascent of the mountain used to entail a strenuous hike, but is now an easy 6-minute ride in the comfortable 60-passenger cars of the Mount Roberts Tramway. Operated by Goldbelt, a Tlingit corporation, the tramway rises from a base alongside the cruise-ship docks and whisks sightseers 2,000 feet up to a center with a restaurant/bar, a gift shop, a museum, cultural film shows, a series of nature trails (bring mosquito repellent!), and a fabulous panorama. Don't miss it, but on the other hand, don't bother if the day is overcast: Many visitors have paid the fees for an all-day pass, reached the top, and been faced with a solid wall of white mist.

At the cruise-ship docks. © **888/461-TRAM** (8726) or 907/463-3412. www.mountrobertstramway.com. All-day pass $27 adults, $13.50 children 6–12, free for children 5 and under. May–Sept Mon noon to 9pm, Tue–Fri 8am–9pm; Sat–Sun 9am–9pm.

Red Dog Saloon This is the place to go for a taste of the scrumptious, locally brewed Alaskan Amber Ale. Look up on the wall behind the bar, where, among other things (many other things), is one of Wyatt Earp's pistols. Also look at the rest of the walls, where you'll see scrawled messages from legions of cruise-ship passengers who came before you.

278 S. Franklin St., right by the cruise-ship docks. © **907/468-3535.** Main courses $10–$17. AE, DISC, MC, V. Year-round daily 9am–11pm.

St. Nicholas Russian Orthodox Church This tiny, ornate, octagonal structure is altogether captivating. It was built in 1893 by local Tlingits, who, under pressure from the government to convert to Christianity, chose the only faith that allowed them to keep their language. Father Ivan Veniaminov had translated the Bible into Tlingit 50 years earlier, when the Russians were still in Sitka.

5th and Gold sts. No phone. $2 donation requested. Lengthy services are sung in English, Tlingit, and Slavic for vespers Sat 6pm and Sun 9am; congregation stands throughout service. Church open for visitors in summer Mon–Sat 9am–5pm; Sun noon–5pm.

ON YOUR OWN: BEYOND THE PORT AREA

Mendenhall Glacier Mendenhall is the easiest glacier to get to in Alaska and the most visited glacier in the world. Its U.S. Forest Service visitor center has glacier exhibits, a 12-minute movie called *Magnificent Mendenhall,* and rangers who can answer questions. Check out the trail descriptions and choose from several that'll take you close to the glacier. The easiest ones are the .3-mile photo trail (which takes about 20 min. and provides an excellent glacial photo op) and the .5-mile Trail of Time, a self-guided nature path (which takes about 1 hr. to complete). The 3.5-mile Eastern Glacier Loop follows the glacial trim line, with a lot of time in the forest. It takes about 2 hours and includes some moderate uphill climbing. If you hike, bring water, sunscreen, and bug spray. Bears occasionally are spotted in the forest. If you do encounter one, stand still but make a lot of noise.

Mendenhall is about 13 miles from downtown, and taxis and local bus services are readily available in town (the bus costs $1.50 each way, taxis about $25) for those who want to visit independently of a tour. If you take a taxi out, make arrangements with the driver to also pick you up—and negotiate a round-trip price before you leave. Or take the MGT (Mighty Great Trips) Mendenhall Glacier Express, a bus that will carry you from the pier to the door of the glacier visitor center and back for $14. No reservation is needed; just walk off the ship and get on one of the buses parked 50 yards away (just past the Mount Roberts Tramway). It's an old school bus painted bright blue—not necessarily the most comfortable way to go—but it has an advantage over city transportation in that it really takes you to Mendenhall Glacier, as opposed to dropping you off at the bus stop more than a mile away. Since it doesn't stop to embark and disembark riders en route, the MGT Mendenhall Glacier Express gets you there in 25 minutes; although the city bus is cheaper, the ride takes closer to an hour. The MGT bus also comes with commentary. Our coauthor Fran once had a Native American driver who shared such wisdom as: "Why does the bald eagle have a white head? Because the raven flies above."

Off Mendenhall Loop Rd. Visitor center ✆ **907/789-0097.** Admission to visitor center $3 adults, free for children 12 and under. May–Sept daily 8am–7:30pm; Oct–Apr Thurs–Sun 10am–4pm.

Glacier Gardens Rainforest Adventure Opened in 1998, this botanical garden was created in an area that had been decimated in a landslide. Privately owned, the garden has since expanded to 50 acres of landscaped gardens with alpine and other flowers and lush rainforest, including an eagle viewing area. A golf cart shuttle takes you past the blooming flowers as you travel up Thunder Mountain, high above Gastineau Channel, and past trees, waterfalls, and ponds. You can get to the gardens by city bus (for $1.50 per ride) or cab (about $18 each way from downtown). There is also a greenhouse area with beautiful plants hanging, a gift shop, and a small cafe serving beverages and sandwiches (locals winter their plants here). Ships also sell pre-booked tours here for those who would rather not travel on their own.

7600 Glacier Hwy. ✆ **907/790-3377.** www.glaciergardens.com. Admission, including guided 1½-hr. golf cart tour, $22 adults, $16 children 6–12, free for children 5 and under. Open daily 9am–6pm.

SHOPPING

Taku Smokeries (✆ **800/582-5122;** www.takustore.com), right off the ship pier at 550 S. Franklin St., has all kinds of smoked fish for sale and gives delicious free samples. They will ship your purchase home for you. **Raven's Journey Gallery,** 435 S. Franklin St. (✆ **907/463-4686**), specializes in Tlingit and other Northwest Indian carvings and masks, whalebone, ivory, basketry, fossil ivory carvings, and jewelry from the Yup'ik and Iñupiat of western and northern Alaska. **Juneau Artists Gallery,** in the Senate Building, at 175 S. Franklin St. (✆ **907/586-9891;** www.juneauartistsgallery.com), is staffed by a co-op of local artists and shows only the members' work: paintings, etchings, photography, jewelry, fabrics, ceramics, and other media. For gifts, try **Annie Kaill's** fine arts-and-crafts gallery, at 244 Front St. (✆ **907/586-2880;** www.anniekaills.com). It's a bit out of the cruise-ship shopping area and is frequented by locals. **Ad Lib,** at 231 S. Franklin St. (✆ **907/463-3031**), also is reliable and oriented to authentic items made in Alaska. Many shops in downtown Juneau are very touristy, so that's a good place to stock up on Alaska T-shirts and trinkets.

11 Icy Strait Point, Icy Strait & Hoonah

Icy Strait Point wasn't on the map a few years ago. The name was coined to describe a new private dock built to handle cruise-ship traffic near the Tlingit city of Hoonah, the largest Tlingit settlement in Alaska, with a population of nearly 1,000. Only now with increasing attractions in the area—including the world's longest and highest Zipline—is the once nonexistent place getting visits from non-cruise travelers, too. So go figure. In fact, the *Anchorage Daily News* recently named the Icy Strait Point ZipRider—an amusement park ride where you zip a mile down a mountain in 90 seconds—as a must-do attraction in the state.

The concept is similar to what the cruise lines did in the Caribbean—with traditional ports (including Juneau) getting full, they created a new venue to get passengers off the ship and onto shore excursions.

Hoonah happens to be strategically located about 22 miles southeast of Glacier Bay National Park. Nature is the calling card here. We're talking prime whale-watching waters. Passengers aboard large ships may well be fortunate enough to see whales on their journey. Those in small ships or whale-watching excursions will have an even better chance, since the small ships have the luxury of going places where the bigger vessels can't, and their size and maneuverability make it possible for them to get closer to the whales.

Onshore around Hoonah is old-growth rainforest, and brown (grizzly) bear sightings are common. Bald eagles are frequently spotted overhead. Fishermen here go after halibut and five species of salmon.

Hoonah is an old blue-collar village, just now being "discovered," although the Huna Tlingits have resided here for thousands of years.

Development-wise, the Northwest Trading Company came to town and opened a store in 1880. A mission and school were created shortly thereafter. The city got its first post office in 1901. Fire destroyed much of the city, including Tlingit artifacts, in 1944. The federal government led a rebuilding effort, and the city was incorporated in 1946.

The cruise dock, built by a Tlingit Indian corporation, opened in 2004 and is now being visited on a regular basis (albeit one shipload at a time) by Royal Caribbean and Celebrity, and occasionally by Princess.

The dock was built to incorporate a historic cannery that dates to 1930—Hoonah once was one of the most productive salmon cannery towns in the state. Fishing and fish processing, along with logging, are still the mainstays of the economy in these parts, and tourism is catching on. If you find your tummy rumbling and seafood on your mind, indulge at the Crab Station, where you can eat fresh Dungeness crab that's come straight out of the water and into a pot.

COMING ASHORE Cruise passengers are tendered into the dock at the Icy Strait Point Cannery, with its shops and restaurants.

INFORMATION There is an information booth (no phone) at the dock. If you're a hiker, here's the place to ask for directions to local beach and forest trails.

BEST CRUISE-LINE SHORE EXCURSIONS

ATV Expedition (2½ hr.; $150 adults and children; minimum 10 yrs.): Traverse the mountains of Chichagof Island in rugged fashion on a 4×4 expedition. You start high in the majestic mountains of Chichagof Island (after a drive by motorcoach through Hoonah). Your guide will provide a little area history and a brief orientation. Then you board a 4×4 Kawasaki Mule off-road vehicle and ride along a trail, taking in the Alaska wilderness, rainforest, and tremendous views of Icy Strait.

Glacier Bay Flightseeing (2 hr.; $310 adults and children): Depart Hoonah Airport on a fixed-wing plane and fly over Point Adolphus and Icy Strait, an important feeding ground for many marine mammals; Glacier Bay (note how land that once held glaciers is now deeply forested); and the awesome delights of Glacier Bay National Park, including the massive Brady Glacier.

Hoonah Sightseeing (1½ hr.; $50 adults, $28 children): Tour the quaint Alaska village, the largest Tlingit settlement in the 49th state. Your guide will explain the village's history, including how the Huna Tlingits had to flee advancing glaciers. Your motorcoach will stop at an old cemetery and you can see a Tlingit shaman gravesite. Modern Tlingit life will also be described in detail.

Hoonah Sightseeing & Tribal Dance Combo (1 hr.; $67 adults, $38 children): Do the tour (above) and then see dancers perform in full regalia at the Native Theater, telling the story of the Tlingits. Learn about the ancient significance of the raven and the eagle.

Remote Wildlife & Brown Bear Search (2½ hr.; $110 adults and children; minimum 8 yrs.): Explore the wilds of Chichagof Island in search of grizzlies. Your motorcoach will travel through Hoonah en route to the Bush country of the Spasski River Valley. Learn about the local flora and fauna on a short hike along gravel and boardwalk-lined paths through a rainforest to viewing platforms overlooking the Spasski River. Keep your eyes out for bears, salmon, bald eagles, and more, though sightings, of course, are not guaranteed.

ZipRider Adventure (1 hr.; $120 adults and children; minimum 10 yrs and 90 lbs.): Ride on the world's longest Zipline, 5,330 feet long with a 1,300-foot vertical drop. You travel at speeds of up to 60 miles per hour. The highest point is 300 feet above the ground. If you dare to look down, you'll enjoy views of Port Frederick, Icy Strait, and your cruise ship. You're harnessed in a seat for this ride; no skill is required.

EXCURSIONS OFFERED BY LOCAL AGENCIES

The setup in Icy Strait Point is tightly controlled by the Hoonah Totem Native Corporation. Tours are offered only in advance, through the cruise lines.

ON YOUR OWN: WITHIN WALKING DISTANCE

Icy Strait Point Cannery Beautifully restored and reopened in 2004, the historic cannery, located right where you get off the tender, once was one of the most productive salmon canneries in the state. Its halls are filled with family-owned shops (27 at last count) and a museum with a 1930s cannery display, as well as a cultural center. The original cookhouse is now open for family-style dining.

ON YOUR OWN: BEYOND THE PORT AREA

Hoonah, meaning "village by the cliff," is the largest Tlingit Indian village in Alaska, and it's just about a mile from the pier. It's an unspoiled little town that sustains itself mostly on fishing and logging. The wilderness is so close that, as you walk along the bay, you'll likely see eagles flying overhead; you may even spot whales from the pier. The town has grocery and hardware stores catering to locals. The atmosphere is much different than in ports used for the tourist trade. Some visitors may like that; others may not. But this is a chance to catch a glimpse of real Alaskan life.

SHOPPING

All the shops at the **Icy Strait Point Cannery** are owned by Alaskans, and you can find local crafts and clever tourist items on sale. You even can have a message canned and shipped to friends back home. In town, **Creations,** 541 Garteeni Hwy. (© **907/945-3478**), carries all the materials and beading supplies a quilter could want.

12 Glacier Bay National Park Preserve

There are about 5,000 glaciers in Alaska, so what's all the fuss about Glacier Bay? Theories on its popularity abound. Some think it's the wildlife, which includes humpback whales, bears, Dall sheep, seals, and more. Some think it's the history of the place, as it was frozen behind a mile-wide wall of ice until about 1870. A mere 55 years later, it was designated as a national park, along with its 3.3 million surrounding acres. The glaciers are thought to be the fastest moving ones in the world, retreating by about 1½ inches a year. Whatever the reason, Glacier Bay has taken on an allure not achieved by other glacier areas.

The first white man to enter the vast (60-plus-mile) Glacier Bay inlet was naturalist **John Muir** in 1879. Just 100 years earlier, when Capt. James Cook and, later, George Vancouver sailed there, the mouth was still a wall of ice. Today, all that ice has ebbed back, leaving behind a series of inlets and glaciers whose calving activity entertains hundreds of cruisers lining the rails as their ships sit for several hours. It can take 200 years for ice that falls off the face of a glacier to reach that point.

Each ship that enters the bay takes aboard a park ranger. The ranger provides commentary about glaciers, wildlife, and the bay's history over the ship's PA system throughout the day. On large ships, the ranger may also give a presentation in the show lounge about conservation; on small ships, he or she will often be on deck throughout the day, available for questions.

Glacier Bay is the world's largest protected marine sanctuary. The bay is so vast that the water contained within its boundaries would cover the state of Connecticut. The

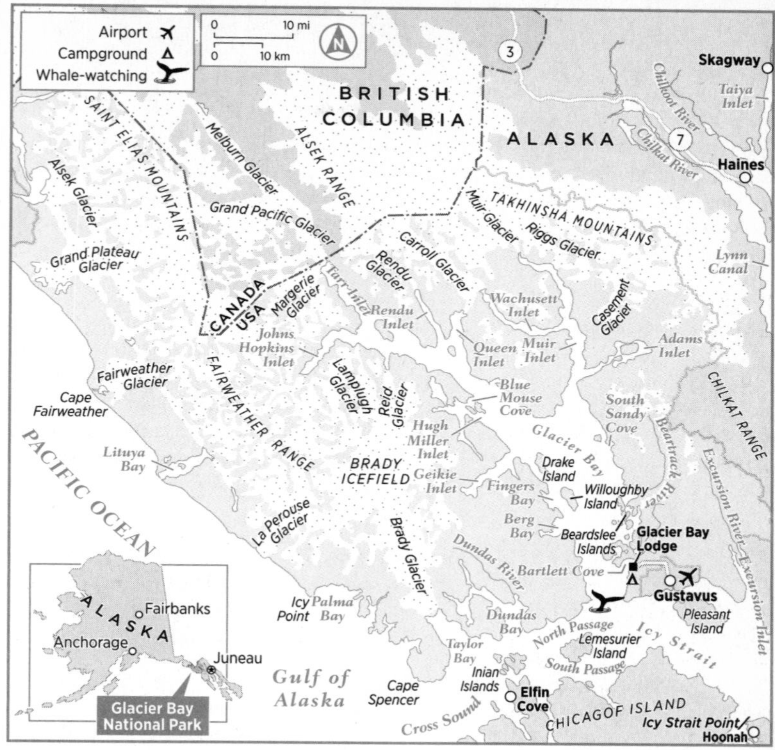

bay is a source of concern for environmentalists, who would like to see cruise ships banned from entering, or at least have their access severely curtailed. The ship operators, on the other hand, argue that no evidence shows that their vessels have any negative impact on the wildlife.

There are numerous glaciers in the park: 16 major tidewater glaciers (those that go all the way to the water) and 30 valley or alpine glaciers (those that compress between two hills, but don't extend all the way to the water). In Tarr Inlet, at the Alaska/Canada border, two notable glaciers meet—Margerie and Grand Pacific. Margerie, on the Alaskan side, is pristine white and very active, calving frequently; Grand Pacific, on the Canadian side of the line, is black, gritty, and not particularly active. The widely differing coloration of the two is caused by the terrain through which each glacier pushes its way to the sea. Margerie cuts through a relatively clean path, while Grand Pacific picks up rocks and dirt along the way.

Visible from much of the bay (on a clear day) is the massive Mount Fairweather (elevation 15,320 ft.). Although Fairweather is taller than any mountain in the Lower 48, it ranks no higher than 19th among Alaska's peaks.

13 Haines

This pretty, laid-back port is an example of Alaska the way you probably thought it would be. It's a small, scenic town with wilderness at its doorstep and only two stop signs. If you're not on one of the few ships that regularly visit Haines (pop. 2,500), you can easily reach the port on a day excursion from **Skagway.** The two communities lie at the northern end of the Lynn Canal, just 17 miles apart by water (350 miles by driving). The trip takes only about 45 minutes by fast ferry and is priced round-trip at $68 adults, $34 children (© **888/766-2103;** www.hainesskagwayfastferry.com). It's well worth taking, especially for those who have "done" Skagway before. But make sure to check return times so you get back to your ship on time.

The thing that's immediately striking about Haines is its setting, one of the prettiest in Alaska. The village lies in the shadow of the Fairweather Mountain Range, about 80 or so miles north of Juneau and on the same line of latitude as the lower reaches of Norway. Framed by high hills, it is more protected from the elements than many other Inside Passage ports. Ketchikan, for instance, gets up to 200 inches of rain in a wet year, Haines a mere 60 inches. That's positively arid by some Southeast Alaska standards!

Haines was established in 1879 by Presbyterian missionary S. Hall Young and naturalist John Muir as a base for converting the Chilkoot and Chilkat Tlingit tribes to Christianity. They named the town for Mrs. F. E. Haines, secretary of the Presbyterian National Committee, who raised the funds for the exploration. The natives called it *Da-Shu,* the Tlingit word for "end of the trail." Traders knew the place as Chilkoot. The military, which came later and built a fort here in 1903, knew it as Fort Seward or Chilkoot Barracks. In 1897 and 1898, the town became one of the lesser known access points (it was less popular than Skagway and Dyea) to a route to the Klondike; it was located at the head of what became known as the Jack Dalton Trail into Canada. At about the same time, gold was discovered much closer to home—in Porcupine, just 36 miles away—and that strike drew even more prospectors to Haines. The gold quickly petered out, though, and Porcupine is no more.

The **old fort** still stands, although its survival was questionable at one point. After World War II, and 42 years of service, it was decommissioned and the future of the place—and of Haines itself, to some extent—was in doubt. So much of the local economy had depended on the spending of the military personnel stationed there. A group of veterans once stationed at Chilkoot Barracks, however, would not let the fort die. In 1947, they bought the 85 buildings standing on 400 acres. They built a salmon smokehouse, a furniture-making plant, and other business ventures. They agitated to have Haines included on the Alaska Marine Highway System. They built the Hotel Hälsingland, established art galleries, and funded Indian arts training programs for local youngsters.

The **Officers' Club Lounge** in the Hälsingland Hotel is a dandy place to stop for a libation. It serves Alaskan and Yukon beers and a house special known as the Fort Seward Howitzer. The descendants of some of these modern-day pioneers still live in homes that their fathers and grandfathers built on the fort grounds. One house on the grounds was sold to a Colorado couple who visited Haines on a cruise ship and decided they wanted to live there. Designated a National Historic Site by the U.S. government in 1972, **Fort William Seward** should be a must-see on your list. All lines invariably include a fort shore excursion in their brochures.

Haines is so small that it can be covered on foot. You can see almost everything in 1 to 2 hours of reasonably flat walking. Start at **Steve Sheldon's museum** about a

Haines

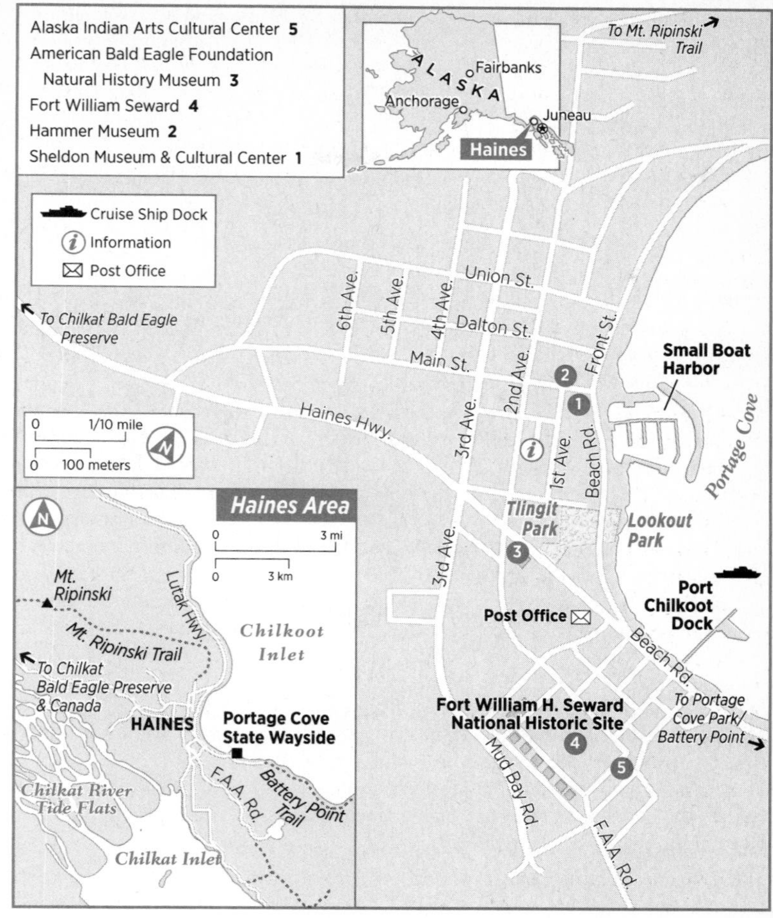

quarter-mile from the pier; turn west up Main Street (the only uphill part of the journey), with its beautiful views of the Chilkat Mountains. Next is the free **Hammer Museum**—dedicated to hammers. Haines' tallest building—all of four stories high—is a little farther on. Turn right onto 2nd Avenue and have a drink or a meal at the **Pioneer Bar & Bamboo Room Restaurant,** or visit the nearby **Old City Hall and Fire Station.** Turn left onto Union Street, past the **Lindholm House** (built in 1912), left onto 3rd Avenue, and right onto Dalton Street, named for Jack Dalton, a turn-of-the-century entrepreneur who helped put Haines on the map. A few blocks later, turn left onto 5th Avenue and then left again onto Main Street toward the Lynn Canal. In no time at all, you're back at the ship.

The town's gold history, its military background, and its Native heritage draw travelers to Haines. So do the **eagles:** The area is a magnet for these magnificent creatures—a couple of hundred are year-round residents. Unfortunately, cruise passengers are unable to experience the annual **Gathering of the Eagles,** which occurs in winter (usually Oct until mid-Feb) and brings as many as 4,000 birds from all over the Pacific Northwest to the area in search of salmon that can't be found anywhere else during these months. During this time, trees along a 5-mile stretch of the river (in an area known as the **Alaska Chilkat Bald Eagle Preserve**) are thick with these raptors—often a dozen or more sharing a limb. But even during the cruise season, you're likely to spot at least an eagle or two. We once spotted eight in various swooping and tree-sitting poses on a bike ride out to Chilkoot Lake (about 10 miles from the cruise-ship pier).

COMING ASHORE Thanks to a newly expanded dock, you no longer have to tender from big ships into Haines. Some smaller ships also come into the Native American-owned ferry terminal which also has a small shop selling souvenirs. A long-discussed plan to add more bathroom and parking facilities to the terminal has been hotly contested by local residents who don't want to give up the beach space. Both docks are within walking distance of many of the town's main attractions.

INFORMATION Pick up some walking tour information on Haines at the **visitor center,** on 2nd Avenue (✆ **800/458-3579** or 907/766-2234). It's open in summer Monday through Friday from 8am to 7pm, Saturday from 9am to 5pm, and Sunday from 11am to 5pm. It's easy to explore the town on foot, or you can rent a bike at **Sockeye Cycle,** on Portage Street, right up the street from the cruise-ship dock (✆ **907/766-2869;** www.cyclealaska.com); it's $14 for a 2-hour rental, $25 for 4 hours, and $35 for the entire day.

BEST CRUISE-LINE SHORE EXCURSIONS

Best of Haines by Classic Motor Car (1 hr.; $64): Explore Haines in style in a 1930s or 1940s six-passenger automobile. The entertaining guides share the history of the area, and you'll get insight into how Haines residents live.

Eagle Preserve Wildlife River Adventure (3½ hr.; $134 adults, $100 children 12 and under): A bus takes you to the world-famous Chilkat Bald Eagle Preserve, where you board small boats specially designed to traverse the narrows of the Chilkat River. Eagle spotting is the thing on this excursion, and you may also see bears, moose, and beavers.

Wilderness Kayak Experience (4 hr.; $119 adults, $59 children 7–12): Located as it is at the top of the Inside Passage, Haines is an ideal place for kayaking. A short bus trip will take you to the launch site, and the goal as you glide in your kayak is to see wildlife—depending on your luck, this might include humpback whales, porpoises, seals, sea lions, sea otters, moose, brown bears, and, of course, Haines' famous bald eagles.

A Taste of Haines (1½ hr.; $69 adults and children): Sample some of the fresh products of Haines on this intimate tour, headed by a local guide. You'll visit Dalton City, a gold-rush town created for the 1989 Disney film *White Fang,* tour Haines Brewing Company (with an annual production of only 350 barrels), and sample ales and stouts with the brewmaster. The tour also includes a visit to Dejon Delights to learn how the experts make smoked halibut and salmon. Samples are provided, and there's time for shopping (see more in "Shopping," below).

EXCURSIONS OFFERED BY LOCAL OPERATORS

Chilkat Guides, on Portage Street (✆ **888/292-7789** or 907/766-2491; www.raftalaska.com), takes a rafting trip twice a day in summer down the Chilkat River to watch eagles. The rapids are pretty easy—there's a chance you may be asked to get out and push—and you'll see lots of eagles. The 4-hour trip includes a snack and costs $94 for adults, $65 for children. **Alaska Nature Tours** (✆ **907/766-2876;** www.alaskanaturetours.net) has a variety of escorted tours, including a 4-hour walking tour of the Chilkat Bald Eagle Preserve ($85 for adults, including lunch, and $70 for children 12 and under).

ON YOUR OWN: WITHIN WALKING DISTANCE

Alaska Indian Arts Cultural Center Located in the old fort hospital on the south side of the parade grounds, the center has a small gallery and a carvers' workshop where you may be able to see totem-pole carving in progress.

On the south side of the parade grounds. ✆ **907/766-2160.** Mon–Fri 9am–5pm and evenings when cruise ships are in town.

American Bald Eagle Foundation Natural History Museum This foundation celebrates Haines' location in the "Valley of the Eagles" with a huge diorama depicting more than 100 eagles. Adjacent is the Alaska Bald Eagle Foundation's new Mew Building, which opened in May of last year and gives visitors the opportunity to get up close and personal with three rehabilitated bald eagles. View the birds in their enclosed aviary, and catch a presentation given by a staff handler.

At Second Ave. and Haines Hwy. ✆ **907/766-3094.** www.baldeagles.org. Admission $3 adults, $1 children 8–12, free for children 7 and under. Mon–Fri 9am–5pm and evenings when cruise ships are in town.

Fort William Seward The central feature of the town, rising right above the docks, Fort Seward was retired after World War II and redone by a group of returning veterans. It's not the kind of place that you think of when envisioning a fort. It has no parapets, no walls, no nothing—just an open parade ground surrounded by large wood-frame former barracks and officers' quarters that have today been converted into private homes, the Hälsingland Hotel, a gallery and studio, and the Alaska Indian Arts Cultural Center (see above). In the center of the sloping parade ground, you'll find a replica of a Tlingit tribal house. Also added—thanks to a local collector—is a harpoon gun on the parade grounds, which is now fired on special town occasions (it looks like a cannon).

The area is just inland from the cruise-ship dock. Open all day.

Hammer Museum You want quirky? Check out this museum, devoted entirely to the hammer. The collection is that of longshoreman Dave Pahl, who amassed his collection while building his homestead over a span of some 20 years. The prize in the collection is an 800-year-old Tlingit war hammer, but hammer lovers will find some 1,400 instruments from all over the world.

108 Main St. ✆ **907/766-2374.** www.hammermuseum.org. Admission $3, free for children 12 and under. Mon–Fri 10am–5pm.

Sheldon Museum & Cultural Center Not to be confused with the Sheldon Jackson Museum in Sitka, this place was established by a local man, Steve Sheldon. Small by some museum standards, it nevertheless has a wonderful collection of Haines memorabilia: Tlingit artifacts, gold-rush-era weaponry, military items, and so on.

Corner of Main and Front sts. ✆ **907/766-2366.** www.sheldonmuseum.org. Admission $5, free for children 12 and under. Mid-May–mid-Sept Mon–Fri 10am–5pm, Sat–Sun 1–4pm. Mid-Sept–mid-May Mon–Sat 1–4pm.

ON YOUR OWN: BEYOND THE PORT AREA

Chilkat Bald Eagle Preserve Haines may be the best place in the world to see bald eagles. And this 48,000-acre park along the Chilkat River is ground zero for the species. From around mid-October to December, some 3,000 eagles reside here. But even during cruise season, you're likely to glimpse a few—a couple of hundred live here year-round. The best viewing is on the Haines Highway, between miles 18 and 21. The preserve is managed by the Alaska State Parks.

Contact the local ranger's office at ✆ **907/766-2292,** or find updated reports at www.alaskastateparks.org.

SHOPPING

Haines is not a big shopping destination, and we like it that way. But shoppers will find a few enticements. The **Dejon Delights Smokery** (✆ **907/766-2505;** www.dejondelights.com), on Portage Street near Fort Seward, sells freshly smoked wild Alaska salmon and halibut, and gives free samples so you know what you're buying. They'll ship your purchases if you don't want to carry them. Stop by the nearby outdoor stand, **The Local Catch,** on Portage Street, for a cup of coffee and sweets (✆ **907/766-3557**). On Portage Street, just up from the cruise-ship pier, **The Wild Iris** (✆ **907/766-2300**) is an art shop selling fine jewelry, including local gold, Eskimo art, watercolors, and silkscreen prints.

14 Skagway

No port in Alaska is more historically significant than this small town at the northern end of the picturesque Lynn Canal. In the late 19th century, a steady stream of prospectors began the long trek into Canada's Yukon Territory, seeking the vast quantities of Klondike gold that had been reported in Rabbit Creek (later renamed Bonanza Creek). Not many of them realized the unspeakable hardships they'd have to endure before they could get close to the stuff. They first had to negotiate either the **White Pass** or the **Chilkoot Pass** through the coastal mountain range to the Canadian border. To do so, they had to hike 20 miles, climbing nearly 3,000 feet in the process, and, by order of Canada's North West Mounted Police, they had to have at least a year's supply of provisions before they could enter the country. Numbed by temperatures that fell at times into the –50s (–40s Celsius), and often blinded by driving snow or stinging hail (they were, after all, hiking through mountain passes that gave Skagway its name—in Tlingit, *Skagua* means "home of the North Wind"), they plodded upward. They ferried some of their supplies partway up, stashed them, and then returned to Skagway before repeating the process with another load, always inching their way closer to the summit. The process took as many as 20 trips for some, and often enough, their stashes were stolen by unscrupulous rivals or opportunistic locals. Prospectors who thought themselves lucky enough to be able to afford horses or mules found their pack animals to be less than sound of limb. One stretch of the trail through the White Pass (the more popular of the two routes through the mountains) is called **Dead Horse Gulch.**

Arduous as it was, that first leg was just the beginning. From the Canadian border, their golden goal lay a long and dangerous water journey away, part of the way by lake (and, thus, relatively easy), but most of it down the mighty Yukon River and decidedly perilous.

The gold rush brought to Skagway a way of life as violent and as lawless as any to be found in the frontier West. The Mounties (the law in Canada) had no jurisdiction in Skagway. In fact, there was no law whatsoever in Skagway. Peace depended entirely on the consciences of the inhabitants—saloonkeepers, gamblers, prostitutes, and desperadoes of every stripe.

The most notorious of the Skagway bad men was Jefferson Randolph "Soapy" Smith, an accomplished con man. He earned his nickname in Denver, Colorado, by persuading large numbers of gullible people to buy bars of cheap soap for $1 in the belief that some of the bars were wrapped in larger denomination bills. They weren't, of course, but the scam made Smith a lot of money. In Skagway, he and his gang engaged in all kinds of nastiness, charging local businesses large fees for "protection," exacting exorbitant sums to "store" prospectors' gear (and then selling the equipment to others), and setting up a telegraph station and charging prospectors to send messages home (though the telegraph wire went no farther than the next room).

The gold-rush days of Skagway had their heroes as well. One of them, city surveyor Frank Reid, put an end to Soapy's reign; he shot Smith dead and was himself mortally wounded in the gunfight. In his honor, the local citizenry erected an impressive granite monument over his grave in the Gold Rush Cemetery; Smith's marker, on the other hand, is very simple, and his remains aren't even underneath it (they're 3 ft. to the left, outside consecrated ground). Perversely, though, it is the villain Smith whose life is commemorated annually on July 8, with songs and entertainment. The women of the gold-rush days are also given tribute—at least, those of ill repute—in a shore excursion called the Ghosts & Goodtime Girls Walking Tour (see below).

Unlike many other Alaska frontier towns, Skagway has been spared the ravages of major fires and earthquakes. Some of the original buildings still stand, protected by the National Park Service. The Klondike Gold Rush National Historic District contains some striking examples of these buildings. Other little touches of history are preserved around town, such as the huge watch painted on the mountainside above town—it was an early billboard for the long-gone Herman Kirmse's watch-repair shop. Also remaining from the old days is the White Pass and Yukon Route narrow-gauge railroad, opened in 1900 to carry late stampeders in and gold out. A ride on the train is a must for visitors. The round-trip to the summit of the pass, following a route carved out of the side of the mountain by an American/Canadian engineering team backed by British money, takes 3 hours from a departure site conveniently located a short walk (or an even shorter shuttle bus ride) from the cruise-ship piers.

Having a sweet little historic town is nice for Skagway's 860 or so year-round residents, of course, but by itself, history doesn't pay the bills. So, though Skagway is trying to hang on to its gold-rush heritage, it's also trying to make money off it. Businesses, including restaurants (a Starbucks!) and jewelry stores have taken over much of the downtown, many of which have gold-rush connotations only in the sense that they've opened to cash in on visitors' "gold."

On a recent visit, a clerk standing outside one of those fancy jewelry stores that have followed cruise passengers here from the Caribbean encouraged us to come in. We know he was only doing his job, but in the past, you could window-shop in Skagway without worrying about being pestered.

For a respite from shopping, check out the $3 beer specials at the 1898 **Red Onion Saloon** (at Broadway and 2nd Ave.), or, down Broadway, test the product at the **Skagway Brewing Company** (www.skagwaybrewing.com), one of the few places in town where you can check your e-mail. For a quick snack, try reindeer sausage at the **Popcorn Wagon,** at 565 Broadway (in front of the Skagway Bazaar), where they also serve popcorn.

COMING ASHORE Most ships dock at the cruise pier, at the foot of Broadway. But if many ships are in town, two other docks are available, and the walk from those is no longer than 10 minutes, with shuttles provided. From the closest point, it's about a 5-minute walk from the pier across the train tracks to downtown, but shuttle buses are also provided. The only street you really need to know about is Broadway, which runs through the center of town and off which everything branches.

After you've docked, take a few minutes to study the paintings of ships' and captains' names and dates, which cover the 400-foot-high cliffs alongside the pier. It's not graffiti; it is a genuine history of the development of the cruise industry in Skagway over the last 4 decades or more. All of the paintings, mostly of shipline logos, were done by crew members from visiting ships. Some of the pictures are placed hundreds of feet up the cliffs. Local authorities have put a stop to it. For several years, it's been a case of "paint a rock, go to jail" and the rock face, which used to be so colorful, is beginning to fade without new creations. Occasionally, some enterprising crew members will attempt to revive the tradition, but they are quickly shepherded away from the cliff.

INFORMATION Maps with routes for walking are available at the **Skagway Visitor Information Center** (✆ **907/983-2854**), at the Arctic Brotherhood Hall, 245 Broadway, between 2nd and 3rd avenues. Located in the restored railroad depot, the **National Park Service Visitor Center,** 2nd Avenue and Broadway (P.O. Box 517, Skagway, AK 99840; ✆ **907/983-2921;** www.nps.gov/klgo), is the focal point for activities in Skagway. Rangers answer questions, give lectures, and show films; five times a day, they lead an excellent walking tour. The building houses a small museum that lays the groundwork for the rest of what you'll see. The park service's programs are free. The visitor center is open May through September daily from 8am to 6pm, and during the rest of the year Monday through Friday from 8am to 5pm.

BEST CRUISE-LINE SHORE EXCURSIONS

Haines Eagle Preserve Float Adventure & Lynn Fjord Cruise (6½ hr.; $207 adults, $115 children 7–12): This outing combines a fjord cruise (45 min. to Haines) with a leisurely raft float (no white-water rapids here) through the Chilkat Bald Eagle Preserve. Essential equipment (boots and life jackets, rain poncho if needed) is provided.

Horseback Riding Adventure (3½ hr.; $163 adults and children; minimum 12 yrs.): Giddy-up on horseback to see the remnants of Dyea, once a booming gold-rush town, and explore the scenic Dyea Valley. Participants, of course, must be able to mount a horse and maintain balance in a saddle.

Skagway Street Car (2 hr.; $42 adults, $22 children 12 and under): This is as much performance art as it is a historical tour. Guides in period costume relate tales of the boomtown days as you tour the sights both in and outside of town aboard vintage 1930s sightseeing limousines. Though theatrical, it's all done in a homey style, as if you're getting a tour from your cousin Martha.

White Pass Scenic Railway (3 hr.; $122 adults, $61 children 3–12): The train makes two round-trips a day, three on Thursday. The sturdy engines and vintage parlor cars of this famous narrow-gauge railway take you from the dock past waterfalls and parts of the famous Trail of '98, including Dead Horse Gulch to the White Pass Summit, the boundary between Canada and the United States. Don't take this trip on an overcast day—you won't see anything. If you have a clear day, though, you can see all the way to the harbor; you might spot a marmot fleeing the train's racket. Or take the train to Fraser, B.C. (in Canada), and get on mountain bikes for the ride back (4 hr.; $150 adults, $75 children 3–12). All of the trains are wheelchair-accessible.

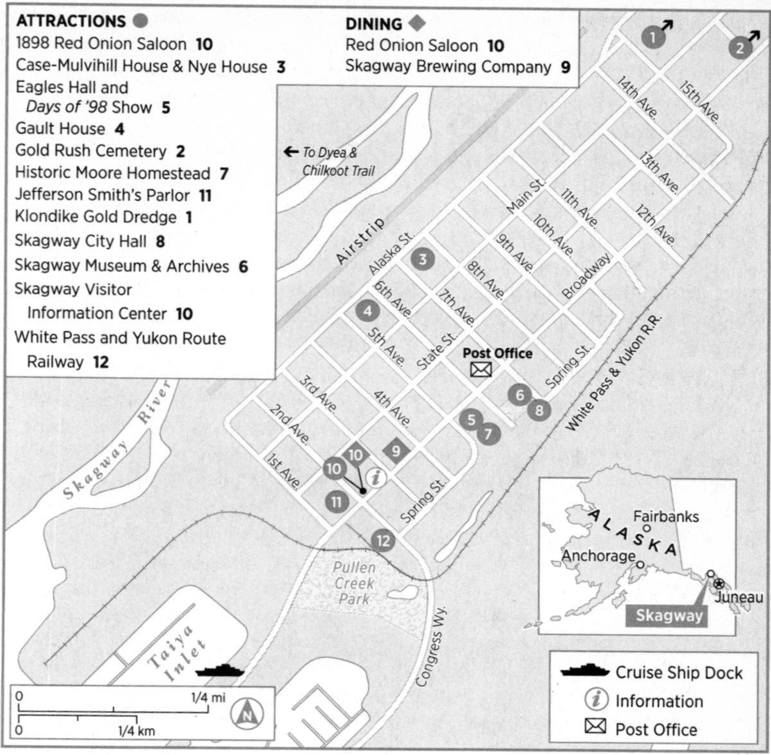

Yukon Jeep Adventure (5 hr.; $159 adults, $105 children 12 and under): Retrace the steps of the gold miners along the Trail of '98 from the comfort of a four-wheel-drive Jeep Wrangler. Interactive headphones permit drivers in the convoy to keep in touch with guides as they describe the events of '98. The convoy passes all of the historic gold-rush sights.

Golden Glass-blowing Experience (3 hr.; $207 adult, $125 child; minimum age 7): Visit a working glass-blowing studio to learn how to blow or mold molten glass. You'll get to create your own ornament, complete with 24K gold.

Ghosts & Goodtime Girls Walking Tour (2 hr.; $40 adults and children; minimum age 16): Take a walking tour of Skagway's streets and back alleys, led by a costumed Red Onion madam, and end with a champagne toast at the infamous Red Onion Saloon. Look out for the brothel's resident ghost.

60 Degrees North Yukon Golf & Scenic Drive (8 hr.; $179 adults and children; golf cart included): Head into the Yukon on the Klondike Highway, a route that runs parallel to the White Pass railroad (and serves up amazing scenery, including deep gulches and mountain peaks), into Canada. Your destination is a 9-hole, regulation par-36 course set at about 60 degrees latitude north, and surrounded by lakes, mountains, and forest. Lunch is served in the log clubhouse.

Melting Glaciers

If you've been promising yourself a trip to Alaska to see the glaciers, you might want to think about doing it fairly soon—before they disappear. Virtually all of the state's thousand or so glaciers are receding—and not slowly, folks. Some of them are fading into the distance at truly astonishing speeds. Most people tend to think of glacier recessions as slow, barely perceptible actions. The word "glacial" suggests just such a process. In fact, the movement can be relatively rapid and is eminently measurable. And studies show that the process is becoming more rapid with each passing year.

Global warming? Who knows? Some people, including glaciologists and other scientists, instinctively point to that phenomenon as the reason that huge chunks of the frontage split away (or "calve"). At the same time, they are convinced that it prevents sufficiently heavy snowfall in the upper regions of the ice field to compact—the action that creates glaciers in the first place.

Others are less anxious to point the finger. It's not global warming, some say, but a cyclical thing, a quirk of nature. They argue that glaciers tend to retreat for years and then gallop forward again. To some extent, that's been true for centuries—but there's been a lot more retreating than advancing in Alaska in the last decade, not to mention the fact that some glaciers that have not significantly pulled back from their termini are not as high as they used to be.

One of the most famous, and most easily accessible of the lot—Mendenhall Glacier, near Juneau—offers one of the most dramatic examples of a receding ice wall. Since 1935, it has withdrawn more than a mile from its original position. And the rate of retreat is accelerating. Depending on whose assessment you accept, Mendenhall is moving back at anything between 30 and 100 feet a year! (Apparently, a factor in determining the rate of retreat is where exactly the measurement is taken.)

EXCURSIONS OFFERED BY LOCAL AGENCIES

Independent tours, representing a number of operators, are sold at a tour center at 7th Avenue and Broadway. Tours are priced in the $45 to $55 range for a 2½-hour city and White Pass Summit tour by van. **Chilkat Cruises** (✆ **888/766-2103;** www.hainesskagwayfastferry.com) has a fast ferry that takes you to Haines in about 45 minutes. They run several trips a day, costing $68 for adults, $34 for children 3 to 12. Gold mining never actually happened in Skagway—it was only a transit point—but the town now gets more gold-rush tourists than any other place.

ON YOUR OWN: WITHIN WALKING DISTANCE

The Case-Mulvihill House, the Gault House, and the Nye House All within a block of one another, these three buildings are striking examples of gold-rush-era Skagway architecture. You can view these three, from the street only, as part of a guided walking tour conducted by officers of the National Park Service.

The Case-Mulvihill House and the Nye House are on Alaska St., btw. 7th and 8th aves. The Gault House is on Alaska St., btw. 5th and 6th aves.

The U.S. Forest Service, which staffs an Interpretive Center at Mendenhall—built less than a decade ago—reports that the rate of retreat is growing year by year. The Interpretive Center, once slap-bang up against the ice wall, is now a 20-minute walk away.

Anybody who has enjoyed the beauty of Columbia Glacier, lapped by the waters of the wildlife-rich Prince William Sound, cannot help but notice that it has grown more distant. Scientists estimate that in a quarter-century, it has retreated by almost 10 miles! And the rate of its back-pedaling has become more pronounced in the last 5 years. Much the same could be said of its nearby neighbor, Valdez Glacier. For years, a day-boat sightseeing company has offered a 26-glacier cruise of the Sound. It still does, but the glaciers just aren't as close as they used to be!

Everywhere in Alaska, glaciers are in retreat, according to scientists attached to the U.S. Geological Survey. Cruise passengers will see the results in Glacier Bay, where Muir Glacier has thinned considerably in the last decade, and at Margerie and Grand Pacific, both of which have lost a bit of their frontage.

In Kenai Fjords National Park and at Portage and the St. Elias Mountain areas, the story is the same—glaciers are receding. Scientists reckon that, in total, probably 95% of the glaciers in Alaska are losing ground. If the believers in a cyclical ebb-and-flow pattern are correct, the ice walls will come charging back. If the global warming doomsayers are right, the retreat will continue until Alaska's glaciers are a thing of the past, at least as visitor attractions.

Catch them now—just in case!

Eagles Hall and Days of '98 Show This is the venue for Skagway's long-running (since 1927) *Days of '98* show, a live melodrama of the Gay '90s featuring dancing girls and ragtime music. Follow the events leading up to the historic shootout that led to the end of Smith's crime reign. Daytime performances are at 10:30am, 12:30pm, and 2:30pm, timed so cruise passengers can attend.

Southeast corner of 6th Ave. and Broadway. ✆ **907/983-2545.** Daytime performances $16 adults, $8 children 15 and under.

Historic Moore Homestead The Moore Cabin was built in 1887 as the home of Capt. William Moore, the founder of Skagway. The cabin was restored recently by the National Park Service.

5th Ave. and Spring St. Free tours 10am–5pm during summer.

Jefferson Smith's Parlor Also known as Soapy's Parlor, Jefferson Smith's Parlor was a saloon and gambling joint opened by the notorious bandit in 1897. The building has been relocated twice, but looks pretty much as it did at the time of Smith's death in a gunfight in 1898.

2nd Ave., just off Broadway.

Red Onion Saloon Located near the Arctic Brotherhood Hall, whose eye-catching facade is constructed of thousands of pieces of driftwood, the Red Onion was a dance hall and honky-tonk bar (ca. 1898) with the obligatory bordello upstairs. The bartenders still serve drinks over the same mahogany counter as did their turn-of-the-century predecessors. The waitresses wear dance-hall outfits, and there's often live entertainment. The establishment bears a striking resemblance to Juneau's Red Dog Saloon; it's just as noisy and as much fun.

205 Broadway, at the corner of 2nd Ave. ✆ **907/983-2414.** www.redonion1898.com. Apr–Oct daily 10am–11pm.

Skagway City Hall This is not, strictly speaking, a tourist site, but as the town's only stone building, it's worth a peek.

Spring St. and 7th Ave.

Skagway Museum & Archives In the historic McCabe College building (built 1899–1900), this museum offers a look at Skagway's history through artifacts, photographs, and historical records. Items on display include a Tlingit canoe and Bering Sea kayaks, as well as a collection of gold-rush supplies and tools, and Native Alaskan items including baskets and beadwork.

7th and Spring sts. ✆ **907/983-2420.** Admission $2 adults, $1 students, free for children 12 and under. May–Sept Mon–Fri 9am–5pm; Sat 10am–5pm; Sun 10am–4pm. Oct–Apr hours vary; call ahead.

ON YOUR OWN: BEYOND THE PORT AREA

The Gold Rush Cemetery This is the permanent resting place of Messrs. Smith and Reid. The cemetery is small and is a short walk from the scenic Reid Falls, named after the heroic one-time surveyor. Aside from Reid's impressive monument, most of the headstones at the cemetery are whitewashed wood and are replaced by the park service when they get too worn. You can get a good look at it from the White Pass & Yukon Rail carriages.

About 1½ miles away from the center of downtown, up State St. (walkable if you have the time and inclination).

SHOPPING

The shops in Skagway are touristy, with many items made outside of Alaska (and most outside the country). But you can find high-end crafts, including Tlingit masks and silver jewelry, at **Inside Passage Arts,** at 340 7th Ave. (✆ **907/983-2585;** www.insidepassagearts.com). **Skagway Artworks,** 555 Broadway (✆ **907/983-3443;** www.skagwayartworks.com), also sells regionally made art, jewelry, and crafts. The **Train Shoppe** (✆ **800/343-7373**), in the White Pass and Yukon Route Depot (at 231 2nd Ave.), has memorabilia for train buffs.

9

Ports & Wilderness Areas Along the Gulf Route

Earlier in this book, we mentioned that going on a Gulf cruise does not mean you miss out on the ports, glaciers, or other natural areas of the Inside Passage. It just means that rather than a round-trip itinerary from, say, Seattle, you are more likely to be doing a one-way routing either north- or southbound between Vancouver and Whittier or Seward (both ports for Anchorage).

Your itinerary may include typical Inside Passage stops and attractions such as Ketchikan, Juneau, Skagway, and Glacier Bay. But there may also be the addition of Gulf ports, including Seward, and such fabulous attractions as Hubbard Glacier and College Fjord.

The big-ship cruise lines offer longer cruises (see details in chapter 5) that allow additional exploration to less visited areas. Small-ship lines can access certain regions more easily, thanks to their shallow drafts, and they also have the flexibility to visit smaller towns and wilderness areas, including on shorter itineraries (details in chapter 6).

See chapter 4 for information on shore excursions and a few tips on debarkation, what to bring along with you while ashore, and little matters such as not missing the boat.

1 Petersburg

Visiting this perfect little fishing town on Mitkof Island in the Frederick Sound is like visiting a slice of Norway. In fact, it was founded in 1890 by Norwegian immigrant Peter Buschmann, who came here to found a cannery and killed himself after living here for only 4 years. But that inauspicious history should not hinder your impression. This is "Alaska's Little Norway," and it's lovely.

Petersburg (pop. 3,055) is the perfect little small town, with an appealing quirkiness—there are so many docks, boardwalks, and wooden walkways that the town almost feels like it's floating on the water. Big cruise ships can't enter the narrow harbor, so cruise passengers who do visit come on small, laid-back ships rather than in big crowds, and that's fine with everyone concerned.

Nordic Drive has businesses catering to its residents, including family-owned grocery and hardware stores. Given the number of blond locals and the neat white clapboard houses decorated with flower boxes, you really might think you're in a fishing village in Scandinavia.

The town is surrounded by water and rainforest. There are wonderful trails for hiking and biking. On the water, humpback whales frolic—sightings are frequent. Nearby LeConte Glacier is a prime place to visit, and the fishing here is terrific.

In fact, the town's economy is based on fishing for salmon and halibut (note the big commercial fishing fleet) and government work—the Stikine Ranger District of the Tongass National Forest is headquartered here.

Ships that visit here usually include a complimentary performance for their passengers of traditional Norwegian folk dances by a costumed local troupe, the Leikarring Dancers, either shipboard or at the Sons of Norway Hall.

COMING ASHORE The small cruise ships that visit here (Lindblad in 2011) use the small, welcoming ferry terminal (✆ **907/772-3855**), with a pier from which to watch the boats and marine animals. It's about a mile to the town center.

INFORMATION The Petersburg Chamber of Commerce **Visitor Information Center,** at the corner of 1st and Fram streets (✆ **907/772-4636;** www.petersburg.org), offers guidance on outdoor activities and distributes trail guides and natural history publications. The center is open in summer Monday through Saturday from 9am to 5pm, Sunday from noon to 4pm; in winter, Monday through Friday from 10am to 2pm.

BEST CRUISE-LINE SHORE EXCURSIONS

Mitkof Island Tour & Rainforest Nature Walk (3 hr.; $40 adults and children): Meet a local guide and learn about life on the edge of North America's largest rainforest. After driving until the road ends, you stroll through old-growth forest, taking in the local flora and fauna. It's an easy walk on a boardwalk past forest, bogs, and a saltwater estuary.

LeConte Glacier & Stikine River Flightseeing (1 hr.; $229 adults and children): Fly over coastal mountains, the Stikine Ice Field, and the mighty glacier, and experience the excitement of a takeoff and landing on water.

EXCURSIONS OFFERED BY LOCAL AGENCIES

The full-service **Viking Travel** agency, corner of Nordic Drive and Sing Lee Alley (✆ **800/327-2571** or 907/772-3818; www.alaskaferry.com), specializes in booking local guides for tours, kayaks, whale-watching, flights, fishing charters, and other activities. **Alaska Sea Adventures** (✆ **888/772-8588** or 907/772-4700; www.yachtalaska.com) offers a 4½-hour LeConte Glacier tour that departs in the morning and afternoon, for $140 per person (two-person minimum).

ON YOUR OWN: WITHIN WALKING DISTANCE

Birch Street This charming little one-lane, one-dock stretch follows the Hammer Slough, the tidal mouth of the creek that runs through town. On the pilings are old, weathered houses that hang over the placid channel. Many have one door opening to the road and another door for the water.

Clausen Memorial Museum Here's the place to learn about Petersburg and its history, although it's mostly geared toward locals. Exhibits include obsolete fishing gear, rugged old nautical equipment, and a model fish trap, outlawed in 1959 when Alaska became a state.

2nd and Fram sts. ✆ **907/772-3598.** www.clausenmuseum.net. Admission $3, free for children 12 and under. Summer Mon–Sat 10am–5pm; winter Tue–Sat 10am–2pm.

Eagle's Roost Park Past the commercial fishing activity of the harborfront, Eagle's Roost Park has a grassy area where you can sit and relax, and a stairway that leads

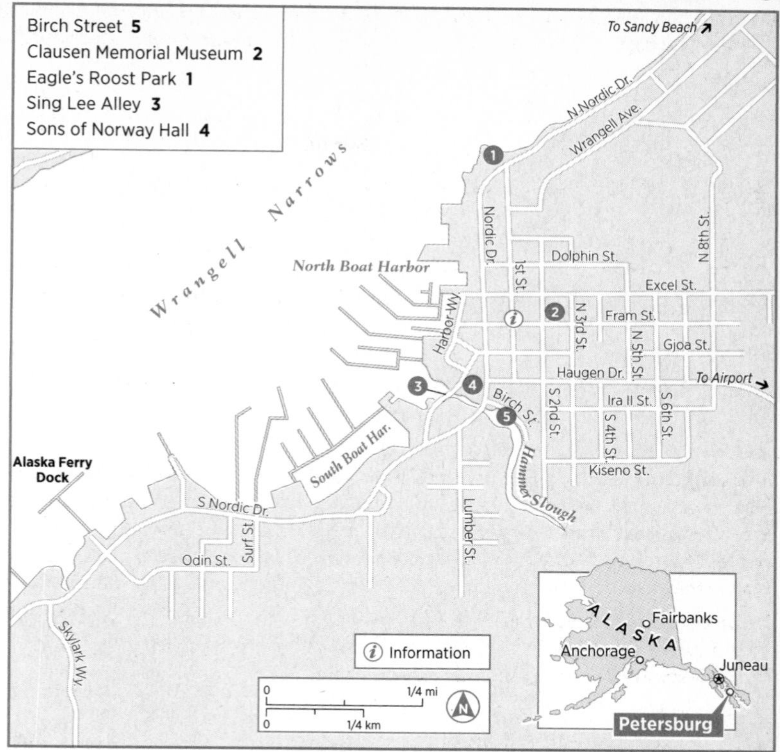

down to the water. At low tide, an interesting but rugged beach walk starts here. Look up in the treetops and you're almost guaranteed to see eagles, which congregate while waiting for the fish waste from the nearby cannery.

Nordic Dr.

Sons of Norway Hall A giant model of a Viking ship used in the Little Norway Festival in May is often parked outside this national historic site, which dates to 1912. Though you can't go inside, the model ship still makes for a nice photo op. On the pilings next door, the **Fishermen's Memorial Park** is a memorial to Petersburg mariners lost at sea and includes a bronze statue of Bojer Wikan, a fisherman and lifelong resident.

23 Indian St., near Sing Lee Alley, on the wooden dock.

ON YOUR OWN: BEYOND THE PORT AREA

Sandy Beach Three miles southeast of town on Sandy Beach Road, this beach does not have fine sand (it's more like fine gravel), nor can you swim in the frigid water. But it's still a pretty spot facing Frederick Sound, and at low tide you can see the outlines of ancient fish traps, dating back some 2,000 years. There are also some petroglyphs on nearby rocks. Finding the traps and petroglyphs isn't easy—it's best if you can get someone to lead you, perhaps by joining the occasional Forest Service walks (information at the Visitor Information Center; see above). If you go at high tide, you can still go beachcombing and maybe spot a great blue heron or two.

SHOPPING

Sing Lee Alley boasts some nice little shops—none of them of the chain variety. You can find a good collection of books on natural history and local culture at **Sing Lee Alley Books,** 11 Sing Lee Alley (© **907/772-4440**); handmade Norwegian knit souvenirs and arts-and-crafts supplies at **Cubby Hole,** 14 Sing Lee Alley (© **907/772-2717**); and canned smoked salmon and smoked halibut, and more fishy products at **Tonka Seafoods,** 22 Sing Lee Alley (© **888/560-3662** or 907/772-3662).

2 Hubbard Glacier

Said to be Alaska's longest ice face accessible by cruise ships—it's about 6 miles across—Hubbard lies at the northern end of **Yakutat Bay.** It also has a rather odd claim to fame: It is one of the fastest moving glaciers in Alaska. So fast and far did it move about a dozen years ago that it quickly created a wall across the mouth of **Russell Fjord,** one of the inlets lining Yakutat Bay. That turned the fjord into a lake and trapped hundreds of migratory marine creatures inside. Scientists still can't tell us why Hubbard chose to act the way it did or why it receded to its original position several months later, reopening Russell Fjord.

Cruise ships in Yakutat Bay get spectacular views of the glacier, which, because of the riptides and currents, is always in motion, calving into the ocean and producing lots of white thunder. It should be noted, however, that only one ship can get close to the glacier at a time, and if another ship is hogging the space, your ship may have to wait or may not get close at all.

There is one footnote to the Yakutat Bay cruise experience: A few years ago, some Alaska residents tried to make visitors pay for the privilege of viewing the glacier. Some of the **villagers of Yakutat,** at the mouth of the bay, tried to impose a $1.50 head tax on all ship passengers cruising past to see Hubbard Glacier—even though ships never call at Yakutat. Ultimately, the ship operators and the villagers reached a compromise. Instead of paying a tax on passengers carried into the bay, the lines now buy fish and other area products for use in the dining room, thereby enriching the locals without having to add to the cost of a cruise berth.

3 Prince William Sound

Located at the northern end of the underside of the Kenai Peninsula, this is truly one of Alaska's most appealing wilderness areas, though it suffered mightily following the *Exxon Valdez* oil spill in 1989. The area has recovered nicely from the ravages of that infamous spill, and today visitors are absolutely guaranteed wildlife—whales, harbor seals, eagles, sea lions, sea otters, puffins, and more.

If your cruise doesn't spend time on the Sound, day cruises are available out of Whittier and Seward. One company, **Phillips' Cruises and Tours,** 519 W. 4th Ave., Ste. 100, Anchorage (© **800/544-0529** or 907/276-8023; www.26glaciers.com), markets what it calls a "26 Glaciers Cruise." All in one day! That tells you about as much as you need to know about the scenic beauty of the sound. The cruise—$139 per adult and $79 per child—is well worth taking.

Another operator, **Major Marine,** 411 W. 4th Ave., Anchorage (© **800/764-7300** or 907/274-7300; www.majormarine.com), offers a slightly more modest cruise on

The Kenai Peninsula & Prince William Sound

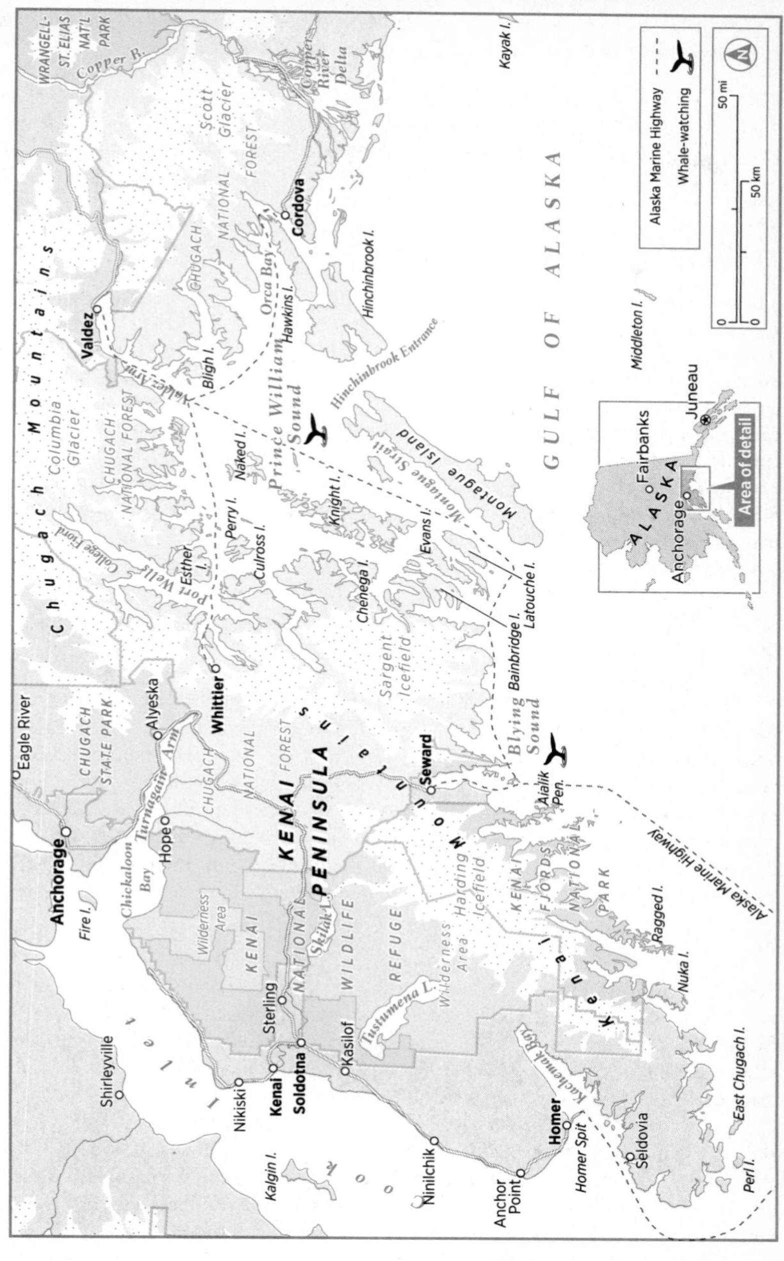

the Sound. It features a *mere* 10 glaciers. The 5-hour cruise costs $107 for adults and $53 for children 11 and under. Food is extra—$19 for a salmon and prime rib buffet.

Perhaps the most spectacular of the sound's ice faces is **Columbia Glacier,** whose surface spreads over more than 400 square miles and whose tidewater frontage is more than 5 miles across. Columbia is receding faster than most of its Alaska counterparts. Scientists reckon it will retreat more than 20 miles in the next 20 to 50 years, leaving behind nothing but another deep fjord—just what Prince William Sound needs.

4 College Fjord

College Fjord is in the northern sector of Prince William Sound, roughly midway between Whittier and Valdez. It's not one of the more spectacular Alaska glacier areas, being very much overshadowed by Glacier Bay, Yakutat Bay (for Hubbard Glacier), and others, but it's scenic enough to merit a place on a lot of cruise itineraries, mostly for **Harvard Glacier,** which sits at its head. On a visit in 2005, our coauthor Fran got within 1,000 feet of the glacier on the *Carnival Spirit,* and it was calving every few minutes. What this may mean in terms of global warming aside, it was an unforgettable sight to behold.

The fjord was named in 1898 by an expedition team that opted to give the glaciers lining College Fjord and their neighbor, Harriman Glacier, the names of Ivy League and other prominent Eastern universities—hence, Harvard, Vassar, Williams, Yale, and so on.

5 Seward

Seward is the main northern embarkation/debarkation port for north- and southbound Alaska cruises. For information on attractions, shore excursions, tours, accommodations, and dining, see chapter 7, "The Ports of Embarkation."

10

Cruisetour Destinations

No matter how powerful your binoculars, you can't see all of Alaska from a ship, and that's why the cruise lines invented the cruisetour. In this chapter, we'll give you information on the most popular cruisetour destinations. See "Cruisetours: The Best of Land & Sea," in chapter 2, for a discussion of the various cruisetour packages offered; for more in-depth information on these destinations, pick up a copy of *Frommer's Alaska 2011.*

1 Denali National Park & Preserve

This is Alaska's most visited—environmentalists say over-visited—wilderness area, with almost one million people a year coming by bus and train to soak up the park's scenic splendor. It used to be difficult to stay overnight anywhere in or near the park, but it's become easier in recent years with the opening of the Talkeetna Alaskan Lodge and the Princess McKinley Lodge—both with spectacular views of the Alaska Range and Mount McKinley. An addition to the McKinley Chalet Resort has brought the room count to 345 in the area around the mountain. That's not a lot by any means, but it has made a stopover at the park much easier. There are, however, times when demand outstrips supply, so book early.

Wildlife is the thing in Denali—somewhere in the realm of 161 bird species, 37 mammal species, and 450 plant species are found there.

The **Alaska Railroad** operates daily between Anchorage and Fairbanks alongside the park, towing the private railcars of Holland America Line and Princess, as well as those of Royal Celebrity Tours (Royal Caribbean and Celebrity Cruises' joint tour product). You can do the tour in either direction. Five years ago, the Alaska Railroad added its own domed viewing cars in addition to its more basic (but less expensive and perfectly adequate) carriages. (Trains do not actually enter the park; they run along its perimeter and deposit passengers at stations just outside the boundary.)

Besides the wildlife, the focal point of the park is North America's highest peak, **Mount McKinley** (also known by its original Native name, *Denali,* which means "the great one"). You could argue that McKinley comprises the two highest peaks in North America: Its north face towers over the Alaska Range at 20,320 feet, while its south face rises to 19,470 feet. Permanently snow-covered mountains dominate the surrounding expanse. There's Mount Foraker, which stands a mere 17,400 feet; Mount Silverthrone, at 13,320 feet; Mount Crosson, at 12,800 feet; and many, many more giant heaps. It's an awesome sight, even from below at one of the nearby lodges. You just have to hope you can see it.

As with all enormous mountains, the Great One creates its own weather system, and foggy seems to be its favorite flavor. Sadly, it's possible to be in the area for days and never catch a glimpse of the Alaska Range. Trust us, though: When you finally

A Mountain by Any Other Name . . .

We've long been taught that the Athabascans of Interior Alaska named the mountain *Denali,* meaning "the high one" or "the great one." But at least one historian contends that the word *Denal'iy* actually referred to a mountain near Anchorage, now known as Pioneer Peak, and means "one that watches," and that the Native word for McKinley, "the high one," is actually *Doleika.* In any event, Alaska Natives seldom made use of the area, as it produced little fish or game, and white men came only in search of gold. In 1896, a prospector named the mountain after William McKinley of Ohio, who was elected president of the United States that year.

All well and good, except that most Alaskans prefer the name Denali and since 1975 have petitioned to officially change it back. Ohio won't allow it. Although congressmen from Alaska and Ohio compromised on the issue in 1980, changing the name of the national park to Denali and leaving the mountain named McKinley, Alaskans have kept pushing for Denali. However, the U.S. Board on Geographical Names has refused to take up the issue. The board has a rule against considering an issue that is also before Congress, and the Ohio Congressional delegation repeatedly introduces a one-paragraph bill stating that the name should stay the same. This bill never goes anywhere, but just introducing it has been enough to thwart any name change.

see it in all its splendor, you'll realize that it's worth the wait. It is one of coauthor Gene's favorite Alaska views.

Most people cannot drive far into the park. Private vehicles are tightly restricted, for environmental reasons, and are allowed only to about mile 15 on the park road. That cuts down on your wildlife viewing chances. However, you can sign up for the park concessionaire's coaches, which are allowed to penetrate much more deeply into the park. The buses have been upgraded in recent years to include drop-down video screens on which the driver shows live video of the animals you see along the road, allowing everyone a better view. The coaches leave from the few local hotels. The drivers of these buses are all experts in the flora and fauna of the area. They always seem to be able to spot Dall sheep on the hillside, or caribou in the tall grass—even bears. When that wildlife is close enough, the driver/guide will ask for quiet so as not to startle the animals. And you'd better be quiet! The tour demands a long day—about 8 hours in not particularly luxurious vehicles—but if the weather holds and the viewing is good, it'll be the best $103 you ever spent ($51.50 for children 14 and under).

2 Fairbanks

Alaska's second largest city (after Anchorage) is friendly, unpretentious, and easygoing in the Alaska tradition, although its downtown area is drab and a little depressing. Fairbanks' major attraction is the *Riverboat Discovery,* 1975 Discovery Dr. (© **866/479-6673** or 907/479-6673), a three-deck stern-wheeler that operates 4-hour cruises twice a day throughout the summer on the Chena (*Chee*-nah) and Tanana (*Ta*-na-naw) rivers. The boat visits a re-created Indian village, a sled-dog training school, and an Athabascan Indian fish camp (with narration), and a flyby is performed by a bush pilot. The cruise costs $55 for adults, $38 for children 3 to 12, and is free for children 2 and under. Sailings are mid-May to mid-September. The vessel used for the cruise is the third in the *Riverboat Discovery* series.

The Binkleys, the family that owns the stern-wheeler, also own **El Dorado Gold Mine,** off the Elliott Highway, 9 miles north of town (✆ **866/479-6673** or 907/479-6673). Here, visitors can pan for gold and, while riding on the open-sided Tanana Valley Railroad, study the workings of the mine just as it was a century ago. It's hokey, but it's good fun, especially for youngsters. Tours, which run daily (call for times), are $35 for adults, $23 for children 3 to 12, and free for children 2 and under. If you buy the Gold Mine tickets at the same time as you do the riverboat cruise, you can save $2 a head off the combined price.

Pioneer Park (formerly **Alaskaland**), at the intersection of Airport Way and Peger Road (✆ **907/459-1087**), is a low-key Native culture–theme park with a couple of small museums, a playground, and a little tour train. It will never be confused with Disneyland. The park is open year-round, but the attractions operate only from Memorial Day weekend to Labor Day, daily from noon to 8pm. And the best part of all? Admission is free.

Your cruisetour may include a tour of the gold mine or a visit to **Gold Dredge No. 8,** a huge monster of a machine that dug gold out of the hills until 1959 and is now on display for visitors. Shore excursions and cruisetours almost always include the *Riverboat Discovery* and the El Dorado Gold Mine.

3 Prudhoe Bay

Prudhoe Bay is at the very end of the Dalton Highway, also known locally as the Haul Road, a 414-mile stretch built to service the Trans-Alaska Pipeline. The road connects the Arctic coast with Interior Alaska and passes through wilderness areas that include all sorts of scenic terrain—forested rounded hills, the rugged peaks of the Brooks Range, and the treeless plains of the North Slope. The route provides lots of wildlife-spotting opportunities, with strong chances of seeing caribou, Dall sheep, moose, and bear.

But the real reason to come way up here is the **Prudhoe Bay Oilfield.** (Indeed, Prudhoe Bay is, essentially, a company town run by oil giant BP, with a population of just 50 people or so, give or take). Although touring an oil field may not be high on your vacation must-do list, the bay complex is no ordinary oil field. It's a historic and strategic site of great importance and a great technological achievement. (And chances are, you'll be the only one on your block who's actually been there!) The industry coexists here with migrating caribou and waterfowl on wet, fragile tundra that permanently shows any mark made by vehicles. (Visits to the oil field were curtailed following the September 11, 2001, terrorist attacks, but a modified version has since resumed under stricter security rules.) Tours (2 hr.; $38 adults, $19 children 12 and under) are operated by the **Arctic Caribou Inn,** P.O. Box 340111, Prudhoe Bay, AK 99734 (✆ **866/659-2368;** www.arcticcaribouinn.com). They will need your name and an identification number that BP can use to run a background check before allowing you on the oil field: A driver's license, passport, or Social Security number

First to the Top

It's the biggest. That's why climbers risk their lives on Mount McKinley. You can see the mountain from Anchorage, more than 100 miles away. On a flight across Alaska, McKinley stands out grandly over waves of other mountains. It's more than a mile taller than the tallest peak in the other 49 states. It's a great white triangle, always covered in snow, tall but also massive and strong.

The first group to try to climb Mount McKinley came in 1903, led by Judge James Wickersham, who also helped explore Washington's Olympic Peninsula before it became a national park. His group made it less than halfway up, but on the trip they found gold in the Kantishna Hills, setting off a small gold rush that led to the first permanent human settlement in the park area. Wickersham later became the Alaska Territory's nonvoting delegate to Congress and introduced the bill that created the national park, but the government was never able to get back land in the Kantishna area from the gold miners. Today, that land is the site of wilderness lodges, right in the middle of the park.

On Sept. 27, 1906, renowned world-explorer Dr. Frederick Cook announced to the world by telegraph that he had reached the summit of Mount McKinley after a lightning-fast climb, covering more than 85 miles and 19,000 vertical feet in 13 days with one other man, a blacksmith, at his side. On his return to New York, Cook was lionized as a conquering explorer and published a popular book of his summit diary and photographs.

In 1909, Cook again made history, announcing that he had beaten Robert Peary to the North Pole. Both returned to civilization from their competing treks at about the same time. Again, Cook was the toast of the town. His story began to fall apart, however, when his Eskimo companions mentioned that he'd never been out of sight of land. After being paid by Peary to come forward, Cook's McKinley companion also recanted. A year later, Cook's famous summit photograph was re-created—on a peak 19 miles away and 15,000 feet lower than the real summit.

In 1910, disgusted with Cook, four prospectors from Fairbanks took a more Alaskan approach to the task. Without fanfare or special supplies—they carried doughnuts and hot chocolate on their incredible final ascent—they marched up the mountain carrying a large wooden flagpole they could

will work. Entry is by advance booking only. There are no walk-ins. Included in the tour is a short stop on the shores of the Arctic Ocean. Brrrrr!

To get here, you usually drive the Dalton Highway one way in buses and then fly back, with either **Fairbanks** or **Anchorage** being the other connecting point. The trip includes an overnight in **Coldfoot.**

Be aware: The bus trip is a long one over not particularly good roads and it's not always terribly comfortable.

plant on top to prove they'd made it. But on arriving at the summit, they realized that they'd climbed the slightly shorter north peak. Weather closed in, so they set up the pole there and descended without attempting the south peak. Then, when they got back to Fairbanks, no one could see the pole, and they were accused of trying to pull off another hoax.

In 1913, Episcopal archdeacon Hudson Stuck organized the first successful climb to reach the real summit—and reported he saw the pole on the other peak. Harry Karstens led the climb (he would become the park's first superintendent in 1917), and the first person to stand at the summit was an Alaska Native, Walter Harper.

Although McKinley remains one of the world's most difficult climbs, about 10,000 people have made it to the top since Hudson Stuck's party. Since 1980, the number of climbers has boomed. Garbage and human waste disposal are a major problem. June 12, 2003, 115 climbers made it to the summit. In 1970, only 124 made the attempt all year; now more than 1,200 try to climb the peak each year, with about half making it to the summit. The cold, fast-changing weather is what usually stops people. From late April into early July, climbers fly from the town of Talkeetna to a base camp at 7,200 feet elevation on the Kahiltna Glacier. From there, it takes an average of about 18 days to get to the top, through temperatures as cold as –40°F (–4°C).

Climbers lose fingers, toes, and other parts to frostbite, or suffer other, more severe injuries. More than 90 climbers have died on the mountain, not counting plane crashes. During the season, the park service has a station for rescue rangers and an emergency medical clinic at the 14,200-foot level of the mountain, and a high-altitude helicopter is kept ready to go after climbers in trouble. In 2002, under pressure from Congress, the park service started charging climbers a $150-a-head fee, defraying a portion of the rescue costs. The park and the military spend about a half-million dollars a year rescuing climbers, and sometimes much more. The cost in lives is high as well. Volunteer rangers and rescuers die as well as climbers. Plane crashes, falls, cold, and altitude all take a toll. Monuments to those who never returned are in the cemetery near the airstrip in Talkeetna.

—Charles Wohlforth

4 Nome & Kotzebue

There's no place like Nome. Well, we had to say it. But, really, this Arctic frontier town is a special place, combining a sense of history, a hospitable and silly attitude (we're talking about a place that holds an annual Labor Day bathtub race), and an exceptional location on the water before a tundra wilderness.

What it does not have is anything that remotely resembles a tourist destination. Anthropological, yes. Touristy, no. It's little more than a collection of beat-up residences

Denali Changes

Been to Denali before? If it's been a few years, you may be surprised by the changes to the park's visitor facilities, which have undergone a major upgrade over the past decade. Among the new additions:

- A complete rebuilding of the Eielson Visitor Center—the more remote of the two visitor centers in the park. Long a small and limited facility, the center was completely demolished in 2005 and rebuilt bigger (but more environmentally friendly) over several years, finally reopening in 2008. Located 66 miles inside Denali's borders and reached by shuttle bus only (cars are not allowed), it has new exhibits and viewing areas. The shuttle bus from the park entrance to the center costs $31 for adults ($15.50 for youth 15 to17; free for children 14 and under).
- A new Murie Science and Learning Center, located near the entrance to the park, which doubles as a visitor center in the winter months (when the regular visitor centers are closed).
- A new main Denali Visitor Center, near the entrance to the park, which includes exhibits and a theater housing an award-winning film, "Heartbeats of Denali." Finished several years ago, the building has won kudos for its environmentally friendly design, including the use of integrated photovoltaic solar panels on its south-facing side and renewable and recycled materials for walls, ceilings, and carpeting. The center is open from mid-May to late September.
- A revamped transit center near the entrance to the park (formerly the Visitor Access Center) where travelers board buses and get permits for campgrounds and backcountry tours.

and low-rise commercial buildings. It looks like the popular conception of a century-old gold-rush town—which isn't really surprising, as that's what it is. But if it seems to be in need of a face-lift, the inhabitants make up for all that by the warmth of their welcome. They're probably glad to see a strange face in the summer, because they know they'll see precious few in the winter when the weather turns ugly and the sun disappears for 3 or 4 months. There are local roads, but no highway link with the rest of the state.

The name Nome is believed to have been an error by a British naval officer in 1850, who wrote "? Name" on a diagram. The scrawl was misinterpreted by a mapmaker as "Nome." The population boom here in 1899 also happened by chance, when a prospector from the 1898 gold rush was left behind due to an injury. He panned the sand outside his tent and found that it was full of gold dust.

Undoubtedly, on your visit, you'll find time to try gold panning. The city also has a still sloppy, gold-rush-era saloon scene, and bargains on **Iñupiat Eskimo** arts and crafts.

Your tour will also visit **Kotzebue** (pronounced *Kot*-say-bue) to the north, one of Alaska's largest and oldest Iñupiat Eskimo villages. Here, you'll tour the **NANA Museum of the Arctic,** run by a regional Native corporation representing the 7,000 Iñupiat people who live in the northwest Arctic region.

To get here, you fly from Anchorage to Nome, then to Kotzebue, and then fly back to Anchorage, as part of itineraries that typically include an overnight in Anchorage and a visit to Denali and Fairbanks.

5 The Kenai Peninsula

The Kenai (*Kee*-nye) Peninsula, which divides Prince William Sound and Cook Inlet, has glaciers, whales, legendary sportfishing, spectacular hiking trails, bears, moose, and high mountains. It's easy to get to, to boot. At least it's not a long way from Alaska's tourist hub, Anchorage, and there's a good road to help you get there. The trouble is that there's an awful lot of traffic on it—not just from tourists, but also from Alaskan locals who drive down from Anchorage on weekends for outdoorsy pursuits. The traffic jams on Friday evenings and Saturday mornings, especially, can make the most jaded Los Angelenos forget the crush on the I-405 at rush hour, or New Yorkers the Lincoln Tunnel. Try to get to Anchorage a day or two before your cruise begins (or stay a day or two afterward) and make the trip in midweek. The scenery alone is well worth the effort. There are two main towns on the peninsula, Kenai and Soldotna, the former slightly bigger than the latter, but neither a major metropolis by any stretch of the imagination.

People from Anchorage come here for the weekend to hike, dig clams, paddle kayaks and, particularly, to fish. There's a special phrase for what happens when the red salmon are running in July on the Kenai and Russian rivers: **combat fishing.** Anglers stand elbow-to-elbow on a bank, each casting into his or her yard-wide slice of river, and they still catch plenty of fish (as well as, occasionally, each other!).

Cruisetours to the Kenai Peninsula include options for fishing, **river rafting,** and other soft adventure activities.

You typically travel here by bus or rail from Seward or Whittier. Princess includes an overnight stay at its own Kenai Princess Lodge, a wilderness resort with a gorgeous setting on a bluff overlooking the river; other cruise lines provide overnight stays at other properties. Some tours combine a visit to the Kenai Peninsula with an overnight in Anchorage.

6 The Yukon Territory

You'll pass plenty of beautiful scenery along the way, but today the real reason to cross the Canadian border into this region is the same as it was 100 years ago: **gold** (or, rather, gold-rush history).

Gold was discovered in the Canadian Klondike's Rabbit Creek (later renamed Bonanza Creek—for fairly obvious reasons) in 1896. In a matter of months, tens of thousands of people descended into the Yukon for the greatest gold rush in history, giving birth to Dawson City, Whitehorse, and a dozen other tent communities. By the turn of the century, the gold rush was on in earnest, and in 1900, the White Pass Yukon rail route opened from Skagway to the Canadian border to carry prospectors and their goods.

Once part of the Northwest Territories, the Yukon is now a separate Canadian territory bordered by British Columbia and Alaska. The entire territory has a population of just over 33,000, two-thirds of them living in **Whitehorse,** the capital of the region since 1953. Located on the banks of the Yukon River, Whitehorse was established in 1900, 2 full years after the stampeders began swarming into Dawson City. Today the city serves as a frontier outpost, its tourism influx also giving it a cosmopolitan tinge complete with nightlife, good shopping opportunities (with some smart boutiques and great outdoor shops), fine restaurants, and comfortable hotels. The up-to-the-minute nature of the town—with the Canada Games Centre, a sports/convention center; its modern Visitor Information Center; and its Waterfront Trolley rail service ($3 one-way) that runs from the Games Centre all the way to the other end of town, allowing passengers to disembark at any of several stations along the way—contrasts it with most of the Yukon.

Dawson City was once the biggest Canadian city west of Winnipeg, with a population of 30,000, but it withered to practically a ghost town after the gold-rush stampeders stopped stampeding. Dawson today is the nearest thing in the world to an authentic gold-rush town, with old buildings, vintage watering holes, dirt streets flanked with raised boardwalks, shops (naturally), and some particularly good restaurants. On a visit to Dawson 2 years ago, we were much impressed by the excellent La Table, in the Aurora Inn at the corner of 5th Avenue and Harper Street, an eatery that compares to the dining spots in the nation's largest cities. There is always, of course, the Dawson staple—Diamond Tooth Gertie's Gambling Hall (full-service bar, poker, blackjack, roulette, and slots), where one can eat a casual meal in truly fun surroundings. There's a $6, good-for-two-nights admission charge for adults—and don't bring the kids! The place is operated by the Klondike Visitors Association and it's all in fun. The proceeds go to maintain the gold-rush-style architecture and ambience of the town. Another establishment worth a visit is Bombay Peggy's Inn & Pub at 2nd Avenue and Princess Street. The pub features—along with a selection of locally brewed libations—artworks by Dawson area artists. (And no, there is no plan to change the name to Mumbai Peggy's!) Take a look also at the city museum, in the Old Territorial Building on 5th Avenue, with one of the most comprehensive narrations found anywhere of the tumultuous years of the gold rush.

If you're on a Holland America cruisetour—highly likely, as that company operates more Yukon cruisetours than any other—you'll travel between Dawson City and the tiny Alaskan town of Eagle via the *MV Yukon Queen II,* a high-speed, 115-passenger catamaran. It makes the trip along the Yukon River in 5 hours, passing through incredibly beautiful wilderness scenery, where the only sign of civilization is the occasional fisherman.

Holland America also has two more Yukon strings to its bow—exclusive rights to enter the UNESCO World Heritage Site known as **Kluane National Park,** a protected Canadian wilderness area that was hitherto all but inaccessible (a few backpackers, campers, and cyclists made up almost the only traffic into the park), and **Tombstone Territorial Park,** about a 90-minute drive from Dawson City.

7 The Canadian Rockies

Canadian Rockies cruisetours typically include travel by bus and/or train between Vancouver and either Seattle or Calgary.

Highlights of the tour include a visit to the parks at **Jasper** and **Banff,** which together comprise 17,518 sq. km (6,832 sq. miles). The parks are teeming with wildlife, with some animals—like bighorn sheep, mountain goats, deer, and moose—meandering along and across highways and hiking trails. There are also coyotes, lynx, and occasional wolves (though they tend to give humans a wide berth), as well as grizzlies and black bears, both of which are unpredictable and best photographed with a telephoto lens.

The two "capitals," Banff and Jasper, are 287km (178 miles) apart and connected by scenic Highway 93 (a destination unto itself). Banff is in a stunningly beautiful setting with the mighty Bow River, murky with glacial till, coursing through town.

The stylish **Fairmont Banff Springs** (✆ **403/762-2211;** www.fairmont.com) was originally built in 1888 as a destination resort by the Canadian Pacific Railroad. Ever since then, tourists have been visiting this area for its scenery and hot springs, plus nearby fishing, hiking, and other outdoor activities. Today, the streets of Banff are also an attraction, lined with trendy cafes and exclusive boutiques with international fashions.

Lake Louise is located 56km (35 miles) north of Banff and is a famed spot, deep green from the minerals it contains (ground by the glaciers above the lake) and surrounded by forest-clad, snowcapped mountains. The village near the lake is a resort destination in its own right. Nearly as spectacular as the lake is the **Fairmont Château Lake Louise,** 111 Lake Louise Dr., Lake Louise (✆ **800/441-1414** or 403/522-3511; www.fairmont.com), built by the Canadian Pacific Railroad and one of the most celebrated hotels in Canada.

Between Lake Louise and Jasper is the **Icefields Parkway,** a spectacular mountain road that climbs through three deep-river valleys, beneath soaring, glacier-notched mountains, and past dozens of hornlike peaks. Capping the route is the **Columbia Icefields,** a massive dome of glacial ice and snow that is the largest nonpolar ice cap in the world.

Jasper isn't Banff. It was born as a railroad division point, and the town does not have the glitz of its southern neighbor. **Jasper National Park** is Canada's largest mountain park and provides an outdoor-oriented experience with opportunities to hike, ride horseback, fish, or even climb mountains.

Appendix A: Alaska in Depth

by Charles Wohlforth

To discover Alaska is something apart from statistics, although the numbers do give you a general idea of scale. If you've driven across the continental United States and realize how big it is, take a map of Alaska and superimpose it on top of the area you crossed and you'll have some notion of the state's size. Alaskans always like to threaten that they'll split in half and make Texas the third-largest state. In 2008, Alaska had a population of just 686,293, according to the U.S. Census Bureau—the fourth least populous state in the Union. If you placed each resident an equal distance apart, each one would be almost a mile from any other. Of course, that couldn't happen. No human has ever set foot in some of the most remote parts of Alaska.

1 A Short Gold Rush History

The biggest event in Alaska history happened 112 years ago: The 1898 Klondike gold rush. If you're coming to Alaska, you'll hear a lot about it. Here's some context for the barrage of anecdotes you can expect.

A small number of prospectors sought gold even before Russia sold Alaska to the United States in 1867. After the American flag went up over Sitka, prospectors slowly worked their way into Alaska's vastness, often led by or in partnership with Natives, who knew the country. Called **sourdoughs** for the yeast and flour mixture they carried to make their bread, these were tough wilderness men, living way beyond the law or communications with the outside world.

A few of them struck it rich. In 1880, a major find on the Gastineau Channel started the city called Juneau and decades of industrial, hard-rock mining there. Finds followed on the Fortymile River, in 1886 (on the Taylor Hwy.); near Circle, in 1893 (on the Steese Hwy.); and near Hope, on the Kenai Peninsula, in 1895 (on the Seward Hwy.). Gold slowly brought more people to Alaska, but not enough to catch the nation's attention.

In 1896, white prospector George Carmack and his Native partners, Tagish Charlie and Skookum Jim, found gold on the Klondike River, a tributary of the Yukon in Canada. Word traveled downriver to the goldfields in Fortymile country, and within 48 hours, that area was empty and claims on the Klondike were being staked. The miners dug gravel from the creek that winter, and when they washed it, it yielded big chunks of solid gold, a massive discovery. Some were instant millionaires at a time when a million dollars really meant something.

It's hard to imagine today the impact of the news on the outside world. The U.S. economy was in a deep depression. The dollar was on the gold standard and the scarcity of that precious metal had caused a deflationary vise that in 1893 brought a banking collapse and unemployment of 18%. Suddenly, in 1897, a steamer arrived in Seattle bearing men from a place called the Klondike, with trunks and gunnysacks full of gold. The supply of money suddenly grew and economic confidence returned. The national economy turned around on the news and, in 1898, some 100,000 people set off for Skagway, Alaska (the easiest jumping-off point for the Canadian interior). They, too, had high hopes of getting rich, plunging off into a trackless wilderness for which they were completely unprepared.

The **Klondike gold rush** marks the start of contemporary Alaska. Before the gold rush, Alaska largely remained as it had been for thousands of years, ruled and inhabited by indigenous people. As late as the 1880 census, the territory had fewer than 500 white residents and not more than 4,000 by 1890. In 1898, the gold stampede began, bringing an instant population. Even the mayor of Seattle left for Alaska. Within a few years, Alaska had cities, telegraph lines, riverboats, and sled dog mail routes. About 30,000 made it all the way to Dawson City, in the Yukon Territory. Only a few of the miners struck it rich, but those entrepreneurs who built the towns and businesses to serve them became prosperous. Suddenly there were saloons and brothels, dress shops and photo studios. Promoters sold credulous public plans for newly laid-out towns on supposed routes to the gold mines, including many that were virtually impassable.

The White Pass above Skagway and the Chilkoot Pass above Dyea carried the most stampeders. Gold seekers arrived in the crazily lawless settlements by steamer from Seattle, got robbed and cheated, and then hauled their goods on their backs over one or other of the passes to Lake Bennett. The Canadian authorities wisely required each stampeder to bring a ton of supplies, a rule that undoubtedly prevented famine but which made the single-file journey over the passes a miserable ordeal. Prospectors sometimes had to make dozens of trips up the trail to get their supplies over the pass. At **Lake Bennett,** the stampeders built boats and rafts, crossed the lake, and then floated down the Yukon River, through the dangerous Five Finger Rapids to **Dawson City**—a 500-mile journey from the sea. Many of them didn't make it.

Imagine the disappointment of those who did when they found, upon arrival, that the gold claims had all been staked and big companies were taking over. Prospectors looking to strike it rich had humbling choices. The smart ones started businesses to make money off the others, and some of them did quite well. Others worked for wages or went home. But many continued their quest for the next big find. Their wild chase for gold drew the modern map of Alaska, founding dozens of towns. Many of these gold-inspired communities disappeared as soon as the frenzy cooled and now are entirely forgotten, or live on only as place names in memory. But some became real cities. **Nome** was born in 1899; **Fairbanks** in 1902; **Kantishna,** now within Denali National Park, in 1905; **Iditarod** in 1908; and many others were born until the rush finally ended with the start of World War I in 1914.

Upon completion of the railroad through the **White Pass** in 1901, Dyea and the Chilkoot Pass were abandoned, but Skagway lived on (see chapter 8).

Even without a rush, there's still gold to be dug. Small-time prospectors are still looking all over Alaska and working their claims, and sometimes someone makes a significant strike. In 1987, a find north of Fairbanks produced as much as 1,000 ounces of the precious metal every day for years.

But there's a bigger, safer business: mining the tourist trade. The rush of visitors each summer dwarfs the number who came in 1898. In the true spirit of the event whose history they celebrate, the gold rush towns of Skagway, Dawson City, Fairbanks, and Nome know there's more money to be made from people than from gold.

2 An Introduction to Southeast Alaska's Native Cultures

This essay was written for us by Jan Halliday, a former editor of Alaska Airlines Magazine *and author of a number of books, including* Native Peoples of the Northwest *(Sasquatch Books) and* Native People of Alaska: A Traveler's Guide to Land, Art, and Culture *(Sasquatch Books), both of which describe Native tours, interpretive centers, museums, art galleries, artists' studios, lodges, B&Bs, and restaurants in their area of coverage, and provide detailed contact information.*

Welcome to the islands of the Inside Passage, the traditional and contemporary home of the Tlingit (pronounced *Klink*-get) Indians. Although the Tlingit's language is related to the language of the Athabascan of Interior Alaska and Canada, and to the language of the Navajo of the American Southwest, no one knows for sure when the group settled on this strip of Alaska coastline and islands. The Tlingit may be descendants of the first wave of ice-age travelers who crossed the Bering Sea from Asia into North America, or they may trace their ancestry from a later wave of immigrants who returned to this fish-rich area from the interior of the North American continent more than 10,000 years ago, after ice-age glaciers retreated.

Until the last century, Tlingits used channels between islands and river passageways through barrier mountains as their highways. In the 1700s, Tlingit paddlers, steering huge cargo canoes carved from cedar logs, were sighted as far south as the Channel Islands off the coast of Los Angeles, reportedly to take slaves. In the 18th and 19th centuries, before epidemics decimated their communities, the Tlingit people were trade partners with the Russians, British, Americans, and interior tribes of Canada, controlling the waterways of Southeast Alaska and demanding tolls for their use. In the 1800s, the Tlingits allowed gold miners to travel over the rugged Chilkoot Pass, between Skagway and the Klondike gold fields, but only after they paid a substantial fee.

Newcomers to Southeast Alaska include the Haida and Tsimshian Indians, who came into Tlingit territory from British Columbia in the last 2 centuries. The Haida, from the Queen Charlotte Islands, settled on Prince of Wales Island in the late 1700s; the Tsimshian Indians, from the Prince Rupert area, settled Annette Island as a utopian Christian community in the late 1800s.

Today many Natives live in small villages on remote islands (such as Angoon on Admiralty Island, Hoonah on Chichagof Island, and Kake on Kupreanof Island) and in centers of commerce such as Juneau, Ketchikan, and Sitka. In smaller villages, away from the bustle of larger towns, you may see Natives drying seaweed in front of their houses on a sheet of plywood or filleting and drying salmon—both of these are traditional foods. But visitors should not expect people, villages, or towns to look as they did when photographers froze their images 100 years ago, any more than you'd expect to see people in Oregon dressed in pioneer garb, making soap over a wood fire. Although many Natives do live traditional subsistence lifestyles, gathering and preserving fish and shellfish, beach greens, and berries, nowadays they also order bulk groceries from Costco in Juneau. The primary source of income for villagers is logging and commercial fishing. All small communities use fuel-burning generators for electrical power and have well-stocked stores, with larger items arriving by barge and cargo jet, and fresh goods arriving daily by smaller planes.

It's important for visitors to remember that Native history and culture was and is influenced by the cultural and economic impact of the Russian, British, and American traders of the early 1800s; the gold miners of the late 1800s; and the timber, fishing, canning, and mining industries of the 20th century. Southeast Alaska clans led (and won) the fight for Native civil rights years before Martin Luther King, Jr., led the civil rights movement for blacks in the 1960s. Many Natives have served in the U.S. military, many own businesses, and several are Alaska state legislators.

In 1971, Natives gained economic clout when the Alaska Native Claims Settlement Act settled the 100-year-old question of aboriginal land rights. Under dispute were 375 million acres of land in Alaska. Under provisions of the act, Congress deeded title to 44 million acres, spread throughout the state, to Alaska Natives, and a payment of close to $1 billion was made to compensate for the loss of the remaining 331 million acres. The act created 13 regional corporations and more than 230 village corporations to receive federal money and manage land on behalf of Native shareholders. In Southeast Alaska, Native corporations, such as Goldbelt (operator of such Juneau-area visitor facilities as Mount Roberts Tramway, Goldbelt Juneau Hotel, and Auk Nu Tours), Cook Inlet Region, Inc., or CIRI (Talkeetna Alaska Lodge, Kenai Fjords Tours, Prince William Sound Glacier Tours, and more), Cape Fox (the Cape Fox Lodge in Ketchikan), and Huna Totem (developer of Alaska's newest cruise destination, Icy Strait Point), have taken the lead in tourism development, investing in first-class hotels, cruise ships, air taxis, and passenger ferry sightseeing boats. Huna Totem Corporation also owns the *Alaskan Southeaster,* a magazine about the region. In Juneau, Goldbelt owns and operates the tram to the top of Mount Roberts and a modern hotel. CIRI owns hotels and sightseeing and tour operations. Sealaska Heritage Foundation, the nonprofit arm of Sealaska, another Juneau-based Native corporation, supports scholarly work, publishing videos, language learning materials, and such books as *Haa Shuka, Our Ancestors: Tlingit Oral Narratives,* by poet Nora Marks Dauenhauer, written in both Tlingit and English. Even small corporations, such as the Organized Village of Kake, have built lovely little hotels for visitors, overlooking beautiful vistas of seacoast and snow-covered mountains.

Alaska Natives don ceremonial regalia (robes decorated with clan insignia and magnificent carved headdresses inlaid with abalone shell) only during celebrations. (The largest of these traditional events, simply called Celebration, is held in Juneau every 2 years for 4 days in June, with clans gathering from throughout Southeast Alaska to celebrate their cultural heritage and perform traditional dances.) As in most of corporate America, Native Alaskans wear business suits when running their corporations, which are located in some of Juneau's finest office buildings.

Having said this, there are many facets of Native culture for you to enjoy in Southeast Alaska. Distinctive Tlingit, Haida, and Tsimshian totemic art is prevalent. In Ketchikan, for example, there are more than 70 standing totem poles, plus a museum dedicated entirely to the oldest poles collected from abandoned Tlingit villages. There are also two traditional clan houses, reminiscent of dozens of large houses that lined the waterfront in the last century, constructed from hand-hewn cedar and adorned with carved house posts and decorated house screens. Both houses are open to the public. You can observe Native carvers working on commissioned masks, canoes, and totem poles at places such as Saxman Village, 3 miles south of Ketchikan, and in private studios. Many Native artists, such as carvers Amos Wallace and Nathan Jackson, and Chilkat blanket weaver Delores Churchill, have their work in private and museum collections throughout the world.

Most towns in Southeast Alaska have fascinating museums filled with artifacts and traditional art. Those with the largest collections are the Alaska State Museum in Juneau and the Sheldon Jackson Museum in Sitka, but smaller museums shouldn't be missed.

Raven and Eagle clan symbols, representing the two major clan divisions to which every Haida, Tsimshian, and Tlingit Native belongs, adorn everything from bags of fresh-roasted coffee to beach blankets and T-shirts. These clan symbols, plus other totem figures, such as salmon, killer whales, frogs, and bears, represent the strong family ties that reach back far into the past and bind contemporary Native people in this region. Rather than describe complicated clan lineage systems in this guide, I suggest you learn firsthand about the clans from Native tour guides and through Native-based shore excursions designed especially for the time frame that cruise-ship passengers have in port—Saxman Village in Ketchikan, Metlakatla's tour and salmon bake, or one of Sitka Tribal Tours' bus or walking tours of the old Russian/Tlingit capital of Alaska.

When I researched my guidebook to the Native peoples of Alaska, I stayed at Native-owned hotels, visited with artists (one of the best places to meet carvers, weavers, painters, silversmiths, and bead workers while they work is at the Southeast Alaska Indian Cultural Center in Sitka), gazed in wonder at museum collections, saw the old Chilkat and Ravenstail woven robes come out from behind the glass windows to be worn, and danced to the resonant beat of box drums at Celebration. I watched the Sheet'ka Kwaan Naa Kahidi Community House, a gorgeous hall modeled after the old clan houses, being constructed in Sitka. I listened as Native guides explained how each totem pole tells a unique family story or honors a fallen clan member. I went fishing with Natives on their charter boats and toured canneries, fish-processing plants, and salmon hatcheries owned by Natives (one had a standing totem pole right in the center of the creek, with an opportunistic eagle perched on top, eyeing the spawning salmon below). In Metlakatla, I scaled Yellow Hill on the boardwalk and stairs that Terry Booth, a Tsimshian, built for his wife years ago, and watched the sun bathe the village in first morning light. They were all unforgettable experiences. I hope your trip will be an unforgettable experience as well.

Appendix B: Alaska on the Wild Side

by Charles Wohlforth

The variety of wildlife found in our 49th state is mind-boggling, whether it rules on land or in the ocean or in the air. The one thing that an Alaska cruise can guarantee is that passengers will see some of these creatures—from the decks of their ship, during organized shore excursions specifically planned to search for them, or even when just walking the streets of the communities their ships visit. Majestic bald eagles, the symbol of this nation, are all over the place and, thankfully, are now well and truly back, after having been placed on the protected species list several years ago. Bears roam the woods, Dall sheep dot the hillsides, and caribou and moose inhabit parts of the Interior of the state. The waters of the Inside Passage, Glacier Bay, and Prince William Sound teem with harbor seals, sea otters, sea lions, and—most spectacularly of all—whales. It is highly unlikely that you will ever take a cruise to Alaska without seeing the telltale flukes and condensation spouts in the vicinity of your vessel.

So that you can recognize what you're seeing, here's a short rundown on the creatures you may encounter along the way.

1 Whale-Watching 101

Imagine standing on the deck of a ship, looking out onto the calm silver waters of an Alaskan bay. Suddenly, the surface of the water pulls back and an immense yet graceful creature appears, moving silently, the curve of its back visible for a moment before the water closes over it again. You wait for it to reappear. And wait. And wait. Then, just as you're beginning to think it's gone forever, the creature leaps straight out of the water, twisting around in midair before falling back with a gigantic kersploosh! That's followed a half-second later by an equally distinctive sound: 1,000 cruise-ship passengers saying "Oooh!," "Aaah!," and "Marty! Marty! Did you see that?!"

On most large cruise ships, the captain or officer on watch will make an announcement when he or she spots a whale, but due to its strict schedule, the ship probably won't be able to stop and linger. A few lines, though (mostly the small-ship lines), feature whale-watching as a major component of their cruises. Their ships visit areas favored by whales—for instance, waters near Petersburg or Sitka, near Gustavus and Glacier Bay National Park, and near Seward and Kenai Fjords National Park. Once in position, they will spend time waiting for an encounter, or will monitor marine-traffic radio broadcasts and deviate from course to go where whale sightings have been reported. Most ships, both large and small, will offer lectures about whales at some point during each cruise.

To get you ready for your whale encounters, we've prepared the following little whale primer. Study up so you'll know what you're looking at.

THE HUMPBACK WHALE These migratory whales spend their summer in Alaska feeding, then swim to Mexican or Hawaiian waters for the winter, where they give birth to their young and then fast until going north again in spring. The cold northern waters produce the small fish and other tiny creatures that humpbacks filter through their baleen—the strips of stiff, fibrous material that humpbacks have instead of teeth. A humpback is easy to recognize by its huge, mottled tail; by the hump on its back, just forward of its dorsal fin; and by its armlike flippers, which can grow to be 14 feet long. Most humpback sightings are of the whales' humped backs as they cruise along the surface, resting, and of the flukes of their tails as they dive.

The Humpback Whale. Maximum length: 53 ft.

Humpbacks weave nets of bubbles around their prey, then swim upward through the schooled fish, mouths wide open, to eat them in a single swoop, sometimes finishing with a frothy lunge through the surface. Feeding dives can last a long time and often mean you won't see that particular whale again, but if you're lucky, the whale may just be dipping down for a few minutes to get ready to leap completely out of the water, a behavior called **breaching.** No one knows for sure why whales do this; it may simply be play. Breaching is thrilling for viewers and, if you happen to be in a small boat or kayak, a little scary (paddlers should group their boats and tap the decks to let the whales know where they are). Humpbacks are highly sensitive to noise, so keep quiet to see longer displays.

Humpbacks tend to congregate to feed, making certain spots with rich supplies of food reliable places to watch them. In Southeast Alaska, the best humpback-watching spots include the waters of **Icy Strait,** just outside Glacier Bay; **Frederick Sound,** outside Petersburg; and **Sitka Sound.** In Southcentral Alaska, **Resurrection Bay,** outside Seward near Kenai Fjords National Park, has the most reliable sightings.

THE ORCA (KILLER WHALE) The starkly defined black-and-white patches of the orca, the ocean's top predator, recall the sharp, vivid look of the Native American art of the Pacific Northwest and Southeast Alaska. Moving like wolves in highly structured family groups called pods, and swimming at up to 25 knots (about 29 mph), orcas hunt salmon, porpoises, seals, sea lions, and even juvenile whales. There's never been a report of one attacking a human being. Like dolphins, orcas often pop above the surface in a flashing, graceful arc, giving viewers a glance at their sleek shape and tall dorsal fin.

Unlike humpbacks and other whales that rely on a predictable food supply, orcas' hunting patterns mean it's not easy to say exactly where you might find them. **Resurrection Bay** and **Prince William Sound** both have pods that are often sighted in the summer, and we saw a pod of orcas from the beach in Gustavus, but they could show up anywhere in the waters of Southeast Alaska. For cruisers coming to Alaska from Vancouver, B.C., a top spot to see orcas is **Robson Bight,** an area in Johnstone Strait (btw. Vancouver Island and mainland British Columbia).

The Orca, or Killer Whale. Maximum length: 30 ft.

THE BELUGA WHALE This small white whale with a cute rounded beak is one of only three types that spend all their lives in cold water rather than heading south for the winter. Belugas are more likely to be mistaken for dolphins than any other whales. However, the beluga is larger and fatter than a dolphin and lacks the dolphin's dorsal fin. Adults are all white, while juveniles are gray. Belugas swim in large packs that can number in the dozens. It is the only whale that can turn its head, and is one of a few species with good eyesight.

The Beluga Whale. Maximum length: 16 ft.

Belugas feed on salmon, making the mouths of rivers with salmon runs the best places to see them. Occasionally, a group will strand itself chasing salmon on a falling tide, swimming away when the water returns. The Cook Inlet group of belugas is the most often seen: If you're in Anchorage after your cruise, take the Seward Highway south of town, and keep your eyes on the **Turnagain Arm,** or watch from the beach near the mouth of the **Kenai River,** in Kenai.

THE MINKE WHALE The smallest of the baleen whales, the minke is generally less than 26 feet long and has a blackish-gray body with a white stomach, a narrow triangular head, and white bands on its flippers. Along with the humpback and (occasionally) the gray whale, it is the only baleen whale commonly seen in Alaskan waters.

When breaching, minkes leap somewhat like dolphins, gracefully reentering the water headfirst—unlike humpbacks, for instance, which smash down on their sides. Also unlike the humpbacks, they don't raise their flukes (the tips of their tails) clear of the water when they dive. Minkes are easy to confuse with dolphins: Watch for the dark skin color to tell the difference.

The Minke Whale. Maximum length: 26 ft.

THE GRAY WHALE Here's one whale you'll probably see only if you take a shoulder-season cruise (in May or very late Sept), and then only if you're lucky. The grays spend their winter months off the coast of California and in the Sea of Cortez (btw. Baja and mainland Mexico), and their summer months off northern Alaska, meaning that cruise passengers sailing in the Inside Passage and Gulf of Alaska can spot one only while it's on its migration.

The Gray Whale. Maximum length: 45 ft.

Like the humpback, grays are baleen whales. They're also about the same size as the humpback, though they lack the humpback's huge flippers. Their heads are pointed, and they have no dorsal fin. Grays will often smack the water with their flukes and are very friendly—it's not uncommon for them to swim right up to a small boat and allow their heads to be patted.

2 Alaskan Wildlife

Large mammals other than humankind still rule most of Alaska—even in the urban areas, there sometimes remains a question of who's in charge. In this section, we'll describe some of the more common forms of wildlife. For visitors, the chances of seeing the animals described below are excellent.

BALD EAGLE Now making a comeback all over the United States, the bald eagle has always been extremely common in Alaska. Every fishing town is swarming with eagles, and they even soar over the high-rise buildings of downtown Anchorage. Only adult eagles have the familiar white head and tail; juveniles of a few years or less have mottled brown plumage and can be hard to tell from a hawk. Eagles are most often seen soaring on rising air currents over ocean or river waters, where they are likely looking for fish to swoop down and snatch, but you also can often see them perched on beach driftwood or in large trees. **Haines** is a prime eagle-spotting area, where thousands of birds congregate in the fall; **Sitka** and **Ketchikan** both have raptor centers where you can see eagles in enclosures.

The eagle represents one of the two main kinship groupings in the matrilineal Tlingit culture (the other group is represented by the raven), so eagles frequently appear on totem poles and in other Southeast Alaska Native art.

Bald Eagle

Raven

RAVEN A member of the Corvidae family, which includes jays, crows, and magpies, the raven is found throughout the Northern Hemisphere and is extremely common in Southeast Alaska. You can tell a raven from a crow by its larger size, heavy bill, shaggy throat feathers, and unmistakable call, a deep and mysteriously evocative "kaw" that provides a constant soundtrack to the misty forests of Southeast Alaska. The raven figures importantly in Southeast Alaska Native stories and in the creation myths of many other Native American peoples. It is portrayed as a wily and resourceful protagonist with great magical powers, an understandable personality for this highly impressive and intelligent scavenger.

BLACK BEAR Black bears live in forests all over Alaska, feeding on fish, berries, insects, and vegetation. In Southeast Alaska, they can be so common that they are sometimes considered pests, and many communities have adjusted their handling of garbage to keep bears out of town. Although not typically dangerous, blackies still deserve caution and respect: They stand about 3 feet tall at the shoulders and measure 5 or 6 feet from nose to tail. Black bears are usually black but can also be brown, blond, or even bluish—color is not the best way to tell a black bear from a brown bear. Instead, look for smaller size, a blunt face, and the shape of the back, which is straight and lacks the brown bear's large shoulder hump. You're liable to find black bears pretty much anywhere in Southeast Alaska where the popular Inside Passage ports are located. Mostly, you will spot them along riverbanks and near salmon streams. On a cruise on the *Island Princess,* I saw one swimming across the mouth of Johns Hopkins Inlet in Glacier Bay. Quite a sight!

Black Bear

Brown Bear

BROWN BEAR Also known as grizzly bears, brown bears are among the largest and most ferocious of all land mammals. Size depends on the bear's food source. In coastal areas where salmon are plentiful, such as Southeast Alaska and Katmai National Park (near King Salmon, Alaska), brown bears can grow well over 1,000 pounds and even approach the 1-ton mark. The largest bears are found on salmon-rich Kodiak Island. Inland, at Denali National Park and on similar tundra landscape (where they feed on rodents, berries, and insects), brown bears top out closer to 500 pounds. Bears can also take larger prey, but that's less common. You can recognize brown bears by their prominent shoulder humps, long faces, and large sizes; color can range from almost black to blond. Among the best places to see them are **Pack Creek** (on Admiralty Island near Juneau), at **Denali and Katmai national parks,** and on bear-viewing floatplane excursions from **Homer.** Of these, Denali is the only inexpensive option.

MOOSE In winter, when they move to the lowlands, moose can be an absolute pest, blocking roadways and eating expensive shrubbery. In the summer, they're a little more elusive, most often seen standing in forest ponds, eating the weeds from the bottom or pruning streamside willows. The largest member of the deer family, with males reaching 1,200 to 1,600 pounds, moose are found primarily in the boreal forest that covers Interior and Southcentral Alaska. You'll be likely to see one if you're on a pre- or post-cruise land package such as the Anchorage-Denali-Fairbanks route. They are unmistakable. As big as a large horse, with bristly, ragged brown hair; a long, bulbous nose; and huge, mournful eyes, moose seem to crave pity—though they get little from the wolves and people who hunt them or from the trains and cars that run them down, and they give little to anyone in their way when they're on the move. Males grow large antlers, which they shed after battling for a mate every fall. Females lack antlers, are smaller, and give birth to between one and three calves each year.

Moose

Caribou

CARIBOU Alaska's barren-ground caribou are genetically identical to reindeer, but were never domesticated as reindeer were in Europe. For Iñupiat and Athabascan people, they continue to be an essential source of food and hides, and caribou hunting remains a necessity. By law, nobody is allowed to kill caribou for sport or recreation in Alaska. Both males and females have antlers that they shed annually. Caribou travel the arctic tundra and Interior foothills, often in herds of thousands of animals, a stunning sight witnessed by only a lucky few, as the migration routes lay in remote regions. However, often you can see caribou in smaller groups of a few dozen at Denali National Park, along the Dalton and Denali highways, and on other northern rural roads above the tree line.

SITKA BLACK-TAILED DEER The Sitka black-tailed deer is a relatively small deer found in the coastal rainforests of Alaska. Males typically weigh in at around 120 pounds and have small antlers. Both males and females sport a reddish-brown coat in summer. They can be found throughout the Southeast, in Prince William Sound, and on Kodiak Island.

Sitka Black-Tailed Deer

Dall Sheep

DALL SHEEP Dall sheep resemble the more familiar bighorn sheep but are smaller, with males weighing up to 300 pounds and females topping out at 150 pounds. Like the bighorn, males have curling horns, which they butt against each other to establish dominance for mating. Their habitat is high, rocky places, where their incredible agility makes them safe from predators. Except in a few exceptional spots (such as on the **cliffs above the Seward Highway** just south of Anchorage on Turnagain Arm), you almost always need strong binoculars to see Dall sheep. **Denali National Park** is a good place to see them in the usual way: from a great distance. Scanning the mountains, look for white spots, and then focus in on them. The sheep often move in herds of a dozen or more.

MOUNTAIN GOAT Another animal that you won't see unless you bring your binoculars, the mountain goat inhabits the same craggy mountain habitat as Dall sheep, including the prime viewing area around Turnagain Arm. From a distance, it's easy to confuse mountain goats with female Dall sheep, but mountain goats are shaggier; have short, straight black horns (which appear in both male and female); have the typical goat beard; and have a much more pronounced hump at the shoulders.

SEA OTTER Possibly number one in Alaska's "cute critter" category, the sea otter is a member of the weasel family (as are minks and river otters) and spends almost all of its life in the water. Extensively hunted for its rich coat from the mid-18th century (when Russian explorer Vitus Bering brought back pelts from his voyage of discovery and initiated extensive Russian settlement of Alaska) until the early 20th century, the sea otter was almost driven to extinction—in 1911, there were probably fewer than 2,000 of them left in Alaska. But by the mid-1970s, that number had risen above 150,000. Adult males weigh between 70 and 100 pounds, while females average 40 to 60 pounds. Adults average 4½ feet in length. Their fur is generally brown to black, often with a silvery or gray tinge, particularly in older animals. You typically see sea otters floating on their backs, sometimes cradling a rock on their stomachs (which they use to crack open shellfish), or sometimes just watching the cruise ships float by.

Mountain Goat

Sea Otter

SEA LION You'll hear 'em—and smell 'em—before you see 'em. An argumentative honking, like cars stalled in traffic, mixes with a low undertone that sounds like elephants with sinus problems. Then the smell hits you—fishy beyond belief. Still, when you get close enough to know what you're smelling, you won't mind because it's quite a sight: Sea lions typically haul out in the hundreds onto small islands, where they loll in the sun, argue, occasionally fight, go fishing, and breed—just like people on vacation. Their bodies are huge, blubbery, tubular affairs that are perfect for the cold northern waters but appear impossibly ungainly on land, over which they bounce and bound on perfectly inadequate-looking front flippers. Still, even on land you wouldn't want to mess with one: The average adult male weighs approximately 1,250 pounds and measures 10½ feet long, while adult females average 580 pounds and are 8½ feet long. Most adult females are brownish yellow, while males typically are a bit darker, some with a reddish coat.

Sea Lion

Index

See also Accommodations and Restaurants Indexes, below.

General Index

Accommodations

Restaurants